Improving Skills Development in the Informal Sector

DIRECTIONS IN DEVELOPMENT
Human Development

Improving Skills Development in the Informal Sector

Strategies for Sub-Saharan Africa

Arvil V. Adams, Sara Johansson de Silva, and Setareh Razmara

THE WORLD BANK
Washington, D.C.

1 2 3 4 16 15 14 13

ISBN (paper): 978-0-8213-9968-2
ISBN (electronic): 978-0-8213-9969-9
DOI: 10.1596/978-0-8213-9968-2

Cover painting: Mavua Lessor, oil on canvas, World Bank Art Collection
Cover design: Naylor Design

Library of Congress Cataloging-in-Publication Data

Adams, Arvil V.

Improving skills development in the informal sector : strategies for Sub-Saharan Africa / Arvil V. Adams, Sara Johansson de Silva, and Setareh Razmara.

pages cm. -- (Directions in development)

Includes bibliographical references.

ISBN 978-0-8213-9968-2 (alk. paper) – ISBN 978-0-8213-9969-9 (ebook)

1. Informal sector (Economics)–Africa, Sub-Saharan. 2. Small business–Africa, Sub-Saharan. 3. Labor–Africa, Sub-Saharan. 4. Labor market–Africa, Sub-Saharan. 5. Vocational education–Africa, Sub-Saharan. 6. Africa, Sub-Saharan–Economic policy. I. Silva, Sara Johansson de. II. Razmara, Setareh. III. World Bank. IV. Title.

HD2346.A57A33 2013
331—dc23

2013015932

Contents

Boxes

Figures

Tables

Foreword

Against a backdrop of steady economic growth despite global economic uncertainty, Sub-Saharan Africa's prospects have been rising in the twenty-first century. More children are surviving infancy and early childhood and are able to attend school, and the burden of infectious diseases is decreasing. As the share of young people in the population is now rising in many African countries, it is more critical than ever to make key investments in human capital—in improved health and education, particularly for women and girls, and robust social safety nets to help cut poverty and keep children in school. As part of this larger effort, countries need to look at what is standing in the way of greater productivity, regardless of what type of work people are engaged in—whether in agriculture, nonfarm household enterprises or in the modern wage sector.

Today, the nonfarm informal sector—the area of focus in this book—is a significant economic force and a major source of employment and earnings in Sub-Saharan Africa. Household enterprises account for most nonfarm employment in the region. With a rapidly growing and youthful work force and continued urbanization, this slice of the economy will continue to play a significant role for job creation and livelihoods in the future. Thus strategies for poverty reduction in the region have to squarely address the constraints that hamper productivity in this sector—including the skills of the workforce.

This book examines the role played by education and skills development in increasing productivity, profitability, and earnings in the nonfarm informal sector, focusing on five African countries—Ghana, Kenya, Nigeria, Rwanda, and Tanzania—that together account for one-third of the nearly 900 million persons living in Sub-Saharan Africa, and where a majority of nonfarm employment is informal. Using household surveys, the book provides an assessment of the size and characteristics of the nonfarm informal sector, of how skills are developed and mapped to activities in the sectors, and of how this results in higher productivity and increased earnings. Moreover, the book reviews the impact of the institutional settings and existing policies and programs in this area.

This book is an important contribution to our understanding of the role of skills in the informal sector in Sub-Saharan Africa. It offers an insightful approach to improving employment outcomes in the informal sector through skills development, with examples of successful interventions taken from international experiences.

Ritva Reinikka
Director, Human Development, Africa Region
The World Bank

Acknowledgments

This report is based on a series of country background studies prepared by (a) Richard Johanson, Marco Ranzani, and Kaviranga Gakuba (for Rwanda); (b) Jutta Franz, Anthony Wambugu, and Elda Onsomu (for Kenya); (c) Richard Johanson, Alexandru Cojocaru, and Goodwill Wanga (for Tanzania); (d) Alberto Behar and Jorgen Billetoft (for Nigeria); and (e) Arvil V. Adams, Quentin T. Wodon, Harold Coulombe, and Setareh Razmara (for Ghana).

The peer reviewers for the report were Luis Benveniste (Sector Manager, EASHE), Amit Dar (Sector Manager, SASHD), John T. Giles (Senior Labor Economist, DECHD), and Alexandria Valerio (Senior Economist, HDNED). The report has benefited from the contributions of many who shared their insights and advice with us throughout the various stages of preparation. Peer reviewers at the concept stage were Sumila Gulyani (AFTU1), Andrew Mason (LCHS), Stephen Mink (AFTSN), and Ivan Rossignol (AFTPS). Others who have provided us with guidance at critical points in the report's preparation have been Harold Alderman, Amit Dar, Peter Darvas, Shantayanan Devarajan, Emanuela Di Gropello, Linda English, Mourad Ezzine, Deon Filmer, Louise Fox, Lucy Fye, Birgit Hansl, Margo Hoftijzer, Dena Ringold, Shobhana Sosale, and Paul Noumba Um.

We owe a special debt of gratitude to the Africa Region chief economist and the Country Units for Ghana, Kenya, Nigeria, Rwanda, and Tanzania for their guidance and support throughout the preparation of this report. The report could not have been completed without the cooperation and contributions of many unrecorded individuals in government agencies and nongovernmental organizations of the five countries. Their contributions of time and access to the household data sets used in the report and the background materials and evaluations of various programs for skills development have greatly enriched this study.

None of the above, however, bears any responsibility for the analyses and findings of this report. The authors alone assume full responsibility for its conclusions. The study was made possible by financial support provided under the grant from the Trust Fund for Environmentally and Socially Sustainable Development donors (Norway and Finland) to the World Bank.

Darcy Gallucio has been responsible for initial editing and technical production of the report with additional editing by Laura Glassman, Publications Professionals LLC. The study was conducted under the general direction of Lynne D. Sherburne-Benz, sector manager, and Yaw Ansu and his successor, Ritva S. Reinikka, sector directors, Africa Human Development. The team also acknowledges the valuable support and guidance of Stefano Paternostro, sector manager. The task team leader has been Setareh Razmara.

About the Authors

Arvil V. Adams is an economist and an international consultant on employment and training issues. He retired from the World Bank in 2005 as Senior Adviser for Social Protection in the Africa Region. Before joining the World Bank in 1989, he was Professor of Economics and Director of the Doctoral Program in Public Policy, George Washington University, from 1979 to 1989 and served as Executive Director of the U.S. National Commission on Employment and Unemployment Statistics from 1977 to 1979. Earlier, he was a faculty member at the Ohio State University and the University of Utah.

Sara Johansson de Silva is an economist and an international consultant whose work centers on how growth, job creation, skills development, and social protection policies can help alleviate poverty. Between 1999 and 2003, she was a Senior Economist at the World Bank, working in the Middle East and North Africa Department on growth, employment, and poverty analysis. Prior to joining the World Bank, she was an economist at the Organisation for Economic Co-operation and Development from 1997 to 1999, where she worked on industrial policy and aid effectiveness. She holds a PhD in economics from the Stockholm School of Economics.

Setareh Razmara is a lead Social Protection specialist in the Human Development group of the World Bank's Sub-Saharan Africa Region. Trained as a macroeconomist, she has focused primarily on poverty analysis, labor markets, social insurance, safety nets, and risk management. Since 1987, she has worked for World Bank programs in the Middle East and North Africa and West Africa. Before joining the World Bank, she was a research assistant in the Center for Policy Alternatives at the Massachusetts Institute of Technology. She holds an MA in economics from the University of Grenoble, France.

Abbreviations

ACWICT	African Centre for Women, Information and Communications Technology
BDS	business development services
BECE	Basic Education Certificate Examination (Ghana)
CBT	competency-based training
CFJ	Centre des Formation Jeunes
CFP	Centre de Formation Professionnelle
DIT	Directorate of Industrial Training (Kenya)
EICV	Household Living Conditions Survey (Rwanda)
EOP	Education Offers Perspective
ET	École Technique
ETO	École Technique Officielle
FBO	faith-based organization
GDP	gross domestic product
GIZ	German Agency for International Cooperation (formerly GTZ)
GLSS	Ghana Living Standards Survey
GNP	gross national product
GTZ	German Agency for Technical Cooperation (now known as GIZ)
HRDF	Human Resources Development Fund (Malaysia)
ICT	information and communication technology
ILFS	Integrated Labour Force Survey (Tanzania)
ILO	International Labour Organization
ILTF	Industrial Levy Training Fund (Kenya)
INTEP	Integrated Training and Entrepreneurship Promotion (Tanzania)
ISA	informal sector association
ISBI	Informal Sector Business Institute
KIHBS	Kenya Integrated Household Budget Survey
KYEP	Kenya Youth Employment Program
LFS	Labour Force Survey (Kenya)

LMI	low and middle income
MoESS	Ministry of Education, Science, and Sports (Ghana)
MoHEST	Ministry of Higher Education, Science, and Technology (Kenya)
MoMYE	Ministry of Manpower, Youth, and Employment (Ghana)
MoYAS	Ministry of Youth Affairs and Sport (Kenya)
MTP	microtraining provider
NBTE	National Board for Technical Education (Nigeria)
NCTE	National Council for Technical Education (Tanzania)
NGO	nongovernmental organization
NLSS	National Living Standard Survey
NUSAF	Northern Uganda Social Action Fund
NYS	National Youth Service (Kenya)
OECD	Organisation for Economic Co-operation and Development
OJT	on-the-job training
OLS	ordinary least squares
SDF	Skills Development Fund (Singapore)
SIDO	Small Industries Development Organization
SITE	Strengthening Informal Training and Enterprise
SSA	Sub-Saharan Africa
SSSCE	Senior Secondary School Certificate Examination (Ghana)
TSS	technical secondary school
TVET	technical and vocational education and training
TVVP	Technical and Vocational Vouchers Program (Kenya)
VTC	vocational training center
VETA	Vocational Education and Training Authority (Tanzania)
VIBINDO	Association of Small Informal Businesses
WB IS	World Bank Busia Informal Sector Vouchers
YDS	Youth Development Scheme
YP	youth polytechnic

Currencies

K Sh	Kenya shilling
RF	Rwanda francs
T Sh	Tanzania shilling
US$	U.S. dollar

Overview

Background

In Sub-Saharan Africa, a significant number of people are engaged in small and household enterprises outside formal wage employment. Although the prospects for economic growth have improved in the region since 2000 along with prospects for the expansion of modern industries and wage employment, household enterprises and small businesses remain a cornerstone of national economies and make up the livelihoods of millions. Of the many definitions of informal employment, this study focuses on small enterprises and self-employment in the nonfarm sector. Over 65 percent of people employed in Sub-Saharan Africa are engaged in farming, but nearly 70 percent of employment outside farming is in the informal sector. Previously expected to be a temporary phenomenon that would diminish in importance as countries progressed on the path to industrialization, the informal sector has instead become a significant and durable feature of Africa's economic landscape.

The nonfarm informal sector has established its role as a major source of employment and earnings for rapidly growing populations. Informality, at least in developing countries, appears to be less the result of cumbersome regulations and mistrust in public institutions and taxation, and more a result of significant pressures on job creation and sustaining livelihoods. From 1985 to 2010, the population 15–24 years of age doubled in the region. At the same time, urban populations almost tripled in tandem with some outflows from farming activities (figure O.1). However, economic growth—and with it the expansion of labor demand in the formal wage sector—has been slower than anticipated. Wage and salaried jobs, generally offering higher earnings and better working conditions, account for much less than half of total employment in the countries of Sub-Saharan Africa, and the share has increased only very modestly in the past 25 years (figure O.2).

The informal sector is likely to continue to absorb the majority of workers in the nonfarm sectors in the future. As seen in figure O.1, demographic trends will continue to put pressure on employment opportunities.

Figure O.1 Youth and Urban Populations in Sub-Saharan Africa, 1985, 2010, and 2035

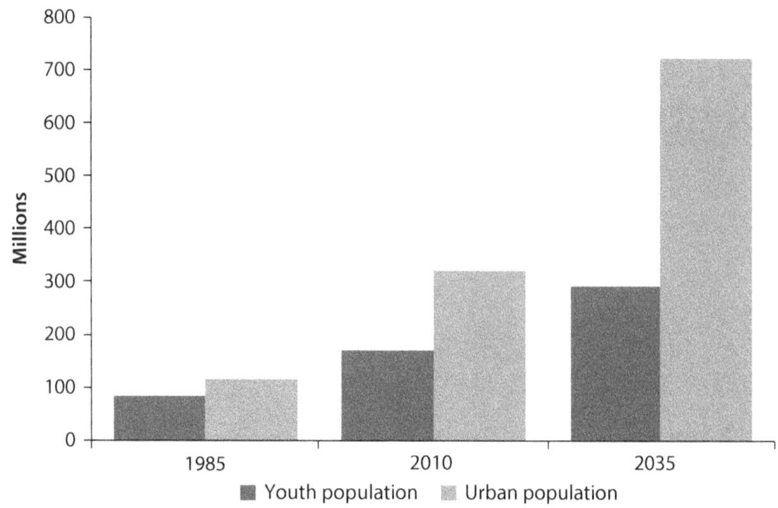

Sources: UN 2010, 2011.

Figure O.2 Wage and Salaried Workers in Sub-Saharan Africa, 1980s–2000s

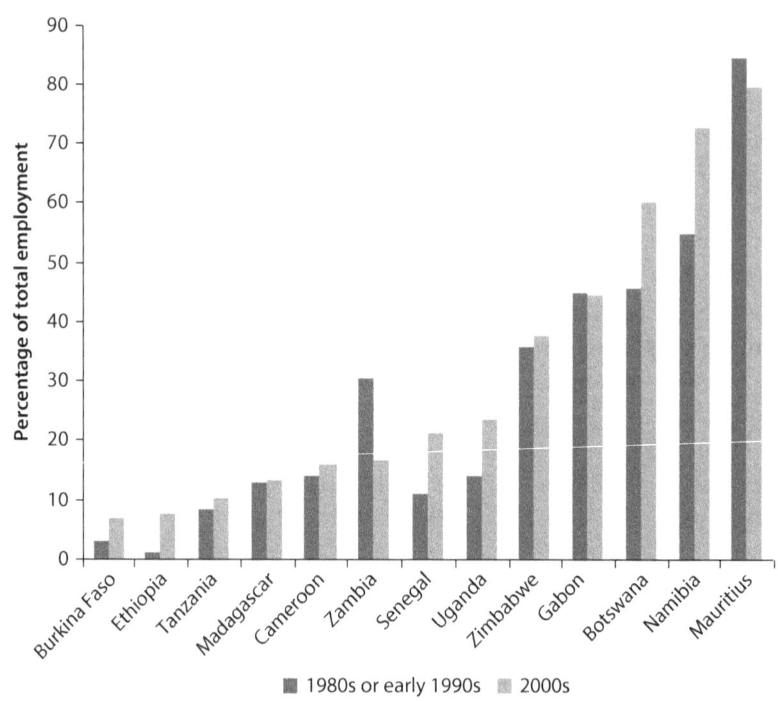

Source: World Bank 2012.

Meanwhile, the changing economic and political environment in Africa holds promise for improving economic growth. Given the small size of the formal sector, however, its labor demand is not likely to be able to match the dynamics in labor supply, even with extraordinary growth rates. Thus, the informal sector will likely continue to provide most of the employment in the nonfarm sector. In the event of a more significant exodus from farming activities, pressures for job creation will be even greater.

Improving the productivity of the nonfarm informal sector is therefore essential for employment, income growth, and poverty reduction in the region. Many factors affect this productivity. Among them are not only access to finance, infrastructure, and an investor-friendly business climate, but also the level of human capital, including skills relevant to the labor market. In this context, the Africa Region of the World Bank launched this study on how workers are prepared with skills for informal sector employment and how governments could encourage further investments in skills alongside other interventions that would raise productivity and earnings in the sector.

This book looks at the experience of skills development in five African countries—Ghana, Kenya, Nigeria, Rwanda, and Tanzania—that together account for one-third of the nearly 900 million people living in Sub-Saharan Africa. The study examines (a) the employment characteristics of the informal sector, (b) its size and impact on poverty, (c) the profile of education and training in the informal and formal sectors and the links with employment and earnings, and (d) the skills development strategies of those working in the informal sector. It draws on household survey data in the five countries as well as institutional analyses of the many programs offering opportunities for skills development.

This book defines the nonfarm informal sector as follows: (a) the self-employed (that is, those working on their own and with additional workers), (b) the contributing family members, and (c) the wage workers in small and household enterprises. Chapter 2 discusses the background for this definition. The empirical analysis of the five country cases shows that the nonfarm informal sector is a significant part of the economic landscape in these countries. The study is well anchored in a larger literature on the informal sector, and its findings are linked to and consistent with this literature. Its findings are therefore expected to be relevant to many other countries in the region, as well as other regions such as South and East Asia.

The book aims to provide insights and messages for a wide audience concerned with skills development. It raises issues relevant to government policy makers, the donor community, and those responsible for labor market institutions that provide information, regulate, and support the intermediation of labor demand and supply, as well as for public and private skills providers, employers, children and their parents, new labor market entrants, and of course those already working in the informal sector.

Main Findings

The study confirms the significance of the nonfarm informal sector as a source of employment and earnings in Ghana, Kenya, Nigeria, Rwanda, and Tanzania; the strong link between education and different labor market opportunities; the limited skill levels available in the informal sector; and the need to continue to focus on skills development in the informal sector to increase productivity and earnings.

Characteristics of Those Employed in the Nonfarm Informal Sector

On the basis of available household surveys in the five country cases, the profile of people employed in the nonfarm informal sector reveals the following:

- *The average income of people employed in the nonfarm informal sector is lower than that of people employed in the formal sector but exceeds earnings in farming.* Although farming remains the largest employer in Sub-Saharan Africa, labor continues to leave the farm in search of other employment. Because Africa does not offer large numbers of low-skilled jobs in manufacturing and construction, as found in East Asia, most migrants find jobs in petty trade and services that still offer welfare gains compared to farming. Although average earnings in the informal sector are lower than those of the formal sector, the earnings display considerable variation, and for some, the earnings of the nonfarm informal sector compare favorably with those in the formal sector (figure O.3).
- *Employment in the nonfarm informal sector is associated with lower poverty.* Higher earnings in the informal sector lead to lower poverty rates than in

Figure O.3 Distribution of Log Monthly Earnings by Formality Status in Nigeria

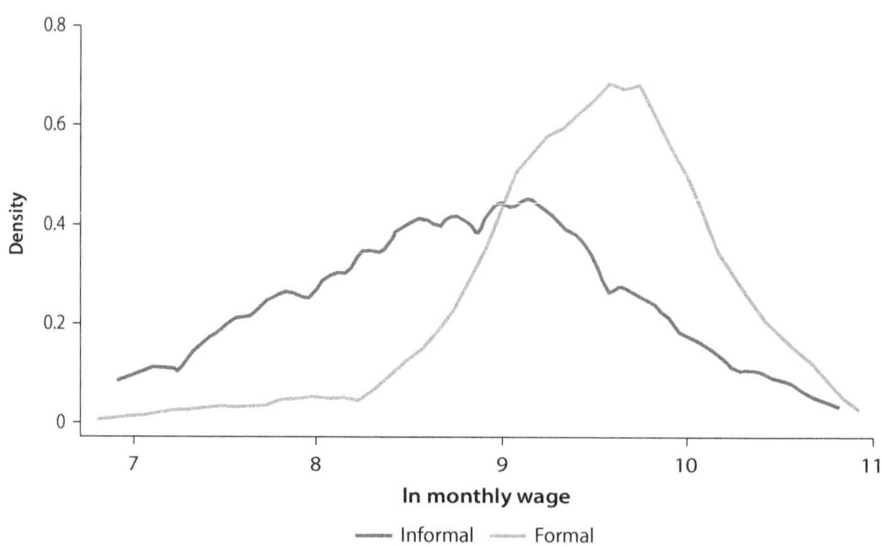

Source: Elaborations based on NBSN (2004).

Figure O.4 Percentage of Population Belonging to the Three Poorest Consumption Quintiles in Formal, Informal, and Farm Sectors of Rwanda and Kenya

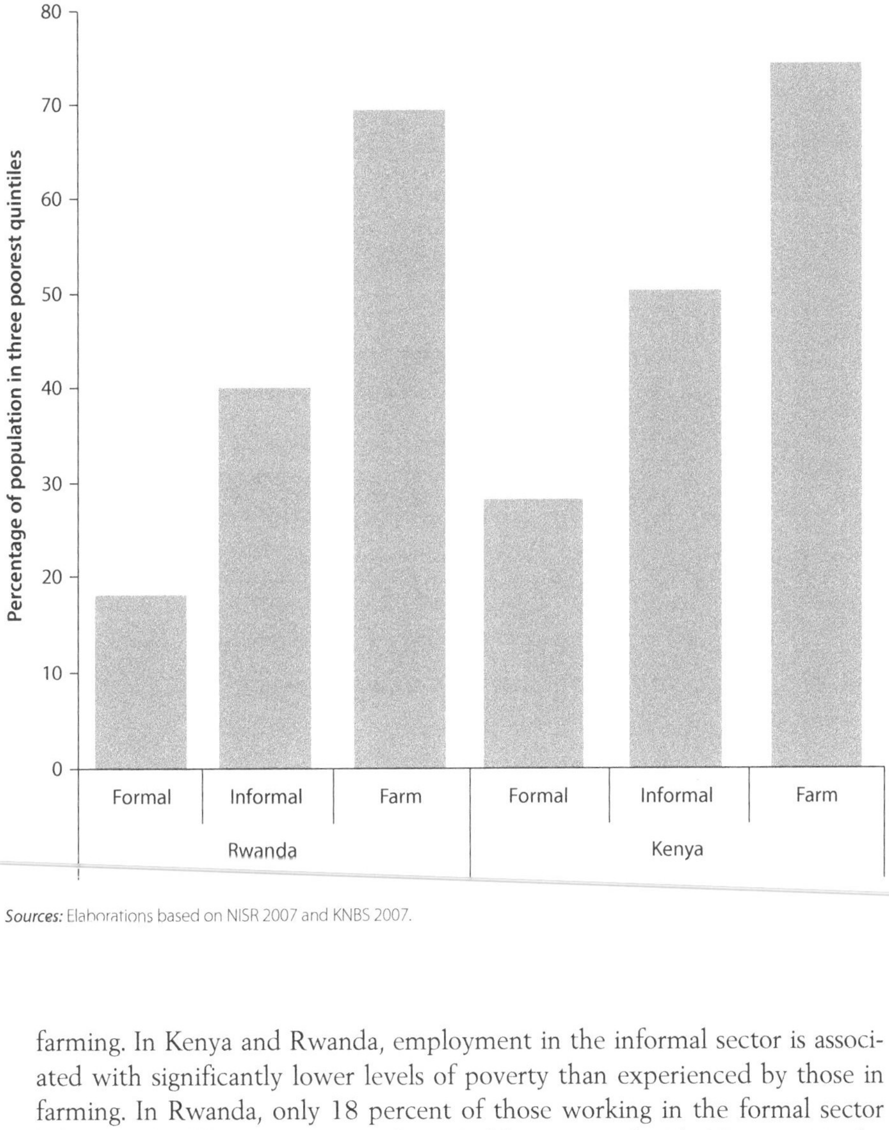

Sources: Elaborations based on NISR 2007 and KNBS 2007.

farming. In Kenya and Rwanda, employment in the informal sector is associated with significantly lower levels of poverty than experienced by those in farming. In Rwanda, only 18 percent of those working in the formal sector belong to the 60 percent poorest households, compared with 40 percent in the nonfarm informal sector and 69 percent in farming; the same pattern is observed in Kenya (figure O.4).

- *Women are more likely to be working in more vulnerable and less profitable occupations and sectors.* The share of women active in the nonfarm informal and formal sectors differs among the countries, indicating the need for a gender focus in efforts to improve economic and social outcomes. Whereas men account for a majority of employment in the informal sector of Kenya, Rwanda, and Tanzania, women play a larger role in Ghana and Nigeria. However, women

Figure O.5 Women Employed in Informal and Formal Sectors of Selected Countries

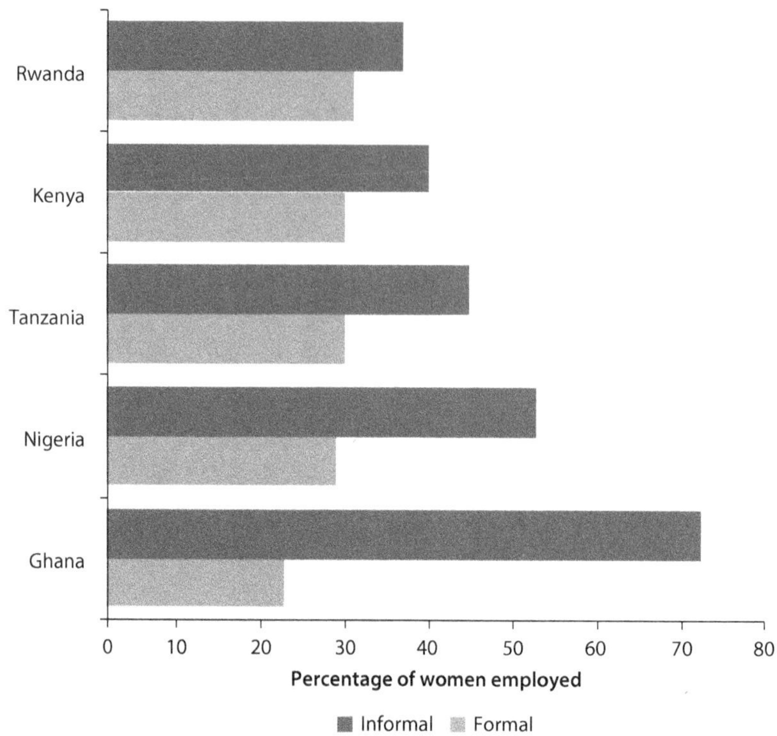

Sources: Elaborations based on GSS 2005–06; KNBS 2007; NBS 2007; NBSN 2004; and NISR 2007.

are everywhere more likely than men to be engaged in farm activities, and for those working in the nonfarm sector, they are more likely to work in the informal than the formal sector (figure O.5). Within the informal sector, they are often confined to lower-earning occupations such as unpaid family work.

- *The reasons for working in the nonfarm informal sector are different in urban and rural areas, and the pattern by age is mixed.* Available information shows that workers are pushed into the informal sector in urban areas whereas they are attracted to nonfarm informal employment in rural areas, perhaps by the higher earnings compared with farming. In Tanzania, the push factors provide the principal reason for working in the informal sector with nearly 7 of 10 seeking additional income or unable to find other work opportunities. For those in rural areas, however, pull factors play an important role in the choice of employment, led by the perception of good business opportunities and the chance to open a business with the limited capital available to them. Age patterns are mixed. In Ghana and Tanzania, the mean age in formal and informal sectors is roughly the same, whereas in Kenya, Nigeria, and Rwanda the share of youth in the informal sector is higher than in the formal sector.

- *Most employment in the nonfarm informal sector is in trade and services.* In Tanzania, more than two-thirds of informal sector jobs are in trade, restaurants, and hotels. These patterns repeat in Ghana, Kenya, and Nigeria. Concentration of the informal sector in trade and services places downward pressure on the earnings of those employed in these sectors. Thus, to diversify employment in the informal sector as a means to reduce this pressure and promote higher earnings, skills will be an important part of the equation.

The Role of Skills in Improving Productivity and Promoting Earning Mobility for People Employed in the Informal Sector

Education and training is an important asset for both formal and informal employment. Overall, the study findings point to the importance of basic education for all, which helps establish a solid foundation for further skills development. The combination of cognitive and noncognitive skills development in primary and lower secondary education provides a foundation for the acquisition of technical skills and the preparation of individuals for employment with secondary and postsecondary education. This foundation is also important to the subsequent reskilling and upgrading of workers later in the life cycle. Employers look for signals of prior education and training in the recruitment process.

The informal sector displays lower education levels than the formal sector, but workers in both sectors have higher education levels than farmers. Overall, analysis of household surveys in the five countries suggests that education is associated with different kinds of employment opportunities; the share of the population with at least a primary education is significantly higher in the formal sector than the informal sector (figure O.6). The case of Tanzania also demonstrates the concentration of advanced education in the formal sector, and in particular the government sector, and the very low levels of education prevalent in farming. A vast majority of informal sector workers have completed primary education, but few have proceeded to secondary levels or higher (figure O.7).

Education translates into additional investments in skills and higher earnings. Skills acquisition is a cumulative process. In Tanzania, people working in the private formal sector are more likely to receive some form of additional training compared with those in the nonfarm informal sector. Almost 80 percent of government employees, who already have high levels of education, receive additional training. Access to basic education and literacy may open the door to postbasic education and provides a signal to employers about the ability of the worker to acquire higher levels of skills and productivity through training from different sources.

In urban and rural areas, traditional apprenticeships are the main source of skills for people in the informal sector, but traditional apprenticeships can also be valued for employment in the formal sector. Their prevalence, popularity, and gender balance differ among countries. In Tanzania, only about 1 in 10 informal operators have been through an apprenticeship; in Rwanda and Nigeria, this figure increases to 1 in 5, while in Ghana, half of those who have entered

Figure O.6 Share of Population with Primary Levels of Education or More in the Formal and Informal Sectors

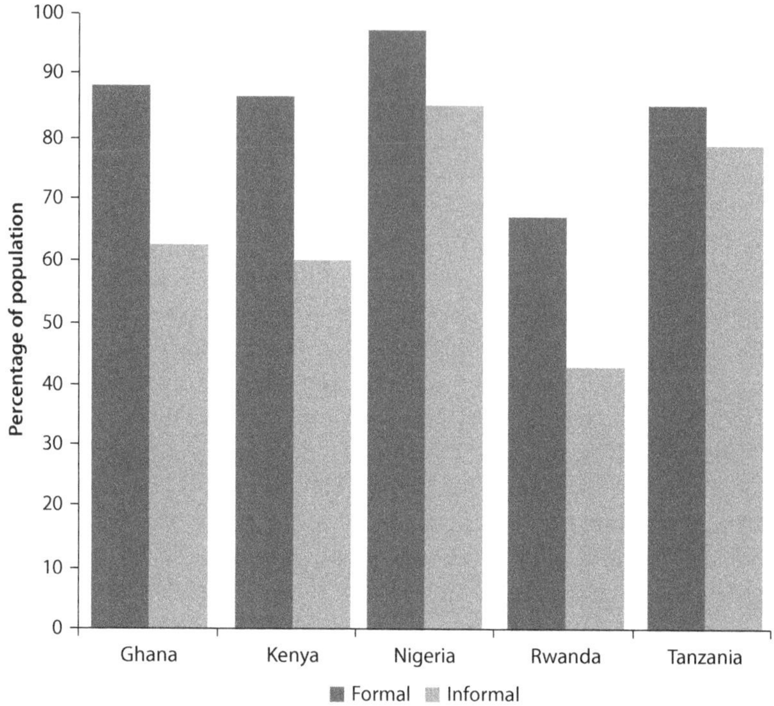

Sources: Elaborations based on GSS 2005–06; KNBS 2007; NBS 2007; NBSN 2004; and NISR 2007.

Figure O.7 Employment by Education Level in Different Sectors of Tanzania

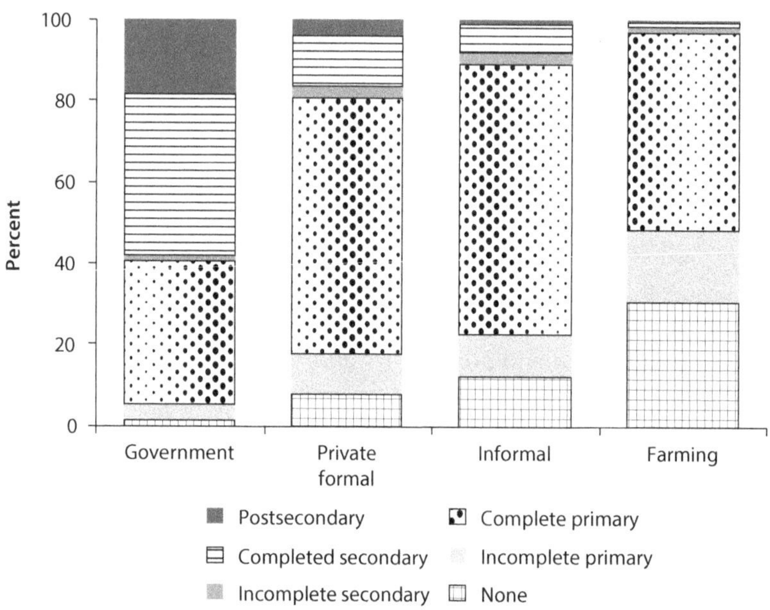

Source: Elaborations based on NBS 2007.

the informal sector are former apprentices. Finding an apprenticeship is easier in urban areas than in rural areas: such residential differences are observed in Ghana, Nigeria, and Rwanda. Apprenticeships in Ghana are the main source of skills for those working in both the informal and formal sectors. However, despite their lower cost compared to formal forms of training, apprenticeships are less accessible to the very poor. Access to apprenticeships also requires some level of basic competencies, and most apprentices have a primary or lower-secondary education (figure O.8).

Education and training are strongly linked to the type of job held. The pattern among the five countries confirms the positive link between education and training and the probability of holding employment off the farm, and similarly, whether an individual is employed in the informal or formal sector. Formal education, and particularly higher education, increases the odds of holding employment in the formal, or wage, sector for all the countries. Those with limited education are more likely to work in the informal sector, but the association between education and informal sector employment weakens at higher education levels (figure O.9). In the five countries, the results point to the strong association between acquiring education, particularly secondary and higher education, and subsequently holding formal sector employment. Lower levels of nonformal training are linked to employment in the informal sector, whereas more advanced training is coupled with employment in the formal sector.

The shortage of higher levels of education is evident in higher returns to this education, especially in the formal sector. Returns to education in the formal sector generally become significant only after completing a lower-secondary or higher level of education, including technical and vocational education. In fact, in Nigeria, returns to higher levels of education account for most of the difference between the average earnings of the formal sector and the informal sector. In both Ghana and Tanzania, evidence shows that primary education is no longer enough to increase earnings (figure O.10). The returns in Ghana show that education influences earnings most in the formal sector and that the payoff begins only with those completing a lower-secondary education. The payoff to primary education may therefore be in promoting labor mobility out of farming into the informal sector with its higher earning opportunities, but once there, no further income gains are made until higher levels of education are attained.

In most countries (Rwanda is an exception), the returns to education are lower in the informal sector than in the formal sector. Several explanations are possible for such a gap being sustained. Skills taught may not be relevant to informal sector needs. Because of the absence of sufficient employment opportunities in the formal sector, some highly educated people may fail to find a job there and are compelled to work in the informal sector, where their skills are not needed. Moreover, noncompetitive wage setting in the public sector may increase returns in the formal sector. Crowding may exist in the informal sector, which depresses earnings, or earnings premiums in large (formal) firms

Figure O.8 Access to Apprenticeship across Groups in Ghana

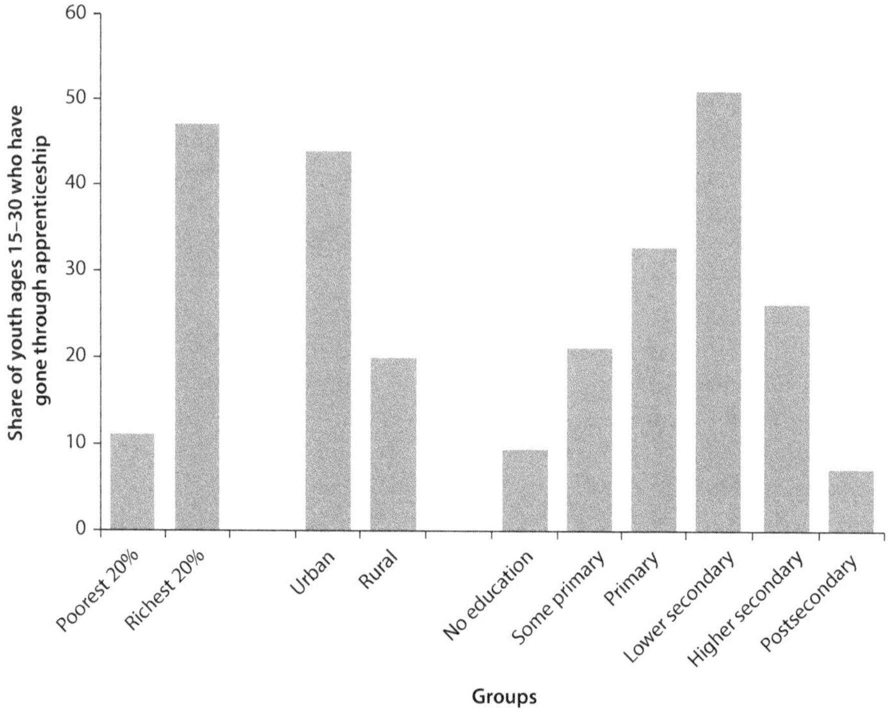

Source: Elaborations based on GSS 2005–06.

Figure O.9 Predicted Probabilities by Educational Attainment in Rwanda

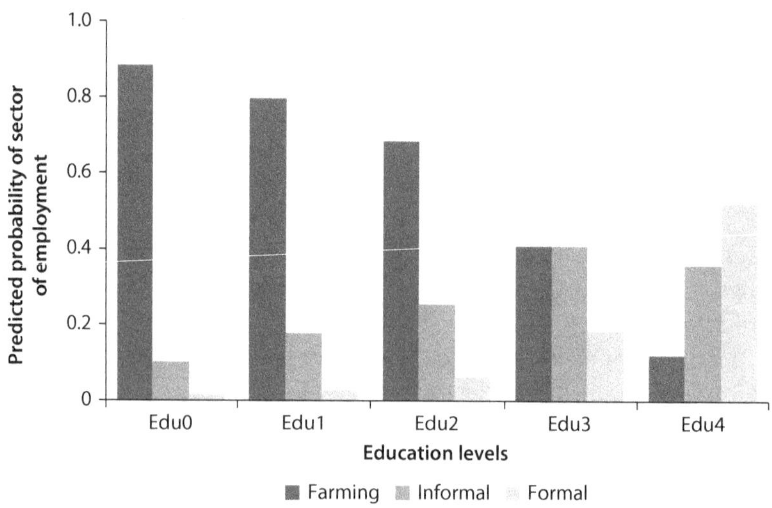

Source: Elaborations based on NISR 2007.

Note: a. The figure presents multinomial logit estimations. b. Education levels are defined as follows: Edu0 = no education; Edu1 = some education but less than completed primary education; Edu2 = completed primary and some lower secondary; Edu3 = completed lower-secondary and some higher-secondary or vocational education; Edu4 = completed higher-secondary or extended vocational education and above.

Figure O.10 Returns to Education for Wage Workers Compared with Nonwage Workers in Tanzania

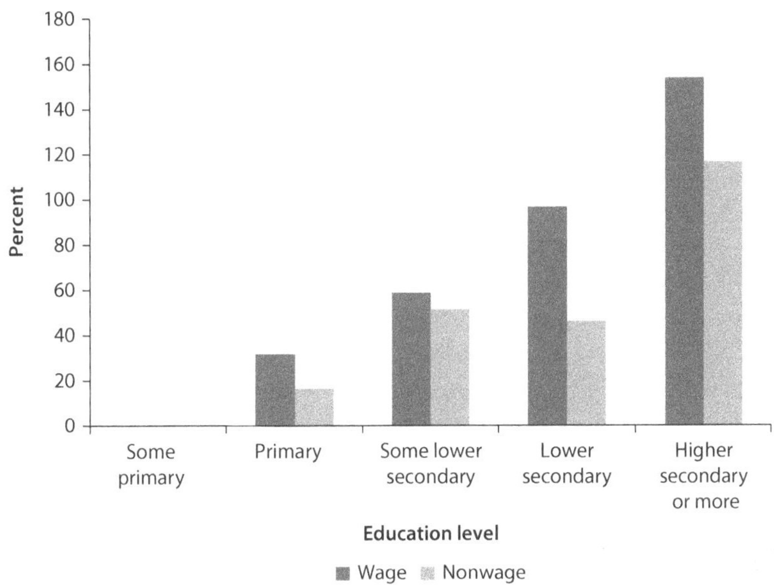

Source: Elaborations based on NBS 2007.
Note: Wages are considered a proxy for formal sector employment.

caused by productivity differences may play a role. Possibly the quality of education available to those destined for the informal sector is inherently lower.

Technical and vocational education in schools is linked to employment in both informal and formal sectors and to higher earnings. Evidence from the five countries confirms the association between training and employment off the farm in both formal and informal sectors. In Nigeria, technical training raises the chances of being in formal sector employment by 26 percent. In Kenya, it raises the probabilities of both formal and informal sector employment compared to farm work. In Nigeria, vocational training does not produce earning gains in either the informal or formal sectors. In Tanzania, lower levels of vocational training are connected with employment in the informal sector, and advanced training can raise the chances of employment in the formal sector. In Rwanda, training does not raise earnings in either sector, although a technical vocational education appears to increase earnings in the informal sector. In Ghana, the returns of secondary technical and vocational education match those of general secondary education in both formal and informal sectors.

The evidence of the impact of traditional apprenticeships on earnings is mixed. Only in Rwanda is there statistical evidence of a positive association between apprenticeships and earnings. The primary effect appears to be opening access to off-farm employment and allowing some to find employment in the formal sector. Although apprenticeships are self-regulated, self-financed, and popular in Sub-Saharan Africa, their effect on earnings is limited because of the low education levels and literacy of those who pursue their skills through this means, the low quality of the training offered by master craftspersons, and the dated technology and production methods used.

Main Policy Recommendations

A strategy to improve productivity and incomes in small businesses and household enterprises of the informal sector needs to consider factors behind the sector's shortfall in skills. These factors include the low education of people in the sector, the unequal access to training experienced by some groups, the presence of inefficient markets encouraging skills development, the lack of interest in the needs of the informal sector shown by public training providers, and the existence of other market constraints to training for informal sector enterprises. Although expanding basic education is necessary to provide the underpinnings for further skills development, complementary measures must deal with the existing large stocks of people already in the informal sector and the number of potential future entrants to the sector. These measures will need to focus on the specific needs and constraints faced by small and household enterprises in enhancing the skills of their workforce. A strategy should include the following elements:

- *Increasing efforts of public skills providers in the informal sector:* Public providers can give more attention to entrepreneurship training, second-chance and literacy education, and short courses for in-service training of those already in the informal sector. To shift attention to the skills requirements of the informal sector, public skills provision needs to move away from supply-driven financing (focused on inputs) to results-based financing that holds providers accountable for training outcomes, especially those of the informal sector (that is, trainees placed, improvements in retention and completion, and services delivered to targeted growth sectors). Moreover, national poverty reduction strategies should not only recognize the importance of the informal sector but also include concrete action plans for addressing the sector's development needs, including skills.

- *Encouraging investments in skills by small and household enterprises:* Reducing barriers to investments in skills by enterprises is an important part of the strategy for promoting higher productivity and incomes in the informal sector. Chapter 4 highlights a list of constraints to skills development faced by small and household enterprises. Lowering financing and information constraints and enabling small enterprises to invest in the skills they need to promote their growth and productivity will reduce the pressure on government to make such investments and allow government to focus on more strategic needs for improving market efficiency and equity.

- *Improving the quality of training offered by master craftspersons in apprenticeships:* Inadequate attention to the quality of apprenticeships poses a problem, as does the absence of market indicators of this quality. Examples of progress are found in Kenya, where master craftspersons receive additional training and access to new technology, thereby improving their capacity as trainers. Steps to promote information about quality through including apprenticeship trades in testing and certification systems can help the market sort among good and bad training for apprenticeships. Examples exist in Ghana of these steps taking place with support from German technical assistance.

- *Expanding second-chance programs for education:* Programs are needed that open further education opportunities for master craftspersons and apprentices. Currently, besides literacy programs, few programs in Sub-Saharan Africa offer second chances for education to the large numbers of individuals without literacy or a basic education in the informal sector. Malawi is an exception with its Complementary Basic Education Program that targets youth and adults. The program serves individuals who leave the formal education system and provides, through community facilities and contract teachers, education credentials accepted as equivalent to those offered by formal education.

- *Providing small firms in the informal sector with information about the benefits of training and competitive sources for obtaining it:* Small enterprises, unlike their larger counterparts, rarely have the specialized expertise and knowledge to identify and design curricula for training programs that are tailored for their workers, who often have less than a secondary education. Thus, to meet small enterprises' learning needs, providing them with information on the benefits of training along with information on providers who offer competitive services will be helpful. Industry associations can play an important role in providing this information to their members. Particularly to promote training among small firms, solutions need to be found to reduce their unit cost of training. Industry associations can play a role there, as well.

- *Encouraging industry associations to play a larger role in skills development for the informal sector:* Strengthening the capacity of small industry associations to play a larger role in skills development for their members can open the door to more information and better, more affordable training services for enterprises in the informal sector. The Micro and Small Enterprises Sector Board, as part of the Kenya Private Sector Alliance, has played an important role in analyzing training needs and designing training for its members as part of a youth empowerment project.

- *Improving information on training providers:* The market for information on skills for the informal sector is underdeveloped. Information on costs, quality, and outcomes associated with training is rarely available for nonformal training programs and traditional apprenticeships. To obtain such information, the performance of various providers needs to be monitored. For instance, simple inclusion of apprenticeships in current testing and certification systems and in national qualification frameworks could provide a tool for comparing skill attainment among different providers and improve the portability of these skills. More attention needs to be given to the rigorous evaluation of training programs, public and private. External technical assistance can help in this area.

- *Promoting competition and innovation in training for the informal sector:* Financing through vouchers in Kenya has created a private supply response serving the skill needs of the informal sector. The use of demand-side financing instruments such as vouchers, training funds, and results-based financing can encourage competition and innovation in training delivery, as can opening markets to private training providers. In Rwanda, the emergence of microtrainers as an innovation has created a new source of skills training for the informal sector. Improving financial services to enterprises in the informal sector also has the potential to encourage private investment in training and stimulate the supply response to this market.
- *Improving understanding of skills and policy effectiveness:* Much work remains to enrich household survey measures of skills, broaden measures of training, and enhance measurement of activity in small enterprises run out of the household. At the other end, emphasis on results-based policy making needs to be supported by program monitoring and evaluation to establish what works, where, and why.

All stakeholders (governments, public and private providers of training, and international development and financing agencies) have roles to play in the implementation of this comprehensive strategy.

- Governments can play an important role in building a market for skills for the informal sector and in supporting basic education. They can also promote efficiency and equity in training markets that serve the informal sector by changing the incentive system to serve market needs for both formal and informal sectors. Governments can use different tools to address both supply and demand constraints through financing, information, quality assurance, and the like. They can lead efforts to strengthen statistical sources and improve program monitoring and evaluation.
- Public providers of skills (including the technical and vocational education offered by ministries of education and the nonformal training offered by other ministries such as labor, youth and sports, industry, and agriculture) can play a larger role in providing skills for the informal sector. They can introduce reforms such as the use of modular curricula for training that offer greater flexibility in delivery and reduce the time needed away from work for those in the informal sector. Although the private sector is more responsive to the informal sector, public providers can offer other services that contribute to the skills needed by those in the informal sector, such as introducing adult literacy, second-chance education, and entrepreneurship courses.

- Private providers of skills that already play an important role in serving informal sector enterprises should be encouraged and their efficiency improved. Evidence shows that private training providers are responsive to increased demand in the informal sector, and better regulation and market information can improve their efficiency. On the supply side, governments and donors can play an important role in strengthening the capacity of informal sector associations for organizing and delivering training. On the demand side, financing through targeted vouchers and training funds can improve equity and access to skills for the informal sector.

- International development and financing agencies can also play an important role in the financing of skills for small and household enterprises and ensure that their assistance focuses on interventions that help improve productivity and incomes for the nonfarm informal sector. Among possible investments are improving the skills and pedagogy of master craftspersons; building the capacity of industry associations to serve the skill needs of the informal sector; offering targeted demand-side financing to promote equity in access to skills, competition, and innovation for the informal sector; supporting public sector reforms in technical and vocational education that expand services to the informal sector; strengthening market institutions that provide information about quality; and supporting rigorous evaluations of programs for skills development serving the small and household enterprises of the informal sector.

References

GSS (Ghana Statistical Service). 2005–06. *Ghana Living Standards Survey (GLSS) V 2005–2006*. World Bank SHIP Harmonized Dataset, GHA_2006_GLSS_v01_M_v01_A_SHIP. http://microdata.worldbank.org/index.php/catalog/1064.

KNBS (Kenya National Bureau of Statistics, Ministry of Planning and National Development). 2007. *Kenya Integrated Household Budget Survey 2005–2006*. Version 1.0 of the KNBS dataset, Government of Kenya, Nairobi. http://statistics.knbs.or.ke/nada/index.php/catalog/8.

NBS (National Bureau of Statistics, Ministry of Finance and Economics Affairs). 2007. *Integrated Labour Force Survey 2006 (ILFS 2006)*. Version 1.0 of the public use datasets (August 2007), provided by the National Bureau of Statistics, Government of Tanzania, Dar es Salaam. http://www.nbs.go.tz.

NBSN (National Bureau of Statistics, Nigeria). 2004. *National Living Standard Survey 2003*. Federal Government of Nigeria, Abuja. http://www.nigerianstat.gov.ng/nada/index.php/catalog/28.

NISR (National Institute of Statistics of Rwanda). 2007. *Enquête Intégrale sur les Conditions de Vie des Ménages 2005–2006 - Overview- 10 -2005-2006 (EICV 2005)*. Version 1.1. NISR, Kigali. http://www.statistics.gov.rw/survey-period/integrated-household-living-conditions-survey-2-eicv-2.

United Nations. 2010. *World Urbanization Prospects: The 2009 Revision Population Database*. United Nations Population Division (accessed August 2012). http://esa.un.org/wup2009/unup/index.asp?panel=1.

———. 2011. *World Population Prospects, The 2010 Revision* (database). Population Division of the United Nations Department of Economic and Social Affairs of the United Nations Secretariat, New York (accessed August 2012). http://esa.un.org/unpd/wpp/index.htm.

World Bank. 2012. *World Development Indicators 2012*. Washington, DC: World Bank. http://data.worldbank.org/data-catalog/world-development-indicators.

CHAPTER 1

Introduction

In This Chapter

The informal sector of Sub-Saharan Africa, represented by small and household businesses in the nonfarm sector, has proven prolific in creating jobs and incomes, cultivating entrepreneurs, and absorbing the large numbers of youth entering the regional workforce each year. Improving its productivity is essential for regional employment and income growth, and skills development is an important part of this equation. This chapter reviews the literature about skills development for the informal sector and the challenges to raising the productivity and incomes of people working in the informal sector.

Background

The informal sector first entered economic development literature in the early 1970s through the International Labour Organization (ILO) and its World Employment Programme (Bangasser 2000). Identified in Kenya and earlier in Ghana, the sector was described as including small household enterprises that operated largely outside the purview of government regulatory and tax authorities. It was set against a formal sector where firms were considered to be in compliance with those same authorities. The informal sector and its firms were understood to be a safety net for people unable to find employment in the formal sector. The informal sector was thought to provide a pool of surplus labor for developing countries that industrialization would in time absorb into the modern wage sector. However, it has since become clear that what was observed as the informal sector is not diminishing in size with industrialization. Instead, the informal sector is holding its own and even growing as a share of employment in countries throughout the world (Verick 2006).

The informal sector today is a global phenomenon and is found in developing and industrialized countries worldwide (Becker 2004; OECD 2009). According to the January 1993 resolution of the 15th Conference of International Statisticians under the ILO, the informal sector represents all unregistered or unincorporated enterprises in the nonfarm sector that are below a certain size and that are operated by self-employed people who work on their own account or who employ contributing family members and, on an occasional basis, wage employees. Individuals who are in these employment categories and who work in small, unregistered enterprises, usually with fewer than 10 employees, are counted in the informal sector (Roubaud and Razafindrakoto 2007). The sector has become part of a growing trend of informal employment spurred by the competition of globalization, one that now includes those working in the modern wage sector without social protection and job security (ILO 2002c, 11–13).[1]

Sub-Saharan Africa's informal sector covers a large share of the nonfarm workforce employed outside the full-time, stable, protected employment of the formal wage sector. Researchers' view of the formal and informal sectors has changed over time as evidence grew that the record of compliance with regulations and taxes has been more mixed than initially described. Experience has shown that compliance is influenced by the benefits of regulations balanced against the cost of compliance.[2] Small and household enterprises in some instances find compliance with selected regulations beneficial. The formal and informal sectors are thus more like points on a continuum that range from full compliance to noncompliance with regulations. Because the informal sector cuts across many industrial sectors, it is often referred to as the *informal economy*.

This book focuses on the nonfarm informal sector because it has been a growing source of employment for youth over the past four decades, as well as for older workers pursuing entrepreneurial goals and others adjusting to structural changes in the region's employment (Bangasser 2000; Becker 2004; Fox and Gaal 2008; Haan 2006; ILO 2002a; Johanson and Adams 2004; Liimatainen 2002). The image of the sector has changed with time. Rather than viewing it as a safety net and a temporary stop while workers search for employment in the modern wage sector, growing numbers of school leavers see the informal sector as a destination that offers opportunities to those wanting to become entrepreneurs[3] and one that can offer job satisfaction as high as formal work. Indeed, expanding entrepreneurship has become one of the options for addressing Africa's sizable youth employment challenge (World Bank 2009b, 1–26).

The nonfarm informal sector in Africa continues to be an important economic feature, accounting for a significant share of national output and the well-being of a growing number of households. Africa's growth has not created enough productive jobs to absorb the 7 million to 10 million young people entering the labor force each year. Unlike other regions, Africa has little open unemployment. Instead, many individuals work in low-productivity jobs in the informal sector (World Bank 2011). The slow pace of job growth in the formal sector and the sector's small size make it unlikely to absorb the growing numbers of youth entering the workforce and those already employed in the informal sector. While continuing to create formal sector jobs, African countries need to increase the productivity—and hence earnings—of people employed in the nonfarm informal sector, many of whom work in household enterprises.

Employment in the nonfarm informal sector is robust and operates in tandem with industrialization. Capturing the scale and characteristics of informal employment and its contribution to national welfare and poverty reduction is a first step for many countries in developing strategies that recognize the informal sector and promote ways to improve its productivity and income. Improving the skills of people employed in the nonfarm informal sector is prevalent among these strategies.

This book sets out to understand how skills are enhanced in the informal sector as part of a larger strategy to improve the economic performance of the sector. The nonfarm informal sector, with its small and household enterprises, promises to remain a part of the economic landscape for the future (Fox and Sohnesen 2012), and the ILO observes that the formal sector is experiencing increasing informalization as a consequence of globalization and competition. Given the cumulative relevance of the informal sector for growth, jobs, and poverty reduction in Sub-Saharan Africa, it makes sense for countries to think about how to improve the productivity and incomes of those working in the nonfarm informal sector. Providing access to skills is one way to do this but requires strategies that can successfully overcome the constraints that impede skills development in small firms.

Public Interest in the Nonfarm Informal Sector

Informal sector activities in Africa hold a significant and, in some cases, dominant share of their respective markets, spanning mining, manufacturing, commerce, finance, and other sectors. Examples are found in countries like Kenya, Nigeria, and Senegal; on the streets and in home-based activities such as vending of food and small merchandise, tailoring of garments, manufacture of furniture, and repair of automobiles; as well as in health care provided by traditional healers. The size of the sector was estimated in 2007 for 43 countries in Sub-Saharan Africa (see figure 1.1). The sector accounted, on average, for 40 percent of gross national product in these countries. The sheer size of the sector has forced governments to acknowledge its existence and importance to the national economy and the welfare of those it employs (ILO 2002c, 24; Schneider 2002). In South Africa, which has a relatively large modern wage sector, the informal economy still contributes over 20 percent of GNP.

Public interest in the informal sector is driven by a series of questions. They include its size and the demographic profile of the people it employs, its contribution to national income accounts, the effect it has on household poverty, the access it provides workers to instruments of social protection to manage different risks, and the factors behind its sustained presence.

The growth of the labor force and the need for jobs have been a key source of interest in the informal sector of Sub-Saharan Africa. Since the 1970s, the sector has filled a gap left by the formal wage sector as a principal source of job creation (see, for example, Becker 2004; Chaudhuri and Mukhopadhyay 2009; Tiwari 2005). Rapid labor force expansion has outpaced job growth in the formal wage sector. Fertility rates behind this expansion have been higher in Sub-Saharan Africa than in other regions, and although these rates are declining, they remain elevated by comparison with other regions.[4]

Figure 1.1 Informal Economy as a Percentage of GNP in Sub-Saharan Africa, 2006–07

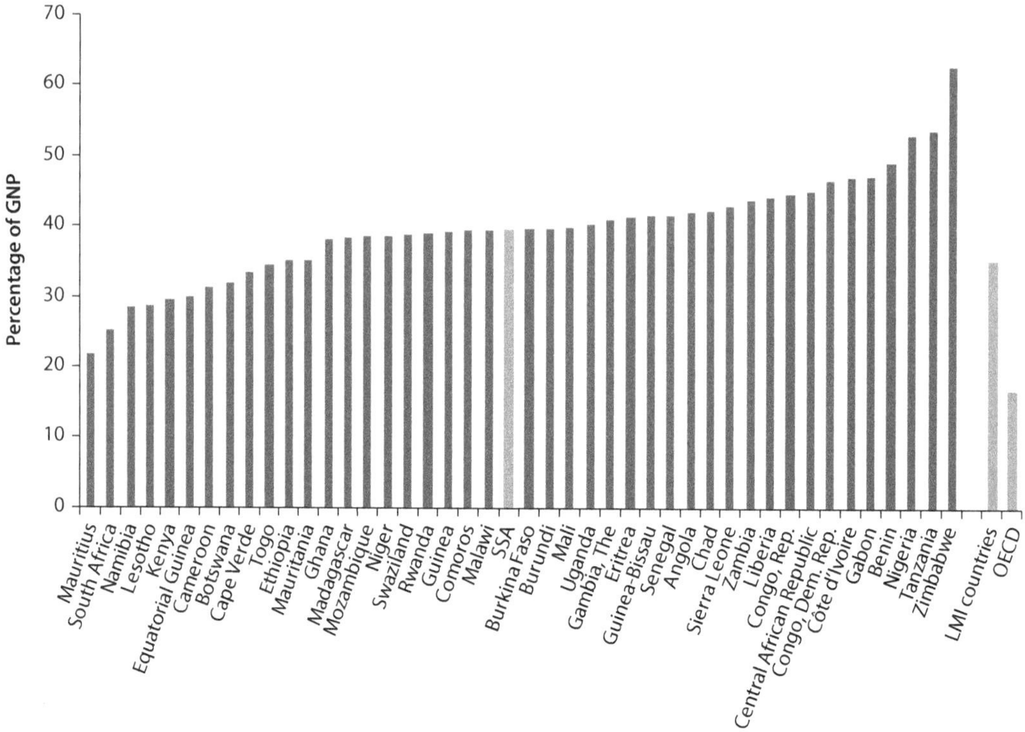

Source: Elaborations based on Schneider, Buehn, and Montenegro 2010.
Note: GNP = gross national product; LMI = low and middle income; OECD = Organisation for Economic Co-operation and Development; SSA = Sub-Saharan Africa.

Sustained population and labor force growth and accelerating rural–urban migration create pressure for job creation, especially for youth. Since 1985, the size of the youth population (defined as 15–24 years of age) doubled in Sub-Saharan Africa, from 85 million to 170 million. During the same period, urban populations almost tripled, from 120 million to 320 million, and the trends are likely to continue in the future (figure 1.2).

Modest economic growth rates have restrained formal sector job creation, which in turn has curbed labor demand and opportunities for higher-earning jobs. Employment opportunities in the formal wage sector have not developed in parallel with the labor force boom. In many countries, economic policies in the past did not foster the enabling environment needed to decisively raise investment, and with it labor demand, in the formal wage sector. Even in recent years, and notwithstanding pockets of regional growth in oil-producing countries and other diversifying economies, the modern wage sector's growth has remained sluggish, and wage jobs still account for less than half of total employment in most countries (figure 1.3). Meanwhile, low income levels and lack of social protection systems mean that few people can afford to be unemployed.[5]

Figure 1.2 Youth and Urban Populations in Sub-Saharan Africa, 1985, 2010, and 2035

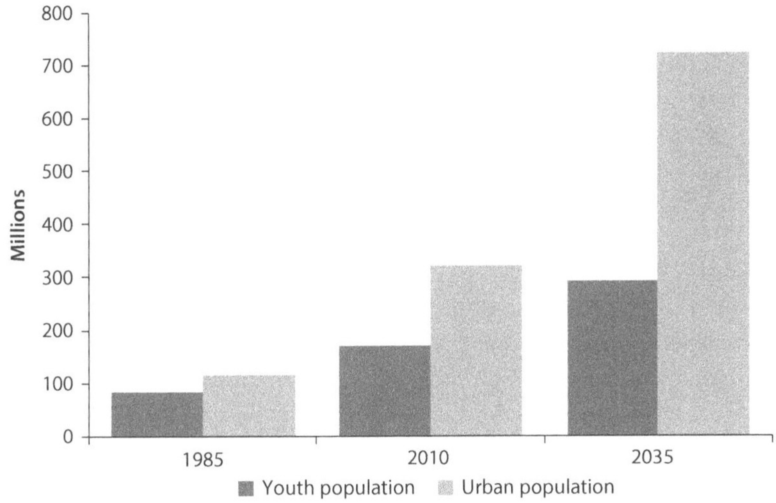

Sources: UN 2010, 2011.

Figure 1.3 Wage and Salaried Workers in Sub-Saharan Africa, 1980s–2000s

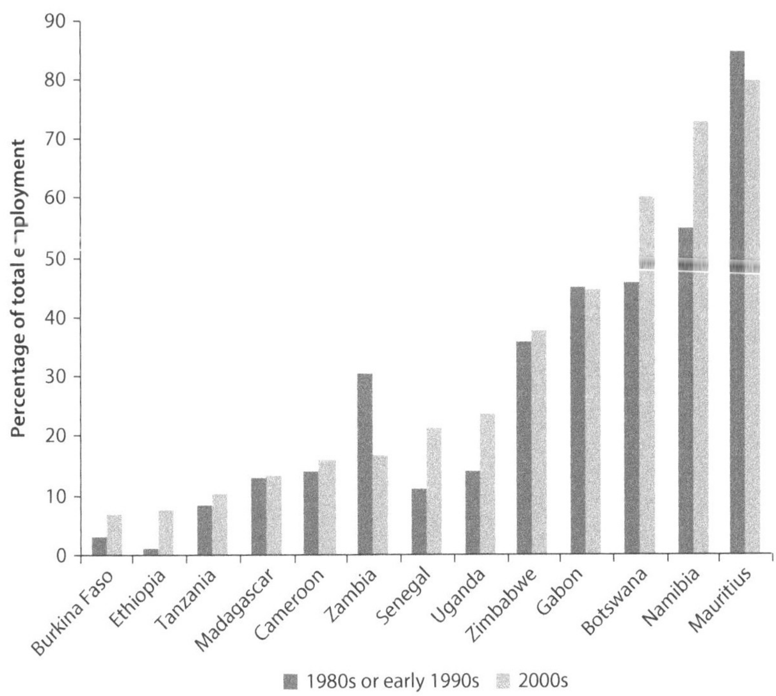

Source: World Bank 2012.

This lack of job creation in the formal sector has meant a majority of people seeking employment outside the farm sector must create their own jobs in small and household enterprises of the informal sector. A majority of the region's population continues to depend on low-productivity farming, while the informal nonfarm sector has become the residual source of employment for growing numbers of youth seeking livelihoods (World Bank 2008). Some people may actively seek entrepreneurial opportunity in the informal sector, but the majority of informal work is likely the result of lack of other earning opportunities. Although the improved policy environment in the 2000s and the resulting prospects for growth hold promise, the small size of the wage sector suggests the informal sector will remain an important economic force for years to come.

Various sources indicate the informal sector is larger in Sub-Saharan Africa than in other regions (ILO 2002c; OECD 2009). Although variation exists between countries, the informal sector accounts for a sizable and often dominant share of nonfarm employment. Using nonfarm self-employment for the latest year available as a proxy for the size of the informal sector, its share reaches over 40 percent for a majority of countries, ranging from nearly 12 percent in South Africa to over 88 percent in Benin, and many of the self-employed operators are women (table 1.1).

A World Bank review of household enterprises in Sub-Saharan Africa (Fox and Sohnesen 2012) confirms that the informal nonfarm sector is an important contributor to economic development in low-income Sub-Saharan Africa as a source of employment, earnings, and household livelihoods. Thus, creating the conditions to grow the sector and implement effective employment strategies will, by necessity, be important for the next two decades. In particular, policies need to focus not only on productivity growth but also on viability.

All indicators point to the importance of the nonfarm informal sector as a source of employment in the region and as a significant presence in the economic landscape. Signs exist of growth that could restore the expansion of the formal wage sector, and the employment and earning standards of the informal sector may not meet the standards established by the formal sector. Nevertheless, the ubiquity of the informal sector is synonymous with the well-being of millions of workers and the vibrancy of their communities. Indeed, among the first questions to emerge, beyond the size of the sector, are its impact on household poverty and the profile of those employed in the sector. The answers to these questions are essential to informing policies for improving the economic performance of Sub-Saharan Africa.

Skills Play Different Roles in the Formal and Informal Sectors

Access to skilled workers and managers is a key ingredient to the success of any business in both the formal and informal sectors. This book focuses on performance-enhancing skills and how knowledge gained through different modes of skills development can improve the productivity and earnings of people who make their living in the informal sector. The literature surrounding

Table 1.1 Self-Employment as a Percentage of All Nonfarm Employment and Women as a Percentage of Self-Employment, Latest Survey Year

Country	*Self-employed in nonfarm employment*	*Women's share in nonfarm self-employment*
Benin	88.7	59.9
Botswana	18.8	44.7
Burkina Faso	69.7	53.6
Burundi	35.6	22.0
Cameroon	43.8	23.1
Central African Republic	57.5	47.4
Chad	72.4	54.0
Comoros	61.0	24.8
Congo, Dem. Rep.	51.8	39.5
Congo, Rep.	38.7	42.6
Ethiopia	73.6	60.9
Ghana	66.9	74.6
Guinea	71.8	31.0
Guinea-Bissau	48.4	35.5
Kenya	61.0	67.6
Lesotho	17.6	56.4
Liberia	40.8	38.7
Madagascar	46.3	45.9
Malawi	33.2	24.5
Mali	83.9	57.2
Mauritius	17.7	33.9
Mozambique	46.5	29.2
Niger	83.7	47.4
Rwanda	25.4	21.9
South Africa	11.6	57.1
Sudan	40.7	12.5
Tanzania	27.5	[illegible]
Togo	68.3	61.0
Zambia	17.9	46.6

Source: OECD 2009, 4–7, table 2.

micro- and small enterprise development emphasizes the importance of access to a range of business development services and finance as a means for achieving these objectives. Lack of access to capital and technology is acknowledged as a constraint to the growth and development of small business, as is the need for access to communications, transportation, marketing, accounting, and other services. At the core of a business's success, however, is the knowledge of the people engaged in its operations and management.

The system for skills development in many countries is designed for an industrial environment; it provides specialized skills in a full-time school setting and takes as long as two or three years for completion. Following national independence in the 1960s for many countries in Sub-Saharan Africa, governments and donors sought to expand access to vocational and technical education to prepare households to take advantage of the new employment expected with industrialization. This training format is not well suited for the typical entrepreneur or contributing family member of today's informal sector.

Skills development for the informal sector is different from that of the formal sector, where large firms have the resources to acquire and sustain a well-educated workforce and to enhance skills with training on and off the job. Small businesses often depend on workers who perform multiple tasks and thus need multiple skills, yet finding this type of training ("multiskilling") and affording its cost often act as constraints to upgrading skills in the informal sector. The ability to absorb and benefit from training starts with a good foundation of formal education. This foundation has proven to be an important variable influencing later skills acquisition.

The acquisition of skills to improve productivity and earnings by small and household enterprises is more difficult than for the typical firm in the formal sector. Small firms lack the specialized knowledge and personnel needed to define skill needs and design appropriate training. In addition, questions surrounding the poverty status of people who work in the informal sector and their ability to finance skills acquisition are important. Not only does taking time off from production to participate in training have a high opportunity cost for small firms, their generated cash flow generally is insufficient to pay for training on or off the job. These costs effectively stifle investments in human capital and obviate the inability of the sector to leverage economies of scale (box 1.1).

How well has public school–based vocational and technical education adapted to the needs of the informal sector with its small and household enterprises? Public provision of skills training has been joined by that of for-profit and nonprofit nongovernmental organizations (NGOs). The quality and responsiveness of this training to the needs of the informal sector have posed similar quandaries. Much of this training capacity is located in larger urban settings where markets are sufficiently large to support profit-making institutions. The location of this capacity is well situated for the urban informal sector but less well

Box 1.1 Why Skills Development Differs in the Informal and Formal Sectors

Sources of difference in small firms in the informal sector:

- High opportunity cost to train.
- Low cash flow to pay for training.
- Greater needs for multiple skills.
- Lack of capacity to identify training needs and design training programs.
- Lack of knowledge about benefits of training.
- Absence of economies of scale for training, driving up cost.
- Limited supply of trainer capacity serving the informal sector.

positioned for small firms operating in rural areas. Just how large is the rural informal sector, and what options does it offer for providing the workforce skills? These are questions of significance to public policy concerned with improving the economic performance of the informal sector.

Enterprises are another source of skills development. In the informal sector, master craftspersons and owners of small businesses provide training for their workers through traditional apprenticeships. The apprenticeships involve commitments by the master craftspersons to the parents or youths to provide training for specified periods in exchange for small fees or the apprentice's labor. The training is recognized for its high relevance to the tasks performed and is self-financing, though subject to questions of quality (Johanson and Adams 2004). Although traditional apprenticeships address many of the constraints to skills development in the informal sector, they suffer weaknesses connected with the use of outdated technologies, limited instructional capacity of the master craftsperson, poor quality of training, and lack of portability of the skills obtained, as well as constraints imposed by the limited education of the apprentices. These issues suggest an agenda for how countries can improve skills development in the informal sector.

What can public policy do today to improve productivity and incomes of small and household enterprises through better access to skills? A useful beginning in answering this question is asking how many governments actually recognize the informal sector for its importance to the economy and have national strategies in place that strive to improve the economic performance of the sector and reduce barriers to its formalization. Removing barriers to business development and growth—including skills—for the informal sector can lead to better resource use and higher incomes, and balancing access to services whether by residence, income, or gender can promote wider opportunities for the poor. Existing literature has touched upon some of these issues; none has delved into the implicit intricacies.

What We Know about Skills and the Informal Sector

Work skills are acquired in different settings (classrooms, workshops, and on the job) and provided by public education and training institutions, private for-profit and nonprofit institutions, and employers through training in and out of the workplace. Training may be taken to qualify for employment or later to upgrade skills and prepare for the introduction of new technology in production. For people working in the informal sector, some or all of these approaches to skills may be used (McGrath and King 1994). Public and private schools play an important role in preparing individuals for creating their own employment by providing them with a technical skill, usually through a technical and vocational education curriculum. A commonly used approach to self-employment is working for another employer and acquiring skills on the job, either informally or through an apprenticeship, before leaving to set up one's own business. Each approach has strengths and weaknesses.

Public Provision of Skills

Surprisingly, public secondary and tertiary schools with technical and vocational education programs have played a smaller role than expected in preparing workers for informal sector employment (Atchoarena and Delluc 2001).[6] Most policies and practices reflect the postindependence thinking of the 1960s, overlooking (or dismissing) 50 years of structural change and growth within the informal sector (Brewer 2004; Filipiak 2007; Haan 2006; Liimatainen 2002; NISER 2007). Structural adjustment programs and tight government budgets contributed in the 1980s and 1990s to the deterioration of facilities and equipment and to the inability of these institutions to update programs and respond to the shift to informal sector employment (ILO 2002b; Johanson and Adams 2004).

Other factors have hindered the public sector's response to the skills challenge of the informal sector. The training offered by the public sector is considered theoretical without sufficient opportunities for practice and biased toward white-collar jobs in the wage sector (Liimatainen 2002). Entry requirements and fees are often too high for this schooling, and the training methods used are better suited to a more literate population. The courses offered fail to meet the multiskilling needs of the highly diverse informal sector. Where public financing is used without accountability for results, the institutions have few incentives to monitor and adjust to changes in the demand for skills (Ziderman 2003). Finally, weak accountability influences not only the responsiveness of the public sector to special needs of the informal sector but, in a more general way, to the changing demand for skills in the formal sector.

The population targeted for public training and its mode of delivery are factors behind the failure to reach out to the informal sector with skills. Public technical and vocational education programs are largely focused on full-time students preparing for entry into the world of work and require sustained periods of time in school. The focus on preservice training is not matched by a focus on in-service training for those already employed. This model proves ill-suited to people among the poor seeking to combine school and work in part-time fashion to provide families with income and similarly to meet the needs of older workers who are unable to afford time away from work for training. A more flexible approach is needed to meet the needs of those finding employment in the informal sector. Good practices can be found where schools have adopted modular, competency-based curricula that permit flexible entry to and exit from training at hours not interfering with the workday.

The Kenyan *Jua Kali* program (Kiswahili for "work under the hot sun") offered training vouchers to people in the informal sector in the mid-1990s and provides an interesting window on the response of public training institutions to the demand for skills these vouchers create. The vouchers were observed to produce a positive supply response to the demand created for skills, though predominantly from NGOs and master craftspersons in the informal sector. New programs were developed, tailored to the needs of voucher recipients, and offered during off hours to fit work schedules. Public institutions showed little interest in adapting their traditional programs to respond to this new source of demand (Adams 2001). The motivation for responding to demand like this with innovative programs was reduced where public institutions were unable to retain locally generated income for quality improvements and incentives for instructors.

The more recent introduction of entrepreneurship education represents an innovation in public secondary and tertiary education institutions that is relevant to the informal sector. These programs help develop attitudes favorable to starting one's own business and provide knowledge and skills for running a business (for example, business law, accounting and bookkeeping, credit and finance, and marketing).[7] Just how well a public sector institution can provide entrepreneurial skills for the private sector is a question meriting more study. Farstad (2002) examined entrepreneurship education programs in secondary and tertiary education institutions in Botswana, Kenya, and Uganda. He found instructors generally well qualified but observed no immediate effect on the numbers of students leaving school to start a business after completing their education.

The fact that students did not immediately start new businesses is not an indicator of failure on the part of these programs, however. Farstad acknowledged that the more traditional route to self-employment starts with an initial period of apprenticeship or wage employment to gain practical experience and build professional self-confidence before setting out to start a new business. In a comparison of graduates of general secondary education programs and those from technical and vocational education programs, he observed that the latter group was more likely to start businesses within a few years of graduation. The technical education provided a skill that was then honed on the job with an apprenticeship and wage employment before launching a new business.

Entrepreneurship education has encouraged schools to think outside traditional patterns of classroom instruction. Periods of mandatory work placement have been introduced along with compulsory development of a business plan subject to examination and grading. In Kenya, entrepreneurship education is delivered with the assistance of Small Business Centers attached to all public postsecondary and some private technical and vocational education institutions. In Botswana, students have benefited from the requirement that they establish and operate a student enterprise. Cooperation between training institutions and private enterprises in curriculum development and training delivery was found to add value in the three countries Farstad studied.

Other options for engaging public education and training institutions in skills development for the informal sector are reviewed in the section below on employers and traditional apprenticeships. The low educational background of many people employed in the informal sector opens opportunities for public sector institutions to give greater attention to adult education and literacy programs and to offer what is called second-chance education tailored to the needs of those who have missed opportunities for early education (Adams 2007; World Bank 2007). Where found, these programs have provided low-cost education to open doors for employment. They have not yet been carefully evaluated for their effect on further training and earnings.

Nongovernment Provision

Although the public sector has been slow to respond to changes in demand for skills brought about by growth of the informal sector, private institutions have been more responsive to this demand (Brewer 2004). Private institutions are of two types, for profit and nonprofit. The for-profit institutions grew in numbers in the 1990s with the decreased capacity of public providers (Atchoarena and Esquieu 2002). Although many are registered trainers and follow official curricula and prepare trainees for government trade tests like their public counterparts, a large number are unregistered, small in scale, and part of the informal sector themselves. They appear as storefront operations that can be observed in any African city.

Tuition and training fees constitute their main sources of income, although registered institutions may receive government subsidies. Largely dependent on fees, for-profit institutions are concentrated in urban markets and found less frequently in rural areas. They are seen as responsive to demands for skills, adjusting quickly to changing needs. The programs offered often require limited investment in equipment and facilities and enable easy market entry and exit for the providers. Business courses are popular, as are information technology programs. Other courses cover tailoring, driving schools, food preparation, auto repair, cosmetology, and the like. Programs in the for-profit sector are often shorter in duration to fit the "just-in-time" learning needs of trainees.

Even though fees are kept low, they still may not be affordable for the poorest of the poor. Quality varies widely where standards are left to the provider (Johanson and Adams 2004). Private for-profit providers could play a larger role in providing training to those in the informal sector. Their programs are demand led, and their sometimes modular, short courses are well suited to a more flexible delivery of skills training for people who cannot afford long spells away from work. Expanding the role of these providers demands attention to the capital market constraints they face and the incentives needed to encourage more services in rural areas and for the poor. The promotion of private training associations could open opportunities for cooperation and reduction of costs while providing a framework for accreditation and quality assurance.

The term *NGO* generally refers to a range of nonprofit organizations that include providers of training (Haan 2006). Faith-based organizations (FBOs) and international agencies play an important role in this capacity along with national and local community-based organizations. NGOs include local branches of strong international and national NGOs with wide coverage and smaller community-based organizations. Training by larger NGOs is sometimes linked to other support services for small business, including microcredit. Small business incubators, operated by NGOs, offer entrepreneurs a package of business services, including training, but have not been carefully studied in Africa. Large church-based training NGOs like Don Bosco and secular NGOs like Opportunities Industrialization Centers are found in a number of African countries.

Many of the smaller faith-based and community-based organizations maintain a strong social emphasis in their training outreach to the rural poor, minorities, women, and people with disabilities. Their training activities tend to have social and cultural rather than economic objectives with the result that their training is of limited value in helping participants enter into self-employment (Haan 2006). Overall, quality is low: traditional trades are the focus with less attention to newer technologies; curricula are outdated; theoretical rather than practical training is offered. Most services are generally free of charge, but some are beginning to charge minimal fees. These NGOs do serve the poor, but they offer little that translates into preparation for self-employment.

What Haan (2006) calls "traditional training NGOs" are larger in size and specialize in skills training. The Jesuit schools are an example. They benefit from international assistance and tend to resemble training provided by the public sector with full-time, center-based training of long duration directed at wage employment in the formal sector. In many respects they look like modern, better-equipped versions of public technical and vocational education schools. The quality of training offered in these traditional training NGOs tends to be better than that found in public institutions, offering more practical experience, but still without a focus on self-employment. These institutions are more likely to reach into rural areas and serve the poor. Their financial base, however, is often limited and insecure.

Enterprise Training

Enterprises employ skilled workers, and they train and provide needed skills and experience for employees to promote competiveness and profitability. The training offered by enterprises tends to be short term in nature and to use the firm's own skilled workers for delivery. In other cases, firms will engage external vendors for delivery. The training may be offered on site in the enterprise, such as an apprenticeship might be, or off site in an institutional setting. With time, some of the workers choose to create their own employment with the acquired skills.

Enterprises in Sub-Saharan Africa are active trainers. The World Bank provides a profile of enterprise training in more than 100 countries worldwide through its Enterprise Surveys. These show considerable variation in enterprise training across regions (see figure 1.4).

Earlier Enterprise Surveys showed that large and modern enterprises trained more, focusing on the educated workforce, whereas smaller firms relied largely on traditional apprenticeships. An earlier version of the Enterprise Surveys in Sub-Saharan Africa, the Regional Program for Enterprise Development, captured training by enterprises in the mid-1990s and the correlates of this training (Biggs, Shah, and Srivastava 1995). Enterprises that were active trainers were large in size measured by employment, active exporters, users of technology, and beneficiaries of foreign direct investment (Johanson and Adams 2004). Regional Program for Enterprise Development surveys in Kenya, Zambia, and Zimbabwe found that the training of workers was selective, with those having higher levels of education more likely to be chosen (Nielsen, Rosholm, and

Figure 1.4 Percentage of Firms Offering Formal Training Programs for Permanent, Full-Time Employees, Latest Year Available

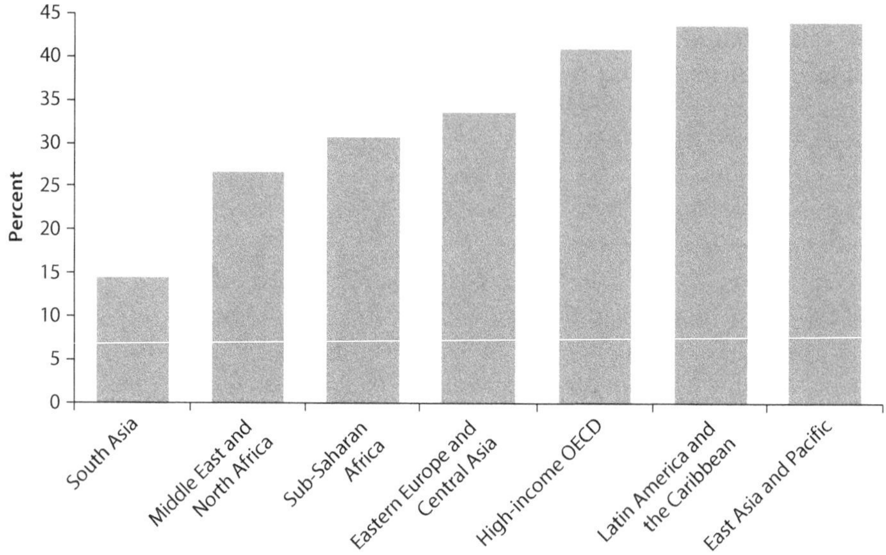

Source: World Bank 2013.
Note: OECD = Organisation for Economic Co-operation and Development.

Dabalen 2007). Only 4.6 percent of firms in Kenya, Zambia, and Zimbabwe with 10 or fewer employees trained, in comparison with 81 percent of firms with 151 employees or more (Nielsen, Rosholm, and Dabalen 2007). The effect of this training was favorable on the output of enterprises and the wages of workers. A 1 percentage point increase in the workers trained from the sample average of 9 percent translated into a 60 percent increase in value added for all firms and a 99 percent increase for micro- and small enterprises. Training was estimated to increase wages on average by 15–21 percent (Biggs, Shah, and Srivastava 1995).

One of the possible solutions to training constraints for the informal sector comes in the form of support for industry associations (see Johanson and Adams 2004). The formation of industry associations and their engagement in training has offered solutions to a number of the problems smaller enterprises face. These associations promote a greater awareness of the benefits of training among small enterprises, help in defining training needs for members and the design of appropriate training programs, contribute to scale economies in the delivery of training and reduce the unit cost to the enterprise, and establish training standards for a sector and certify the skills acquired as a means to promote the quality of the training offered. This role is already played by construction associations and many others, and could be expanded. However, there has been little rigorous examination of the effect of these associations on skills development in the informal sector.

Traditional Apprenticeships

Traditional apprenticeships are by far the most frequent form of skills training in Africa for the informal sector, with a concentration in West and Central Africa. Filipiak (2007), Haan (2006), and Liimatainen (2002) estimate that up to 70 percent of urban informal sector workers in Africa have been trained through the traditional apprenticeship system. The Ghana Statistical Service, for example, found 207,000 youths registered as apprentices in 2002, while in this same period, a much smaller number, just over 50,000 youths, were enrolled by public and private providers (World Bank 2009a).

Traditional and formal apprenticeships have fundamentally different structures. Traditional apprenticeships in the informal sector consist of private contractual arrangements between a parent or apprentice and a master craftsperson who agrees to provide practical training in the workplace, ranging from several months to three or four years in duration, and subsequently to certify the training in return for a fee or reduced earnings for the apprentice while learning.[8] Formal apprenticeships are registered with a government agency, usually a ministry of labor, and administered by employers and worker organizations.

Traditional apprenticeships have both strengths and weaknesses. They are self-financing and self-regulating and provide practical, hands-on training with good prospects for employment after the training. At the same time, traditional apprenticeships suffer from weak education among the entrants, where literacy is an issue. Few participants pass beyond a lower-secondary education and many will not have completed a primary education. In addition, choices of trades follow gender biases. Master craftspersons, in turn, do not provide theoretical knowledge alongside practical experience and, more often than not, teach outdated technologies. Pedagogy varies, and few market standards are available to judge the quality of the training provided (Johanson and Adams 2004).

These apprenticeships are available in a wide range of trades, mostly in blue-collar occupations, and are a substitute for school-based instruction.[9] Most trades offered by public and private training institutions can be mastered through a traditional apprenticeship. The flexibility of apprenticeships in combining work and learning, their affordability and self-financing, their connection with future employment, and their generally lower entry standards make them attractive as a source of skills to disadvantaged youth. Haan (2006) reports apprenticeships are less evident in eastern and southern Africa than in West and Central Africa, with youth sometimes described in the former merely as helpers. Still, in countries such as Kenya, Tanzania, and Zimbabwe, he finds large numbers of youths who are acquiring skills in informal enterprises under the guidance of a master. In Kenya, available information indicates that some 40–60 percent of informal sector operators acquire their skills through apprenticeship.

In Ghana, the use of apprenticeships is increasing for youth 15–30 years of age, as measured by Ghana's Living Standards Surveys in 1991/92 and 2005/06 (World Bank 2009a). The share entering an apprenticeship has been rising for young men and women, reaching just over one-quarter of the population, but with a higher growth rate for young women. Apprenticeships are more evident in urban than in rural areas. Education levels for youth are rising as a consequence of Ghana's efforts to provide basic education for all, and the share of those following their education with an apprenticeship is also rising at each level of education except postsecondary. Although individuals with a technical or vocational education are likely to acquire their skills in an institutional setting, those with a general education are more likely to pursue skills through an apprenticeship.

An apprenticeship opens opportunities for employment not only in the informal sector but also in other types of employment. In the Ghana surveys, 4 of 10 people working in the private informal sector as self-employed or wage workers in 2005 acquired their skills through an apprenticeship. Reflecting the growing importance of traditional apprenticeships, 51 percent of youth in nonfarm self-employment in 2005 acquired their skills in this manner, a rate twice that of the earlier period. With consumption levels used as a proxy for family income, apprenticeships in Ghana were accessible to all income groups but favored those who were better off. People in the lowest consumption quintile demonstrated much lower rates of participation in apprenticeships.

Should traditional apprenticeships form part of a strategy for skills development in Sub-Saharan Africa? Small, informal sector firms that acquire skilled workers through apprenticeships are unlikely to contribute in a significant way to the export-led development strategies of most countries. Moreover, the ability to leverage large numbers of apprentices is constrained by the number of skilled craftspersons available. These considerations aside, improving traditional apprenticeships can contribute in a positive way to employment and poverty reduction. Small firms with more productive workers have the potential to become suppliers of intermediate products in value chains leading to exports. People employed in the informal sector earn more than those in the farm sector, and improving their productivity through skills can further contribute to poverty reduction (Fox and Gaal 2008).

It is reasonable, however, to question whether emphasis on skills alone will improve the productivity and incomes of people who are employed in the informal sector. The improvement of financial services and access to credit are often listed as critical needs in surveys of small businesses, along with secure worksites and access to new technologies and business services (Liimatainen 2002; Riley and Steel 2000). NGOs play an important role in providing these services to micro-, small, and medium-size enterprises, often providing a menu of services alongside training. Working through informal sector employer associations, as noted earlier, can further assist in organizing services, particularly in skills training, by using their collective size to reduce the cost of training needs assessments, establish competency standards, develop curricula, and certify skills obtained in traditional apprenticeships.

Financing Mechanisms of Skills Development

Government policies that encourage enterprises to invest in skills subsidize the cost of this investment through various measures. The incentives vary in how they affect the actual amount of training done. Twenty-one countries in Sub-Saharan Africa have introduced training funds financed by payroll taxes, and others, such as in Namibia, have been proposed (Ziderman 2003). These funds reimburse enterprises for the cost of qualified training undertaken. Governments and training funds also use training vouchers to subsidize the cost of training by enterprises and individuals (Patrinos 2002). Offered to master craftspersons and workers in the informal sector, vouchers can help pay for training selected by the worker. The cost of training is also subsidized by governments that allow enterprises to deduct eligible training costs from their income for tax purposes or that provide tax credits for qualified training expenses.

Training levies on payrolls are used globally to mobilize additional resources for skills development (Ziderman 2003). The fairness of the levy is judged on the taxation principle that those who benefit from the resources spent on training should be the ones to pay. Payroll levies have been used to finance the provision of training by national training organizations, as found in such Latin American countries as Brazil, Colombia, and República Bolivariana de Venezuela, as well as direct training by enterprises, where a levy-grant system is adopted and administered through a training fund. Enterprises are reimbursed in a levy-grant system for the cost of qualified training expenditures by these funds. This is the dominant model found in Sub-Saharan Africa.

The effect of these funds on training by the informal sector, however, is modest. Most funds exempt smaller enterprises (fewer than 50 employees) from the payment of a levy because of the higher administrative cost of enforcing compliance, effectively limiting their application to the small firms in the informal sector. Dar, Canagarajah, and Murphy (2003) in a review of international experience with training funds find that small employers do not benefit substantially from these schemes. The financial incentives offered are insufficient to offset the other factors mentioned earlier that deter training by small enterprises. As a result, training funds with levy-grant schemes tend to favor larger enterprises and the training of more highly educated and skilled workers in these enterprises.[10]

Tailored approaches are needed to involve the informal sector. Exceptions exist, nevertheless, as found in Malaysia and Singapore. Both countries recognized the low participation of small enterprises in their levy-grant funds and set out to address the problem. Among the solutions offered were subsidies for conducting training needs assessments, preapproved training courses not requiring costly application and justification, and the use of excess training capacity of large enterprises to provide training for smaller firms. Singapore offered training vouchers to enterprises with fewer than 50 employees that could be used to pay up-front training costs to ease cash flow problems. The vouchers helped Singapore's Skills Development Fund reach 65 percent of the enterprises with 10–49 workers and 14 percent of those with fewer than 10 workers (Hirosato 1997). Limited evidence is available in Sub-Saharan Africa on the initiatives of national training funds to reach small enterprises in the informal sector.

Other voucher programs have been introduced to encourage training in the informal sector (Johanson and Adams 2004). The Kenyan Jua Kali voucher program, mentioned earlier, was successful in its pilot stage in expanding the supply of training to workers in the informal sector and lowering costs. Evidence showed its positive effect on the earnings of participants and the strengthening of the capacity of local Jua Kali associations responsible for distribution of the vouchers. In scaling up, problems were encountered with governance that led to high administration costs (Adams 2001; Riley and Steel 2000). Ghana offered a similar voucher program targeted at informal sector enterprises in the early 1990s that largely failed because of lack of attention in the design to the marketing and distribution of the vouchers (Johanson and Adams 2004).

In summary, how various financial incentives affect training is not well documented for enterprises in the informal sector. Worldwide, countries allow enterprises to deduct the cost of training from their income as a cost of business before taxes, but for the informal sector, where small enterprises may not earn sufficient income to pay taxes or may avoid taxes altogether by not being registered, these deductions provide a limited incentive for training. The same result applies to tax credits that are targeted to selected enterprises in return for agreed training and employment actions. Where the credit can be refunded to the enterprise in the absence of a tax liability, it may serve as an added incentive for training and even registration of the enterprise but once again may not be sufficient to prompt small enterprises in the informal sector to train. Yet, although evidence is scarce, the case of Uganda shows that the effect of removing credit constraints for training and business material can be significant (Blattman, Fiala, and Martinez 2011).

Objectives and Structure of This Book

This book uses the experience of five African countries to examine (a) the industrial features of the informal sector, (b) the size and effect of the sector on livelihoods, (c) the demographic profile of employment in the sector, (d) the effect of formal education and training on the likelihood of employment by sector and the earnings therein, and (e) the strengths and weakness of strategies for providing skills to people working in the informal sector. Ghana, Kenya, Nigeria, Rwanda, and Tanzania were selected because of the presence in each country of household surveys that enabled us to take a new, more quantitative look at the informal sector. These countries account for one-third of the 853 million people living in Sub-Saharan Africa. Ghana and Kenya in particular have formed the backbone of much of the research on the informal sector. The study combines the household analysis with institutional analysis of programs for skills development in each country.

The nonfarm informal sector has played an important role in all five countries over the past decade, a period of strong economic growth for all. Kenya's gross domestic product (GDP) growth, although disrupted in 2008 by postelection violence, has since recovered and is on an upward trajectory. Ghana's economy has continued its expansion from the 1990s, driven by exports, public investment, and domestic consumption. In recent years, Nigeria has seen important economic improvements with GDP growth exceeding 7 percent. Its nonoil, farming, manufacturing, and telecommunication sectors have outpaced the growth of its oil-mining sector. Rwanda emerged from the 1990s and a national crisis and is now experiencing GDP growth over 4 percent, driven by the expansion of services. Tanzania, in turn, has managed to reverse its slow growth of the 1990s with GDP per capita growth currently close to 4 percent annually.

Part I of this book contains a synthesis of the findings from the five countries and recommendations for improving access to skills in the nonfarm informal sector. It highlights the critical role of formal education in shaping the flow of labor into the two sectors and their earnings. The importance of formal education is stressed as a foundation for access to further skills development in these sectors, and examples are offered of how constraints to skills development in small and household enterprises can be overcome. Part I has three chapters, beginning with chapter 2 that defines and describes employment in the formal and nonfarm informal sectors. Chapter 3 examines the effect of formal education and training on employment in the two sectors. Chapter 4 summarizes the institutional analysis of programs for skills development and offers recommendations to overcome constraints to skills development in small and household enterprises and to enhance the economic performance of the informal sector. Part II of this book contains the five country case studies whose evidence underpins the findings of part I.

The book aims to provide insights and messages for a wide audience concerned by skills development. It raises issues relevant to government policy makers, the donor community, and those responsible for labor market institutions that provide information, regulate, and support the intermediation of labor demand and supply, as well as for public and private skills providers, employers, children and their parents, new labor market entrants, and of course those already working in the informal sector.

Notes

1. The broader concept of informal employment is contained in the resolution adopted in December 2003 by the 17th Conference of International Labor Statisticians (Hussmanns 2004).
2. Noncompliance also may occur in a firm that produces a good or service that is illegal.
3. A study by Falco and others (2012) on subjective measures of job satisfaction in Ghana suggests job satisfaction for many people employed in the informal sector may be as high or higher than for formal sector workers.
4. Average fertility rates have declined from 6.7 births per woman in the 1970s and 1980s to just below 5 today; however, they remain almost twice as high as for other developing regions (World Bank 2012).
5. Aterido and Hallward-Driemeier (2010) show that in Sub-Saharan Africa, poor business environments are in fact associated with high employment growth, but that growth is in low productivity microenterprises.
6. In a study of the informal sector in seven African countries, Filipiak (2007) estimates that on-the-job training, self-training, and traditional apprenticeships account for

95 percent of training in the informal sector. Senegal, for example, has some 400,000 youth in apprenticeships compared with 7,000 in technical and vocational education and training. Monk, Sandefur, and Teal (2007), using a household survey, find that 80 percent of training in Ghana is acquired through on-the-job training and traditional apprenticeships.

7. Although curricula for entrepreneurship education are often locally developed, other packages have been developed and tested by donors, for example, ILO's Start and Improve Your Business program and GTZ's *Competency-Based Economies through Formation of Enterprises* (Haan 2006).
8. Haan and Serriere (2002) estimate that fees for traditional apprenticeships average about US$70 per year. The ILO in 2006 estimated fees to average US$160, ranging from US$22 to US$616. In 2005, Palmer (2007) estimated the average apprenticeship fee in the Ashanti Region of Ghana to be US$42 with a range from US$13 to US$173.
9. In South Africa, a new learnership scheme has been adopted to broaden the present apprenticeship system beyond traditional blue-collar trades to include white-collar occupations in the service sector as well as the informal sector (Gill, Fluitman, and Dar 2000).
10. Given the tendency noted earlier for large enterprises to train without subsidies, training funds are subject to criticism for their high deadweight effects. That is, the funds pay firms to train that would train without the subsidy. At the same time, these funds correct for a "free rider" problem that transfers the cost of training more evenly across firms of all sizes and types.

References

Adams, Arvil V. 2001. "Assessment of the Jua Kali Voucher Program." World Bank, Washington, DC. http://siteresources.worldbank.org/EDUCATION/Resources/278200-1099079877269/547664-1099079934475/547667-1135281552767/Jua_Kali_Pilot_Voucher_Program.pdf.

———. 2007. "The Role of Youth Skills Development in the Transition from School to Work: A Global Review." Human Development Network Children and Youth Department Discussion Paper 5, World Bank, Washington, DC.

Atchoarena, David, and André Marcel Delluc. 2001. *Revisiting Technical and Vocational Education in Sub-Saharan Africa: An Update on Trends, Innovations, and Challenges.* IIEP/Prg.DA/1,320. Paris: International Institute for Educational Planning for the World Bank.

Atchoarena, David, and Paul Esquieu. 2002. *Private Technical and Vocational Education in Sub-Saharan Africa: Provision Patterns and Policy Issues*. New Trends in Technical and Vocational Education Series. Paris: International Institute for Educational Planning/UNESCO.

Aterido, Reyes, and Mary Hallward-Driemeier. 2010. "The Impact of the Investment Climate on Employment Growth: Does Sub-Saharan Africa Mirror Other Low-Income Regions?" Policy Research Working Paper 5218, World Bank, Washington, DC.

Bangasser, Paul E. 2000. "The ILO and the Informal Sector: An Institutional History." Employment Paper 2000/9, International Labour Organization, Geneva.

Becker, Kristina Flodman. 2004. *The Informal Economy*. Stockholm: Swedish International Development Agency.

Biggs, Tyler, Manju Shah, and Pradeep Srivastava. 1995. "Technological Capabilities and Learning for African Enterprises." Technical Paper 288, African Technical Department Series, World Bank, Washington, DC.

Blattman, Christopher, Nathan Fiala, and Sebastian Martinez. 2011. "Employment Generation in Rural Africa: Mid-term Results from an Experimental Evaluation of the Youth Opportunities Program in Northern Uganda." Social Protection Discussion Paper 1120, World Bank, Washington, DC.

Brewer, Laura. 2004. "Youth at Risk: The Role of Skills Development in Facilitating the Transition to Work." Skills Working Paper 19, International Labour Organization, Geneva.

Chafa, Jones. 2002. "Informal Sector Programmes in TEVETA of Malawi." Paper presented at the Training for Survival and Development in Southern Africa Seminar, Nordic Network of UNEVOC Centres, Oslo, November 14–15.

Chaudhuri, Sarbajit, and Ujjaini Mukhopadhyay. 2009. *Revisiting the Informal Sector: A General Equilibrium Approach*. New Delhi: Springer.

Dar, Amit, Sudharshan Canagarajah, and Paud Murphy. 2003. "Training Levies: Rationale and Evidence from Evaluations." World Bank, Washington, DC. http://siteresources.worldbank.org/INTLM/Resources/TrainingLevies.pdf.

Falco, Paolo, William Maloney, Bob Rijkers, and Mauricio Sarrias. 2012. "Heterogeneity in Subjective Wellbeing: An Application to Occupational Allocation in Africa." Policy Research Working Paper 6244, World Bank, Washington, DC.

Farstad, Halfdan. 2002. *Integrated Entrepreneurship Education in Botswana, Uganda and Kenya: Final Report*. Oslo: National Institute of Technology.

Filipiak, Ewa. 2007. "Vocational Training in the Informal Sector: The Outcomes of a Field Survey in Seven African Countries." PowerPoint presentation prepared by the Research Department, Agence Française de Développement, Paris.

Fox, Louise M., and Melissa Sekkel Gaal. 2008. *Working Out of Poverty: Job Creation and the Quality of Growth in Africa*. Washington, DC: World Bank.

Fox, Louise, and Thomas Pave Sohnesen. 2012. *Household Enterprises in Sub-Saharan Africa: Why They Matter for Growth, Jobs, and Livelihoods*. Washington, DC: World Bank

Gill, Indermit Singh, Fred Fluitman, and Amit Dar, eds. 2000. *Vocational Education and Training Reform: Matching Skills to Markets and Budgets*. New York: Oxford University Press for the World Bank.

Haan, Hans Christiaan. 2006. *Training for Work in the Informal Micro-enterprise Sector: Fresh Evidence from Sub-Sahara Africa*. Dordrecht, Netherlands: Springer.

Haan, Hans Christiaan, and Nicholas Serriere. 2002. "Training for Work in the Informal Sector: Fresh Evidence from West and Central Africa." Occasional Papers, International Training Centre of the International Labour Organization, Turin, Italy.

Hirosato, Yasushi. 1997. "Skills Development Fund: A Preliminary Assessment of a Financing Alternative for Enterprise-Based Training in the Context of APEC." APEC Discussion Paper 17, GSID, Nagoya University, Nagoya, Japan.

Hussmanns, Ralf. 2004. "Measuring the Informal Economy: From Employment in the Informal Sector to Informal Employment." Working Paper 53, Bureau of Statistics, International Labour Office, Geneva.

ILO (International Labour Organization). 2002a. "ILO Compendium of Official Statistics on Employment in the Informal Sector." STAT Working Paper 1, International Labour Office, Geneva.

———. 2002b. *Decent Work and the Informal Economy: Abstracts of Working Papers.* Employment Sector, International Labour Office, Geneva.

———. 2002c. *Women and Men in the Informal Economy: A Statistical Picture.* Employment Sector, International Labour Office, Geneva.

Johanson, Richard K., and Arvil V. Adams. 2004. *Skills Development in Sub-Saharan Africa.* Washington, DC: World Bank.

Liimatainen, Marjo-Riita. 2002. "Training and Skills Acquisition in the Informal Sector: A Literature Review." Working Paper 9, InFocus Programme on Skills, Knowledge, and Employability, Informal Economy Series, International Labour Organization, Geneva.

McGrath, Simon, and Kenneth King, with Fiona Leach and Roy Carr-Hill. 1994. "Education and Training for the Informal Sector." Education Research Paper 11, U.K. Department for International Development, London.

Monk, Courtney, Justin Sandefur, and Francis Teal. 2007. "Apprenticeship in Ghana." Department of Economics, Centre for the Study of African Economies, University of Oxford.

Nielsen, Helena, Michael Rosholm, and Andrew Dabalen. 2007. "Evaluation of Training in African Enterprises." *Journal of Development Economics* 84 (1): 310–29.

NISER (Nigerian Institute of Social and Economic Research). 2007. "Report of Baseline Study on Employment Generation in the Informal Sector of the Nigerian Economy." African Capacity Building Foundation/International Labour Organization Project on Strengthening the Labor Market Information and Poverty Monitoring System in Africa, Nigerian Institute of Social and Economic Research, Ibadan, Nigeria.

OECD (Organisation for Economic Co-operation and Development). 2009. *Is Informal Normal? Towards More and Better Jobs in Developing Countries.* Paris: OECD.

Palmer, Robert. 2007. "Skills Development, the Enabling Environment and Informal Micro-Enterprise in Ghana." Doctoral thesis, University of Edinburgh.

Patrinos, Harry. 2002. "A Review of Demand-Side Initiatives in Education." World Bank, Washington, DC. http://www-wds.worldbank.org/servlet/WDSContentServer/WDSP/IB/2003/11/03/000112742_20031103154746/Rendered/PDF/269590Patrinos0Review1of1Demandside.pdf.

Riley, Thyra, and William Steel. 2000. "Kenya Voucher Program for Training and Business Development Services." Africa Region Private Sector Group, World Bank, Washington, DC. http://info.worldbank.org/etools/docs/library/74184/winter2002/proceedings/pdfpapers/mod6ws.pdf.

Roubaud, François, and Mireille Razafindrakoto. 2007. "The Informal Sector in the LDCs: An Economic and Statistical Perspective." PowerPoint presentation to the Economic and Social Commission of Asia and the Pacific, Bangkok, March 29. http://www.unescap.org/stat/isie/reference-materials/Data-Collection/Methodology/The-informal-sector-in-LDCs-ESCAP-2007.pdf.

Schneider, Friedrich. 2002. "Size and Measurement of the Informal Economy in 110 Countries around the World." Paper presented to a workshop of the Australian National Tax Center, Australia National University, Canberra.

Schneider, Friedrich, Andreas Buehn, and Claudio E. Montenegro. 2010. "Shadow Economies All over the World: New Estimates for 162 Countries from 1999 to 2007." Policy Research Working Paper 5356, World Bank, Washington, DC.

Tiwari, R. S. 2005. *Informal Sector Workers: Problems and Prospects*. New Delhi: Anmol Publications.

UN (United Nations). 2010. *World Urbanization Prospects: The 2009 Revision Population Database*. United Nations Population Division (accessed August 2012). http://esa.un.org/wup2009/unup/index.asp?panel=1.

———. 2011. *World Population Prospects, the 2010 Revision* (database). Population Division of the United Nations Department of Economic and Social Affairs of the United Nations Secretariat, New York (accessed August 2012). http://esa.un.org/unpd/wpp/index.htm.

Verick, Sher. 2006. "The Impact of Globalization on the Informal Sector in Africa." Economic and Social Policy Division, United Nations Economic Commission for Africa and Institute for the Study of Labor, Addis Ababa. http://www.iza.org/conference_files/worldb2006/verick_s872.pdf.

World Bank. 2007. *World Development Report 2007: Development and the Next Generation*. Washington, DC: World Bank.

———. 2008. *Africa Development Indicators: 2007*. Washington, DC: World Bank.

———. 2009a. "Ghana: Job Creation and Skills Development Draft Report." Vol. I: Main Report. Report No. 40328-GH, World Bank, Washington, DC. http://ddp-ext.worldbank.org/EdStats/GHAstu09a.pdf.

———. 2009b. "Youth and Employment in Africa: The Potential, the Problem, the Promise." In *Africa Development Indicators 2008/2009*. Washington, DC: World Bank.

———. 2011. "The Challenge of Employment in Africa: Raising the Productivity of the Informal Sector." *Africa's Pulse* 4. http://siteresources.worldbank.org/INTAFRICA/Resources/Africas-Pulse-brochure_Vol4.pdf.

———. 2012. *World Development Indicators 2012*. Washington, DC: World Bank. http://data.worldbank.org/data-catalog/world-development-indicators.

———. 2013. Enterprise Surveys (database), World Bank, Washington, DC (accessed January 2013). http://www.enterprisesurveys.org.

Ziderman, Adrian. 2003. *Financing Vocational Training in Sub-Saharan Africa*. Africa Region Human Development Series. Washington, DC: World Bank.

PART 1

Findings and Actions

CHAPTER 2

Employment in the Informal Sector

In This Chapter

The nonfarm informal sector can be defined in various ways. On the basis of available data from household surveys in Ghana, Kenya, Nigeria, Rwanda, and Tanzania, this book uses the following definition: (a) the self-employed (for their own account and with workers); (b) contributing family members; and (c) wage workers in small, unregulated enterprises of the nonfarm sector. Of the nearly 36 million people working off the farm in the five countries, 7 of 10 work in the informal sector. People who find employment in the informal sector fare better in earnings than those who remain on the farm and earn more than some who work in the formal wage sector. The informal sector is disproportionately urban in character but has a significant rural presence. Women are prominently represented, as are youths. Trade and other services dominate.

Introduction

After four decades of study, the informal sector continues to elicit diverging views about how to define it, measure and classify it, and most important, how to respond to it (Andrews, Caldera Sánchez, and Johansson 2011; Bangasser 2000). The International Labour Organization (ILO) has been at the center of all these debates. As a concept explained in chapter 1, the informal sector has moved from a presumed temporary phenomenon in developing countries, expected to diminish in size with industrialization, to one that is more permanent in light of today's development patterns. Although interest in the informal sector focuses largely on developing countries, the Organisation for Economic Co-operation and Development has demonstrated the growing importance of the sector in industrial countries (OECD 2009). Whatever the measure used, the sector shows no signs of disappearing. The efforts of the ILO in the 1990s to construct a survey-based measure of this employment and its significance to national incomes have encountered difficulties in producing uniform indicators suitable for comparison among countries because the informal sector manifests itself in different ways in different countries. The ILO through the Delhi Group on Informal Sector Statistics continues to work on this measurement problem (Hussmanns 2004).

More recent initiatives by the ILO, joined by the Organisation for Economic Co-operation and Development, have attempted to move understanding of the concept forward to take into account changes brought by a global economy by introducing alongside the informal sector the concept of informal employment. *Informal employment* is offered as a broader concept that includes people counted in the informal sector plus people working in the formal sector without the benefit of job security and social protection. The broader concept emerges from a growing awareness of globalization and the increasing vulnerability of those working in the formal sector (Hussmanns 2004). The ILO described the *informal economy* as "all economic activities by workers and economic units that are—in law or in practice—not covered or insufficiently covered by formal arrangements" (Hussmanns 2004, 2).

Distinction between these concepts is important because their policy responses differ. In the case of the nonfarm informal sector, the unit of interest is the *enterprise* and people working therein; whereas for informal employment, the unit of interest is the *worker* and the conditions under which the worker is employed. For the informal sector, policies address factors leading to the growth and productivity of employment in small and household enterprises, specifically the regulatory and investment climate surrounding these enterprises and the factor markets that serve their productive needs. In the case of the informal employment, policies address these factors and a larger set of cross-national pressures that promote informality in work arrangements, including pressures to reduce labor costs.

This chapter and this book are concerned with the first of these concepts, the informal sector and its contribution to growth and incomes: emphasis is on the enterprise. Using data available from household surveys in our five selected countries of Sub-Saharan Africa, we set about the task of trying to measure the informal nonfarm sector and provide demographic and social profiles of people employed in the sector. The household surveys illustrate the difficulty of comparing statistics on the informal sector from country to country. The ILO's own efforts to compare the informal sector in Sub-Saharan Africa substantiate these complexities.[1] By comparing results from different definitions of the informal sector, this book points to a readily available subset of questions in all household surveys of labor force activity that provide robust measures of those employed in the informal sector.

This study uses household surveys in each country to construct estimates of the nonfarm informal sector's employment for comparison (see table 2.1). The official definition of the informal sector explained in chapter 1 is contained in the January 1993 resolution of the 15th International Conference of Labour Statisticians under the ILO. A more detailed account of the different building blocks in the ILO definition is provided in this chapter's annex 2A. It combines the characteristics of nonfarm enterprises with those of employees collected in household and enterprise surveys to estimate the scope of the informal sector (Roubaud and Razafindrakoto 2007). The ILO definition begins by sorting

Table 2.1 Household Surveys Used for Analysis of the Informal Sector

Country	Survey name	Years Earliest	Years Latest
Ghana	Ghana Living Standards Survey (GLSS)	1991/92	2005/06
Kenya	Labour Force Survey (LFS)	1998/99	n.a.
	Kenya Integrated Household Budget Survey (KIHBS)	n.a.	2005/06
Nigeria	National Living Standard Survey (NLSS)	2003/04	n.a.
Rwanda	Household Living Conditions Survey (Enquête Intégrale sur les Conditions de Vie des Ménages; EICV)	1999/2000	2005/06
Tanzania	Integrated Labour Force Survey (ILFS)	2000/01	2005/06

Note: n.a. = not applicable.

enterprises into the informal sector. The following criteria are used for the sorting: (a) unincorporated enterprises owned by individuals or households not operating as separate legal entities from the household; (b) enterprises producing goods and services for sale; (c) enterprises below a size threshold that is nationally determined (for example, fewer than 10 employees); (d) enterprises that are not registered under specific forms of legislation (for example, business licenses, taxation, social protection for workers); and (e) enterprises engaged in nonfarm activities. Enterprises matching these criteria are classified in the nonfarm informal sector. Where data are available, efforts have been made to compare different definitions of the informal sector in the country cases prepared for this study.

This study focuses largely on own-account workers and microenterprises. Hans Haan (2006) in his seminal study of the informal sector differentiated these enterprises into three groups. The largest is what he called the subsistence type of self-employment characterized by part-time (seasonal) operations using traditional technologies and local materials. These firms represent small and household enterprises serving primarily local markets and are a particularly important source of income for poor rural workers. Many of the self-employed working on their own account, including women, fall into this category. The second group is formed by microenterprises of up to 10 workers with contributing family members and apprentices, using a mix of technologies and serving rural and urban markets. The third group, which is smaller in number, comprises enterprises with 10–50 workers, using some modern technologies, closely connected with formal enterprises, and exhibiting growth potential. Within the enterprises, employment is classified according to the ILO definition as follows: (a) self-employed working on own account; (b) self-employed with other workers; (c) unpaid contributing family members; (d) wage workers employed in these enterprises; and (e) members of producers cooperatives. Because of the nature of the African economies, this book's analysis focuses largely on the first two of Haan's informal sector groups.

The construction of these measures is data-intensive, and not all countries and household surveys supply the building blocks needed. Table 2.2 illustrates the data available on employment status and enterprise characteristics in our five countries and differences among the countries. Using the available data, we have

Table 2.2 Differing Accessibility to Data for Classifying Employment in the Informal Sector among Countries and Their Household Surveys

	Ghana	*Kenya*	*Nigeria*	*Rwanda*	*Tanzania*
Employment module data	*GLSS 2005/06*	*KIHBS 2005/06*	*NLSS 2003/04*	*EICV 2005/06*	*ILFS 2005/06*[a]
Occupational status					
Working employer	X	X	X	X	X
Own account	X	X	X	X	X
Contributing family member	X	X	X	X	X
Wage worker for self-employed		X	X	X	X
Employment conditions					
Access to benefits (social protection)	X		X	X	X
Type of contract	X				X
Characteristics of firm where employed					
Size of firm	X				X
Self-identified informal	X			X	
Keeps accounts					X
Enterprise module data, including firm size, registration, and earnings	X	X	X	X	

Sources: GSS 2005–06; KNBS 2007; NBS 2007; NBSN 2004; and NISR 2007.
Note: EICV = Household Living Conditions Survey (Rwanda); GLSS = Ghana Living Standards Survey; ILFS = Integrated Labour Force Survey (Tanzania); KIHBS = Kenya Integrated Household Budget Survey; NLSS = National Living Standard Survey (Nigeria).
a. Tanzania has a short informal sector module for firms identified as private with fewer than 10 employees and does not keep accounts. It is a labor force survey and does not have an enterprise module allowing for calculating enterprise profits and the like.

attempted to replicate the ILO definition or come as close as possible by using information on enterprises and employment status in the estimation process. The largest share of people employed in the nonfarm informal sector turns out to be those who are self-employed working on their own account, representing about half of those employed in the sector. In the chapters of part II, we have separately constructed measures of the informal sector relying solely on the status of the worker and excluding characteristics of the enterprise to form a comparison with the ILO enterprise-based measure. The objective is to assess how much additional information is provided by the more complex measure that includes characteristics of the enterprise.

Nigeria is a typical case for measurement. We have examined alternative definitions of the informal sector that begin with using only the employment status of the worker and then add characteristics of the enterprise to produce the more complex measure of the informal sector combining enterprise and worker status. Four versions of the definition have been constructed for nonfarm employment:

- Self-employed (own account or employing wage workers) or contributing family member.
- Self-employed (own account or employing wage workers), contributing family member, or working in a cooperative.

- Self-employed (own account or employing wage workers), contributing family member, or working in a cooperative and employed by a private firm with fewer than 10 employees and receiving no benefits.
- Self-employed (own account or employing wage workers), contributing family member, or working in a cooperative and employed by a private firm with fewer than 10 employees.

The first of these definitions includes only nonwage workers (self-employed and contributing family members) as representing the informal sector. People not falling into this category are treated as being in the formal sector. The expanded versions include workers in cooperatives and wage workers in enterprises with fewer than 10 employees and receiving no benefits. Nonwage workers by themselves account for 68 percent of nonfarm employment in Nigeria. Adding wage workers in small private sector enterprises with fewer than 10 workers pushes this percentage to 73 percent. In our sample of countries, wage workers are generally a small share of informal sector employment. This pattern is repeated in Ghana, Kenya, and Tanzania—but not in Rwanda where the share of nonwage workers in nonfarm employment is 45 percent.

We have chosen to use the following parameters in this study to define the informal sector: (a) the self-employed (own account and with workers), (b) contributing family members, and (c) wage workers in informal sector enterprises. The criteria distinguishing wage workers vary among the five countries on the basis of differences in questions asked in household surveys. In Kenya, for example, these are wage workers who work for the self-employed. In Nigeria, they are wage workers working in private firms with fewer than 10 employees. In Rwanda, they are wage workers without social benefits, and in Tanzania, they are wage workers in private enterprises with fewer than 10 employees and no written accounts. The presence of wage workers in an informal sector enterprise may already signal something different and more promising about the enterprise, separating it from enterprises where the self-employed work for their own account. The ability to pay workers may suggest something about the profitability of the enterprise and signal its potential for further growth (Haan 2006).

The inclusion of wage workers in the informal sector is a choice made to bring the measurement in closer alignment with the ILO definition of the informal sector. However, we find that inclusion of these workers has little effect on our analysis of who works in the informal sector and their earnings mainly because informal sector enterprises with wage workers, excluding the unusual example of Rwanda, represent on average only 13 percent of informal sector employment in our sample. We have chosen the broader definition that includes these wage workers, but for cases where the data are not available, we note that use of the self-employed and contributing family members, representing nonwage workers, provides a reasonably robust proxy for examining the informal sector. We have used the broader definition to compare the profile of the formal and informal sectors. In chapter 3, we explore how education and skills influence entry into employment and earnings in both sectors.

Table 2.3 Total Employment[a] by Sector of Work

Sector	*Ghana*	*Kenya*	*Nigeria*	*Rwanda*	*Tanzania*
Total	6,900	9,737	53,697	3,971	18,780
Farm	3,408	4,856	31,818	3,048	13,991
Nonfarm	3,492	4,881	21,879	923	4,789
Formal	985	1,404	6,172	190	2,550
Informal	2,507	3,477	15,707	733	2,239
Nonfarm as percentage of total	51	50	41	23	26
Informal as percentage of nonfarm	72	71	72	79	47

Sources: Elaborations based on GSS 2005–06; KNBS 2007; NBS 2007; NBSN 2004; and NISR 2007.
a. Employment numbers are in thousands and rounded.

The resulting estimates of the informal sector illustrate the sector's importance to employment (table 2.3). In the five countries, more than 23 million people are employed in the informal sector; Nigeria alone accounts for 15.7 million. The share of nonfarm employment in the informal sector ranges from 71 percent in Kenya to 79 percent in Rwanda, but drops to 47 percent in Tanzania.[2] The transition toward an industrial economy has progressed at a faster pace in Ghana and Kenya where the share of nonfarm employment roughly matches the share of farm employment. Nigeria is not far behind with nonfarm employment accounting for 40 percent of total employment. Rwanda and Tanzania, in contrast, are still largely agrarian with only about 25 percent of total employment in the nonfarm sector. The informal sector and its employment accounts for a significant share of economic activity in each country, leading to questions about who is employed in the sector.

The study focuses on primary occupation only. Many households are involved in farm and nonfarm activities simultaneously, and some undertake multiple activities ("enterprises") within the informal sector. This stepwise diversification away from farming into more productive ventures is not captured by our study as long as farming remains the most important occupation. Therefore, the importance of nonfarm activities in rural areas may be understated.

A Profile of Those Employed

The movement from an agrarian to an urban industrial society is a pattern of development observed in all countries worldwide over history. The countries of Sub-Saharan Africa are no exception. As the transition takes place, the share of farm employment falls while that in nonfarm activities increases. The pace of the transition varies from country to country, as observed in table 2.4 where we have more than one survey over the past decade for comparison. As labor moves out of farming, we see the growing importance of self-employment in the nonfarm sector taking its place. People leaving farming are crowding into self-employment. Over much of the past four decades, this crowding has been the consequence of the region's failure to produce wage employment in the formal sector and of structural reforms that have reduced wage employment in the public sector.

Table 2.4 Growth of Nonfarm Employment and Self-Employment

Country	*Farm employment as a percentage of total employment*		*Self-employment as a percentage of nonfarm employment*	
	Earliest survey	*Latest survey*	*Earliest survey*	*Latest survey*
Ghana[a]	53	52	60	63
Kenya[b]	52	47	66	74
Rwanda[c]	90	77	23	31
Tanzania[d]	82	75	57	62

Sources: GSS 1991–92, 2005–06; KNBS 1999, 2007; NBS 2002, 2007; and NISR 2001, 2007.
a. Ghana Living Standards Survey 1991/92 compared with 2005/06.
b. Labour Force Survey 1998/99 compared with Kenya Integrated Household Budget Survey 2005/06.
c. Household Living Conditions Survey (Rwanda) 1999/2000 compared with 2005/06.
d. Integrated Labour Force Survey (Tanzania) 2000/01 compared with 2005/06.

For many youths, self-employment has become the safety net absorbing those searching for their first job.

Farming is the largest employer in Sub-Saharan Africa, but labor continues to move off the farm in search of other employment. Some of this labor remains in rural areas, but much of it moves into urban areas. The marginal product of labor in farming is often low because of the crowding of large families on small farms with limited access to technology and capital per worker. The potential of greater earnings and the expectation of finding more productive employment in the nonfarm sector entice younger household members to pursue opportunities off the farm. For those leaving the farm, the first stop is often a job in the informal sector. The slow growth of the formal sector constrains opportunities for employment as do the qualifications of those searching for work. Africa does not offer the large number of low-skilled jobs found in manufacturing and construction observed in East Asia. Instead, migrants leaving farms often wind up in petty trade and services where barriers to entry are low. Even this employment offers welfare gains over farming work.

The household surveys reveal that the average income of people employed in the informal sector, although lower than in the formal sector, exceeds earnings in farming by a substantial margin (see figure 2.1). These earnings are unadjusted for other factors affecting incomes, such as education; however, chapter 3 shows that even after adjusting for differences in personal characteristics, the earnings advantage of employment in the nonfarm informal sector remains when compared with farming. Where surplus labor in farming is present, policies promoting labor mobility off the farm improve the incomes of migrants. Employment in the informal sector plays a positive role in this respect. This pattern points further to the value of understanding these small enterprises and those who are employed in them and the means by which their productivity and incomes are enhanced.

Workers in the public and private formal sectors have earnings distributions that fall to the right of those in farming and the informal sector (for both wage and self-employed). However, the earnings distributions of these groups overlap, indicating that some people in the informal sector have earnings exceeding those

Figure 2.1 Informal Sector Earnings Compared with Farm Sector Earnings in Kenya, Ghana, Nigeria, and Rwanda

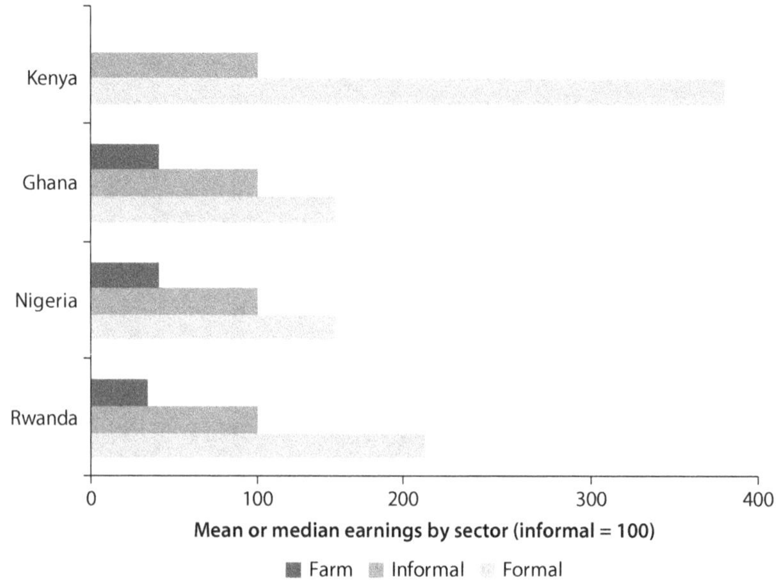

Sources: Elaborations based on GSS 2005–06; KNBS 2007; NBSN 2004; and NISR 2007.
Note: Farm earnings are not available for Kenya.

in the formal sector (figure 2.2, panel a). This pattern is also observed in Kenya (figure 2.2, panel b) and, though not shown here, in Nigeria and Rwanda.

Off-farm employment in the informal sector is linked to higher consumption and lower poverty. Using Rwanda and Kenya, employment in the informal sector is associated with higher levels of consumption than experienced by those working in farming. Employment in the formal sector reduces poverty even further, and 64 percent of those working in the formal sector in Rwanda belong to the richest consumption quintile; only 18 percent belong to the three poorest consumption quintiles (table 2.5). What we learn from these comparisons is that structural changes in employment are taking place in our sample of countries as labor is shifting out of farming. A growing share of labor is finding its way into self-employment off the farm in the small enterprises of the informal sector, and in so doing, incomes and consumption levels are rising. Even larger gains are possible if productivity in the informal sector is increased and barriers to mobility between the two sectors are lowered.

The nonfarm informal sector, although present in rural areas, tends to be concentrated in urban communities. The estimates of its size given here are for primary jobs, but the informal sector also provides secondary jobs for some in rural areas, supplementing farm earnings. Kenya has a particularly large share of its informal sector in rural areas (figure 2.3).

Gender plays an important role in nonfarm informal sector employment. In Rwanda, even though the labor force participation of men is greater than that of women, women still comprise 45 percent of employment in the informal sector

Figure 2.2 Distribution of Wages and Earnings in Ghana and Kenya

a. Distribution of wages and earnings by sector of employment in Ghana, 2005/06

Source: World Bank 2009.

b. Distribution of earnings by formality status in Kenya, 2005/06

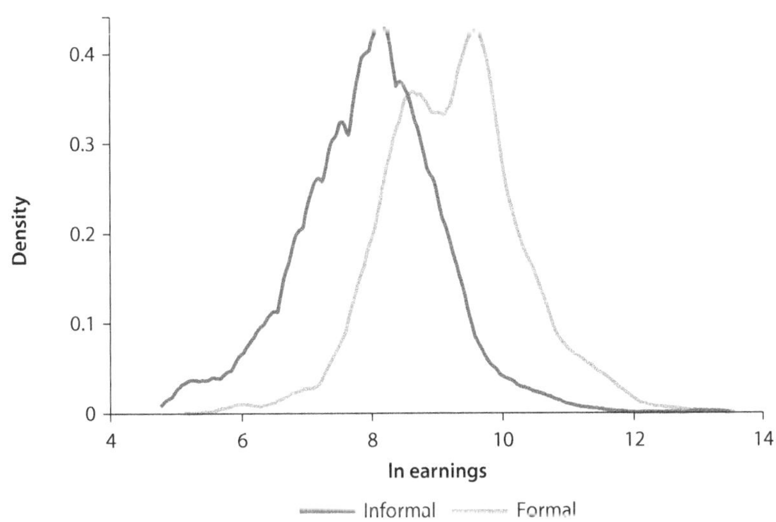

Source: Elaborations based on KNBS 2007.

Table 2.5 Distribution of Employed by Sector and Household Consumption Quintile, Rwanda and Kenya

	Rwanda			*Kenya*		
Quintile	*Formal*	*Informal*	*Farm*	*Formal*	*Informal*	*Farm*
Poorest	2	12	23	5	16	24
Second poorest	6	14	23	10	15	26
Third poorest	9	14	23	13	19	24
Second richest	18	21	20	26	23	18
Richest	64	39	11	50	27	7
Total	100	100	100	100	100	100
Percentage belonging to three poorest quintiles	18	40	69	28	50	74

Sources: Elaborations based on NISR 2007 and KNBS 2007.
Note: Because of rounding, some columns may not total exactly.

Figure 2.3 Urban Share of Formal and Informal Sector Work in Nigeria, Ghana, Tanzania, and Kenya

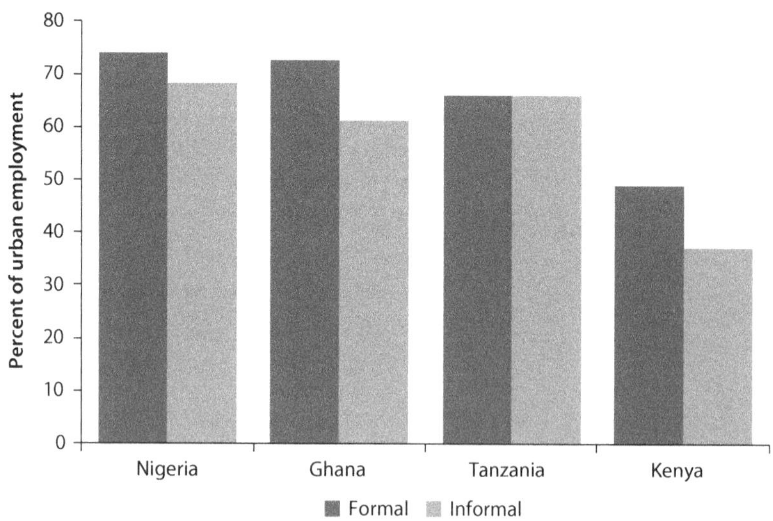

Sources: Elaborations based on GSS 2005–06; KNBS 2007; NBS 2007; and NBSN 2004.

of the capital city, Kigali. Their share in rural areas is lower, although it still accounts for nearly one of every three women employed in the informal sector (figure 2.4).

The gender balance of the informal sector varies among the five countries, indicating the need for a gender focus in efforts to improve sector outcomes. Men account for a majority of employment in the informal sector of Rwanda, Kenya, and Tanzania; women play a larger role in Nigeria and Ghana (figure 2.5, panel a).

In all the study countries, women maintain a higher share of employment in the informal sector than they do in the formal sector (figure 2.5, panel b). In Ghana, for example, women hold three of four jobs in the informal sector while

Figure 2.4 Women's Share of Informal Sector Work by Area in Rwanda

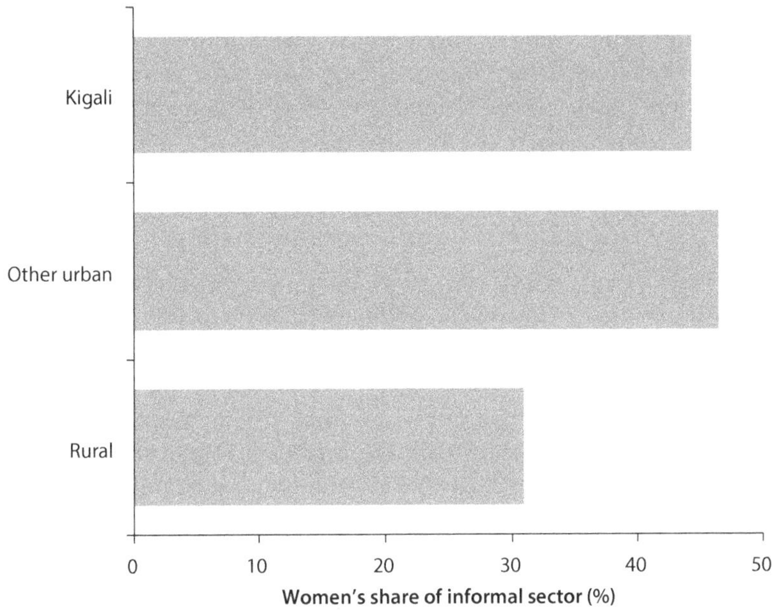

Source: Elaborations based on NISR 2007.

Figure 2.5 Gender Distribution of Employment

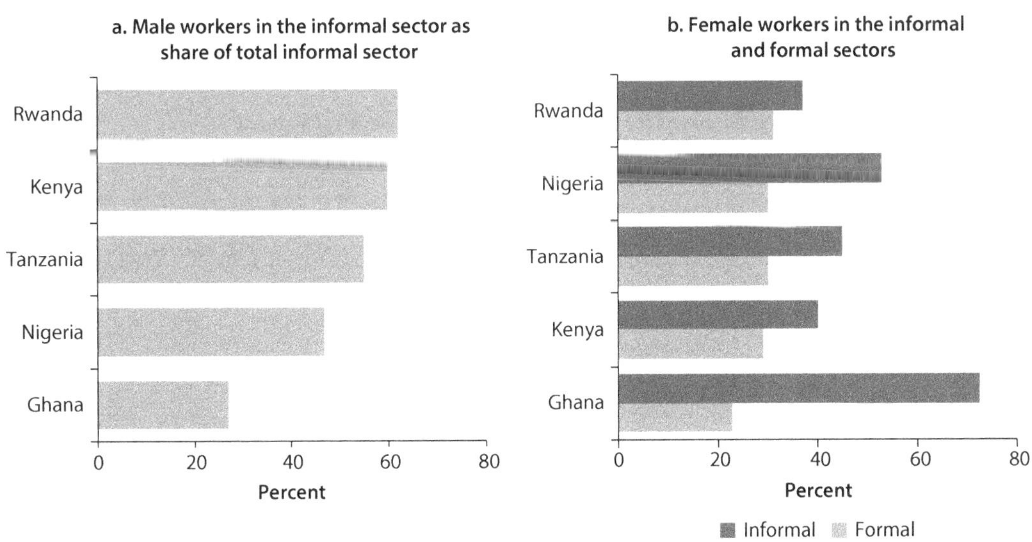

Sources: Elaborations based on GSS 2005–06; KNBS 2007; NBS 2007; NBSN 2004; and NISR 2007.

accounting for only one of four in the formal sector. The propensity of women to find their way into the informal sector in contrast to their male counterparts contributes to the gender imbalance of incomes for the two groups. The informal sector is thus an important source of employment for women, with this particularly evident in Ghana and Nigeria. The informal sector and its small enterprises play an important role in determining the welfare of women.

Lack of other options is a major reason for choosing the informal sector. Tanzania's 2006 household labor force survey (ILFS 2006, see NBS 2007) offers a look at reasons for choosing to work in the informal sector. The reasons are split between factors pushing workers into the informal sector for lack of better opportunities and those pulling workers into this sector to take advantage of its opportunities. Push factors provide the principal reason for working in the informal sector with nearly 7 of 10 people working there because of their need for additional income or because they are unable to find other work. For others, however, pull factors play an important role in the choice of employment, led by the perception of good business opportunities and the chance to open a business with the limited capital available to them. The push factors dominate in urban areas where few jobs are found and the alternative is to start a new business. The pull factors are stronger in rural areas where workers are attracted to employment in the nonfarm informal sector because of the higher earnings in comparison with the likely alternative of employment in the farm sector (table 2.6).

Confronted with a formal sector unable to produce the jobs needed to absorb the influx of youth 15 years of age and older into the region's labor force, youth often find their first employment in the informal sector as helpers and

Table 2.6 Main Reasons for Entering the Informal Sector in Tanzania

	Percentage of respondents			
Reasons	*Rural*	*Dar es Salaam*	*Urban (excluding Dar es Salaam)*	*Tanzania*
Push factors	60	72	73	68
Cannot find other work	27	45	39	37
Family needs additional income	32	27	34	31
Pull factors, attractive sector	18	13	12	14
Good income opportunities	16	10	10	12
Desire to be independent	2	3	2	2
Pull factors, convenient sector	18	9	11	13
Does not require extensive capital	10	4	7	7
Can keep production costs low	1	1	1	1
Can choose hours and place of work	2	1	1	2
Can combine business and household responsibilities	5	2	2	3
Other	4	7	5	5

Source: Elaborations based on NBS 2007.
Note: Because of rounding, columns may not total exactly.

Figure 2.6 Informal Sector Jobs for Youth

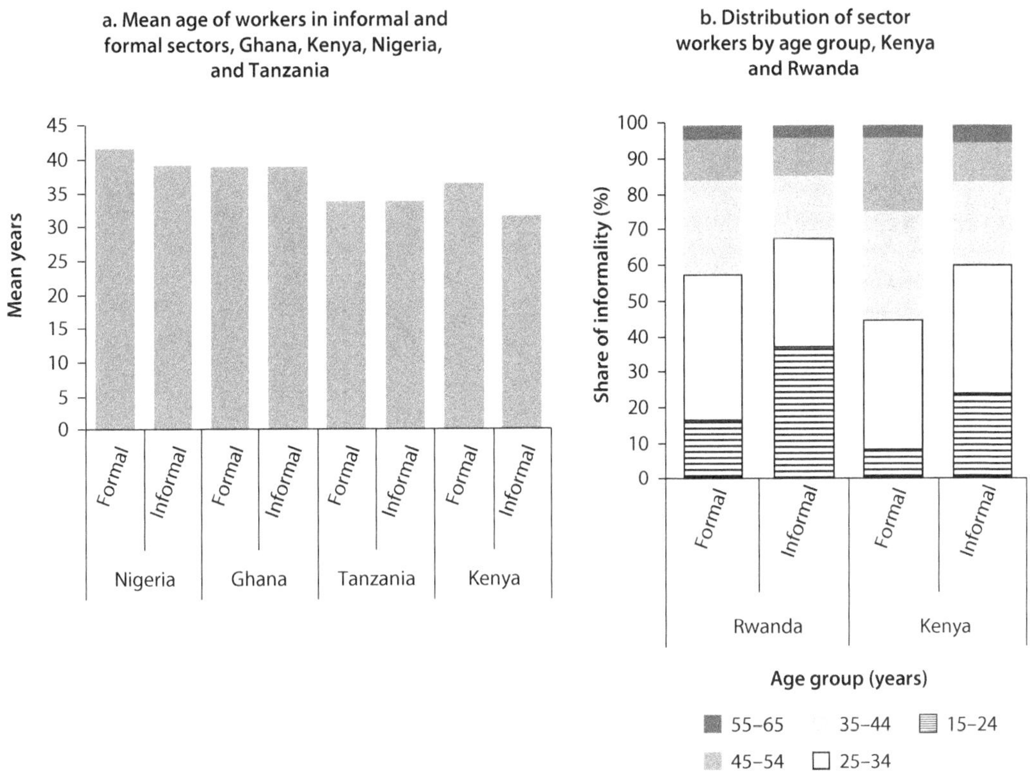

Sources: Elaborations based on GSS 2005–06; KNBS 2007; NBS 2007; NBSN 2004; and NISR 2007.

apprentices. Some with more education or resources are able to start their own businesses, but the typical pattern involves working first for an employer to gain skills and experience before attempting to launch one's own business. That being said, figure 2.6, panel a, shows a mixed pattern of sector employment by age. The mean age in formal and informal sectors is roughly the same in Ghana and Tanzania, while a slightly younger informal sector is evident in Nigeria, Kenya, and Rwanda (not shown in figure). Kenya and Rwanda show a sizable number of young persons in the informal sector compared with those in the formal sector (figure 2.6, panel b).

With cross-section data, Rwanda displays a difference in the age distribution of employment in the two sectors (see figure 2.7). In rural and urban areas, more than 80 percent of youth begin in the informal sector, and only 20 percent start their careers in the formal sector. At all ages, the share of informal sector employment exceeds that of the formal sector. A curious pattern is evident in urban areas, suggesting that the share of those entering the formal sector rises with age and then levels off. Without longitudinal data, we cannot determine whether mobility exists across sectors over time, or whether the data reflect a cohort effect tied to conditions favoring formal sector employment before the civil

Figure 2.7 Difference in Age Distribution of Nonfarm Workers, Informal vs. Formal Sector and Rural vs. Urban, in Rwanda

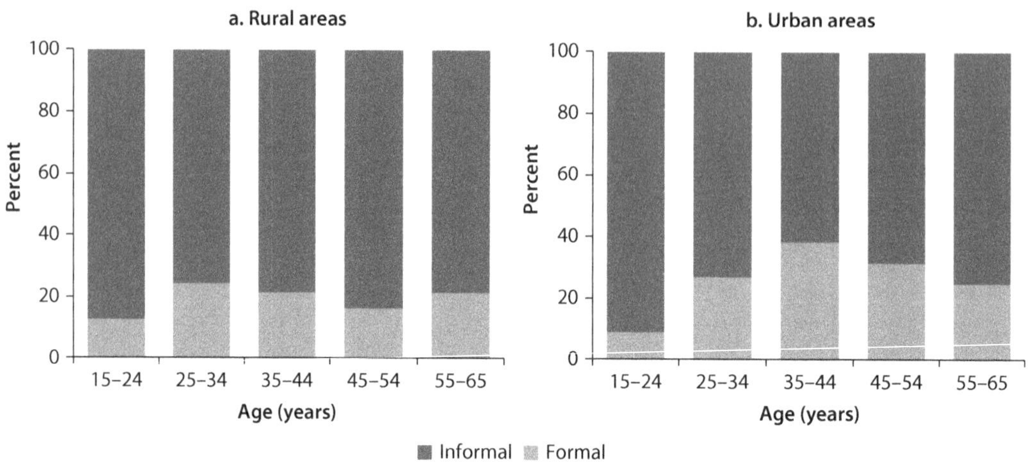

Source: Elaborations based on NISR 2007.

conflict of the 1990s. This pattern observed in urban areas is not repeated in rural areas. Kenya offers a similar pattern for youth to that observed in Rwanda.

Trade and services account for the largest share of employment in informal sector enterprises. In Tanzania, more than two-thirds of informal sector jobs in 2006 were in trade, restaurants, and hotels. Wholesale and retail trade was the main activity in the informal sector among both men and women. The pattern in Rwanda in 2006 was similar with 63 percent of the informal sector employed in trade and services. Women were more likely to be in trade, whereas men exhibited more diversity with a quarter employed in construction and manufacturing. These patterns are repeated in Ghana, Kenya, and Nigeria. Hans Haan (2006), earlier in the decade, found a similar pattern in other countries. From this pattern, he argued that the concentration of the informal sector in trade and services placed downward pressure on the earnings of people employed in these sectors. He recommended efforts to diversify employment in the informal sector to reduce this pressure and promote higher earnings. Skills were an important part of the strategy for meeting this objective.

Main Conclusions

The household surveys from five African countries, representing one-third of the continent's population, were used to measure and describe people employed in the nonfarm informal sector. Farming continues to be Africa's primary source of employment. The World Bank estimates it accounts for about 65 percent of the region's employment. The share, however, has been declining as capital and technology have substituted for labor in farming. This pattern will continue with time as farm productivity improves and surplus labor in farming is released.

The formal sector until now has been unable to supply the jobs needed to absorb the movement of labor off the farm and to employ the numbers of youth newly entering the workforce each year (7–10 million). The nonfarm informal sector and self-employment have provided a safety net of employment for the African economy and particularly for those who cannot find employment in the formal sector. These informal sectors have also provided new opportunities, particularly because their earnings can match or exceed those in the formal sector. This factor not only further bolsters the argument to improve the sector's productivity, but it also sheds light on the innovative and resourceful cohorts previously tamped down.

The informal sector accounts for two-thirds to three-quarters of nonfarm employment. In Rwanda, the percentage reaches 90 percent. The average earnings in this employment exceed that in farming but fall below earnings in the formal sector. These averages, however, obscure the fact that the earnings distributions overlap and that people can find jobs in the informal sector with earnings that match and even exceed earnings in the formal sector. The informal sector also plays a positive role in the reduction of poverty as observed in Ghana and Kenya. The persistence of informal sector employment over time and the positive role it plays in reducing poverty support our initiative to improve the productivity of the enterprises and the incomes of people employed in the sector, while also looking for ways to lower barriers to mobility between the informal and formal sectors.

As shown by Tanzania, as many as 3 of 10 people who work in the nonfarm informal sector are drawn to this employment as a preferred choice. The evidence from earnings distributions in Ghana and Kenya back this finding by showing that earnings in the informal sector can match and exceed those in the formal sector, thus providing an incentive for retaining employment in the informal sector. Actions to improve incomes and the mobility of those engaged in the informal sector will need to take on board a number of findings in this chapter as a guide to these actions. Chapter 3 reveals how education and training influence in a positive fashion incomes and the mobility of people employed in the informal sector.

The available data also stress the importance of a strong gender focus. Women are more likely to be employed in the informal sector than in the formal sector in our set of countries. Women account for large numbers of those self-employed working on their own accounts, particularly in rural areas.

For some, the nonfarm informal sector is an urban phenomenon. The data show that with the likely exception of Kenya, the largest share of this employment is located in urban areas, but it is found in rural areas as well. This finding is important in defining the sector and measuring its scope. Enterprises matching the definition given for the informal sector are present in both rural and urban areas. Actions to improve the productivity of these enterprises and the incomes of those employed in them therefore need to reach both areas. An issue that has received less attention in the literature is the one raised by Haan (2006), referring to the concentration of the informal sector in trade and services, thereby depressing earnings in both. Our data on the distribution of employment back up this finding and suggest the importance of encouraging industrial diversification, for example, by providing the skills and business development services to open opportunities in manufacturing where small firms have the potential to enter the supply chain of larger, formal sector enterprises.

The informal sector is now a prominent feature of Sub-Saharan Africa's economic landscape with no signs of disappearing. When first recognized in Sub-Saharan Africa in the 1970s, the informal sector was conceived by economists as a temporary staging point for surplus labor waiting to be absorbed by the industrialization expected in the postindependence era. The sector was identified with small, loosely regulated household enterprises employing mainly family members with limited connections to modern technology. Forty years later, however, the sector has diversified in the scale of its activities. The inability of the region to expand employment off the farm in the formal sector in this period has contributed to the growth of the informal sector as a source of employment for increasing numbers of youth seeking their first job. In the chapters that follow, we examine evidence from our five countries for how the productivity of informal sector enterprises can be improved and mobility between the informal and formal sector increased.

Annex 2A: Employment in the Informal Sector: The Building Blocks

The January 1993 resolution of the 15th Conference of International Labour Statisticians of the ILO combines the characteristics of nonfarm enterprises with those of employees collected in household and enterprise surveys to estimate the scope of the informal sector (Roubaud and Razafindrakoto 2007). The enterprise characteristics attempt to capture the correlates of regulation or nonregulation by introducing questions about the size of the firm, its registration status with government authorities, and in some cases whether the firm offers workers social protection benefits. The features of household enterprises as production units are intersected with the employment status of workers in these enterprises to capture whether members of a household in an informal sector enterprise are self-employed working on their own account, self-employed hiring other workers, unpaid family members contributing to the enterprise, members of producers' cooperatives, or wage workers.

To obtain all the building blocks of the informal sector requires a household survey with an enterprise module to enumerate the presence and characteristics of nonfarm household enterprises. Among our five countries, Ghana offers a good example of a country with a set of periodic household surveys, each with a nonfarm household enterprise module. Interestingly, for a country that once had a ministry responsible for the informal sector, Kenya's Integrated Household Budget Survey (KIHBS) 2005/06, unlike its earlier Labour Force Survey (LFS) 1999 household survey, does not include a module for measuring the nonfarm informal sector, leaving it unable to compare informal sector employment across the two survey periods. Comparative analysis of the informal sector is often limited by the comparability of statistics available.

Greater consultation is needed in national definitions of informal sector activity and household questionnaire design. The comparison is fraught with differences tied to the availability of data and the national setting. The ILO's own efforts to produce these estimates earlier in the decade identified a number of areas contributing to differences in the estimates among countries (ILO 2002):

- Criteria used to define the informal sector vary, for example, employment size of the enterprise and use of registration status.
- Branches of economic activity covered differ, particularly in respect to inclusion or exclusion of farm activity.
- Differences exist in inclusion and exclusion of groups such as paid domestic employees employed by households or producers of goods for own final use by their household.
- Inclusion or exclusion of persons with a secondary job in the informal sector differs.
- Inclusion or exclusion of persons engaged in professional or technical activities differs.
- Geographic coverage varies; some surveys include urban areas only.

Notes

1. Only nine Sub-Saharan countries offer estimates of informal sector employment, and these estimates differ from one another in definition (ILO 2002).
2. The numbers reported working in Tanzania's informal sector are the same as those reported by its National Bureau of Statistics. The national definition of the informal sector is the same as that used in this study.

References

Andrews, Dan, Aida Caldera Sánchez, and Åsa Johansson. 2011. "Towards a Better Understanding of the Informal Economy." Economics Department Working Paper 873, OECD Publishing, Paris. http://dx.doi.org/10.1787/5kgb1mf88x28-en.

Bangasser, Paul E. 2000. "The ILO and the Informal Sector: An Institutional History." Employment Paper 2000/9, International Labour Organization, Geneva.

GSS (Ghana Statistical Service). 1991–92. *Ghana Living Standards Survey III 1991–1992*. World Bank SHIP Harmonized Dataset, GHA_1991_GLSS_v01_M_v01_A_SHIP. http://microdata.worldbank.org/index.php/catalog/1066.

———. 2005–06. *Ghana Living Standards Survey (GLSS) V 2005–2006*. World Bank SHIP Harmonized Dataset, GHA_2006_GLSS_v01_M_v01_A_SHIP. http://microdata.worldbank.org/index.php/catalog/1064.

Haan, Hans Christiaan. 2006. *Training for Work in the Informal Micro-enterprise Sector: Fresh Evidence from Sub-Sahara Africa*. Dordrecht, Netherlands: Springer.

Hussmanns, Ralf. 2004. "Measuring the Informal Economy: From Employment in the Informal Sector to Informal Employment." Working Paper 53, Bureau of Statistics, International Labour Office, Geneva.

ILO (International Labour Organization). 2002. "ILO Compendium of Official Statistics on Employment in the Informal Sector." STAT Working Paper 1, International Labour Office, Geneva.

KNBS (Kenya National Bureau of Statistics, Ministry of State for Planning National Development and Vision 2030). 1999. *Labour Force Survey—1999.* Version 1.2 of the public use dataset (November 2008), provided by the National Data Archive, Government of Kenya, Nairobi. http://statistics.knbs.or.ke/nada/index.php/catalog/22.

KNBS (Kenya National Bureau of Statistics, Ministry of Planning and National Development). 2007. *Kenya Integrated Household Budget Survey 2005–2006.* Version 1.0 of the KNBS dataset, Government of Kenya, Nairobi. http://statistics.knbs.or.ke/nada/index.php/catalog/8.

NBS (National Bureau of Statistics, Ministry of Finance and Economics Affairs). 2002. *Integrated Labour Force Survey 2000–2001 (ILFS 2000–2001).* Version 1.0 of the public use dataset (January 2002) provided by National Bureau of Statistics, Government of Tanzania, Dar es Salaam. http://www.nbs.go.tz.

———. 2007. *Integrated Labour Force Survey 2006 (ILFS 2006).* Version 1.0 of the public use datasets (August 2007), provided by the National Bureau of Statistics, Government of Tanzania, Dar es Salaam. http://www.nbs.go.tz.

NBSN (National Bureau of Statistics, Nigeria). 2004. *National Living Standard Survey 2003.* Federal Government of Nigeria, Abuja. http://www.nigerianstat.gov.ng/nada/index.php/catalog/28.

NISR (National Institute of Statistics of Rwanda). 2001. *Enquête Intégrale sur les Conditions de Vie de Menage 2000–2001 (EICV 2001).* Version 1.0. NISR, Kigali. http://www.statistics.gov.rw/survey-period/integrated-household-living-conditions-survey-1-eicv-1.

———. 2007. *Enquête Intégrale sur les Conditions de Vie des Ménages 2005–2006 – Overview- 10 -2005–2006 (EICV 2005).* Version 1.1. NISR, Kigali. http://www.statistics.gov.rw/survey-period/integrated-household-living-conditions-survey-2-eicv-2.

OECD (Organisation for Economic Co-operation and Development). 2009. *Is Informal Normal? Towards More and Better Jobs in Developing Countries.* Paris: OECD.

Roubaud, François, and Mireille Razafindrakoto. 2007. "The Informal Sector in the LDCs: An Economic and Statistical Perspective." PowerPoint presentation to the Economic and Social Commission of Asia and the Pacific, Bangkok, March 29. http://www.unescap.org/stat/isie/reference-materials/Data-Collection/Methodology/The-informal-sector-in-LDCs-ESCAP-2007.pdf.

World Bank. 2009. "Ghana: Job Creation and Skills Development Draft Report. Vol. I: Main Report." Report No. 40328-GH, World Bank, Washington, DC. http://ddp-ext.worldbank.org/EdStats/GHAstu09a.pdf.

CHAPTER 3

The Role of Skills in the Informal Sector

In This Chapter

A synthesis of our five country case studies finds that education and skills development influence labor mobility off the farm and earnings attainment. The findings emphasize the importance of basic education for all as a foundation for further skills development. The failure to build a strong foundation is shown to have consequences for acquiring additional skills. Secondary and higher education are strong correlates of employment in the formal sector, whereas a primary education or less often translates into employment in the informal sector. Traditional apprenticeships are not only a key to employment in the informal sector but also open opportunities in the formal sector. The direct effect of these apprenticeships on earnings, however, is mixed. Technical and vocational education and training (TVET) offers entry into both sectors and leads to higher earnings. Earnings generally increase with education in both sectors but more so in the formal sector, as explained by market factors.

Introduction

Education and skills development are well known to play a key role in economic growth. By improving worker productivity, supporting more informed livelihood choices, and enabling better management of household activities, education and skills are particularly important for the development, economic diversification, and transformation of low-income countries. Economists have recognized and written about the role of human capital and workforce skills in the production of goods and services since the 1950s (see Becker 1964; Mincer 1958; Schultz 1961). Early in the 1960s, the World Bank began lending for education along with its support for infrastructure, recognizing the need for a skilled workforce in developing countries to operate and maintain the infrastructure (Heyneman 2003). The lending initiatives focused on diversified secondary education and included TVET. The latter was viewed as a way of democratizing education and expanding opportunities for skills and employment beyond that which was available to the elite.

In Sub-Saharan Africa, growing expectations of industrialization followed the independence movements of the 1960s and the awareness of a need to produce more skilled labor for these nascent industries. However, the reality that followed was different. Initially, large numbers of children had no way to pursue a secondary education because they lacked access to primary schools. Rapid population growth put significant pressure on expanding schooling, with consequences for the quality of provision. Moreover, questions emerged from employers, parents, and educators about the relevance, quality, and cost of TVET. A review by the World Bank of this education in the late 1980s culminated with a shift of policy in 1991 that encouraged promotion of private provision of skills and reforms to improve the effectiveness and efficiency of public provision (Middleton, Ziderman, and Adams 1991).

At the same time, increased emphasis was placed on expanding access to basic education. The Education for All movement emerged in 1990 and with it the expansion of international support for primary education. Consequently, support for TVET fell in relative terms. At the same time, the failure of state-managed economies resulted in cutbacks in government administrations and enterprises, with negative consequences for employment. Private investment, including that from abroad in foreign direct investment, was insufficient to replace the cutback in government spending and produce the jobs needed by people emerging from schools and training centers.

Access to primary education has increased quite dramatically, but many African children still are not able to finish primary levels of education. Growing numbers of children entered primary schools as Education for All took hold, along with better country macroeconomic management and conditions for investment. As a result, girls' primary net enrollment rates increased from 53 percent to 73 percent between 1999 and 2010 (World Bank 2012). Notwithstanding these achievements, many children continue to drop out of school before finishing primary levels, especially in the poorest of the countries on the African continent. For those able to complete a primary education, large numbers are unable to continue their education for lack of space in secondary education.

Raising skill levels is one of a number of important challenges to future regional growth and poverty reduction. Raising agricultural productivity and ensuring environmentally sustainable approaches to development are joined by the need to address the effects of HIV/AIDS. Sustaining an investment climate that is favorable to economic growth and industrialization is important, as is raising productivity of the region's large informal sector and opening pathways for these small and household enterprises to grow and enter the formal economy. The literature on this topic centers on (a) improving the regulatory climate faced by such enterprises and (b) increasing their access to business development services, with credit and financial services at the fore (Fox and Sohnesen 2012). This chapter looks further at the role played by skills acquired through education and training and their influence on entry into the informal and formal sectors and on the earnings of people in each sector.

What Is Meant by Skills?

Skills development takes place at different stages of the life cycle for different purposes and occurs in a number of institutional settings. Skills for work and life are the result of learning in settings that range from public and private schools to the nonschool domains of home, community, and workplace. Skills are acquired by learning to perform various tasks with different degrees of proficiency. Three types of skills (see, for example, Cunha and Heckman 2009; Hanushek and Woessmann 2008; Heckman and Rubenstein 2001) are recognized:

- *Cognitive skills* are the mental capabilities required to learn successfully academic subjects such as math, science, and reading. When an individual performs well academically, it is a reflection of the acquisition of cognitive skills such as concentration, perception and interpretation, memory, and logical thinking. Various mental disabilities such as attention disorders are known to impede the acquisition and exercise of cognitive skills in the process of learning.

- *Noncognitive skills* are sometimes overlooked and involve a different set of acquired abilities. James J. Heckman and Alan B. Krueger in their 2004 book *Inequality in America: What Role for Human Capital Policies?* stress that the most persistent, self-disciplined, adaptable students and professionals often have the ability to outperform those with higher levels of cognitive skills. These "overachievers," by virtue of their noncognitive skills, are able to outperform their counterparts who possess higher levels of cognitive skills. Noncognitive skills are sometimes described as "soft" skills and include persistence, emotional maturity, verbal and nonverbal communication, and interpersonal skills. Noncognitive skills influence the overall behavior of an individual and are acquired in the home, at schools, in the community, and in the workplace.

- *Technical skills* combine cognitive and noncognitive skills in performing various tasks. These skills involve acquired expertise for performing certain functions and achieving specific outcomes. Some examples of technical skills include the ability to diagnose and treat diseases, to use information technology in the design and manufacture of products, to operate and maintain heavy equipment, and to design and produce garments. Each task involves specialized technical knowledge or expertise to achieve a specific outcome. This knowledge is acquired at different times in the life cycle for different purposes. It can be acquired early in the life cycle for the purpose of pursuing a first job. It can come later with efforts to stay current with technological change in an existing job or in acquiring new skills for a change of employment.

The acquisition of these skills takes place in many settings, public and private.

- Cognitive skills are shaped early in the life cycle, for example, by family, nutrition, and nurture in early childhood and by formal education.
- Noncognitive skills, in contrast, are acquired from birth onward by observing the behavior of family members and peers, participating in community activities, obtaining classroom experience, and learning in the work environment from the behavior of others. Learning to work with others to achieve goals, for example, occurs in settings such as a playschool, an athletic event, a school project, a community activity, or a work setting.
- Technical skills may come from formal education; a training center outside formal education; or the workplace through an apprenticeship, enterprise-based training, or experience on the job.

The combination of cognitive and noncognitive skills in primary and lower-secondary education provides a foundation for the acquisition of technical skills and the preparation of individuals for employment with secondary and postsecondary education. This foundation is also important to the subsequent reskilling of workers later in the life cycle. Employers look for signals of the presence of these skills in the recruitment process. Years of schooling and academic performance are often used as indicators of cognitive skills. Noncognitive skills are more difficult to detect, and references from teachers, community members, and prior employers are used for this purpose as well as assessments of the performance of individuals in job interviews, their involvement in extracurricular activities, and a record of prior accomplishments in family, community, and work settings.

Looking at the Effects of Skills

This chapter and its analysis of skills acquired through education and training are concerned with how skills can influence the productivity and incomes of people employed in the informal sector. The chapter suggests strategies for improving productivity and incomes in the small and household enterprises of the informal sector for reducing poverty. It also examines the role of skills in promoting mobility between the informal and formal sectors. The case of Tanzania referred to in chapter 2 offers evidence that as many as 7 of 10 people employed in the informal sector are there for lack of choices; the question is what role do skills play in creating those choices? Economists contend that an enterprise's entry into the formal sector is constrained by costly regulations and market failures attached to credit and financial markets, but in this study, we look further at the role of skills as a constraint to the choice of employment (Fox and Sohnesen 2012).

The available data, however, have drawbacks pertaining to accurate analysis of links between skills, employment, and earnings. Household surveys of employment and earnings, like those used in this study, generally do not measure cognitive, noncognitive, and technical skills. Instead, they are often limited to questions about participation in different sources of skills development (for example, schools) and, at best, training programs, apprenticeships, and on-the-job training. Better measures of skills, if available, would quantify not just participation in a program for skills development but also indicators of the actual skills attained.

Few household surveys contain measures of actual skills attainment. Possible indicators of skills attainment might include the completion status of a program, test scores and level of skills certification, scores on standardized tests, and academic degrees received. In most cases, indicators of learning and achievement are not available, and one is forced to rely on simple measures of participation in education or training—yes or no—or time spent in the program. The only exceptions are literacy and numeracy skills, which are sometimes available but clearly measure only a very basic level of skill. Much of the early human capital literature that gauges the effect of formal education on earnings, for example, uses the years of schooling completed rather than a standardized indicator of learning outcomes. Moreover, information on noncognitive and other complementary skills is not available.

This chapter relies on indicators of education and training participation in the household surveys of Ghana, Kenya, Nigeria, Rwanda, and Tanzania to correlate this participation with entry into informal and formal sector employment and the earnings in each of these sectors. The first question addressed is whether education and training from different providers are associated with the choice of formal and informal sector employment. We examine this question with data on education and training from the household surveys by first comparing the education and training profiles of people employed in the formal and informal sectors. We have controlled statistically[1] for factors influencing employment in the two sectors to assess how the years of schooling and participation in different training programs correlate with the likelihood of working in the informal sector.

We also examine the relationship between education and earnings. Once an individual has established employment in a sector, a second question is how education and training correlate with his or her earnings. Are the economic returns to education and training in the enterprises of the informal sector comparable to those of the formal sector, as they should be if markets are working to allocate labor and skills to their best use, or do the returns differ and imply structural barriers to labor and capital mobility that would equate these returns? Earnings of people employed in each sector are regressed on the years of schooling and the different providers of training available to compare economic returns to education and training. As explained in this chapter, steps are taken to control for unobserved characteristics that influence earnings in the informal and formal sectors and may bias the observed outcomes. Schooling measures are available for all five countries, but the measures of training available differ (table 3.1).

Table 3.1 Training Measures in Five Country Household Surveys

Type of training measured	*Ghana 2005/06*[a]	*Kenya 2005/06*[b]	*Nigeria 2003/04*[c]	*Rwanda 2005/06*[d]	*Tanzania 2005/06*[e]
Formal/nonformal education					
Formal education	X	X	X	X	X
Vocational education	X	X	X	X	X
By type and trade					X
Short-term courses	X		X	X	X
By type and trade	X		X	X	X
Literacy course	X		X	X	
Achieved literacy/numeracy	X	X	X	X	X
Enterprise-based training					
Apprenticeships	X		X	X	X
By type and trade	X		X	X	X
On-the-job training					X

Sources: GSS 2005–06; KNBS 2007; NBS 2007; NBSN 2004; and NISR 2007.
Note: Skills and employment in the informal sector are measured.
a. Ghana Living Standards Survey (GLSS) 2005–06.
b. Kenya Integrated Household Budget Survey (KIHBS) 2005–06.
c. Nigeria Living Standard Survey (NLSS) 2003.
d. Rwanda Integrated Household Living Conditions Survey (EICV) 2005–06.
e. Tanzania Integrated Labour Force Survey (ILFS) 2006.

The Profile of Skills in the Informal Sector

The profile of education and training in the informal sector is similar when compared across the five countries and with the formal sector. The following trends are observed:

- Literacy rates are high in each of the five countries but are lower for people employed in enterprises of the informal sector and for women.
- Years of schooling are lower in the informal sector than in the formal sector, with both higher than education levels in farming.
- Years of schooling is a strong predictor of subsequent access to vocational training but an inverse predictor for apprenticeships.
- Years of schooling and vocational training are both closely associated with employment in the formal sector.
- Apprenticeships are the principal source of skills for the informal sector, but apprenticeships also serve the formal sector.
- Gender differences are evident in education and training, and these differences in skills carry over to the sector of employment for women.
- Skills from all sources are more readily accessible in urban than rural areas, raising the question of whether this is a supply or demand phenomenon.

Although the ability to read and write is an essential skill for many business activities and for further skills development, adult literacy rates in Sub-Saharan Africa are among the lowest in the world. The United Nations Educational,

Figure 3.1 Literacy Rates in the Informal and Formal Sectors, Nigeria and Kenya

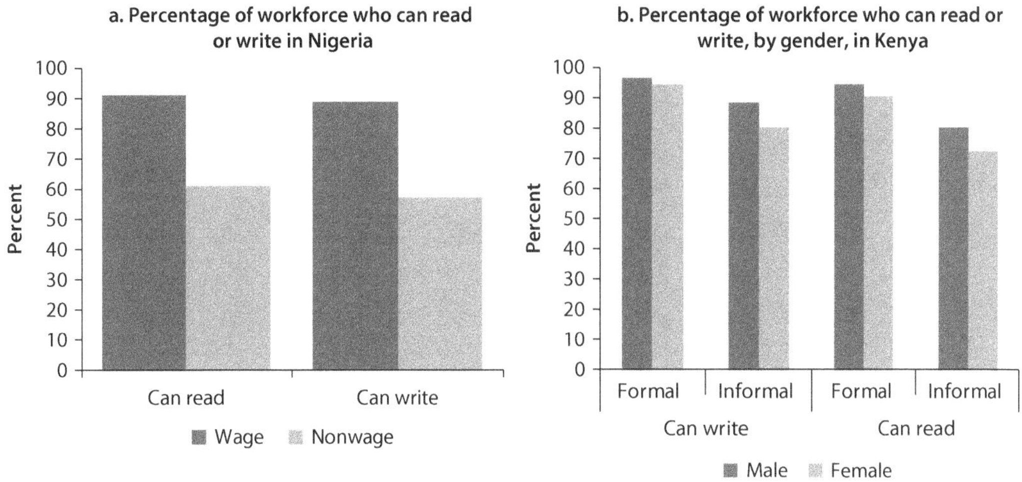

Sources: Elaborations based on KNBS 2007 and NBSN 2004.

Scientific and Cultural Organization (UNESCO) reports the regional average adult literacy rate as being 63 percent and the youth literacy rate as 66 percent for the period 2005–10. In our five country cases, literacy rates are above average, ranging from under 67 percent in Nigeria to over 84 percent in Kenya. However, the comparison of literacy rates in the formal and informal sectors of both countries (figure 3.1) reveals those working in the informal sector are less likely to be able to read or write than those in the formal sector. In Kenya, these rates are lower for women than men (figure 3.1, panel b). Similar patterns are evident in the other three countries. Rising enrollment and completion rates in primary education over the past decade are expected to improve literacy rates for future labor force entrants; for adults already employed, nevertheless, illiteracy is a problem, especially for the informal sector.

The informal sector displays lower education levels than the formal sector, but both sectors have education levels that exceed those of farming. Because literacy is an outcome of schooling, not surprisingly, education patterns are consistent with those observed for literacy. Overall, the data suggest that different levels of education are coupled with different kinds of employment opportunities. As shown in figure 3.2, panel b, 17 percent working in the private formal sector of Tanzania have completed a secondary education or higher. The figure rises to 58 percent for people working in government, reflecting the large number of university graduates in government positions. The informal sector in turn employs only 8 percent with a secondary education or higher, and the percentage drops to less than 2 percent for farming. The lower levels of education in farming are evident with 31 percent not having attended school in Tanzania. In Rwanda, the percentage is 27 percent, and in Ghana, it is 45 percent.

Skills acquisition shows evidence of being a cumulative process linked to years of schooling. Economists have taken note of the cumulative nature of skills

Figure 3.2 Education Levels in the Informal, Formal, and Farming Sectors, Rwanda and Tanzania

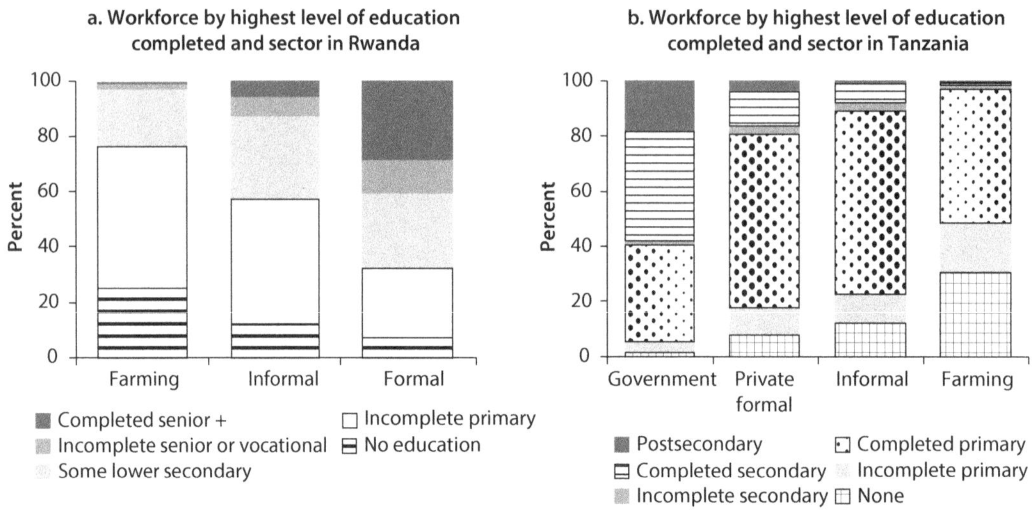

Sources: Elaborations based on NISR 2007 and NBS 2007.

Figure 3.3 Training and Formal Education in the Formal Sector, Especially Government, in Tanzania

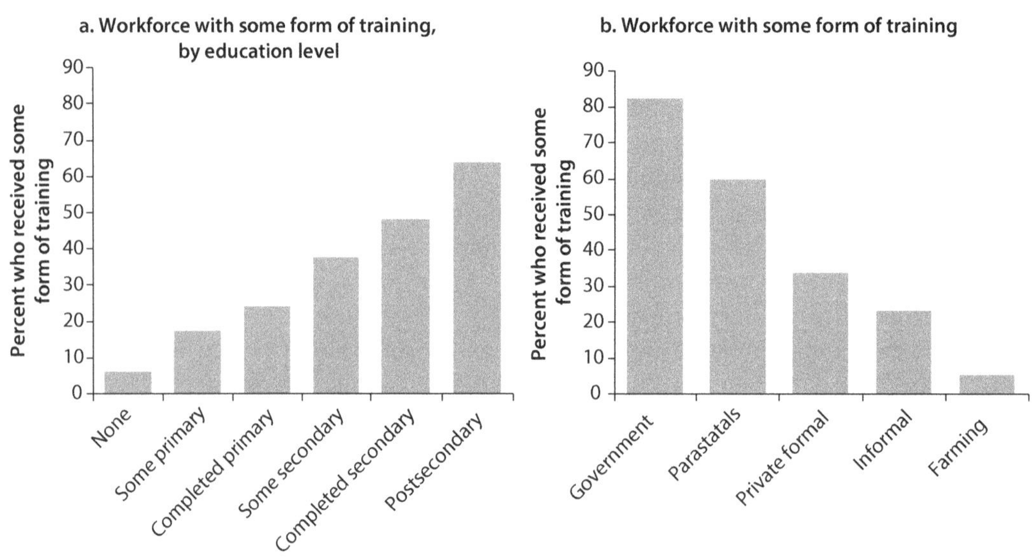

Source: Elaborations based on NBS 2007.

development over the life cycle of workers with those building a foundation of education early in life being more likely to continue this investment later in the life cycle (Cunha and others 2005). Literacy is a basic requirement for further school-based education and many other forms of training. The importance of an early foundation in education is demonstrated in figure 3.3, panel a, for Tanzania.

It shows the percentage of those answering a question about whether they have participated in vocational training. Only 5 percent of people without any education have subsequently participated in a vocational training program, whereas the percentage rises with each level of education. People who acquire education early are more likely to continue investing in their own skills or find others such as employers to invest in them later.

Education translates into further investments in skills, and the differences in education by sector are connected with patterns of vocational training. For Tanzania, figure 3.3, panel b, shows the percentage of the workforce by sector of employment answering "yes" to the question about whether they have participated in some form of vocational training. Five percent or less of those engaged in farming answered affirmatively. The chances of participation in vocational training were higher for those working in the informal sector, with slightly over 20 percent indicating they had received some form of training. However, those working in the private formal sector with their higher levels of education were more likely to have received some form of training compared with people working in the informal sector. Government with its very high level of education shows more than 80 percent receiving training.

The informal sector trains in ways that are different from the formal sector. In the informal sector, traditional apprenticeships primarily provide training. Other sources of training provide the skills for the formal sector (see figure 3.4, panel a). Traditional apprenticeships involve agreements between a master craftsperson and a parent or apprentice to provide training in the workplace for a specified period in return for a small fee, reduced wages, or both. At the conclusion of the training, the apprentice is recognized

Figure 3.4 Apprenticeship Use in Formal and Informal Sectors, Selected Countries

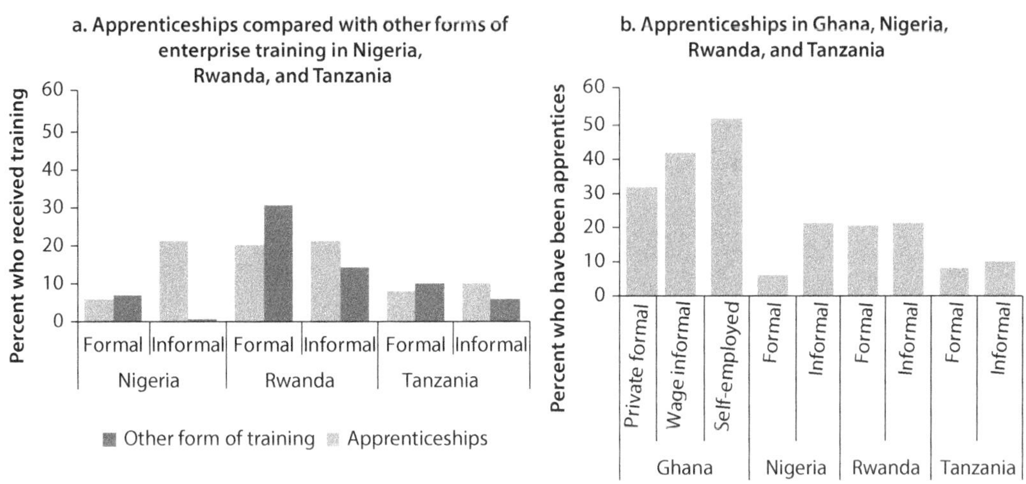

Sources: Elaborations based on GSS 2005–06; NBS 2007; NBSN 2004; and NISR 2007.
Note: Data for Ghana refer only to youth 15–30 years of age.

as a journeyman and may continue working for the master craftsperson or leave to work with another enterprise or start her or his own small business. The government or worker organizations do not regulate traditional apprenticeships, unlike formal apprenticeships in industrial countries. Traditional apprenticeships are self-regulated and self-financing and are, therefore, a popular source of skills for people engaged in the informal sector. As figure 3.4, panel b, shows, those trained by apprenticeship also find their way to employment in the formal sector.

In both urban and rural areas, traditional apprenticeships are the main source of skills for people in the informal sector. Table 3.2 reveals residential differences in access to skills by source of training for people employed in the informal sector of Tanzania. For those who have received training, traditional apprenticeships dominate as a source of skills development. Traditional apprenticeships and on-the-job training are the most likely sources of skills in the informal sector. The chances of having attended a school or acquired a certificate from a training center are lower. In Tanzania, finding an apprenticeship is easier in urban than in rural areas. If one resides in a rural area, skills are less likely to be acquired through an apprenticeship; rather, they are obtained by learning on the job. Perhaps reflecting the tendency of schools and training centers to locate in urban areas near pockets of industry and large population centers, a smaller share of those in rural areas working in the informal sector acquire their skills from these sources. The residential differences in access to apprenticeships observed in Tanzania are also found in Ghana, Nigeria, and Rwanda (see figure 3.5).

Opportunities for access to apprenticeships vary not only by place of residence but also by gender. In Ghana, virtual parity exists in access to apprenticeships for young women and men, but in Nigeria and Rwanda, differences are seen (figure 3.5). Young men are more likely to have been through an apprenticeship than young women in both countries. As noted in chapter 2, women in Nigeria and Ghana were found to account for a larger share of employment in the informal sector than men. Even with the larger presence of women in

Table 3.2 Types of Training within the Informal Sector in Tanzania, 2006
Percent

Type of training, conditional upon having been trained	*Urban*	*Rural*	*Total*
Informal apprenticeship	46.8	39.4	45.0
On-the-job training	22.6	35.6	25.7
Vocational certificate	15.4	13.4	14.9
College or academic certificate	12.3	8.8	11.4
Diploma	1.4	0	1.1
Advanced diploma or university degree	0.5	0	0.4
Other	1.0	2.8	1.5
Total	100.0	100.0	100.0

Source: Elaborations based on NBS 2007 data.

Figure 3.5 Share of Group Who Have Been Apprentices, by Residence Area and Gender, in Ghana, Nigeria, and Rwanda

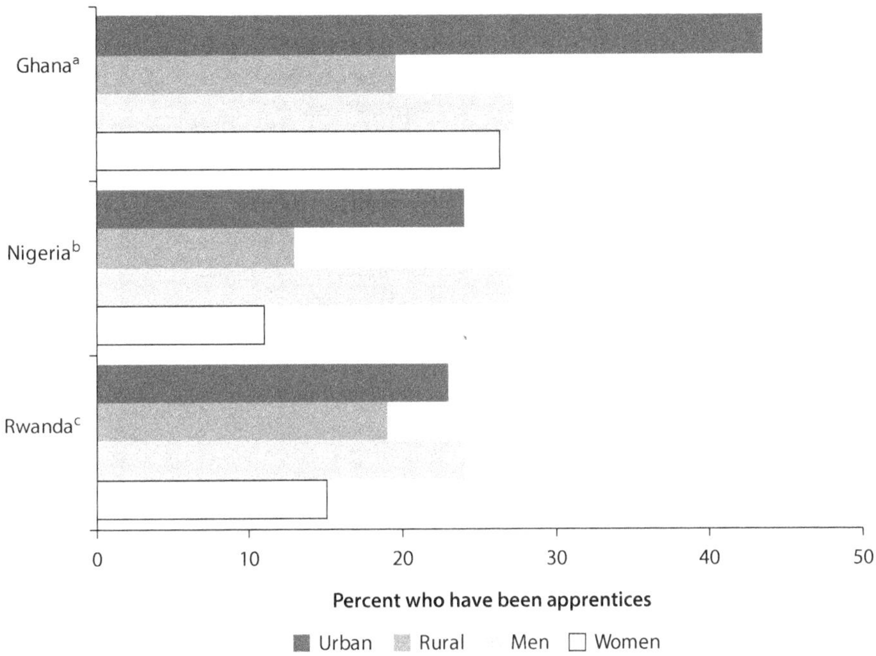

Sources: Elaborations based on GSS 2005–06; NBSN 2004; and NISR 2007.
a. Formal and informal, youth 15–30 years of age.
b. Informal only.
c. Formal and informal.

the informal sector in Nigeria, these women are notably less likely to have access to skills through an apprenticeship. The lower access to skills development is compounded on the demand side of labor markets by occupational segregation because women and men access very different forms of apprenticeships (see chapter 4). Gender is as important an issue in skills as in employment.

Apprenticeships in Ghana are the main source of skills for people working in both the informal and formal sectors. Ghana provides a particularly rich description of those who have completed an apprenticeship among youth 15–30 years of age (table 3.3). The popularity of traditional apprenticeships is reflected in the share of youth who have completed an apprenticeship, 27 percent, and the share who have passed through a technical or vocational education program, only 2 percent. Fully 51 percent of youth who were working off the farm and self-employed acquired skills through an apprenticeship. Smaller, but still significant, numbers of youth working for wages also completed an apprenticeship in both the informal and formal sectors.

Apprenticeships are less accessible to the very poor. Because an apprentice can pay for his or her training by accepting lower wages, in principle

Table 3.3 Percentage of Youth Having Gone through TVET and Apprenticeships in Ghana
Percent

Criteria	*TVET*	*Apprenticeships*	*Criteria*	*TVET*	*Apprenticeships*
All	2	27	All	2	27
Location			Sector of employment		
Urban	4	44	Wage public sector	4	12
Rural	1	20	Wage private formal	8	32
Gender			Wage private informal	2	41
Male	2	27	Self-employed nonfarm	0	51
Female	2	26	Self-employed farm-paid	3	20
Age (years)			Self-employed farm-unpaid	0	9
15–19	0	11	Level of education		
20–24	2	31	No education	..	9
25–29	3	32	Some primary	..	21
Consumption quintile			Primary	..	33
Poorest	1	11	Lower secondary	..	51
Second poorest	1	18	TVET	..	20
Third poorest	1	28	Higher secondary	..	26
Second richest	3	37	Postsecondary	..	7
Richest	4	47			

Source: Elaboration of World Bank 2009.
Note: Youth is defined as 15–29 years of age; .. = negligible; TVET = technical and vocational education and training.

apprenticeships are thought to be more accessible to low-income youth, but table 3.3 offers evidence to the contrary by looking at the percentage of those with an apprenticeship in consumption quintiles. The percentage with an apprenticeship in Ghana systematically rises by consumption quintile: the top consumption quintile is four times more likely to have participated in an apprenticeship than the bottom consumption quintile. This pattern is not limited to apprenticeships. The same holds true for TVET in Ghana. In a separate analysis by the World Bank, the share of youth in the highest consumption quintile with a technical and vocational education, 4.3 percent, is seven times higher than that in the lowest consumption quintile (World Bank 2009).

Access to apprenticeships is also related with some (albeit low) level of basic competencies. All the patterns described in table 3.3 for Ghana are evident in Nigeria (table 3.4). Skills in the informal sector are more likely to have been obtained through an apprenticeship. Men and urban dwellers are more likely to participate in these apprenticeships than women. Although some evidence indicates that apprenticeships are primarily a source of skills for people with limited education, Nigeria demonstrates that apprenticeships can be popular at all levels of education in the informal sector. Illiteracy is a barrier to acquiring skills through an apprenticeship in both the formal and informal sectors. In cases where a basic education has provided individuals with the ability to read and write, access to apprenticeships is more widely available.

Table 3.4 Correlation of Low Levels of Education and Functional Capacities with Holding Apprenticeships in the Informal Sector of Nigeria
Percent

	Apprenticeships		*On-the-job training*	
Education and other criteria	*Formal*	*Informal*	*Formal*	*Informal*
Male	6	27	8	1
Female	2	11	3	0
Urban	6	24	7	2
Rural	4	13	6	0
Education ≥ 10 years	4	24	7	5
Education < 10 years	11	27	2	0
Received OJT	6	5	n.a.	n.a.
No OJT	5	5	n.a.	n.a.
Can read	5	27	7	1
Cannot read	4	8	4	0
Can calculate	5	27	7	1
Cannot calculate	5	8	4	0
Can write	5	26	7	1
Cannot write	5	11	4	0

Source: Elaborations based on NBSN 2004.
Note: OJT = on-the-job training; n.a. = not applicable.

As shown in table 3.3, having obtained some level of education is associated with a higher probability of having been through an apprenticeship. Together with the evidence that those who often are most excluded from basic education—the poorest, the rural population, and women—do not access apprenticeships, this evidence suggests that some minimum competencies are necessary to access even traditional apprenticeships. The relationship is best described as a *U* shape, with the likelihood of an apprenticeship in the informal sector increasing with some education and decreasing for higher levels of education (see figure 3.6).

Overall, this profile of skills emphasizes the importance of a good quality basic education as a foundation for acquiring skills over the life cycle. The profile points to the weak foundation of education for people who are now employed in the informal sector, including low levels of literacy. For want of a strong foundation in education, people in the informal sector are more likely to acquire skills through a traditional apprenticeship. However, access to these apprenticeships is uneven. People living in rural areas face greater difficulty in finding an apprenticeship than those living in urban areas. Women constitute a large part of the informal sector, but they are less likely to participate in an apprenticeship than men. The concentration of women in trade and services in the informal sector (observed in chapter 2), where apprenticeships are less common, is expected to be part of the explanation for this pattern. Finally, even though apprenticeships are self-financing, access to them is lowest among the very poorest of households.

Figure 3.6 Education Levels Needed for Apprenticeships, Ghana and Rwanda

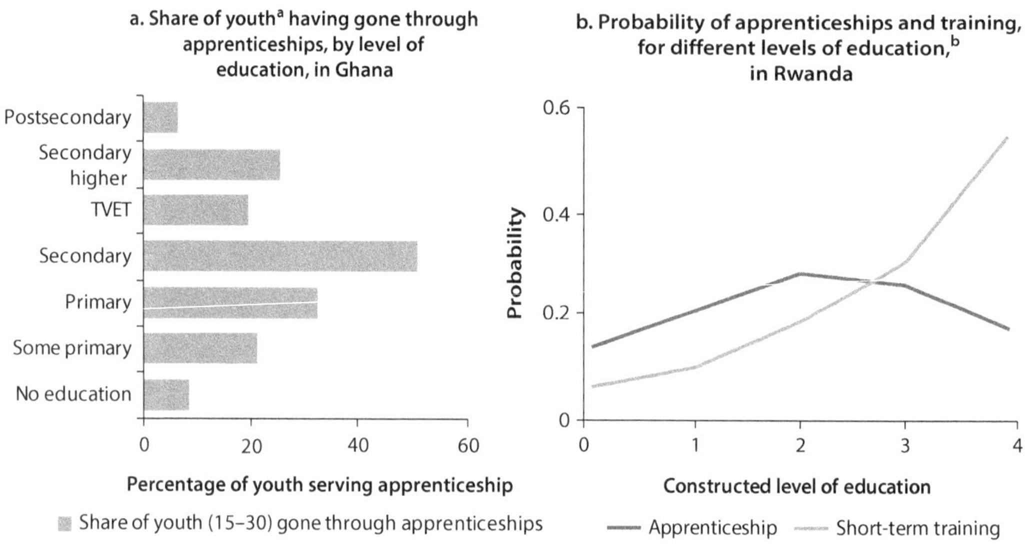

Sources: Elaborations based on GSS 2005–06; NISR 2007.
Note: TVET = technical and vocational education and training.
a. Youth is defined as 15–30 years of age.
b. Constructed level of education is defined as follows: Edu0 = no education; Edu1 = some education but less than completed primary education; Edu2 = completed primary and some lower secondary; Edu3 = completed lower-secondary and some higher-secondary or vocational education; Edu4 = completed higher-secondary or extended vocational education and above.

Sector of Employment

Education and training may affect a worker's earnings by influencing first the type of employment obtained and then the productivity of the worker in the employment and his or her earnings. Multivariate analysis is used to provide a better understanding of the relationship between skills and employment. Focusing on simple correlations can be insufficient: for example, are women less likely to be in the formal sector because they have had less access to education or because of some other gender-specific characteristic? Moreover, education can influence earnings in two different ways. First, a certain level of education or training may be required to get a job in a particular sector. For example, the government sector may predominantly hire university graduates, or operating as an informal self-employed mechanic may be difficult without an apprenticeship. Second, a certain level of education may raise the productivity of a person and thus increase his or her earnings.

The likelihood of employment in the informal and formal sectors and the relationship to education and training are estimated using data from the household surveys. Each of the country chapters explores the correlation between education and training, on the one hand, and sector of employment held, on the other, by estimating the probability of attaining employment in the informal and formal sectors, controlling for years of schooling, various forms of training, and other demographic characteristics. The analysis compares people employed off the farm in the informal and formal sectors with those employed in farming. It then estimates the relationship between education and training on the probability of employment in the formal or informal sectors, controlling for personal and situational factors that might influence this probability.[2]

Education and training exhibit a strong and statistically significant association with the type of job held.[3] The patterns differ on various points among the countries, although overall they are remarkably robust in showing the positive effect of education and training on the probability of obtaining employment off the farm, and similarly, whether an individual is employed in the informal or formal sectors.[4] The results for Tanzania (see box 3.1) are generally matched in the other countries studied, although some differences are found based on data available (see annex 3A, table 3A.1). Formal education and particularly higher education are associated with an increase in the odds of later holding employment in the formal, or wage, sector for all of our countries. People with limited education, usually with less than a primary education, are more likely to wind up employed in the informal sector. The stylized evidence in our five countries points to the importance of education, particularly secondary and higher education, for increasing the chances of later holding formal sector employment. In Nigeria, to determine the probability of formal rather than farm employment, we compared people with a general secondary education to those with a technical and vocational education. Both forms of secondary education increase the odds of holding employment in the formal sector by about one-third. In Ghana, the odds of doing this for technical and vocational education are higher than those for general secondary education. More specifically the results suggest the following:

- Education is linked with a higher probability of employment off the farm. With higher levels of schooling, the chances are much better for finding employment in both the public and private formal sectors than in the informal or farm sectors.
- Training also makes a difference. The results for different forms of training are equally interesting. In Tanzania, people with training of any type are more likely to be employed off the farm than those without training.
- Apprenticeships are correlated with off-farm employment, especially in the informal sectors. In Tanzania, the probabilities are about even across the sectors. In other countries, apprenticeships are associated with informal sector work, whereas the links to formal sector work are low or nil.
- In Tanzania, on-the-job training or training recognized with a vocational certificate or a college certificate is associated with informal sector employment, whereas higher levels of training at the diploma or advanced diploma levels are not associated with informal sector employment.

Box 3.1 Education, Training, and Sector of Employment in Tanzania

The Tanzania case study confirms strong links between education and training, on the one hand, and the probability of work in the informal or formal sector, on the other. The formal sector in Tanzania is divided into two parts representing the public and private formal sectors. Government employment in the public sector, with its large professional cadre, contains a more highly educated workforce than the private formal sector. Probabilities of employment in the two formal sector strata are estimated alongside the probability of employment in the informal sector. The comparison in each case is with people employed in farming.

Multinomial logit regressions (see table B3.1.1) show the following:

- The chances of women finding employment off the farm in the informal sector of Tanzania are lower than those of men.
- They also indicate that living in an urban area increases significantly the odds of finding employment in the informal sector, and age increases the chances of employment off the farm in formal and informal sectors, but the odds of this increase at a decreasing rate.

Table B3.1.1 Entry into Sectors and Role of Apprenticeships: Selected Results from Multinomial Logit Equations in Tanzania

Variables	*Government*	*Private formal*	*Informal*
Age	1.355***	1.005	1.084***
Age squared	0.713***	0.961***	0.900***
Female	0.549***	0.361***	0.716***
Education (baseline: no education)			
Incomplete primary	3.141***	1.153	1.112
Completed primary	5.466***	1.743***	1.723***
Incomplete secondary	7.271***	1.536**	1.550**
Completed secondary	49.063***	4.695***	3.338***
Advanced secondary/university	73.021***	6.271***	3.588***
Training (baseline: no training)			
On-the-job training	16.698***	4.465***	2.699***
Informal apprenticeship	3.345***	2.941***	2.986***
Vocational certificate	13.524***	5.482***	3.560***
College certificate	45.179***	5.832***	2.101***
Diploma	24.187***	4.170***	1.114
Advanced diploma/university degree	18.050***	3.314**	0.255**
Other training	6.502***	2.167***	0.567*
Urban	6.876***	9.988***	12.058***
Constant	0.000***	0.032***	0.011***
Observations	34,671	34,671	34,671

Source: Elaborations based on NBS 2007.
Note: Weighted regression. Relative odds ratios presented instead of coefficients: baseline category is farming. Quarter and region dummies included but not reported.
Significance level: * = 10 percent; ** = 5 percent; *** = 1 percent.

box continues next page

Box 3.1 Education, Training, and Sector of Employment in Tanzania *(continued)*

- The more interesting results are for education and training. Examining the table by column, starting with the informal sector, higher levels of schooling correspond to higher levels of employment off the farm. A higher-secondary or university education is associated with higher odds of informal sector employment over farming (by a factor of 2.5 times). Yet comparing the informal sector with the private formal sector, a higher-secondary or university education nearly doubles the odds for employment in the private formal sector.

- Although advanced training at the diploma level is not strongly associated with employment in the informal sector when compared with farming, it is in the case of the formal sector. This result is observed in both Tanzania and Nigeria. In Rwanda, in contrast, training at all levels is found not to be associated with the sector of employment.
- Access to training from all sources, including advanced training, is more strongly associated with formal sector employment compared with informal sector employment. The exception is apprenticeships, for which the association is roughly the same across formal and informal sectors. We need to keep in mind this does not show causation, because the odds of obtaining training are higher in the formal sector than in the informal sector. Thus, whether training that provides a diploma, for example, increases the chances of formal sector employment or vice versa is undetermined. What we can see is that training beyond formal schooling is generally associated with employment off the farm and more so with employment in the formal sector compared with the informal sector, except for apprenticeships.
- Under the generic heading of vocational training, ample evidence from the five countries shows the link between training and employment off the farm in both formal and informal sectors. In Nigeria, this training is associated with a 26 percent higher likelihood of formal sector employment. In Kenya, it improves the chances for both formal and informal sector employment compared with farm work.

Apprenticeships, as already noted, are the principal source of skills for the informal sector. However, we see evidence that people with apprenticeships are also able to find their way into the formal sector. In Ghana, the question of whether apprenticeships substitute for formal education was examined by creating a variable that intersects participation in an apprenticeship with different levels of education. The results in table 3.5 show a modest positive association between an apprenticeship and employment off the farm in the formal and informal sectors for those with a primary education or less. The effect is larger in rural than in urban areas. The more surprising result is for people with

Table 3.5 Entry into Sectors and Apprenticeships: Selected Results from Multinomial Logit Equations in Ghana

	Wage		*Self-employed nonfarm*	
Variables	*1991/92*	*2005/06*	*1991/92*	*2005/06*
Urban				
Apprenticeships low education	1.819***	1.054	1.383*	1.283*
Apprenticeships medium education	0.909	0.743**	2.058**	1.573***
Apprenticeships high education	1.617	1.099	1.401	4.678***
Rural				
Apprenticeships low education	1.047	4.06***	1.277	2.14***
Apprenticeships medium education	0.984	1.43*	1.647**	1.90***
Apprenticeships high education	0.346	1.24	2.375	2.95

Source: Elaborations based on World Bank 2009.
Significance level: * = 10 percent, ** = 5 percent, *** = 1 percent.

a university education. The most recent survey year in Ghana, 2005/06, shows the odds of holding employment in the informal urban sector have increased sharply for those with a university education and an apprenticeship. As seen, apprenticeships are associated with government or formal private sector employment in Tanzania. This may reflect difficulties in finding employment in the formal sector; university graduates are using apprenticeships and entering the informal sector.

Earnings

Once an individual is employed, education and training are expected to enhance the worker's productivity and, in doing so, increase his or her earnings. To assess how further investments in education and training might raise productivity and earnings of workers in the informal sector, we ran separate regression equations in each country for those employed in the two sectors. These earnings are regressed on measures of education and training plus other individual or situational factors in each country that might influence earning outcomes. We have already noted a pattern of selection into the formal and informal sectors based on education and training as well as on other personal characteristics. Thus, we have used these findings to correct for selection bias in the earnings equations. The steps taken to control for this bias use a two-stage estimation procedure.[5] For comparison, ordinary least squares (OLS) regressions were estimated for some countries, and the results are generally similar.[6] The outcomes are reported in table 3A.2. The importance of these controls seems to vary by country with no significant effects in Ghana and Rwanda but observed effects in Nigeria and Kenya, where education and training significance is increased with controls for selection bias, especially in the formal sector of Kenya.

Lower levels of education and forms of training are associated with off-farm employment but have little or no further effect on earnings. Even with differences in specification of the earnings functions and estimation methods, the patterns around education, vocational training, and apprenticeships are similar, and some consistent patterns emerge. Although literacy is linked to employment off the farm, its direct effect on earnings is modest. In stylized form, the years of schooling increase earnings in all five countries, but more so in the formal than in the informal sector. The returns to a year of schooling in Kenya for people employed in the formal sector in 2005/06 were 18 percent, compared with 8.3 percent in the informal sector. If correction is made for selection bias, the returns to education in the formal sector increase to 23 percent, leaving unchanged the returns in the informal sector, thus widening the gap in returns between the two sectors.

The evidence generally shows higher marginal returns for each level of education in the formal sector compared with the informal sector. In Ghana, Nigeria, and Tanzania, each completed level of education pays off less in the informal than in the formal sector, while in Kenya, additional years of schooling are positively associated with earnings in the formal sector but have no effect in the informal sector. However, Rwanda provides an exception because returns to education in the informal sector exceed those in the formal sector.

There are a number of hypotheses for higher returns for each level of education in the formal sector, but we are unable to distinguish among them. The possibility exists, for example, of labor market segmentation with barriers to labor mobility between the formal and informal sectors. Employment in the formal sector could be rationed, leaving large numbers to crowd into the informal sector, thereby placing downward pressure on earnings in this sector. As already noted, education may play a role in perpetuating this segmentation. Other explanations could include lower quality of education for those who find their way to the informal sector. The education curriculum that tends to focus on skills for moving into higher education may not be well suited to entrepreneurial activities. Differences in returns may also reflect wage premiums found in larger enterprises of the formal sector and the possibility of wages in the formal sector being driven by public sector wage policies that are not competitively determined.

Returns also increase with level of education, especially in the formal sector. Rwanda shows that returns to education in the formal sector become significant only after completing a lower-secondary or higher level of education, including TVET. There is evidence of convexity in returns in other countries, among them Nigeria, where the returns to higher levels of education account for most of the difference between the average earnings of the formal sector when compared with the informal sector. In Ghana, the argument is made that primary education is no longer enough. The success of Education for All has produced numbers of primary school graduates that drive down the returns to this education. The returns in Ghana show that education is most strongly associated with earnings in the formal sector and that the correlation is significant only beginning with those completing a lower-secondary education. The payoff to primary education may therefore be in promoting labor mobility out of farming into the informal sector with its higher earning opportunities, but once there, workers make no further income gains until they attain higher levels of education.

The findings on vocational training in its different forms and sources are mixed among the five countries.

- In Tanzania, as shown previously, lower levels of vocational training are connected with employment in the informal sector, and advanced levels of training do not increase the chances of this employment, but advanced training has higher chances of being linked to employment in the formal sector. The earning functions, perhaps reflecting the variety of training sources organized under the heading of vocational training, do not give us a clear picture of how the training affects earnings. However, training in all forms has robust effects on earnings in the formal sector with returns only for a vocational or college certificate in the informal sector. These two forms of training not only influence access to the informal sector but also influence earnings in a positive manner.
- In Rwanda, training is not linked to earnings in either sector, although a technical and vocational education appears to be associated with higher earnings in the informal sector.
- In Ghana, no separate estimates exist for vocational training and earnings, but estimates of secondary technical and vocational education show returns that match those of general secondary education in both formal and informal sectors.
- In Nigeria, vocational training is not found to be related with earning gains in either the informal or the formal sectors.
- In Kenya, the results for vocational training are influenced by selection bias. Vocational training is not statistically significant in either the formal or informal sector earning functions. However, much like the case for higher education in Kenya, when selection bias is corrected, the returns become significant, but only at the margin. It is difficult to make much from these findings for vocational training because of the diversity of training sources wrapped up in this variable.

People who complete apprenticeships do not see an increase in their earnings. The earlier results in this chapter showed apprenticeship was linked to employment in the informal sector, with significant numbers also finding their way into the formal sector. Once these people are employed, however, the actual effect on earnings is disappointing. In Ghana, apprenticeships do not correspond to higher earnings. In Nigeria, the effect of apprenticeships on earnings is found to be as weak as it is in Tanzania. Rwanda is an exception because apprentices are shown to earn as much as 22 percent more in the informal sector than those who have not completed an apprenticeship. However, there is no observed impact on earnings in the formal sector for those with apprenticeships.

Main Conclusions

Employment off the farm in the informal and formal sectors is strongly associated with education. This chapter emphasizes the importance of education and training and of establishing a solid foundation of education for all who enter the workforce in Sub-Saharan Africa. Failing to do so leads to long-term adverse consequences for skills acquisition, the type of employment held, and one's subsequent earnings in employment. This chapter breaks apart the links between education and employment into education's effect on the type of employment held, and once employed, on what one earns. Although causality cannot be inferred, some minimum education appears to be linked to employment off the farm. However, the failure to attain more than a primary education increases measurably the chances of winding up in the informal sector compared to the formal sector, and once one is working in this sector, the earnings are likely to be lower than the earnings of people who make their way into the formal sector.

The use of modern technologies for competitiveness requires additional education. Although primary schooling is linked to informal sector and off-farm work, it is unlikely to open doors to the formal sector. Secondary and higher education appear to be the passport today for entry into the formal sector of the countries in this study. These higher levels of education do not guarantee better jobs in the formal sector; however, without this education, the chances of finding this employment are significantly reduced. Although many factors will influence whether a small and household enterprise grows and becomes part of the formal sector, what is clear from our findings is that the education of the enterprise's workforce will play a critical role in this transition. An enterprise whose workforce has only a primary education or less will face a barrier to entry into the formal sector. Providing broader access to secondary and more advanced education thus has to be part of the strategy for expanding employment in the formal sector.

Education and training can also influence earnings. Generally, more education is linked to higher earnings in both sectors, although the payoff may be lower in the informal sector. This chapter offers a number of hypotheses for this finding that range from market segmentation with years of schooling as a segmenting force to other factors on the supply and demand sides of labor markets. On the supply side is the quality of education available to people who find themselves in the informal sector and the type of curriculum offered in schools and its relevance to entrepreneurial activity. On the demand side are the wage premiums found in larger enterprises in the formal sector and the likelihood of wages in the formal sector being driven by public sector wages that are not competitively determined. The latter hypothesis proves interesting in light of the large share of public sector employment in the formal sectors of our five countries.

Access to education at all levels takes on added importance when looking at the effect of schooling on where one works and what one is paid. The influence of gender, residence, and household income on schooling access is part of the story behind the demographic profile of employment in the informal sector. Overall, access to different levels of education and training shows the following:

- Access to basic education and literacy plays a role in future skills development by opening the door to postbasic education and providing a signal about the ability of the worker to acquire higher levels of skills and productivity through training from different sources.
- Training outside schools is closely aligned with where one works.
- Apprenticeships are the ticket to employment in the informal sector, but their value for employment in the formal sector is also evident in some countries.
- Lower levels of nonformal training can open pathways to employment in the informal sector, while training in more advanced skills is essential to employment in the formal sector.
- Technical and vocational education in schools, often criticized for its cost and relevance, influences access to employment in both sectors and higher earnings.

The dominant source of skills for the informal sector, traditional apprenticeships, offers a mixed picture of their effect on earnings. Only in Rwanda did we find statistical evidence of this effect. The primary effect appears to be on the access these apprenticeships offer to employment off the farm in the informal sector and for some to find employment later in the formal sector. One can ask why this self-regulating, self-financing source of skills, popular to many in Sub-Saharan Africa, is not producing a larger, more observable impact on earnings. Part of the answer to this question doubtless rests in the limited education and literacy of those who pursue their skills through this means. Addressing this issue would call for attention to second-chance education and adult literacy programs. Other reasons may be found in the quality of the training offered by master craftspersons, the dated technology and production methods often used and taught, and a market for these skills that suffers from information asymmetries about what skills have actually been acquired.

The following chapter draws on the review of skills development programs in our five countries, especially programs focused on the informal sector, as well as experience in other countries. It identifies strategies that address the constraints to skills development in the informal sector (chapter 1) and that may offer a pathway to improving the productivity of these enterprises and those who work in them.

Annex 3A: Summary of Education and Training Impact on Sector of Employment and Individual Earnings by Country

This annex summarizes the results of the study's multinomial logit and earnings regressions in each of the five countries. Table 3A.1 describes whether education and training in its different forms is statistically related in each country to the likelihood of being employed in the formal and informal sectors. Table 3A.2 describes whether earnings in each sector are correlated with the type of education and training received in each country.

Table 3A.1 Multinomial Logit Regressions on Occupational Choice/Sector Entry: Main Results with Respect to Skills[a]

	Wage worker/formal		*Self-employed/informal*	
Country: group	*Formal education/TVET*	*Apprenticeships/other training*	*Formal education/TVET*	*Apprenticeships/other training*
Ghana: Urban, 25–64 years of age, W/S-E	• No significance below secondary; significant and increasing effects from secondary onward • TVET effect higher than secondary, lower than postsecondary	• No significant effect from apprenticeships	• Significant entry effect as of higher secondary • Much weaker entry effect than in wage sector	• Significant entry effect from apprenticeships (especially medium and high education)
Ghana: Rural, 25–64 years of age, W/S-E	• Significant effects from all levels of education	• Significant effect from low-level apprenticeships	• Significant entry effects as of lower levels of education	• Significant effects from apprenticeships (especially low and medium education)
Kenya: 15–65 years of age, F/IF	• Years of schooling determinant of entry • TVET stronger determinant than years of schooling	• Literacy no impact	• No significant effect of years of education	• Literacy increases probability of entry • TVET increases probability of entry but less than in formal sector
Nigeria: 15–65 years of age, W/SE and F/IF[b]	• Positive and increasing entry effect of education • TVET same effect as secondary general on entry	• No effect of apprenticeship • Positive effect of other training • Positive effect of literacy/ numeracy	• No effect of education except senior secondary • No effect of TVET	• Strong positive effect of apprenticeship • No effect of literacy • No effect of other training
Rwanda: 15–65 years of age, F/IF	• Strong and increasing effect of education • TVET no effect	• Apprenticeship small effect • Training no effect	• Positive effect of education but wears off (senior secondary and above less effect than some secondary); smaller effects than in formal sector • TVET no effect	• Apprenticeship stronger effect than in formal sector (but less than completed primary) • Training no effect

table continues next page

Table 3A.1 Multinomial Logit Regressions on Occupational Choice/Sector Entry: Main Results with Respect to Skills[a] *(continued)*

	Wage worker/formal		*Self-employed/informal*	
Country: group	*Formal education/TVET*	*Apprenticeships/other training*	*Formal education/TVET*	*Apprenticeships/other training*
Tanzania: 15–65 years of age, W/SE and F/IF[c]	• Education has a significant effect as of completed primary, exponentially increasing (very fast for government sector)	• Apprenticeship effect significant, but less than completed secondary education	• Education is a significant determinant of entry as of completed primary, increasing but much less than for formal	• Apprenticeships stronger effect than education below completed secondary but less than TVET
	• TVET effect strong	• Other training highly significant, about same as TVET	• TVET more significant than training but much less than in wage sector	• Positive effect of other training but less than apprenticeships

Note: TVET = technical and vocational education and training.

a. Likelihood of being in sector, agriculture is the base outcome. For definitions of formal/informal, see country chapters. W/S-E: Comparing wage workers with self-employed. F/IF: Comparing formal wage workers with informal wage and self-employed.

b. Same results irrespective of whether W/S-E or F/IF are compared.

c. Same results for W/S-E and F/IF, except that effect of education does not wear off significantly for informal (including informal wage workers) as for self-employed group.

Table 3A.2 Earnings Regressions: Main Results with Respect to Skills[a]

	Wage/formal		*Nonwage/informal*	
Country: group	*Formal education/TVET*	*Apprenticeships/other training*	*Formal education/TVET*	*Apprenticeships/other training*
Ghana: Urban, 25–64 years of age, W/S-E, sample selection	• Significant and increasing returns to formal education from secondary/TVET onward	• Negative effect of apprenticeships at higher education	• Weak significance of secondary-plus education; lower than wage earners	• No significance
Ghana: Rural, 25–64 years of age, W/S-E, sample selection	• Only postsecondary significant	• Negative effect of apprenticeships at medium levels of education	• No significance	• No significance
Ghana: Urban, 25–64 years of age, W/S-E, OLS	• Significant and increasing effects from secondary higher/TVET onward	• Negative effect of apprenticeships at higher levels of education	• Significant returns from secondary lower and onward (lower than wage earners at postsecondary, higher at lower secondary)	• No significance
Ghana: Rural, 25–64 years of age, W/S-E, OLS	• Significant and increasing effects from secondary lower and onward	• Positive effect of apprenticeships at low education levels	• Significant returns until lower secondary; no significance at higher levels	• No significance
Kenya: 15–65 years of age, F/IF, sample selection	• Years of education positive and stronger than for informal sector • TVET positive and stronger than for informal sector	• Literacy no significance	• Years of education very small impact • TVET stronger impact	• Literacy small positive impact
Kenya: 15–65 years of age, F/IF, OLS	• Years of education positive and stronger than for informal sector • TVET not significant	• Literacy no significance	• Years of education very small impact • TVET stronger impact	• Literacy no significance
Nigeria: 15–65 years of age, W/S-E, sample selection	• Positive effects of education from secondary onward • TVET not significant	• No significance of training or apprenticeships • Literacy significant	• No significance	• No significance of training or apprenticeships • Literacy not significant
Nigeria: 15–65 years of age, W/S-E, OLS	• Positive effects only at postsecondary level	• No effects of apprenticeships, training, or literacy	• Positive effects only at postsecondary level, weaker than in formal sector	• No effects of apprenticeships or literacy • Small effect of training

table continues next page

Table 3A.2 Earnings Regressions: Main Results with Respect to Skills[a] *(continued)*

	Wage/formal		*Nonwage/informal*	
Country: group	*Formal education/TVET*	*Apprenticeships/other training*	*Formal education/TVET*	*Apprenticeships/other training*
Nigeria: 15–65 years of age, F/IF, sample selection	• Only (weakly significant) positive effects of education at postsecondary level • TVET not significant	• No significance of training or apprenticeships • Literacy weakly significant	• No significance	• No significance of training or apprenticeships • Literacy weakly significant
Nigeria: 15–65 years of age, F/IF, OLS	• Positive effects only at postsecondary level	• No effects of apprenticeships, training, or literacy	• Positive effects only at postsecondary level, weaker than in formal sector	• No effects of apprenticeships, training, or literacy
Tanzania: 15–65 years of age, W/S-E, sample selection	• Significant and exponentially increasing returns from completed primary onward • TVET effect stronger than completed primary but less than higher levels of education	• Positive effects of informal apprenticeships • Positive effects of on-the-job training (higher than apprenticeships)	• Positive effect of education but wears off (senior secondary and above less effect than some secondary); smaller effects than in formal sector • TVET stronger than completed primary education, less payoff than in formal sector	• No significance of apprenticeships or training
Rwanda:15–65 years of age, F/IF, sample selection	• Significant effect only at secondary levels and beyond • TVET not significant	• No significance	• Significant effects from all levels compared to none • TVET positive (but less than primary education)	• Apprenticeships positive and significant
Rwanda:15–65 years of age, F/IF, OLS	• Significant effect only at secondary levels and beyond • TVET not significant	• No significance	• Significant effects at all levels, as high or higher than formal sector • TVET positive (but less than primary education)	• Apprenticeships positive and significant • No effect from training

Note: TVET = technical and vocational education and training; OLS = ordinary least squares.
a. W/S-E: Comparing wage for wage workers with earnings for self-employed. F/IF: Comparing wage for formal wage workers with wages for informal wage and earnings for (formal) self-employed.

Notes

1. We used logit analysis.
2. Although education and training may be positively linked to the likelihood of entering a sector, or increase productivity and earnings in that sector, the reasons behind these effects may be more complex. Omitting relevant variables can result in biased results and inadequate policy prescriptions, in this case an exaggerated emphasis on education to improve outcomes. A key problem, discussed in chapter 2, is the difficulty of measuring ability, rather than educational outcomes. If innate ability could be controlled for, the effects of education might be smaller. Moreover, family background may condition educational attainment, as well as preferences or chances of obtaining a certain job. The importance of this latter variable was tested for Ghana, where survey information is available on parental education. Controlling for father's education did not materially change returns to education, however.
3. The multinomial logit equation is run for three sectors, generally with farming as the reference category, with independent variables such as years of schooling, training, and different control variables. The regression coefficients (odds ratios) are determined for informal and formal sectors. They represent the change in the odds of being in either sector associated with changes in the respective independent variable; values of the ratio above 1.0 represent a positive effect on the chances of informal or formal sector employment, whereas values below 1.0 represent a negative impact on the chances of informal or formal sector employment. As an example, a coefficient for a completed primary education of 1.723 for the informal sector indicates that people with this primary education have a 72.3 percent higher probability of working in the informal sector than in farming. The results need to be statistically significant to conclude that education makes a difference in the chances for employment off the farm in the informal sector.
4. The failure of surveys to break out the training by source leads to ambiguity in assessing the effect of the different training sources on the chances of leaving the farm to find employment in either the formal or the informal sector. A reason for this result is that household sample surveys are unlikely to produce a sample of sufficient size for small training programs to allow reliable estimates of outcomes. Such a sample could be available, however, where large, national training programs are involved. Overall, our surveys identify apprenticeships in all countries except Kenya. Other sources of training, as illustrated by Tanzania, may include nonformal training offered by various line ministries, by for-profit and nonprofit institutions, and by employers. These sources of training are generally grouped together in household surveys under the heading of vocational training. Usually, the survey asks questions about participation in vocational training of six months or less, which includes short courses and training offered on the job by employers.
5. The two-step procedure follows methods initially developed by Heckman (1976). The estimation of an earnings function for the informal sector may be biased by the self-selection of workers into the informal sector. The same problem in reverse would arise for estimates of an earnings function for the formal sector. The two-step procedure estimates the earning functions, taking into account first the sample selection bias estimated with the multinomial logit function for each sector. The correction may not produce unbiased results in cases where specification problems exist in the multinomial logit function. In this case, Puhani (2000), in a survey of the literature on the appropriateness of different sample-selection correction procedures, argues that

a Heckman-like procedure can do more harm than good and recommends using OLS for estimation of the earnings function.

6. This is based on the conventional Mincer (1958) specification of the earnings function in natural log form.

References

Becker, Gary. 1964. *Human Capital: A Theoretical and Empirical Analysis, with Special Reference to Education*. New York: National Bureau of Economic Research.

Cunha, Flavio, and James J. Heckman. 2009. "Formulating, Identifying, and Estimating the Technology of Cognitive and Non-Cognitive Skill Formation." Working Paper 16, China Center for Human Capital and Labor Market Research, Central University of Finance and Economics, Beijing.

Cunha, Flavio, James Heckman, Lance Lochner, and Dimitriy V. Masterov. 2005. "Interpreting the Evidence of Life Cycle Skill Formation." Working Paper 11331, National Bureau of Economic Research, Cambridge, MA.

Fox, Louise, and Thomas Pave Sohnesen. 2012. "Household Enterprises in Sub-Saharan Africa: Why They Matter for Growth, Jobs, and Livelihoods." World Bank, Washington, DC.

GSS (Ghana Statistical Service). 2005–06. *Ghana Living Standards Survey (GLSS) V 2005–2006*. World Bank SHIP Harmonized Dataset, GHA_2006_GLSS_v01_M_v01_A_SHIP. http://microdata.worldbank.org/index.php/catalog/1064.

Hanushek, Eric A., and Ludger Woessmann. 2008. "The Role of Cognitive Skills in Economic Development." *Journal of Economic Literature* 46 (3): 607–68.

Heckman, James J. 1976. "The Common Structure of Statistical Models of Truncation, Sample Selection and Limited Dependent Variables and a Simple Estimator for Such Models." *Annals of Economic and Social Measurement* 5 (4): 475–92.

Heckman, James J., and Alan B. Krueger. 2004. *Inequality in America: What Role for Human Capital Policies?* Cambridge, MA: MIT Press.

Heckman, James J., and Yona Rubenstein 2001. "The Importance of Noncognitive Skills: Lessons from the GED Testing Program." *American Economic Review* 91 (2): 145–49.

Heyneman, Stephen P. 2003. "The History and Problems in the Making of Education Policy at the World Bank 1960–2000." *International Journal of Education Development* 23 (3): 315–37.

KNBS (Kenya National Bureau of Statistics, Ministry of Planning and National Development). 2007. *Kenya Integrated Household Budget Survey 2005–2006*. Version 1.0 of the KNBS dataset, Government of Kenya, Nairobi. http://statistics.knbs.or.ke/nada/index.php/catalog/8.

Middleton, John, Adrian Ziderman, and Arvil Van Adams. 1991. *Vocational and Technical Education and Training: A World Bank Policy Paper*. Washington, DC: World Bank.

Mincer, Jacob. 1958. "Investment in Human Capital and Personal Income Distribution." *Journal of Political Economy* 66: 281–302.

NBS (National Bureau of Statistics, Ministry of Finance and Economics Affairs). 2007. *Integrated Labour Force Survey 2006 (ILFS 2006)*. Version 1.0 of the public use datasets (August 2007), provided by the National Bureau of Statistics, Government of Tanzania, Dar es Salaam. http://www.nbs.go.tz.

NBSN (National Bureau of Statistics, Nigeria). 2004. *National Living Standard Survey 2003*. Federal Government of Nigeria, Abuja. http://www.nigerianstat.gov.ng/nada/index.php/catalog/28.

NISR (National Institute of Statistics of Rwanda). 2007. *Enquête Intégrale sur les Conditions de Vie des Ménages 2005–2006 - Overview- 10 -2005-2006 (EICV 2005)*. Version 1.1. NISR, Kigali. http://www.statistics.gov.rw/survey-period/integrated-household-living-conditions-survey-2-eicv-2.

Puhani, Patrick A. 2000. "The Heckman Correction for Sample Selection and Its Critique." *Journal of Economic Surveys* 14 (1): 53–68.

Schultz, Theodore W. 1961. "Investment in Human Capital." *American Economic Review* 51 (1): 1–17.

World Bank. 2009. *Ghana: Job Creation and Skills Development Draft Report*. Vol. I: Main Report. Report No. 40328-GH, World Bank, Washington, DC. http://ddp-ext.worldbank.org/EdStats/GHAstu09a.pdf.

———. 2012. *World Development Indicators 2012*. Washington, DC: World Bank. http://data.worldbank.org/data-catalog/world-development-indicators.

CHAPTER 4

Strategies for Improving Skills in the Informal Sector

In This Chapter

The main factors behind the shortfall in skills for the informal sector are (a) the low education of people in the sector, (b) unequal access to training, (c) underdeveloped markets, (d) lack of attention from public training providers to the needs of the informal sector, and (e) market constraints to training for the small and household enterprises of the informal sector. A comprehensive strategy to improve productivity and incomes in the small and household enterprises of the informal sector needs to weigh all these factors. This chapter identifies the features of a comprehensive strategy for improving the productivity and earnings of the informal sector through skills development with examples of successful interventions taken from international experience and the five study countries.

Introduction

Chapter 3 illustrates, with household survey data, how skills, acquired through education and training, are associated with earning and incomes. First, skills are linked to the choice of sectors in which one is employed, and second, to the earnings one attains in each sector. Informal sector work is generally characterized by low levels of education (perhaps enough to build basic capacities like literacy). People who complete no more than a primary education may choose not to work on the farm, but they are not likely to find employment in the formal wage sector and instead wind up pursuing employment in the small and household enterprises of the informal sector. Completing a secondary or higher education does not guarantee employment in the formal wage economy, but a measurable connection exists between higher levels of education and formal wage employment where good economic management and policies are creating these jobs. In both sectors, higher levels of education are observed together with higher earnings, but when compared with the formal sector, the payoff to additional education appears to be lower in the informal sector for a variety of market-related reasons explained in chapter 3.

Different levels of education and sectors of employment also show differences in subsequent patterns of skills development. Whereas apprenticeships are generally available to people in the informal sector with a primary education or less, other forms of vocational training are associated with those who have a secondary education or more and hold employment in the formal wage sector. Vocational training is offered by different providers—public and private, for profit and nonprofit, training centers and employers—and is generally combined in household surveys and reported in the aggregate as "vocational training." Access to vocational training is shown in the household surveys to be more likely for those with a secondary or higher education and employment in the formal wage sector than for those who hold employment in the informal sector. Thus, education is linked not only to employment in the formal wage sector but also to the wider range of options for skills development and the earnings that come with this employment. The evidence supports the cumulative nature of skills development over the life cycle from the literature in chapter 1.

The evidence of the previous chapter suggests that improving the skills of people employed in the informal sector is important to increasing the productivity and incomes of small and household enterprises. The evidence in chapter 3 points clearly to the importance of ensuring basic education as a basis for further practical or theoretical skills development. However, chapter 4 focuses more narrowly on different training programs and institutions that are, or could be, catering to the informal sector. In each of the countries for this study, reviews were undertaken of training programs offered by public and private providers with the goal of identifying programs that reach out to the informal sector and address the constraints to skills development described in chapter 1. This chapter looks across the five countries of Ghana, Kenya, Nigeria, Rwanda, and Tanzania and to international experience for programs that show promise in addressing the constraints to skills development for the informal sector and raising the productivity and earnings of those employed in the sector.

Employment and earnings in the informal sector can be attractive and can match and even exceed those of the formal sector, as evidenced in chapter 2, which points to data illustrating the overlapping earnings distributions in the informal and formal sectors in Rwanda and Ghana. Education opens the door to opportunities and to later skills development options that improve earnings. Vocational training in different forms, on the job and off, is more likely to be accessible to people with higher levels of education than to those with only a limited education. Apprenticeships in the five countries are the option for those who lack a strong educational foundation. The option value of education[1] and the incentives it provides to households and employers to invest in further skills development is an underappreciated feature of formal schooling. Together, these findings emphasize the importance of Education for All and laying a foundation for learning, but even more, the importance of expanding access to further schooling for those who complete a primary education and offering second-chance options for those who left formal schooling early.

The five country studies provide the evidence for strategies to improve skills in the informal sector. The country case studies that follow this chapter examine education and training programs that attempt to reach the informal sector in particular. Coverage included technical and vocational education in ministries of education and nonformal training offered by ministries of labor, industry, agriculture, and youth. These nonformal programs produce credits that do not transfer toward further education but provide a skill qualification. The country studies attempt to capture experience from private for-profit and nonprofit training institutions and employers, including those offering apprenticeships. Private provision of training in countries such as Ghana, Rwanda, and Tanzania exceeds public capacity. Other specialized programs related to skills development, such as second-chance education, adult literacy, and entrepreneurship education, were examined along with comprehensive programs offering skills and business development services for self-employment, often with the support of nongovernmental organizations (NGOs) and international development agencies.

The review collected knowledge about the costs and benefits of the training programs and their link to the informal sector (see annex 4A for program descriptions). It looked for rigorous assessments of what does and does not work in addressing constraints to skills development in the small and household enterprises of the informal sector. The results were disappointing. The institutional review of training programs reveals an array of training options, but only a modest number have some form of tracer studies that can indicate labor market impact, and almost no programs could be called rigorously evaluated using random experimental or quasi-experimental evaluation designs. The number is even smaller for those targeting skills specifically for the informal sector. Most of the programs observed are for entry-level training for youth, helping them acquire skills and services for entering self-employment. Apprenticeships provide the majority of this training. Fewer programs are found for in-service training that upgrades the skills of adults already employed in the informal sector and increases their productivity. The chapter contains lessons taken from this review and highlights specific programs that show some potential for success in addressing the constraints to training for the informal sector.

Factors behind the Shortfall in Skills for the Informal Sector

The informal sector is distinguished by the low education levels of the people employed. Chapter 3 demonstrates that skills development is an important part of the story not only for improving productivity and earnings in the informal sector, but also for opening opportunities for employment and higher earnings in the formal sector. Education improves labor mobility and the chances for finding employment off the farm and increasing earnings. People with limited education and literacy are observed to have fewer choices in employment and are more likely to remain in farming or pursue employment in the enterprises of the informal sector. They lack the qualifications sought for employment in the formal sector, and they are unable to pursue more advanced levels of education. The skills they need to work with the limited technology available to them are acquired informally and with traditional apprenticeships that emphasize learning through hands-on experience. People with more education, represented by a secondary education or higher education, are able to acquire further skills and improve their earnings in the informal sector, using more advanced levels of technology, but also find better chances for employment in the formal sector.

Some groups lack equal access to skills. For employment in the informal sector, residence, gender, and household consumption or income are factors correlated with access to skills. The profile of education and training in chapter 3 provides evidence of this. Apprenticeships are more prevalent in urban than rural areas. People pursuing skills in the informal sector in rural areas are less likely to find an apprenticeship and are more apt to rely on informal measures involving observation and experience on the job to acquire their skills. The lack of industry in rural areas compounds the problem. The Tanzania chapter illustrates this pattern. Limited opportunities for skills in rural areas provide another reason for migration to urban areas. Women account for a large share of employment in the informal sector (a majority in countries such as Nigeria and Ghana), but they are less likely to participate in an apprenticeship as a source of skills for this employment. This pattern is partly explained by women's concentration in trade and services where apprenticeships are less likely to be used. Even with the advantages of self-financing, the very poorest are the least likely to participate in apprenticeships.

The market for skills in the informal sector is underdeveloped. The popularity of the traditional apprenticeship is evident in all the study's countries. Sorting among the different providers of vocational training and determining which ones offer skills that are in demand at a fair cost for their quality has its challenges, but doing so for apprenticeships in the informal sector is even more difficult. The number of master craftspersons offering apprenticeships is large. The supply is fragmented, and few market instruments compare cost, quality, and outcomes. Evidence in the country chapters refers to the frequent absence of curricula, variation in training standards, poor instruction, and failure to teach theory. In industrial countries, formal apprenticeships are offered with the oversight of worker organizations and employers, thereby providing better opportunities for quality control and assurance of outcomes. None of these features is present in the free market for apprenticeships of the informal sector, and the potential for abuse and wastage is present. Simple instruments for gauging quality, such as testing and certification of apprentice skills, are underused or missing altogether. Markets for skills in the informal sector rely on informal sources of information, often from friends and family.

The informal sector receives little attention from public training providers. Kenya and Rwanda illustrate the limited response of public providers. In both countries, public providers of skills are found to be slow in responding to the specialized needs of the informal sector for skills and in offering flexible modes of delivery. Whether for lack of budgetary incentives or institutional flexibility, public providers have retained a focus on traditional technical and vocational education and training, providing industrial skills for young persons looking for their first job. Less attention is given to those who lack basic education and literacy, multiskilling, entrepreneurship education, and skills upgrading for those in service. In Tanzania, the national development and poverty reduction plans acknowledge the informal sector, but the Vocational Education and Training Authority (VETA) does not include the informal sector among the issues addressed in its most recent corporate plan. Similarly, the informal sector is not part of Rwanda's Education Sector Strategic Plan or its National Technical and Vocational Education and Training policy. The informal sector is off the radar for many public providers of skills.

Small enterprises in the informal sector are less likely to train than larger enterprises, and when training is done, the approach is different. This pattern is illustrated in chapter 1 by drawing on evidence from the Organisation for Economic Co-operation and Development. The factors behind the pattern are the market failures and structural impediments that depress the economic returns to investing in the skills of workers in small enterprises. The higher cost of investing in skills for small enterprises plays a role in reducing returns. The constraints to investing in skills by small and household enterprises of the informal sector are outlined in chapter 1 and are repeated here in table 4.1, along with strategies that address the constraints. The main constraints to skills development in small and household enterprises in the informal sector are as follows:

- *The cost structure for skills development in small enterprises is different from that observed in larger enterprises.* Enterprises of all sizes are able to recruit skilled labor at market wages and realize further gains in productivity and profits by adding to the skills of these workers. Enterprises invest in skills that are tailored to the needs of the enterprise. Gains in productivity are typically shared with the worker in the form of higher wages as an incentive for acquiring the additional skills. Table 4.1 illustrates factors behind the different training cost structure faced by small enterprises. For example, time spent in training during regular production hours can be more costly in forgone production for small firms. Strategies for addressing the higher opportunity cost for training in small enterprises may include offering training during evenings and weekends or when demand for goods and services is low to reduce the indirect cost of the training in forgone production.

- *Capital market failures and the inability of small firms to generate the cash flow needed to finance investments in skills are another constraint to training by small enterprises in the informal sector.* In Nigeria, illiteracy and poverty were rated by 57 percent of respondents as the most important constraints to training in informal sector enterprises. Larger firms often have better access to capital markets and cash flow for this investment. Strategies addressing this constraint

Table 4.1 Constraints to Skills Development in the Informal Sector and Strategies to Address the Constraints

Constraints for the informal sector	*Strategies to address constraints*			
High opportunity cost to firms for training	Training combined with production (apprenticeships and other forms of enterprise-based training)	Training in nonworking hours or when production is low because of demand	Short, modular competency-based training (CBT) courses reducing time for training	Tax credits and training allowances offsetting training costs
Low cash flow of firms for paying direct cost of training	Training combined with production (apprenticeships and other forms of enterprise-based training)	Training vouchers from government and financing agencies	Financing by training fund	Reform of financial markets, thereby improving services to small businesses
Multiskilling needs of the firm	Training combined with production (apprenticeships and other forms of enterprise-based training)	Competitive grants for development of new curricula for training in multiple skill sets (multiskilling)	Short, modular CBT courses for entrepreneurship skills	Use of industry associations to identify and deliver training for multiskilling
Lack of skills in firm for training design	Vouchers for training needs analysis	Off-the-shelf courses and curriculum in training centers	Subsidized technical assistance from a training fund	Standard courses by industry associations
Information failures on benefits of training	Advocacy of benefits by industry associations	Monitoring and evaluation by training funds and industry associations	Short-term subsidies for well-evaluated demonstration programs	
Limited supply catering to informal skill needs	Vouchers for master craftspersons and apprentices, creating a competitive market for informal sector training	Creating a window in training funds for the informal sector	Transfer of management of ineffective public training to industry associations	Introduction of performance-based budgeting with indicators to improve public response to informal sector
Absence of economies of scale for training driving up cost	Using industry associations to train	Partnering of industry associations with training providers to reach scale	Partnering with larger employers to use their training capacity	

include financial market reforms to improve financial services available to small businesses and diversification of financing, thereby shifting some of the costs of training to workers. Apprenticeships are an example because they are often financed through small fees paid by the worker and his or her family and by the acceptance of below-market wages during the period of training. The value of the trainee's production during the training that exceeds his or her wages can be used to offset some of the cost of investment in the worker's skills.

- *Finding providers of training that offer multiskilling for the informal sector is difficult.* Training centers and schools train for a particular occupation or trade, whereas in a small enterprise workers need the know-how to perform a number of different tasks. The self-employed owner of a small household enterprise is frequently responsible for purchasing raw materials, producing goods and services, managing inventory, taking care of marketing and sales, doing financial accounting, and managing personnel. Workers with multiple skills are important to the small enterprise, unlike larger enterprises that can employ workers with specialized skills for these various functions. Strategies for multiskilling are often homegrown in the enterprise through on-the-job training in the different activities or through an apprenticeship that includes structured hands-on training in activities the worker needs to perform. Finding training providers that offer multiskilling is difficult, although industry associations that conduct a training needs analysis for their smaller members may identify this need and develop specialized programs offering a range of entrepreneurial skills.
- *Financial and technical constraints impede investment in skills.* Small enterprises, unlike larger counterparts, lack the expertise to carry out training needs assessments and design suitable training programs. Information failures lead small and household enterprises to discount the value of training and subsequently underinvest in it. The scale of training in smaller enterprises can increase the unit cost of the training above that paid by larger enterprises. Lack of supply and competition among providers serving the specialized training needs of smaller enterprises, particularly in rural areas, may further increase the cost of training. These factors act as constraints to the efforts of small enterprises to train and improve their productivity and incomes. Table 4.1 identifies strategies for confronting many of these constraints. Recognition by policy makers of these constraints is essential to adopting policies that will engage the small enterprises of the informal sector in building a base of skills for improving productivity and incomes.

Few existing programs address these constraints comprehensively. Most programs and training institutions de facto train for the informal sector, simply because that is where most of the nonfarm jobs are. However, the program review shows that training programs in the five countries often fail to consider the specific informal sector constraints (table 4A.1). Several programs offer multiskilling in as far as they combine some form of entrepreneurial training with technical training for a specific trade. Others address affordability constraints by subsidizing training, by providing a combination of production for sale and training, or by accepting payments in kind. Overall, however, programs are generally less geared toward raising the training capacity for the informal sector by stimulating private sector supply or training trainers, providing flexible modes and times of training to adapt to those in service who wish to upgrade their skills, or raising awareness of the positive payoff to training.

Strategies for Skills Development in the Informal Sector

A comprehensive strategy that takes into consideration the constraints the sector faces is required for skills development in the informal sector. The preceding discussion identifies factors that are behind the shortfall of skills development in the informal sector. A comprehensive strategy to improve productivity and incomes in the small and household enterprises of the informal sector needs to consider each of these factors. No ready-made formulas automatically translate into success in different national or regional contexts, however. The importance of different constraints has to be weighed on a country-by-country basis, starting with ensuring a good quality basic education for all and opening opportunities where demand exists for secondary and higher education. The comprehensive strategy needs to promote equity in access to skills training that serves rural areas, women, and low-income populations. In some cases, this will be addressed through broadening supply, and in others, through demand-side interventions that address market discrimination and capacity to pay for skills in demand. Improving efficiency in the market for skills reaching the informal sector is likely to pay large dividends because market institutions that promote this efficiency through better information on quality, cost, and training outcomes are underdeveloped in all the countries examined. Governments are well able to play a role in promoting equity and efficiency.

Financing of public skills provision can affect its response to the informal sector. The strategy needs to look at reforms in public skills provision that shift attention to the requirements of the informal sector. The informal sector accounts for a large and growing share of employment off the farm in the five studied countries of Sub-Saharan Africa. Kenya's Vision 2030 development strategy recognizes small and medium-size enterprises representing the informal sector as one of its five growth sectors. Some of the factors behind the failure of the public sector to respond to the informal sector are highlighted in chapter 1. Holding public providers accountable for serving the informal sector is probably best encouraged through their financing. Moving away from supply-driven financing focused on inputs, such as the number of training centers built and equipped, instructors hired, and programs offered, to financing formulas based on accountability for training outcomes, such as trainees placed, improvements in retention and completion, and services delivered to targeted growth sectors, can encourage needed reforms. National development and poverty reduction strategies not only need to recognize the importance of the informal sector but also should include action plans for addressing the sector's development needs, including skills.

Promoting Private Investment in Skills

A key to the success of any strategy intended to promote higher productivity and incomes in the small and household enterprises of the informal sector is the removal of barriers to private investment that promote these outcomes. Reducing barriers to investments in skills by enterprises is an important part of the strategy for promoting higher productivity and incomes in the informal sector. For example, the Youth Opportunities Program in Uganda shows the promising effect of removing credit constraints to acquiring training and business materials (box 4.1). Lowering constraints and enabling enterprises to invest in the skills they need to promote their growth and productivity frees government from this role and allows it to focus on more strategic needs for improving market efficiency and equity. Table 4.1 identifies constraints to investment faced by small enterprises and highlights strategies for responding to these constraints. It draws on experience in the five countries studied and from international experience looking for programs that have been carefully evaluated for their effect on training outcomes. Lessons are drawn from this experience for lowering barriers to private investment in skills by the small and household enterprises of the informal sector.

Box 4.1 Removing Credit Constraints Encourages Skills Development

In 2006, the government of Uganda introduced a Youth Opportunities Program as an extension to an existing Northern Uganda Social Action Fund (NUSAF). By offering cash grants to be used for training and business materials, the program intended to raise incomes and employment among young adults (15–35 years of age) by alleviating critical financial constraints to credit and skills development.

Applicants were required to organize into groups of 10–30 people and submit a grant proposal for training and business material for (mostly) individual or joint businesses. Many of the participants were poor and low skilled, although the program attracted middle-class youth as well. They aimed to enter relatively small-scale businesses such as tailoring, mechanics, or hairdressing. Evaluations of the program using a control group who qualified for, but did not benefit from, a grant highlight both a strong demand for training and the importance of resource constraints. Nearly four of five of those receiving grants entered some form of vocational training, compared with less than one in five in the control group. Since starting their business, grant recipients spent four to five times more than control group members on new acquisitions of business equipment. Two years after the grant was made, recipients valued their stock of business assets at US$390, compared with US$158 for the control group (at 2010 market exchange rates). Two-thirds of recipients worked in a skilled trade, compared with one-third in the control group, and grant recipients worked more hours per month. On average, incomes of recipients exceeded those of nonrecipients by 50 percent, and they saw high returns on investment.

The success of the NUSAF approach appears to lie in meeting an unmet demand for training, in the self-targeting approach, and in the discipline imposed by group organization.

Source: Blattman, Fiala, and Martinez 2011.

Improving the Quality of Training Offered by Master Craftspersons in Apprenticeship

The weaknesses of traditional apprenticeships identified in the literature review of chapter 1 are evident in the five countries studied. The search for strategies to address constraints to skills development in small and household enterprises of the informal sector reveals some promising results, yet it also highlights constraints that are overlooked or given less attention. Improving the quality of training offered by master craftspersons in apprenticeships is a popular strategy (box 4.2). Examples are found in Kenya, where the design reduces the opportunity cost of time spent in training by master craftspersons and subsidizes their direct cost. More comprehensive, expanded versions of these programs offer a range of business development services and credit along with training. Tanzania's Integrated Training and Entrepreneurship Promotion (INTEP) program offers an example. Similar comprehensive programs are observed in the other countries. These comprehensive programs show evidence of working to improve productivity and incomes in small enterprises; however, questions remain about their high cost and sustainability. The initiatives depend heavily on support from

Box 4.2 Improving the Skills of Master Craftspersons Enhances Apprenticeships

The Kenya Micro and Small Enterprise Training and Technology Project, completed in 2002 and financed by the World Bank, offered vouchers to offset the cost of training and access to new technology. The vouchers covered 50–70 percent of training costs for master craftspersons and apprentices, and other vouchers offered access to technology and specialized management and marketing services. The program targeted women as beneficiaries and was implemented by a nongovernmental agency. More than 32,000 people were trained, of whom 60 percent were women. After use of the vouchers, employment, assets, and income showed significant increases: 80 percent were able to grow their business, compared with 13 percent for the control group; 61 percent added business assets, compared with 21 percent in the control group; and 59 percent of women seeking to enter the program had started a business.

The Kenya Youth Empowerment Program, also financed by the World Bank, was launched in 2011, implemented by a public-private partnership of the Kenya Private Sector Alliance and the government of Kenya. Its goal is to provide youth with training and internship experience in growth sectors that include micro- and small enterprises. Master craftspersons are expected to offer training to youth who want to work in the informal sector. To encourage the participation of enterprises in training, the program offers master craftspersons training at the program's expense to upgrade their business skills and improve their capacity as trainers. The training is offered after working hours to reduce the time away from business. After completion of the first program cycle, a beneficiary assessment found high levels of satisfaction and calls for more training opportunities by master craftspersons. The program will be evaluated again in the future using a control group.

Sources: KEPSA 2012; Phillips and Steel 2003.

Box 4.3 Comprehensive Programs with Skills and Other Business Development Services Can Improve Outcomes for Small and Household Enterprises

Five different programs with different objectives for skills development were reviewed in Rwanda and their lessons summarized. The programs included KURET-Rwanda by World Vision and CARE-NIPS, which both aimed at providing higher earning opportunities to vulnerable youth through skills acquisition; Education Offers Perspective (EOP), which targeted preservice training for labor market entrants and upgrading informal sector operators; and two vocational centers, Centre de Formation Professionnelle and Centre de Formation de Jeunes, that provided preemployment and in-service training. The conclusions from this review were as follows:

- Local market surveys of training demand prior to interventions are important in providing relevant training. Relying on trainee demand is not enough and risks lowering posttraining employability.
- The benefits of training and skills upgrading need to be better marketed, especially to active informal sector operators whose willingness to pay for skills acquisition otherwise may be limited.
- Cost is a problem for access, including for in-service training.
- Training through production, with artisans, appears to pay off better than formal vocational training in terms of skills acquisition, and employability and earnings, although the varying quality of master craftspersons' pedagogical and technical skills is a problem.
- Upgrading skills requires attention to achieving specific competencies.
- Programs are more effective if they provide a complete package, including multiskilling (especially business training), access to finance packages, and follow-up business services, given that most graduates will end up being self-employed.
- Women remain occupationally segregated. Specifically, they are virtually all in tailoring, which has very limited earning opportunities; thus, finding ways of broadening their access to different types of occupations is important to raise productivity and income.

Most program evaluations are missing information on cost-effectiveness and for judging sustainability. There are clear benefits for the more intensive and expensive approaches that include local market demand surveys up front, comprehensive skills packages, posttraining accompaniment, and access to packages with business services and finance. However, these also tend to be staff intensive and thus costly, and affordable only in the context of ample donor funding.

Source: Johanson and Kayiranga Gakuba 2011.

donors and financing agencies, which support is infrequently sustained by governments after the external financing disappears (box 4.3).

Providing Second Chances for Education

Improving the skills of master craftspersons as trainers and opening pathways to new technologies are important to strengthen apprenticeships, but programs that open further education opportunities for master craftspersons and apprentices are less frequently found. Formal education is shown to pay off in added productivity and earnings for people in the informal sector and to open new opportunities in the formal wage sector. For the large numbers without literacy or a basic education in the informal sector, few programs offer second chances for this education. Second-chance programs for education are frequently found in Latin America and are largely missing in Sub-Saharan Africa, although literacy programs are present to a varying degree. Malawi is an exception with its Complementary Basic Education Program (box 4.4). These programs reach not

Box 4.4 Second-Chance Education Programs Open Opportunities for Further Education and Earnings Opportunities in Malawi

Completing primary school remains a major challenge in Malawi. Over half of children starting primary school drop out before Standard 5. Only a small proportion makes it to secondary school. In 2010, Malawi had 319,000 out-of-school adolescents, a large number for a small country.

To give youth a chance to acquire skills, the government, initially with donor backing, set up the Complementary Basic Education program, which has now been mainstreamed into government operations. The program targets youth 9–17 years of age who either have never enrolled in school or had dropped out before completing Standard 5.

A pilot program was launched in 2006 in three districts. By 2011, the program was operational in six rural districts. The districts had high dropout rates, and the program reached 10,000 children and youth. The plan is to roll out the program nationally in 2012. Half of those reached initially are 14 years of age or older. Almost one in five had never been to school. Only about one-third of older participants are female.

Local nongovernmental organizations (NGOs) implement the program, recruiting and training local facilitators under 35 who have a secondary school qualification. Local recruitment provides jobs and role models for poor local youth. The program has smaller class sizes than formal primary schools, and learner centers have the benefit of being located centrally within villages and are managed by communities.

The curriculum covers basic literacy and numeracy skills, designed around the primary curriculum, as well as more practical skills, including agriculture and the environment, livelihoods and entrepreneurial skills, healthy living, and citizenship. The course is designed so that graduates of the three-year program can reenter Standard 6 in a formal primary school if desired.

The program has been successful in ensuring young people acquire basic skills, with participants often performing better than children in formal primary schools. Over half of learners in the first three-year cycle either completed the program or left early to reenter primary school. For those completing three years in the program, about one-third passed at a level equivalent to Standard 5 of the formal curriculum in numeracy. By contrast, a recent survey found that less than 1 percent of Standard 5 school pupils attained grade-level competency in mathematics.

Source: UNESCO 2012.

only youth but also adults. They serve people who have left the formal education system and provide them with education credentials accepted as equivalent to those offered by formal education. They use community facilities in off hours and contract teachers to reduce the cost of delivery.

Showing Small Firms in the Informal Sector the Benefits of Training

Solutions can be found for other constraints to skills development in small and household enterprises of the informal sector. As described previously, improving the technical and pedagogical skills of master craftspersons and opening pathways to an education credential for master craftspersons and apprentices strengthens apprenticeships and enhances the effectiveness of this instrument for promoting skills development in the small and household enterprises of the informal sector. However, other constraints persist to reduce training in small enterprises. These enterprises, unlike their larger counterparts, rarely have the knowledge needed to identify and design curricula for training programs. Information on the benefits of training may be absent along with providers who offer competitive services to small enterprises, tailored to meet the learning needs of workers who often have less than a secondary education. Unless enterprises can combine their training needs and create programs large enough to be economical, the unit cost of training for small firms may be prohibitive. Solutions to these problems can be found; some are already in use in Sub-Saharan Africa.

Opening a Window for the Informal Sector in Training Funds to Support Small Enterprises as Part of a Value Chain

Training funds, described in chapter 1, can be effective in responding to the needs of small and household enterprises by providing the specialized skills needed to conduct training needs assessments and design or deliver training on a scale suitable to the needs of these enterprises. Training funds are present in Kenya, Nigeria, Tanzania, and more recently Ghana. They are used widely throughout Sub-Saharan Africa and other regions and typically are financed by payroll taxes and external funding agencies. Tanzania's VETA, for example, is financed by a 2 percent tax on payrolls. Ghana is setting up a new training fund with support from the World Bank. Funds that are financed by payroll taxes in the formal sector can be used to procure training services for targeted groups in a competitive manner and to finance training in enterprises through a levy-grant system. Training funds supporting only firms that pay the tax are used to spread the cost of training fairly among firms and reduce the free-rider problem of some firms choosing not to train, and instead, to hire skilled workers from enterprises that do train.

Usually, small firms do not participate in training funds. The reasons, explained in chapter 1, are tied to the high cost of administration and compliance in collecting taxes from these firms. Kenya's Directorate of Industrial Training, which is responsible for administration of its Industrial Levy Training Fund (ILTF), found in a survey of 168 manufacturing enterprises that training enterprises outperform nontraining enterprises. However, although Kenya's informal sector is estimated to account for 30 percent of the nation's gross domestic product, the ILTF did not provide training services to this sector. The informal sector is largely ignored by the ILTF, although the law authorizing the fund does not discriminate against the informal sector. Training funds in Malaysia and Singapore, in contrast, have found ways to encourage small enterprises to pay the payroll tax and participate in these funds (box 4.5). For small firms falling below the minimum size eligible for paying the tax, donors can offer support through training funds.

Strengthening the Capacity of Small Industry Associations to Play a Larger Role in Skills Development for the Informal Sector

Industry associations represent another way to confront training constraints in small enterprises of the informal sector. As explained in chapter 1, these associations are able to provide specialized knowledge of training needs to member enterprises, advocate for the benefits of training, set training standards, create a market for training providers through competitive procurement of services, and organize training for members to take advantage of economies of scale (box 4.6). Haan and Serriere (2002) explain the role these associations have played in West and Central Africa in strengthening apprenticeship and other training in the informal sector. They give an example in Ghana for dressmakers and carpenters, but the institutional analysis of training providers in the other countries studied was unable to identify similar examples. Strengthening the capacity of small industry associations to play a larger role in skills development for their members can open the door to better, more affordable training services for enterprises in the informal sector.

Encouraging Private Providers for Skills Development for the Informal Sector

Private providers of training, as noted earlier in chapter 1, have been more responsive to the skill needs of the informal sector than have public providers. Thus, encouraging private providers to do more for skills development in the informal sector needs to be part of a comprehensive strategy. Experience in Kenya with the Technical and Vocational Vouchers Program (TVVP) launched in 2008 illustrates how demand-side financing with market information can improve choices for skills development and help build a private supply response to meet the skill needs of people who will seek employment in the informal sector (box 4.7). The program uses a random experimental design to test several hypotheses. It examines whether information on the earnings associated with different trades makes a difference in training choices. It tests what happens when recipients of vouchers are given a choice between public and private providers of training. The program with the use of vouchers illustrates the impact of cost and ability to pay on training decisions and suggests the potential for vouchers to open more training opportunities for women and the poor on equity grounds.

Improving Market Efficiency with Information about Training Providers

The market for information in each of the countries studied is underdeveloped. The chapter on Nigeria refers to the absence of instruments monitoring

Box 4.5 Singapore and Malaysia Provide Incentives to Increase Training by Smaller Firms

Singapore established its Skills Development Fund (SDF) in 1979, and Malaysia created the Human Resources Development Fund (HRDF) in 1992. These funds are financed by a 1 percent levy on wages, and grants are given to eligible enterprises to encourage the training of employees. The goal of these funds, as part of a national development strategy, is to expand the resources available for training and to engage employers in developing a more flexible and adaptable workforce. Both funds include special incentives to encourage smaller firms to train. Smaller firms tend not to have capacity for assessing training needs and designing appropriate programs to meet those needs. Releasing key employees for training often harms production and leads to higher training costs for these firms. The small scale of training required adds to this cost, thus discouraging smaller firms from training in comparison with larger ones.

Singapore offered a training voucher to companies with fewer than 50 workers. Working like a discount voucher, it allowed firms to pay 30–50 percent of training costs up front while the SDF supports the balance. The voucher helped small enterprises ease cash flow problems when investing in staff training as well as reducing the amount of administrative procedure. The voucher helped SDF reach 65 percent of enterprises with 10–49 workers and 14 percent of those with fewer than 10 workers. In Malaysia, large enterprises with excess training capacities are encouraged to offer training places to employees of other enterprises, particularly small and medium-size enterprises that do not have the expertise and resources to formulate and run their own training programs. Small enterprises sending workers to these programs are eligible for training grants from the HRDF.

SDF grants were extended to enterprises to engage external consultants to conduct company-wide training needs analyses leading to the submission for financing of a worker training plan to the SDF. Companies with at least 51 percent local ownership could apply for grants covering 70 percent of the consultancy fee subject to a maximum. Although available to all firms, this grant helped smaller firms access the specialized resources needed to assess training needs and design appropriate training programs. Malaysia's HRDF offered similar support, helping companies select the most suitable programs to plan for skills development of all employees. This support helped employers formulate annual training plans that led to only one application for a training grant rather than one every time they wanted to train.

The SDF made available a wide range of preapproved public courses for companies to subscribe to under its Approved-in-Principle system. This program was effective in attracting small companies that had neither the expertise nor the critical mass to conduct such programs on their own. Malaysia's HRDF offered a similar Approved Training Program. Employers could select any Approved Training Program course and send employees for training without prior approval of the Human Resources Development Council and claim for reimbursement, subject to terms and conditions set by the council for completion of the training program. With many smaller firms employing workers without education, the SDF and the HRDF also supported programs providing the equivalent of a primary six levels of functional literacy and numeracy and further access to English and mathematics at the secondary education level.

Source: Adapted from Hirosato 1997.

Box 4.6 What Role Can Informal Sector Associations Play in Training?

Associations of informal sector operators exist in many African countries although their level of organization and influence in many instances remain weak. Their roles can range from risk pooling and information sharing to more ambitious approaches, including organizing training, providing financial assistance to start-ups, and the like. Different countries (for example, Benin and Ghana) show that these informal sector associations (ISAs) can play a role in increasing access to training, improving its quality, and enhancing the market value of training as follows:

- Determine training needs: ISAs can become a partner in identifying skills gaps and help prepare curricula.
- Supervise quality of training: ISAs can help monitor the quality and output of training services.
- Certification: ISAs can provide trade tests and certification of skills acquired in different forms of training.
- Information and outreach: ISAs can provide outreach activities to raise awareness of the importance of training for productivity and earnings; they can channel information about access to different forms of training.

Source: Haan and Serriere 2002.

the quality of training and assessing trainee skills on completion and the effect of this lack on the portability of skills across the country. Information on costs, quality, and outcomes associated with training is rarely available for nonformal training programs and missing altogether for traditional apprenticeships. In Kenya's TVVP, counseling and information on sources of training providers and the earning outcomes in male trades alone was sufficient to increase young women's pursuit of these trades by 10 percent, measured against a control group. Ghana, Nigeria, and Tanzania are developing national qualification frameworks that would test and certify skills obtained from different providers, including traditional apprenticeships. National qualification frameworks have proven difficult to implement but would address questions about the equivalency of skills from different providers and enable prospective trainees to make better training choices. The simple inclusion of apprenticeship trades in current testing and certification systems would provide a tool for comparing skills attainment among different providers and improve the portability of these skills. Ghana, with external technical assistance, is implementing this approach.

Requiring That Governments and Private Organizations Play an Important Role in Providing Market Information

Providing market information is a tool for quality assurance and market development that could help small businesses and trainees sort among providers of skills training. Market information is especially important to voucher and other demand-driven programs where enterprises and trainees as consumers need

Box 4.7 Vouchers and Information Improve Choices in Skills and Help Create a Supply of Private Training Providers

The Technical and Vocational Vouchers Program launched in 2008 in western Kenya (Busia) is a research project focusing on factors affecting demand for skills development and the economic and social impact of skills development. Among youth who applied for the project, 50 percent were randomly selected to receive a voucher, with the remaining 50 percent serving as a control group. Of those receiving vouchers, half were given restricted vouchers that could be used only in public institutions.

Although final results are still pending, some preliminary analysis points to interesting results from a policy perspective:

- High costs of accessing technical and vocational education are potentially a significant barrier to access to skills development. Of the voucher holders, 75 percent attended training, compared with 4 percent of the control group.
- Private training appears to increase the choice in the training market and improve chances that youth find a provider that matches their needs and individual circumstances. The share of unrestricted voucher holders making use of the voucher was 10 percentage points higher than the share for holders with the restricted voucher.
- There is more evidence of the need for a large supply of institutions that flexibly can accommodate individual constraints, including family considerations. When asked for reasons for choosing a specific program, almost half of the youth indicated "proximity to home," and almost a third the "ability to find accommodation nearby training center."
- Information on training supply and labor market contexts is low. Participants turned out not to be properly informed about labor market outcomes, including the likely returns.
- Vocational training can serve as an effective second-chance program for youth with low educational achievements. Participants with at most completed primary were more likely to finish their education than those with secondary levels of education.
- Systematic information on returns to training is not yet available, but very preliminary indications are that training helps in shortening job search and increasing remuneration (especially for women).

Source: Hicks and others 2011.

information to sort by quality, cost, and outcomes among the choices of training providers available. Requiring public and private training organizations to conduct and publish tracer studies that account for the placement record and starting salaries of people completing their programs can furnish information that would help enterprises and youth choose cost-effective options for training. It would also doubtless create pressures for reform where the results are disappointing. Licensing and setting minimum standards for operating a training program can screen out private providers who do not offer effective, good quality services. Accreditation systems that establish higher standards for performance can further help enterprises and youth sort among providers of training services in terms of quality and relevance. Accreditation systems can be maintained not only by government bodies, but also by private industry groups that wish to distinguish their services from others in the market place.

Expanding the Supply of Training for the Informal Sector to Promote Competition and Innovation

Private providers in Kenya and Rwanda have proven to be more responsive to the needs of the informal sector for skills, showing a willingness to innovate in a manner that addresses constraints of financing and cost for training in small and household enterprises. Rwanda's microtrainers show a willingness to innovate (box 4.8). Demand-side financing instruments such as vouchers or grants by training funds to small enterprises to train can help promote this private market by creating new purchasing power for enterprises and stimulate a supply response to the need for training by smaller firms. Opening capital markets and improving financial services to enterprises in the informal sector also has the potential to encourage private investment in training and stimulate the supply response to this market.

Building a Knowledge Base

Much more knowledge is needed about the role of skills in the informal sector and what policies could be effective in promoting skills and productivity in different contexts. Household surveys need to be enriched to better measure skills and training. In particular, different forms of training—vocational formal training, apprenticeships, short-term training, on-the-job training—need to be captured with more detail. Work has begun to provide richer measurements of skills, both cognitive and noncognitive, for example, through the World Bank's STEP Skills Measurement Surveys. Moreover, although the emphasis on results-based policy making is increasing, a serious lack of information on program effectiveness still exists. Full randomized, controlled trials may not be feasible in all settings. However, better monitoring and evaluation of processes and outcomes is necessary to understand what can be done and how to improve the access of informal sector operators to skills development and increase the effect on productivity of this skills development.

Defining Roles and Responsibilities for Reforms

Governments can play an important role in building a market for skills for the informal sector and by supporting basic education. This book shows that the market for skills serving the informal sector is underdeveloped. The market lacks institutions providing the information needed for decision making by consumers of training services and employers, especially for choosing among apprenticeships. Employers lack information on the level of skills attained by workers completing apprenticeships. Information asymmetries arising from this information gap lead to inefficiencies in the labor market. National skills testing and certification systems can be strengthened to include certification for apprenticeship trades. Governments can take other steps to improve the flow of information in training

Box 4.8 Rwanda's Innovative Microtrainers Offer an Alternative for the Informal Sector

A survey of training providers (financed by the German Organization for Technical Cooperation, GTZ) was undertaken in 2009. The survey provides unique material in that it attempted to identify all organized types of training providers and provide information on them using an extensive questionnaire.

The survey showed that private providers of training dominate the training market in Rwanda, accounting for 9 of 10 trainees enrolled. Public providers account for only 1 of 10 trainees. Training is generally financed through apprentice fees and income from sales of goods and services. With the exception of training in commerce and business, employment outcomes were generally reported to be favorable, with four of five graduates finding a job. These private providers differ from the public providers in several respects: they accommodate a higher share of female trainees—possibly because one-third focus on tailoring—and have considerably fewer trainees per teacher or instructor. Courses average one year in duration, with about 70 percent of the time dedicated to practical activities. They are comparatively better connected to labor markets with practical rather than theoretical training and produce directly for the market.

The survey also identified an innovative approach to training. Microtraining providers (MTPs) have 12 or fewer trainees enrolled, on average only 6 trainees per provider, and 3 trainees per teacher or instructor. MTPs account for less than 10 percent of total private enrollment registered in the survey but nonetheless enrolled twice as many trainees as the public technical and vocational education and training institutions. They are young institutions (half were established between 2006 and 2009); half of them are individual proprietorships, and the other half are associations or cooperatives. Four of five MTPs derive income through tuition, and four of six from sales of goods and services.

MTPs are different from informal sector firms offering traditional apprenticeships. Many informal sector enterprises have workers called apprentices (three fourths of whom appear to receive some compensation for their work) who learn skills without any organized curriculum. The main business of the informal sector enterprise is production of goods or services. In contrast, MTPs have trainees who pay fees. The main business of microtrainers is training; they follow organized curricula and often use special-purpose training materials. Two-thirds of the microtrainers supplement their income with some production, which helps keep tuition fees down (and, in the case of very poor people, may take the place of tuition). Microtrainers issue certificates of completion or achievement to their graduates; apprentices may receive a letter from the business owner.

One can fairly assume that this MTP segment is serving women to a greater extent than any other type of provider, including traditional apprenticeships, and MTPs are concentrated in a few areas. Two-thirds of enrollment is in tailoring (45 percent), carpentry (14 percent), and beautician services (8 percent). Compared to traditional apprenticeships, MTPs provide a clear curriculum (designed by the MTP), offer fixed-length courses (though the length varies among providers), and charge a fee. Like traditional apprenticeships, MTPs provide a certification at the end of the training period.

box continues next page

Box 4.8 Rwanda's Innovative Microtrainers Offer an Alternative for the Informal Sector *(continued)*

These findings indicate that the training market is diverse in Rwanda and that a large segment of private training providers are responding to strong popular demand for skills acquisition; in particular, they appear to compensate for lack of female places in public training institutions. They make up the overwhelming majority of training providers in the country, and their numbers suggest ease of access for clients. A vast majority is fee based, which suggests people are willing to pay to acquire skills. They focus on practical training and link to demand for services and goods (and skills), because two-thirds also derive income from production of goods. They operate, apparently successfully, without government regulation or support.

Compared to formal vocational training, these providers specifically address some of the skills acquisition problems inherent in the informal sector, including the low level of income and limited cash flow to pay for training (through production of goods and services), and similarly the opportunity cost of training. However, MTPs are less good at addressing the need for multiskilling (for example, providing business skills to future self-employed individuals). They are also generally limited to preservice training and consequently do not cater to people who need to upgrade existing skills. Although employment outcomes appear relatively good, no clear evidence indicates how well the skills provided actually correspond to demand. The high demand for tailoring in what appears to be a rather saturated market suggests that there may be weak links in some areas. Finally, MTPs do not operate in a standardized context of qualifications.

Source: Johanson and Kayiranga Gakuba 2011.

markets, including the promotion of accreditation systems for private training providers responding to the informal sector. These systems can be developed voluntarily by groups of private trainers and by government bodies providing indicators of quality and training outcomes. Government support of private training with vouchers, for example, can be restricted to accredited training providers.

Government can promote efficiency and equity in training markets that serve the informal sector. Actions like those above that improve information on training quality, cost, and outcomes in the market place will improve efficiency in the market. Government can also promote equity by enhancing the access to skills of marginalized groups based on rural residence, gender, and income. It can promote greater access to training by these groups through targeted financing of vouchers and other demand-side financing instruments for private providers and by introducing performance-based budgeting for public training providers using performance indicators of service to the informal sector. Using markets to encourage private and public provision focused on the needs of the informal sector can promote competition, lower prices, and innovation in services. Government support for basic education for all is essential to laying a foundation for skills development leading to better employment in the informal and formal sectors. Finally, government, through better information and appropriate regulation, can play a role in protecting all consumers of training services and in developing an efficient and effective private training market.

Public providers of skills can play a larger role in providing skills for the informal sector by introducing reforms. Chapter 1 identified many of the factors affecting the response of the public sector to the needs of the informal sector. Reforms introducing modular curricula for training can open options offering greater flexibility than offered by current delivery modes. Rather than requiring two or more years to attain a degree or skill qualification, a modular approach allows the delivery of skills in shorter time bands that are more suitable not only to the just-in-time learning needs of people working in the informal sector, but also for in-service training and upgrading the skills of those in the formal sector. Organizing training in modular form focused on specific competencies can reduce the cost of a worker's time away from production and remove this important constraint to developing skills in the informal sector. The building of skill qualifications in modular steps can serve the trainee who is willing to invest in longer periods of training, as well as those needing to upgrade specific skills quickly and return to work. Curriculum reforms like this are an important step to increasing the flexibility of public provision and building capacity to serve small and household enterprises of the informal sector. The modular, competency-based curriculum is also well suited to developing a lifelong learning framework.

Public providers of training can offer other services that contribute to skills needed by people in the informal sector. These providers include not only the technical and vocational education offered by ministries of education, but also the nonformal training offered by other ministries, such as labor, youth and sports, industry, and agriculture. Introducing adult literacy, second-chance education, and entrepreneurship courses into the programs offered by these public training providers can enhance the relevance of their training to those in the informal sector who lack a basic education and requisite entrepreneurial skills. Special programs for people who want to pursue self-employment that combine skills in production management, accounting, sales and marketing, and human resources along with technical skills can add to their readiness for starting a business. Public providers have proven to be slow in responding to the needs of the informal sector with their focus on longer-term training for finding a first job. Opportunities exist to broaden the market served by offering courses relevant to self-employment and in-service training. As explained above, governments can encourage the introduction of programs like these through their financing for public provision of training.

Private providers of skills already play an important role in serving informal sector enterprises and can be encouraged to do more. Strengthening the capacity of informal sector associations (ISAs) for organizing and delivering of training is possible and can be done by donors and governments. Demand-side financing through vouchers and training funds, if carefully targeted, can improve equity and access to skills for the informal sector. The added purchasing power in the market provided by this financing can create incentives for a private supply response. The evidence from several countries in the study suggests the responsiveness of private training providers to increased demand in the informal sector.

The demand encourages competition, lower prices, and innovation in service delivery for enterprises in the informal sector. Helping workers and trainees sort out good training from bad training in this market remains important. The study evidence suggests that private training capacity exceeds that of the public sector in most countries of Sub-Saharan Africa, and better regulation and market information can improve the efficiency of private provision.

Finally, international development and financing agencies can play an important role in the financing of skills for small and household enterprises. International development and financing agencies are already supporting efforts to improve productivity and earnings in the informal sector through skills development programs and comprehensive programs offering an array of business development services and credit to small and household enterprises. The discovery of this study is just how little can be said about the impact of these programs on beneficiaries for lack of rigorous evaluations. The study points to a number of activities that show promise for improving productivity and incomes in the informal sector through skills. Beyond support for basic education and expansion of secondary and higher education in line with market demand, the study provides a strategic framework for improving productivity and incomes in the informal sector that can be supported by external aid. This support should be accompanied by efforts to evaluate results in a rigorous manner and share the knowledge widely.

The assistance given by international development and financing agencies can focus on a number of interventions that promise improvements in productivity and incomes for the informal sector. Among the interventions identified in this report are efforts needed to reach those in the informal sector with literacy and second-chance education programs. Helping build a foundation of basic education for the large numbers in the informal sector who lack this foundation opens new opportunities for income and further skilling. Beyond this, the list is lengthy and includes (a) improving the skills and pedagogy of master craftspersons; (b) building the capacity of industry associations to serve the skill needs of the informal sector; (c) opening and financing windows in training funds for training in small and household enterprises; (d) offering targeted demand-side financing to promote equity in access to skills and a competitive supply of skills training for the informal sector; (e) supporting public sector technical and vocational education reforms that expand services to the informal sector; (f) strengthening market institutions that provide information and promote greater market efficiency in training for the informal sector; and (g) supporting rigorous evaluations of programs for skills development serving the small and household enterprises of the informal sector.

Annex 4A: Programs That Address Some of the Informal Sector Training Constraints

The following table provides examples of programs that have tried to address some of the informal sector training constraints discussed in this chapter.

Table 4A.1 Examples of Programs Addressing Informal Sector Training Constraints

Program	*Constraint addressed*
Kenya	
Kenya Youth Employment Project (KYEP)	Training of master craftspersons provided in evening hours (opportunity cost)
	Scholarships for trainees/interns and allowances for informal sector master craftspersons to provide places (cash flow, opportunity costs)
	Attachments in informal sector are preceded by training master craftspersons in entrepreneurship, production, marketing, human resources development, and coaching/training methodologies (training capacity)
World Bank Busia Informal Sector Vouchers (WB IS)	Providing informal sector operators with vouchers to partially cover training costs (cash flow)
	Stimulating demand, which was met by a newly emerging type of training providers (within the informal sector) (supply for informal sector needs)
African Centre for Women, Information and Communications Technology (ACWICT)	Combined technical with entrepreneurial and life skills (multiskilling)
Informal Sector Business Institute (ISBI)	Linking training to microcredit scheme (low cash flow)
	Providing "street MBA" (business skills) to informal sector operators (multiskilling)
Technical and Vocational Vouchers Program (TVVP)	Inviting youth to apply for vouchers (information failures)
Nigeria	
Start Your Own Business	Business training for potential informal sector operators (multiskilling)
Shell Youth Development Scheme (YDS)	Technical and business training (multiskilling)
Rwanda	
Combating Exploitive Child Labor through Education in Kenya, Rwanda, and Ethiopia Together (KURET)	Business development services (multiskilling)
Education Offers Perspective (EOP)	Training of trainers in entrepreneurship (training capacity)
Tanzania	
The Small Industries Development Organization (SIDO)	Provides a range of training programs in business and technical areas to informal sector, also provides specific business training to graduates VETA (multiskilling)
SIDO/Vocational Education and Training Authority (VETA)	Accepts in-kind contributions as payments (cash flow, opportunity cost)
	Generates master craftspersons who take on traditional apprentices (training capacity)
Integrated Training and Entrepreneurship Promotion (INTEP)	Provides technical and business skills plus literacy, if needed (multiskilling)
	Subsidized training schemes (cash flow, opportunity cost)

Note

1. Acquiring some human capital provides a person with the option to continue to further studies (human capital accumulation) or not, that is, to make the decision about further education once more information is available. The value of the option increases with higher variability of the returns to education.

References

Blattman, Christopher, Nathan Fiala, and Sebastian Martinez. 2011. "Employment Generation in Rural Africa: Mid-term Results from an Experimental Evaluation of the Youth Opportunities Program in Northern Uganda." Social Protection Discussion Paper 1120, World Bank, Washington, DC.

Haan, Hans Christiaan, and Nicholas Serriere. 2002. "Training for Work in the Informal Sector: Fresh Evidence from West and Central Africa." Occasional papers, International Training Centre of the International Labour Organization, Turin, Italy.

Hicks, Joan, Michael Kremer, Isaac Mbiti, and Edward Miguel. 2011. "Vocational Education Voucher Delivery and Labor Market Returns: A Randomized Evaluation among Kenyan Youth, Final Report for Spanish Impact Evaluation Fund (SIEF) Phase II." Policy Note Human Development Network, World Bank, Washington, DC.

Hirosato, Yasushi. 1997. "Skills Development Fund: A Preliminary Assessment of a Financing Alternative for Enterprise-Based Training in the Context of APEC." APEC Discussion Paper 17, GSID, Nagoya University, Nagoya, Japan.

Johanson, Richard, and Théogène Kayiranga Gakuba. 2011. "Rwanda: Training for the Informal Sector." Unpublished, Africa Department, World Bank, Washington, DC.

KEPSA (Kenya Private Sector Alliance). 2012. "Beneficiary Assessment of Kenya Youth Empowerment Project (KYEP) Training and Internship Component." March.

Phillips, David A., and William F. Steel. 2003. "Evaluating the Kenya Voucher Programme." *Small Enterprise Development* 14 (4).

UNESCO (United Nations Educational, Scientific and Cultural Organization). 2012. *Education for All Global Monitoring Report 2012: Youth and Skills: Putting Education to Work*. 2nd ed. Paris: UNESCO. http://unesdoc.unesco.org/images/0021/002180/218003e.pdf.

PART 2

Country Case Studies

CHAPTER 5

Skills Development in the Informal Sector: Ghana

In This Chapter

Since the 1990s, Ghana has seen buoyant and pro-poor growth coupled with broadened access to basic education. Although the share of nonfarm employment has remained stagnant, at about half the population, recent years have seen an increasing and indeed dominant role for the nonfarm informal sector, while public sector employment has diminished as a result of economic reforms. The informal sector is predominantly urban and, unlike formal wage work, dominated by female operators. Informal sector activities have a lower risk of poverty than farm activities, but higher than formal sector activities. A large share of youth build basic skills through apprenticeships and on-the-job training; they have limited access to formal technical and vocational education. Improving the quality of apprenticeship training will be part of a strategy to improve the employment and earnings of those in the informal sector.

Introduction

Ghana has seen high growth rates and significant poverty reduction since the 1990s,[1] with growth in gross domestic product (GDP) averaging over 5 percent. The main drivers have been a combination of export opportunities in mining and cocoa, domestic consumption, and public investment, with solid macroeconomic management that has attracted foreign aid and remittances to finance part of the investments. Importantly, decisive productivity improvements were registered in the farm sector. This strong economic performance resulted in substantial poverty reduction, among both nonfarm and farm households: total poverty levels were almost halved between 1991 and 2006.[2]

Despite earnings increases, the broad labor market structure has remained static. Of Ghana's adult population (ages 25–64), nearly half already worked outside the farm sector as of 1990. However, between 1991/92 and 2005/06, the share of adult workers engaged in farming employment did not fall, and in real numbers, high workforce growth implied that the farm sector actually experienced an increase of 1.2 million workers, compared with 1.5 million in the nonfarm sector. Thus, even though employment-to-population ratios are high, poverty is not low, because workers remain concentrated in the sectors with the highest poverty levels, especially farming and trade (figure 5.1).

With half the workers engaged in low-productivity farming, high rural poverty rates, and continued expansion of the working-age population, Ghana still faces important social and economic challenges for the future (table 5.1). Strong achievements—solid economic performance, stable economic management, improved access to education—need to be reinforced with further reforms to improve productivity and earnings and to facilitate worker access to better-earning sectors. Improving skills is one of the key pillars of strengthening

Figure 5.1 High Economic Growth and Low Earning–High Poverty Occupations in Ghana

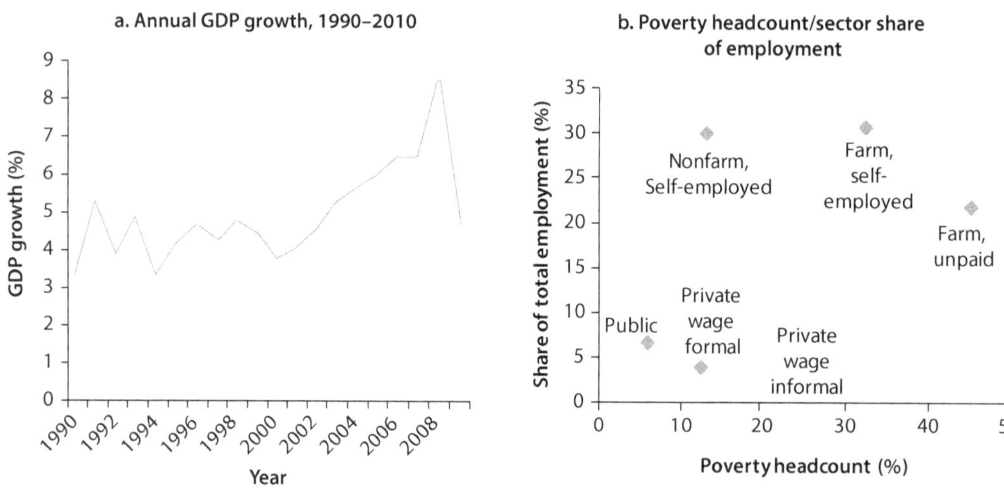

Sources: World Bank 2009, 2010.
Note: GDP = gross domestic product.

Table 5.1 Key Indicators, Ghana

Indicator	*Percentage*
Growth 2000–10	
Average GDP	5.8
Average GDP per capita	3.3
Annual working-age population	2.8
Employment-to-population ratio	67.0
Farm, share of employment	49.0
Farm, share of GDP	28.0
Rural Poverty Headcount Index	39.0
Urban Poverty Headcount Index	11.0
Income, share held by lowest 20 percent	5.0

Sources: World Bank 2009, 2012.
Note: Data are for 2010 or latest available. GDP = gross domestic product.

productivity of small enterprises and individual workers and for raising Ghana's competitiveness. Although access to formal education has increased, a majority of Ghanaian youth still enter the labor market without having completed basic levels of education. Increasingly, they are engaged in small-scale, informal activities in the nonfarm sector. Without a massive expansion of the formal sector work, the nonfarm informal sector will likely be increasingly important for employment. Better preparing youth and adults for these jobs requires a deeper understanding of the characteristics of this sector, the links between earnings and the sector, and how skills affect earnings indirectly and directly, as well as the options for strengthening the supply of skills.

This chapter provides an overview of nonfarm informal and formal employment in Ghana, with a focus on skills availability and its implication for earnings opportunities. More particularly, the chapter discusses the nonfarm informal sector and how to define it, its key characteristics, skill levels among different types of workers, and how this affects earnings. It also presents an overview of the current supply of education and other forms of training and its effect on the ability of young and adult workers to increase their productivity and earnings.

Skills, Employment, and Earnings

Self-employment has increased in Ghana, and a majority of youth and adults work in the informal sector. This section provides a socioeconomic profile of workers in the formal and informal sectors and analyzes the links between earnings and education. Even though the focus is on nonfarm work, the farm sector is at times included for the sake of comparison.

Measuring the Informal Sector in Ghana

Ghana has the advantage of having several household surveys that are broadly comparable over time. This analysis is based on different rounds of the Ghana Living Standards Survey (GLSS) from 1991/92 and 2005/06 (GSS 1991–92, 2005–06). Although data are available for 1998/99, youth employment is not comparable between that survey and the other two, because the former does not account for joint work and school activities. In what follows, the discussion focuses on the most recent outcomes (2005/06) but invokes 1991/92 data for a better understanding of trends. Results for youth and adults are presented separately.

As discussed in earlier chapters, different analytical approaches exist to defining the informal sector; in practice, choices may be constrained by questionnaire and data limitations. A first possible division is between wage and nonwage employment (self-employment and family workers). It may also be possible to distinguish informal forms of wage employment. The GLSSs allow not only for distinguishing between wage and nonwage work, but also for identifying both formal and informal wage employment (here defined as workers without written contracts).

Although the share of nonfarm employment has remained static, self-employment has increased among adult workers within the nonfarm sector.

The share of nonfarm employment is high in Ghana compared with several other and poorer African countries (table 5.2). Nevertheless, adult workers (25–64 years of age) were, in 2005/06, not more likely to work in the nonfarm sector than 15 years earlier. The share of nonfarm work among youth (15–24 years of age) has increased, although active youth are still more likely to work on the farm than older workers. Within nonfarm employment, however, a small shift has occurred away from public and toward private wage and nonwage employment, for both youth and adult workers. In total, three of four youth and three of five adults in nonfarm employment are self-employed.

A vast majority of youth and about two-thirds of adults are involved in informal sector work. Using self-employment as a proxy for informal sector work, two-thirds of Ghana's adult employed population in the nonfarm sector and nearly three-quarters of the equivalent youth population are in the informal sector (table 5.3). If informal wage work—defined as wage workers without a written contract—is included, some 72 percent of adults and 86 percent of youth are in informal activities. With this broader definition, informal sector work increased between 1991 and 2005, for both youth and adults.

Table 5.2 Share of Employment in Ghana by Occupational Status, Youth and Adult
Percent

	Workers 15–24 years of age		*Workers 25–64 years of age*	
Occupational status	*1991/92*	*2005/06*	*1991/92*	*2005/06*
All wage	27	28	40	37
Public wage	10	3	26	14
Private wage	17	26	14	23
Formal	7	12	9	14
Informal	10	14	5	9
Self-employed	73	72	60	63
Public	10	3	26	14
Private	90	97	74	86
Nonfarm share of employment	29	39	47	48

Source: Elaborations based on World Bank 2009.

Table 5.3 Share of Nonfarm Work in Ghana by Formality, Youth and Adult
Percent

	Workers 15–24 years of age		*Workers 25–64 years of age*	
Formality of employment sector	*1991/92*	*2005/06*	*1991/92*	*2005/06*
Formal	17	15	35	28
Public	10	3	26	14
Private	7	12	9	14
Informal	83	86	65	72
Wage	10	14	5	9
Self-employment	73	72	60	63

Source: Elaborations based on World Bank 2009.

Comparing the Formal and Informal Sectors

Significant differences emerge between workers in the formal and informal sectors. The informal sector employs more women, and although most are in urban areas, they have a significant rural presence as well. Poverty is lower in the informal sector than in the farm sector, but higher than in the formal sector.

Demographics

Most of the self-employed in the nonfarm sector are women, and most are based in urban areas. Whereas three of four wage workers are men, three of four self-employed workers are women. Although a majority of self-employment takes place in urban areas, almost 40 percent of the self-employed live in rural areas. Compared with people in wage work, more of the self-employed are located outside Accra, the capital (table 5.4).

Informal sector activities have a lower risk of poverty than farm activities, but higher than formal sector activities. As seen in figure 5.2, poverty is more than twice as high for nonwage workers and informal wage workers than for formal sector workers, whether private or public. Nevertheless, the levels of poverty remain significantly lower than poverty in farm activities; the poverty rate of nonfarm informal workers is one-third that of farm workers. Importantly, since 1991, poverty has fallen among all categories of employed—and more so than among the unemployed or the inactive. The significant reduction in poverty in total thus is related not to a structural shift into occupations that offer less risk of poverty, but to improvements in earnings and reductions in poverty in all categories of work, including farming and informal activities.

Skills and Access to Different Occupations

The level of education differs significantly between wage and nonwage workers, and between farm and nonfarm occupations.[3] Education levels are highest in the wage sector, where 1 of 5 workers has been through postsecondary education and where fewer than 1 in 10 has no education at all (table 5.5). Among the self-employed, 1 in 4 remains without any education. However, half the nonwage workers have more than primary levels of education. This stands in contrast with

Table 5.4 Shares within Sector Employment in Ghana, by Characteristic
Percent

		Self-employed	
Characteristic	*Wage*	*Nonfarm*	*Farm*
Age	39	39	43
Female	23	73	38
Urban	73	61	12
Accra	34	21	0
Forest	37	42	48
Coastal	18	19	19

Source: Elaborations based on World Bank 2009.

Figure 5.2 Poverty Rates in Ghana, by Labor Market Status

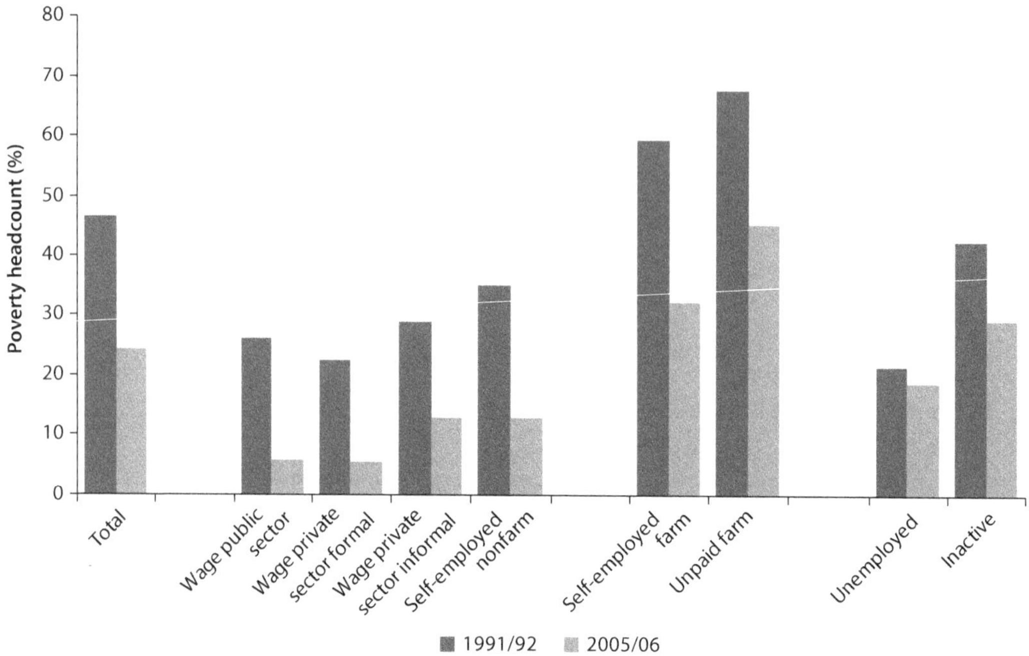

Source: Elaborations based on World Bank 2009.

Table 5.5 Share of Workforce 25–64 Years of Age in Ghana, by Level of Education and Occupation
Percent

	Nonfarm		Farm
Education	*Wage*	*Self-employed*	*Self-employed*
None	7	24	45
Some primary	4	12	13
Primary	8	14	14
Lower secondary	38	38	26
Technical and vocational education and training	8	4	1
Higher secondary	14	5	2
Postsecondary	21	2	0

Source: World Bank 2009.

the farm self-employed, where less than 30 percent have reached levels higher than primary education and where almost half still have no education.

Access to formal technical and vocational education and training (TVET) is very limited. Table 5.6 shows the share of youth (15–30 years of age) that has been through TVET and apprenticeships, respectively. Overall, only 2 percent of youth 15–30 years of age has been through TVET. As shown, the share is highest in the private formal wage sector, where 8 percent has been through TVET.

Table 5.6 Share of TVET and Apprenticeships among Youth 15–30 Years of Age in Ghana
Percent

Characteristics	*TVET*	*Apprenticeships*	*Characteristics*	*TVET*	*Apprenticeships*
All	2	27	All	2	27
Location			Sector of employment		
Urban	4	44	Wage public sector	4	12
Rural	1	20	Wage private formal	8	32
Gender			Wage private informal	2	41
Male	2	27	Self-employed nonfarm	0	51
Female	2	26	Self-employed farm, paid	3	20
Age			Self-employed farm, unpaid	0	9
15–19 years	0	11	Level of education		
20–24 years	2	31	No education	..	9
25–30 years	3	32	Some primary	..	21
Consumption quintile			Primary	..	33
Poorest	1	11	Lower secondary	..	51
Second poorest	1	18	TVET	..	20
Third poorest	1	28	Higher secondary	..	26
Second richest	3	37	Postsecondary	..	7
Richest	4	47			

Source: Elaborations based on World Bank 2009.
Note: .. = negligible; TVET = technical and vocational education and training.

Women appear to have the same access as men, but TVET is almost exclusively an urban phenomenon and is accessed by students from more affluent families.

Instead, a large share of youth builds basic skills through informal apprenticeships and on-the-job training. The percentage of youth 15–30 years of age participating in an apprenticeship has increased since 1991, and currently, about one of every three youths in this age group has experience as an apprentice. Apprenticeships are more than twice as frequent among urban as rural youth, and both women and men have access to this form of training.

Some minimum level of education appears important to access an apprenticeship, but youth with high levels of education are less likely to use apprenticeships. The likelihood of apprenticeships increases with each level of education at the lower levels of education but peaks in the group with lower-secondary levels of education and is much smaller for those with a higher-secondary or postsecondary education.

Apprenticeships are much more frequent among nonfarm informal sector workers than among formal sector workers. Although workers with an apprenticeship are present in all types of employment, they are more frequently found in nonfarm self-employment and wage employment in the informal sector. Significant numbers also show up in wage employment in the private formal sector.

Education influences earnings indirectly by presupposing access to different sectors. Multinomial logit functions help discern the influence of skills on access to different sectors of occupations while controlling for other personal worker characteristics (sex, age, region, and so on). Largely, these estimations confirm the importance of higher levels of education in the wage sector compared with the nonwage sector. As shown in table 5A.1, in annex A in this chapter, in urban areas, the likelihood of becoming a wage worker increases with the level of education.[4] Individuals with a basic education, however, are more likely to be self-employed in the nonfarm sector. The larger effect of basic education observed in 2005/06 could reflect the growing importance of this level of education to being able to establish one's own business, but it is also consistent with the hypothesis of expanding numbers of youth completing a basic education who are unable to find wage employment and are left to create their own employment. Family background (which could influence both access to education and access to specific types of employment) does not materially change the results.

Investing in education is generally associated with moving out of the farm sector to wage or self-employment in the nonfarm sector. The probability of finding wage employment in rural Ghana also rises with the level of education, and in 2005/06, the chances of finding wage employment with a postsecondary education increased sharply (table 5A.2). Though not reported here, the influence of education on the likelihood of becoming self-employed in farming, primarily in subsistence activities, is weaker than for self-employment in the nonfarm sector. In general, having less than a secondary education raises the chances of self-employment in farming, but by substantially less than the chances of self-employment in nonfarming.

TVET exerts a positive influence on wage employment in particular. The likelihood of holding wage employment is slightly higher for those with TVET than for those with a higher-secondary education, although the premium to TVET has fallen over time. The effect on the probability of obtaining wage employment in rural areas is generally lower than that in urban areas, yet it appears to have become a major factor influencing nonfarm self-employment in rural areas.

Apprenticeship offers a pathway to self-employment but is less effective than TVET in opening doors to wage employment. When other factors are controlled for, an apprenticeship does not appreciably increase the chances for wage employment. Evidence indicates that apprenticeship may have this effect for those with low levels of education but not for those with higher levels of education. Formal education is a better investment for increasing the chances of obtaining wage employment. However, an apprenticeship does enhance the probability of becoming self-employed in the nonfarm sector. The relationship has also strengthened over time.

Skills and Earnings

The difference in poverty across employment categories expresses gaps in earnings opportunities. In Ghana, large gaps in earnings between different types of workers characterize the labor market, with public sector employment paying the highest wages. Figure 5.3 shows a clear hierarchy in wages, with wage workers in the public sector faring best, followed by wage workers in the private formal sector, wage workers in the private informal sector and self-employed workers not in farming, and finally, self-employed workers in farming.

Figure 5.3 Distribution of Wages and Earnings in Ghana

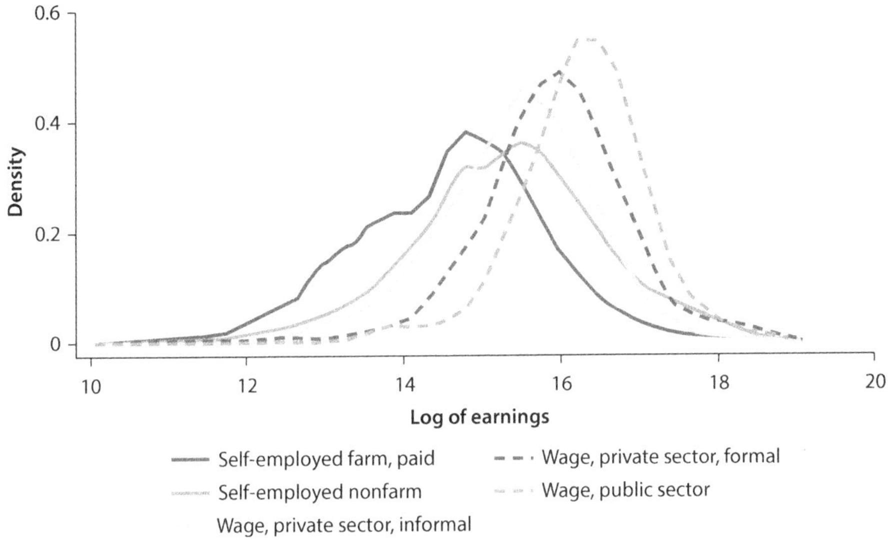

Source: World Bank 2009.

Formal sector workers not only have better-paid jobs but also usually bring home other valuable job attributes, such as job security, worker protection, access to pensions, paid leave, and other forms of benefits (a comparison with 1991/92 data also suggests that the public sector wage premium has increased over time).

The informal nonwage sector in particular encompasses both high and low earners. Earnings in informal employment, especially for nonwage workers, are much more heterogeneous, suggesting that this is indeed a sector with a wide variety of opportunities, from distress work to profitable entrepreneurial activities. The groups of wage workers with the highest earnings tend to have a distribution of earnings with a limited spread (less variance in earnings between individuals).

Disparities also are found in earnings by region, socioeconomic group, sector of activities, gender, age, and skills. For example, women earn consistently less than men, regardless of their employment status; the earnings-age profile follows an inverse *U*-shape pattern; in general, earnings increase with education; earnings in the urban sector are higher than those in the rural sector; farm workers have consistently the lowest earnings; and earnings in the manufacturing and trade sectors are at the tail end of the earnings distribution.

Education is linked to higher earnings in wage employment but to a lesser degree in self-employment. For wage workers in urban settings, secondary and postsecondary levels of education generally translate into higher earnings (tables 5A.3–5A.6), but the level and significance of these results depend on area (urban vs. rural) and specification of the estimations.[5] If sample selection is accounted for, the effect of education is less significant for the informal sector and the level of impact is smaller than in the formal sector. Without taking into account sample selection, the effect of secondary and tertiary education, as well as TVET, is similar across formal and informal sectors. For the self-employed, education has a weaker effect in rural than in urban areas.

There are no private economic returns to primary education in Ghana, pointing to the need for opening up further education opportunities. Evidence in the past has favored primary education over alternative investments in higher levels of education. Continuing to invest in good quality primary education remains important but more from the perspective of the options it opens for postprimary education. Alone, primary education, and in most cases lower-secondary education, does not yield statistically significant earnings gains compared with workers who have no education. However, the additional completion of a higher-secondary education or TVET provides earnings gains for the formal sector in particular. Further gains are found for those with postsecondary education, especially for wage employment, supporting the argument for investment in postbasic education.

Participation in an apprenticeship is not statistically associated with higher earnings in rural or urban areas. Although apprenticeships do increase the chances of becoming self-employed in the nonfarm sector, they do not translate into higher earnings when compared with earnings of the self-employed without an apprenticeship. The relationship is examined for those with an apprenticeship and different levels of education without identifying a positive impact of apprenticeship on earnings. Instead, for the three categories of employment, apprenticeship is frequently associated with having a lower level of earnings when compared with the earnings of people without an apprenticeship.

Beyond education and skills, other socioeconomic factors influence earnings. Men earn more than women, but the gender wage gap is smaller for wage workers than for the self-employed in rural and urban areas. As observed earlier, men are a majority of those employed in the wage sector and farm self-employment. However, only one of four persons in nonfarm self-employment in urban areas is male, yet their earnings are higher than those of women in this employment category and differences are statistically significant. The decline of formal employment, unionization, and public sector employment in the wage sector, earlier, also has implications for earnings. The first two enjoy an earnings premium while holding other factors such as education constant; the declining share of workers in wage employment with these features translates into fewer workers who will realize the higher earnings associated with this employment. Family background—in the form of father's education—does not affect the results on earnings, however.[6]

Acquiring Skills for the Job Market in Ghana

Where do children, youth, and workers get their skills, and what are the key areas in terms of strengthening the skills system? This section presents an overview of key issues in the formal and nonformal education systems. The main conclusion is that access has been expanded, especially at the levels of primary and lower-secondary education, but that a major share of youth still ends up in the labor market with only primary levels of education. Given the very limited supply of

TVET, those who wish to acquire skills are predominantly in traditional apprenticeships, but their quality and relevance may vary significantly.

Education

Ghana has made progress in increasing young people's access to basic education. Gross primary enrollment rates (thus including overage and underage youth) increased from 77 percent in the early 2000s to 106 percent in 2009. With more primary graduates, demand for and access to postprimary levels of education have increased significantly. Gross enrollment rates in lower-secondary education have increased by one-third, from 58 to 78 percent, since 1999. Primary completion rates now reach 88 percent, up from about 70 percent in the early 2000s (table 5.7).

However, national enrollment rates hide disparities across and within regions and to some extent between sexes. Data from 2006/07 show that the Northern and Upper West Regions had primary enrollment rates 10 percentage points below those of the national average. Encouragingly, gender disparities in primary enrollment (whether measured by net or gross enrollment rates) have been eradicated in the past decade; secondary enrollment rates remain slightly higher for males than for females.

The growth in enrollment in public primary schools and higher completion rates have put pressure on the quality of education at both the primary and secondary levels. The expansion in enrollment in public schools has led to higher recruitment of teachers, yet many lack appropriate training. Students in public primary schools also face crowded conditions and poor infrastructure.

Higher-secondary enrollment, likewise, is expanding with conditions similar to basic education. Higher-secondary gross enrollment rates almost doubled between 1999 and 2009 but remain at 35 percent. Regional disparities and some gender disparities also exist, with female gross enrollment trailing behind that of men. Crowding, poor infrastructure of school buildings, and lack of trained teachers remain significant problems at this level, as well.

Quality problems, poverty, and high growth in child and youth populations imply that many children and youth still enter the labor market much before adulthood. Difficult conditions are reflected in the low pass rate for those taking the Basic Education Certificate Examination (BECE) and the Senior Secondary

Table 5.7 Education Statistics, Ghana

Indicator	*1999*	*2009 or latest available*
Primary gross enrollment rate (%)	77	106
Primary completion ratio (%)	—	88
Out-of-school children, primary (thousands)	1,198	828
Lower-secondary gross enrollment rate (%)	58	78
Higher-secondary gross enrollment rate (%)	19	35
Vocational and technical as percentage of secondary	2	3
Tertiary gross enrollment rate (%)	6	9

Source: World Bank 2012.
Note: — = not available.

School Certificate Examination (SSSCE). Sixty-two percent passed the BECE in 2005/06, a figure that has been relatively stable since 2002/03 but with great regional variation, and with boys performing better than girls; 59 percent passed the SSSCE. Those failing the BECE and the SSSCE join others who drop out or simply never enroll and who must enter the labor market with limited education and skills. Low pass rates and low enrollment rates at higher-secondary levels imply that a vast majority of individuals younger than 18 years of age are active in the labor market, with weak skills foundations.

Formal and Nonformal Sources of Skills Development

Beyond the formal education system, the government provides skills training through TVET institutions. These institutions serve the need for intermediate, advanced, and technical skills with entry requirements varying from none to passing the BECE or the SSSCE. There are two main public systems: (a) the Ghana Education Service in Technical Training Institutes under the Ministry of Education, Science, and Sports (MoESS), and (b) the National Vocational Training Institutes run by the Ministry of Manpower, Youth, and Employment (MoMYE). In addition, other technical ministries offer sector-specific training programs, as do community (for-profit and nonprofit) institutions. The number of formal public training institutes is relatively small with some 200 centers, including 26 under the MoESS and 137 under the MoMYE, training approximately 32,500 trainees per year (Darvas and Palmer 2011). A much larger number of private and mostly faith-based centers, both for-profit and nonprofit, enroll a similar number of trainees as the public institutes (430 centers train approximately 34,000 youth per year).

TVET reaches only a small share of the population, making up a marginal share (3 percent) of total enrollment in secondary levels of education. As shown earlier, just over 2 percent of youth 15–30 years of age have been through a TVET program. Access to TVET, like that for secondary and higher education, favors those who come from better-off families.

The upgrading of instructors is important to public and private TVET institutions, as is the improvement of workshops. Only about half of TVET instructors hold the Teacher's Certificate A (from a three-year teacher training college), with a slightly higher percentage in public than in private centers (57 percent, compared with 43 percent). About 84 percent of teachers in public and private centers have obtained the minimum technical qualification of a Technician II Certificate or above. Of the public centers responding, 46 percent of TVET instructors report they hardly ever have in-service training, and another 23 percent say they have this training only once a year. The figures for private TVET institutions are 43 and 23 percent, respectively. Furthermore, in 2005/06, only 12 percent of public training centers and 29 percent of private training centers described themselves as "well equipped." In contrast, 37 percent of public training institutions and 12 percent of private institutions described their facilities as "poorly equipped" or with "no equipment." Public training sites in 2006/07 reported that 18 percent of their classrooms needed major repairs, compared with 37 percent of those in private institutions. Some public and private institutions offer high-quality training, but they are exceptions.

Programs available for helping youth make the transition to employment are not carefully evaluated. Rigorous evaluations using appropriate control and treatment groups are not available for training programs. Moreover, only a few programs have introduced tracer studies to track placement and earnings of graduates, and those that have lack adequate coverage. The evidence available is largely anecdotal and generally unfavorable. Furthermore, public training capacity in Ghana, like that in many other countries, focuses heavily on the skills needs of the small formal sector and, with few exceptions, does not address the need for entrepreneurial skills in the much larger informal economy.

Given the diversity of TVET providers, finding little coordination in the use of scarce public resources is surprising. Although the National Coordinating Committee for TVET under the MoESS is charged with coordinating public and private providers, it shows little evidence of success, with many different bodies and vested interests involved. The legal framework surrounding the TVET sector is itself fragmented. Recent government actions, supported by donors, have taken steps to strengthen TVET coordination.

Traditional Sources of Skills Development

Informal enterprises in Ghana are active trainers offering traditional apprenticeships and on-the-job training. As seen previously, apprenticeships in one form or another are a common form of skills development for youth. Traditional apprenticeships consist of private contractual arrangements between a parent or apprentice and a master craftsperson. The latter agrees to provide practical training in the workplace, ranging from several months to three or four years, and subsequently to certify the training in return for payment of a fee or payment of reduced earnings to the apprentice while he or she learning.

Enterprise-based training reaches more persons than public training institutions. Although numbers are difficult to come by, Atchoarena and Delluc (2001) report 80–90 percent of all basic skills training comes from traditional or informal apprenticeships in Ghana, compared with 5–10 percent from public training institutions. A 2006 urban-based labor market survey in Ghana, conducted by the Center for the Study of African Economies in conjunction with the Ghana Statistical Office, found one-third of individuals 16–65 years of age had some form of training (Monk, Sandefur, and Teal 2009). Apprenticeship was by far the most common form, with 55 percent being either current or past apprentices. Enterprises in the formal sector also provide short-term training to workers beyond formal apprenticeships, helping upgrade skills and introduce new technologies. On-the-job training was the second most common form of training in the 2006 survey, with 25 percent having received such training. The training offered by enterprises favors those with higher levels of general education (Rosholm, Nielsen, and Dabalen 2007). Formal vocational training trailed in importance, with 16 percent receiving their training from this source. Almost all training programs taken at vocational training institutes can be mastered through traditional apprenticeship.

Because traditional apprenticeships form a major source of skills for youth in Ghana, their quality is an issue. In many countries and business environments, traditional apprenticeships serve the informal sector well, yet are proving too narrowly focused to cope with the increasing pace of technological change, skills upgrading, and expanding markets. Their main strengths lie in their practical orientation, self-regulation, and self-financing. However, traditional apprenticeships in Ghana have many weaknesses: (a) they are gender-biased by occupation, generally with women in lower-paid segments[7]; (b) they exclude applicants from the very poorest households unable to finance modest fees; (c) they are based on traditional technologies because master craftspersons fail to keep up with technological change; and (d) they depend on the master craftsperson for their standards and quality assurance, which vary widely. Almost all apprentices and masters lack formal vocational or technical training, and few have more than nine years of formal schooling (Monk, Sandefur, and Teal 2009).

Conclusions

The informal nonfarm sector is increasing in importance as a major source of employment for youth and for women. Half of Ghana's adult population, and two in five youth, make their living in the nonfarm sector and particularly in informal activities. A majority of the nonfarm workers are in small, informal activities, and women are especially likely to be self-employed rather than wage workers. Earnings opportunities are higher and poverty rates lower in the nonfarm informal sector compared to farm work. At the same time, poverty rates remain more than double those of informal wage work. Raising the productivity and earnings of this sector is critical to raising the overall well-being and competitiveness in the country. Building means to increase skills is central to this effort, as shown in the payoff to postbasic skills in terms of accessing sectors and raising earnings.

Ghana has taken important steps toward opening access to education and introducing TVET reforms. Although progress has been made in opening access to basic education, quality remains a challenge, because a large majority of youth leave the formal education system without a solid educational foundation. Opportunities for further formal education, however, are limited, and most skills development for youth will, de facto, take place through apprenticeships. The pressure for expansion at postbasic levels is backed by analysis of household data showing that postbasic education opens access to better-paying jobs and higher earnings.

The challenge will be sustaining the gains made in basic education and improving quality while responding to growing demand for postbasic education. Quality notwithstanding, a school-based TVET investment compares well in employment and earnings outcomes with the alternative of a higher-secondary education for those who expect to enter the labor market on completion. Given the expected higher unit cost of these programs, reforms need to focus on strengthening their link with market demand, ensuring a good match of skills and jobs in an economy that is increasingly led by the private sector, and on providing incentives for the efficient use of resources for skills development.

The role of TVET can be strengthened by improving its quality and relevance to enhance its image and outcomes and by improving articulation within the education and training systems. Opening vertical and horizontal pathways between these two systems can provide space for youth to move between general secondary and vocational programs and from TVET to higher levels of education. Curriculum reforms that blend general and vocational content can do this, as can accelerating development of the National Qualifications Framework. The latter will take time, however, and intermediate steps can be taken by engaging employers in setting skills standards and building capacity to test and certify the training available against these standards, including skills in traditional apprenticeships.

Strengthening of the traditional apprenticeships may have positive benefits for earnings. Although traditional apprenticeships have little direct influence on earnings, they offer an entry into nonfarm activities and, as such, to better earnings opportunities. Traditional apprenticeships are probably not the future for skills development in Ghana, with its aspirations for becoming a middle-income country, but they are an important means for improving the current welfare of workers. Care needs to be taken to strengthen the system and increase the productivity of workers with apprentices, without distorting a reasonably well-functioning system. The focus should be on increasing the quality of training and strengthening the value of a completed apprenticeship by (a) bringing literacy to master craftspersons and apprentices; (b) upgrading the technical and pedagogical skills of master craftspersons; (c) opening access to new technologies for master craftspersons; and (d) certifying apprenticeship skills as a guide to their quality.

Greater accountability for performance needs to be introduced, especially within the public sector. Subjecting institutions to competition for public financing and placing public and private institutions on equal footing for receiving this financing can change the incentives for performance. Vouchers, for example, can subject training institutions to competition for resources directly from the beneficiary. Performance-based budgeting is another tool requiring training institutions to compete for public financing where performance may consider such training outcomes as reduced dropouts, higher skill certification rates, and job placement, along with training inputs such as the number of classes and workshops, number of instructors, and number of programs offered. Moving to funding formulas that focus as much on the outcomes and performance of the providers as on the inputs and holding managers accountable for results can change the incentives in a meaningful way to alter the outcomes. Moreover, encouraging public training institutions to earn more revenue through the design and delivery of customized training for employers can further improve incentives for performance.

Annex 5A: Tables

This annex presents the multinomial regression results that explain the effects of different levels and forms of education and training on the sector and type of employment and earnings, for urban and rural areas separately.

Table 5A.1 Entry into Sectors, Multinomial Logits: Urban Areas

	Urban, age group 25–64								
	1991/92			*1998/99*			*2005/06*		
Variable	*Wage earner*	*Self-employed, farm*	*Self-employed, nonfarm*	*Wage earner*	*Self-employed, farm*	*Self-employed, nonfarm*	*Wage earner*	*Self-employed, farm*	*Self-employed, nonfarm*
Some primary	1.247 (0.78)	1.718* (1.83)	1.266 (0.85)	1.201 (0.57)	1.009 (0.03)	1.244 (1.05)	1.398 (1.52)	1.425 (1.54)	1.426** (2.17)
Primary	0.991 (0.03)	1.115 (0.37)	0.738 (1.47)	1.760** (2.02)	1.195 (0.75)	1.139 (0.68)	1.321 (1.28)	1.006 (0.03)	1.322* (1.92)
Lower secondary	2.878*** (4.33)	0.815 (0.74)	0.808 (1.08)	4.439*** (5.87)	0.689 (1.48)	1.080 (0.46)	2.706*** (5.63)	0.684* (1.84)	1.133 (0.92)
TVET	14.85*** (4.21)	3.489 (1.54)	1.412 (0.47)	7.856*** (6.15)	0.000 (117.58)	1.360 (1.18)	3.763*** (5.57)	0.166*** (3.61)	0.981 (0.10)
Higher secondary	5.544*** (5.26)	0.575 (0.93)	0.503* (1.85)	7.382*** (6.59)	0.272*** (2.74)	0.903 (0.40)	2.813*** (4.62)	0.365*** (2.87)	0.575*** (2.85)
Postsecondary	5.601*** (5.41)	..	0.175*** (3.57)	11.64*** (7.69)	0.195*** (3.22)	0.676 (1.59)	9.072*** (8.73)	0.091*** (4.24)	0.524*** (2.63)
Apprentice, low education	1.819*** (2.62)	0.749 (1.16)	1.383* (1.89)	1.691** (2.29)	0.657 (1.59)	1.329* (1.88)	1.054 (0.29)	0.746 (1.50)	1.283* (1.71)
Apprentice, medium education	0.909 (0.50)	0.671 (1.38)	2.058*** (4.00)	0.737 (1.53)	0.703 (1.12)	1.927*** (4.22)	0.743** (2.24)	0.656* (1.77)	1.573*** (4.09)
Apprentice, high education	1.617 (1.09)	..	1.401 (0.65)	0.966 (0.09)	1.110 (0.13)	3.349*** (3.37)	1.099 (0.31)	2.429* (1.75)	4.678*** (6.25)
Number of children ages 0–6	1.208 (1.29)	1.169 (0.72)	1.247* (1.78)	0.605** (2.52)	1.188 (0.85)	0.700*** (3.07)	0.796* (1.73)	1.074 (0.36)	1.059 (0.51)
Number of children ages 0–6 squared	0.976 (0.57)	0.969 (0.52)	0.948 (1.51)	1.085 (1.06)	0.953 (0.61)	1.092** (2.16)	1.065 (1.15)	0.946 (0.80)	0.990 (0.23)
Number of children ages 7–14	0.854 (1.40)	0.767** (1.97)	0.896 (1.50)	1.120 (0.76)	0.976 (0.20)	1.074 (0.78)	0.835** (2.25)	0.916 (0.57)	0.944 (0.72)
Number of children ages 7–14 squared	1.005 (0.20)	1.033 (1.44)	1.028** (2.24)	0.941 (1.48)	0.981 (0.51)	0.991 (0.36)	1.017 (0.81)	1.003 (0.07)	1.003 (0.12)

table continues next page

Table 5A.1 Entry into Sectors, Multinomial Logits: Urban Areas *(continued)*

	Urban, age group 25–64								
	1991/92			*1998/99*			*2005/06*		
Variable	*Wage earner*	*Self-employed, farm*	*Self-employed, nonfarm*	*Wage earner*	*Self-employed, farm*	*Self-employed, nonfarm*	*Wage earner*	*Self-employed, farm*	*Self-employed, nonfarm*
Age	1.436*** (7.02)	1.277*** (3.47)	1.288*** (5.03)	1.385 (6.57)***	1.245*** (4.37)	1.291*** (7.11)	1.416*** (9.20)	1.472*** (6.63)	1.462*** (11.77)
Age squared	0.996*** (6.52)	0.997*** (3.12)	0.997*** (4.94)	0.996*** (6.22)	0.998*** (3.77)	0.997*** (7.12)	0.996*** (9.26)	0.996*** (6.15)	0.996*** (11.62)
Married	1.853*** (4.16)	1.573** (1.98)	1.570*** (3.69)	1.867*** (3.88)	0.828 (1.23)	1.567*** (4.05)	1.257** (2.16)	1.368* (1.85)	1.201** (2.06)
Men	3.642*** (7.36)	4.024*** (6.01)	0.564*** (4.39)	3.566*** (8.76)	3.872*** (6.59)	0.616*** (3.65)	4.435*** (15.05)	4.400*** (10.57)	0.850* (1.85)
Accra	1.421 (1.10)	0.024*** (3.68)	1.811** (2.04)	1.583* (1.85)	0.241** (2.30)	1.749** (2.19)	2.168*** (3.36)	0.043*** (5.96)	1.387 (1.50)
Forest	1.122 (0.39)	1.195 (0.39)	1.512 (1.48)	1.346 (1.23)	2.080** (1.99)	1.530* (1.70)	1.615** (2.11)	1.610 (1.49)	1.513** (2.03)
Coastal	1.085 (0.28)	1.103 (0.18)	1.549 (1.50)	0.974 (0.10)	1.208 (0.40)	1.254 (0.80)	1.496 (1.50)	1.160 (0.38)	1.353 (1.26)
Father, primary	0.714 (1.08)	0.718 (0.76)	0.734 (1.17)	1.332 (1.05)	0.667 (0.92)	0.984 (0.07)	0.967 (0.17)	1.150 (0.58)	0.803 (1.17)
Father, middle school	0.988 (0.07)	0.437*** (2.89)	0.766** (1.68)	0.974 (0.19)	0.448*** (3.47)	0.790** (2.23)	1.009 (0.09)	0.703* (1.94)	1.092 (0.92)
Father, postmiddle	0.971 (0.13)	0.097** (2.29)	0.838 (0.74)	0.928 (0.32)	0.494* (1.77)	0.880 (0.75)	0.785 (1.70)	0.346*** (3.25)	0.911 (0.70)
Number of observations		2,247			3,104			5,006	

Source: Adams and others 2009.
Note: Urban areas, workers 25–64 years of age. T-statistics in parentheses. .. = negligible; TVET = technical and vocational education and training.
Significance level: * = 10 percent; ** = 5 percent; *** = 1 percent.

Table 5A.2 Entry into Sectors, Multinomial Logits: Rural Areas

	Rural, age group 25–64								
	1991/92			1998/99			2005/06		
Variable	*Wage earner*	*Self-employed farm*	*Self-employed nonfarm*	*Wage earner*	*Self-employed farm*	*Self-employed nonfarm*	*Wage earner*	*Self-employed farm*	*Self-employed nonfarm*
Some primary	2.275*** (3.29)	1.446** (2.31)	1.648*** (2.78)	0.556* (1.67)	0.905 (0.79)	1.310* (1.95)	1.851*** (2.74)	1.230* (1.84)	2.261*** (5.65)
Primary	1.437 (1.19)	1.382** (2.12)	1.413* (1.75)	1.021 (0.06)	1.086 (0.62)	1.447** (2.40)	2.188*** (3.23)	1.150 (1.05)	1.794*** (3.91)
Lower secondary	4.055*** (4.74)	1.262 (1.42)	1.735*** (2.85)	3.278*** (3.38)	0.940 (0.46)	1.497** (2.56)	5.280*** (6.91)	1.142 (1.00)	2.418*** (5.58)
TVET	3.971* (1.94)	0.525 (1.35)	1.486 (0.72)	2.201 (1.11)	0.588 (1.48)	0.638 (0.68)	20.12*** (6.67)	0.830 (0.48)	10.54*** (6.10)
Higher secondary	4.866*** (2.83)	0.426* (1.78)	1.101 (0.17)	6.354*** (4.42)	0.636* (1.71)	1.165 (0.43)	13.61*** (8.30)	0.698 (1.35)	2.092* (1.94)
Postsecondary	12.50*** (6.83)	0.082*** (3.88)	0.294 (1.54)	25.14*** (8.34)	0.356*** (3.19)	0.594 (1.28)	68.60*** (11.71)	0.194*** (3.91)	1.884 (1.50)
Apprentice, low education	1.047 (0.17)	0.780 (1.63)	1.277 (1.50)	1.864** (2.11)	1.069 (0.49)	1.706*** (3.64)	4.061*** (6.63)	1.165 (1.30)	2.142*** (5.31)
Apprentice, medium education	0.984 (0.07)	0.838 (0.92)	1.647** (2.43)	0.743 (1.55)	0.887 (0.78)	1.567*** (3.04)	1.425* (1.81)	0.822 (1.32)	1.901*** (3.33)
Apprentice, high education	0.346 (1.31)	0.227 (1.38)	2.375 (0.92)	0.673 (0.91)	1.190 (0.38)	2.284* (1.83)	1.241 (0.37)	1.952 (1.04)	2.948 (1.47)
Number of children ages 0–6	0.758* (1.90)	1.258*** (2.64)	0.908 (1.02)	0.842 (1.30)	1.052 (0.64)	1.087 (0.96)	0.823 (1.49)	0.972 (0.46)	0.941 (0.72)
Number of children ages 0–6 squared	1.031 (0.97)	0.938*** (3.52)	1.019 (0.92)	1.053 (1.41)	1.005 (0.24)	0.968 (1.17)	1.031 (0.93)	0.999 (0.07)	0.982 (0.87)
Number of children ages 7–14	0.859 (1.15)	0.975 (0.33)	0.918 (0.93)	1.035 (0.32)	1.073 (0.97)	0.968 (0.45)	0.769*** (2.64)	0.927 (1.24)	0.869* (1.81)
Number of children ages 7–14 squared	1.013 (0.51)	0.979 (1.46)	1.004 (0.19)	0.986 (0.58)	0.982 (1.09)	1.002 (0.14)	1.044* (1.92)	1.016 (1.12)	1.027 (1.55)

table continues next page

Table 5A.2 Entry into Sectors, Multinomial Logits: Rural Areas *(continued)*

	Rural, age group 25–64								
	1991/92			*1998/99*			*2005/06*		
Variable	*Wage earner*	*Self-employed farm*	*Self-employed nonfarm*	*Wage earner*	*Self-employed farm*	*Self-employed nonfarm*	*Wage earner*	*Self-employed farm*	*Self-employed nonfarm*
Age	1.485*** (6.56)	1.175*** (4.35)	1.127** (2.50)	1.429*** (5.76)	1.231*** (7.36)	1.204*** (4.92)	1.319*** (5.17)	1.183*** (6.74)	1.149*** (3.98)
Age squared	0.996*** (6.24)	0.998*** (3.60)	0.999** (2.46)	0.996*** (5.58)	0.998*** (6.49)	0.998*** (5.02)	0.997*** (5.16)	0.998*** (6.18)	0.998*** (4.17)
Married	1.189 (0.79)	0.947 (0.39)	1.136 (0.74)	1.281 (1.23)	0.835** (2.06)	0.970 (0.27)	0.778* (1.67)	1.167* (1.69)	0.981 (0.20)
Men	14.76*** (10.88)	7.560*** (13.19)	0.992 (0.05)	6.723*** (9.12)	3.974*** (12.62)	0.944 (0.44)	7.284*** (12.70)	4.393*** (13.97)	0.481*** (6.24)
Accra	..	..	..	..	..	..	..	..	..
Forest	2.687*** (4.03)	1.930*** (3.89)	0.859 (0.70)	4.214*** (4.55)	2.316*** (4.12)	1.441* (1.66)	2.896*** (4.42)	2.739*** (5.68)	1.494** (2.21)
Coastal	3.203*** (3.88)	1.792*** (2.74)	1.667** (2.11)	7.479*** (6.61)	1.554* (1.87)	2.978*** (4.37)	7.127*** (6.39)	3.925*** (6.22)	3.438*** (5.65)
Father, primary	0.683 (1.11)	0.752 (1.17)	1.152 (0.54)	1.325 (0.90)	0.887 (0.61)	0.921 (0.34)	1.321 (0.98)	1.042 (0.21)	1.277 (1.33)
Father, middle school	0.903 (0.40)	0.547*** (3.35)	1.058 (0.33)	1.222 (1.12)	0.715*** (2.73)	0.927 (0.57)	0.985 (0.09)	1.113 (0.99)	1.251* (1.68)
Father, postmiddle	1.167 (0.38)	0.578 (1.63)	0.624 (1.03)	1.492 (1.54)	0.718 (1.39)	1.663** (2.32)	1.050 (0.16)	0.850 (0.81)	0.756 (1.10)
Number of observations		4,201			5,567			7,973	

Source: Adams and others 2009.
Note: Rural areas, workers 25–64 years of age. T-statistics in parentheses. .. = negligible; TVET = technical and vocational education and training.
Significance level: * = 10 percent; ** = 5 percent; *** = 1 percent.

Table 5A.3 Earnings Regressions (OLS): Urban Areas

	Urban, age group 25–64								
	1991/92			*1998/99*			*2005/06*		
Variable	*Wage earner*	*Self-employed farm*	*Self-employed nonfarm*	*Wage earner*	*Self-employed farm*	*Self-employed nonfarm*	*Wage earner*	*Self-employed farm*	*Self-employed nonfarm*
Some primary	−0.240 (0.70)	−0.222 (0.59)	−0.125 (0.68)	0.027 (0.08)	0.122 (0.39)	−0.238 (1.70)	−0.004 (0.02)	0.183 (0.76)	0.077 (0.62)
Primary	0.047 (0.16)	0.740 (1.64)	0.161 (0.72)	0.597 (1.63)	0.564 (1.56)	0.025 (0.17)	0.128 (0.80)	0.161 (0.60)	0.018 (0.13)
Lower secondary	0.480 (1.57)	0.143 (0.25)	−0.014 (0.04)	0.537 (1.65)	0.833 (1.44)	0.143 (0.73)	0.329* (1.93)	0.955** (2.39)	0.221 (1.47)
TVET	0.810 (1.57)	−0.199 (0.19)	−0.568 (0.74)	0.000 (0.00)	..	0.000 (0.00)	0.848*** (3.73)	1.494 (1.48)	0.344 (1.53)
Higher secondary	0.916* (1.93)	0.200 (0.16)	0.307 (0.42)	1.036** (2.53)	2.275** (2.11)	0.829** (2.52)	0.839*** (3.57)	0.572 (0.80)	0.448* (1.88)
Postsecondary	1.457*(1.81)	..	1.650** (2.23)	1.182** (2.40)	2.210 (1.54)	0.907** (2.00)	1.904*** (4.46)	0.971 (0.59)	0.771* (1.81)
Apprentice, low education	−0.134 (0.49)	−1.028** (2.38)	−0.184 (0.98)	−0.239 (0.77)	−0.638* (1.90)	−0.068 (0.53)	−0.090 (0.58)	0.238 (0.87)	0.141 (1.27)
Apprentice, medium education	−0.283 (1.08)	−0.626 (1.06)	0.016 (0.06)	−0.246 (1.19)	−0.881 (1.63)	−0.064 (0.40)	−0.082 (0.63)	−0.536 (1.26)	−0.089 (0.71)
Apprentice, high education	−0.021 (0.12)	..	−0.643*** (3.40)	−0.351 (1.16)	−1.437 (1.08)	−0.081 (0.33)	−0.459** (2.11)	0.419 (0.48)	−0.244 (0.83)
Experience	0.070** (2.05)	−0.089 (1.38)	−0.004 (0.12)	0.037* (1.85)	−0.008 (0.13)	0.057*** (2.61)	0.041*** (2.73)	0.038 (0.69)	0.028 (1.46)
Experience squared	−0.001 (1.50)	0.002 (1.74)*	0.000 (0.11)	0.000 (1.30)	0.000 (0.50)	−0.001*** (2.75)	−0.001** (2.39)	−0.001 (0.97)	0.000 (1.38)
Married	0.185 (0.98)	−0.181 (0.60)	−0.058 (0.34)	0.030 (0.29)	0.017 (0.06)	0.096 (0.96)	−0.010 (0.15)	0.259 (1.39)	−0.015 (0.23)
Men	0.186 (0.48)	1.258 (1.38)	0.034 (0.07)	0.353 (1.25)	1.290* (1.64)	0.518** (2.00)	0.414* (1.78)	0.663 (0.92)	0.155 (0.63)

table continues next page

Table 5A.3 Earnings Regressions (OLS): Urban Areas *(continued)*

	Urban, age group 25–64								
	1991/92			*1998/99*			*2005/06*		
Variable	*Wage earner*	*Self-employed farm*	*Self-employed nonfarm*	*Wage earner*	*Self-employed farm*	*Self-employed nonfarm*	*Wage earner*	*Self-employed farm*	*Self-employed nonfarm*
Formal job	0.420** (2.36)	−0.265 (0.52)	−0.654** (2.36)	0.217* (1.75)	0.211 (0.41)	0.063 (0.44)	0.180*** (2.81)	..	−0.421 (1.16)
Union	−0.003 (0.03)	..	0.081 (0.32)	0.317*** (4.51)	..	0.039 (0.05)	0.144*** (2.86)	..	−0.183 (0.18)
Public	0.097 (0.85)	..	..	0.078 (1.12)	..	..	0.095 (1.68)	..	..
Accra	0.435 (1.38)	−1.617 (1.25)	0.391 (1.29)	0.462*** (3.16)	−0.421 (0.61)	0.218 (1.41)	0.499*** (3.57)	−0.390 (0.30)	−0.001 (0.00)
Forest	0.116 (0.65)	−0.308 (0.91)	0.054 (0.32)	0.236* (1.87)	0.130 (0.39)	−0.129 (1.01)	0.183 (1.84)	−0.138 (0.60)	0.193* (1.80)
Coastal	−0.017 (0.09)	−0.075 (0.21)	0.261 (1.55)	0.154 (1.30)	−0.392 (1.48)	−0.310** (2.36)	0.253** (2.32)	−0.140 (0.53)	0.116 (0.96)
_m1	−0.149 (0.30)	2.292 (0.95)	−0.645 (0.40)	0.129 (0.37)	1.152 (0.49)	−0.999 (0.85)	−0.204 (0.74)	3.158 (1.55)	−1.090 (1.20)
_m2	−0.499 (0.57)	0.423 (0.47)	−0.852 (0.61)	0.234 (0.33)	−0.018 (0.02)	−1.308 (1.30)	−1.413*** (3.41)	0.313 (0.39)	−0.520 (0.81)
_m3	−0.619 (0.41)	−1.246 (0.34)	0.034 (0.05)	−0.474 (0.55)	−3.522 (1.32)	−0.945** (2.12)	−1.450* (1.87)	1.404 (0.58)	−0.180 (0.46)
_m4	−0.996 (0.82)	5.347** (2.17)	0.299 (0.20)	−0.237 (0.33)	−0.358 (0.18)	−2.334** (2.44)	−1.462*** (2.86)	−0.426 (0.25)	0.149 (0.22)
Constant	1.915 (1.45)	5.930** (1.96)	4.310*** (3.78)	4.149*** (4.42)	3.002 (1.25)	4.605 (6.21)	5.281*** (6.62)	7.067*** (3.40)	7.007*** (11.81)
Number of observations	631	186	817	640	315	1,209	1,413	408	1,745
R^2	0.289	0.067	0.071	0.246	0.090	0.089	0.319	0.064	0.077

Source: Adams and others 2009.
Note: Rural areas, workers 25–64 years of age. T-statistics in parentheses .. = negligible; TVET = technical and vocational education and training.
Significance level: * = 10 percent; ** = 5 percent; *** = 1 percent.

Table 5A.4 Earnings Regressions (OLS): Rural Areas

	Rural, age group 25–64								
	1991/92			*1998/99*			*2005/06*		
Variable	*Wage earner*	*Self-employed farm*	*Self- employed nonfarm*	*Wage earner*	*Self-employed farm*	*Self- employed nonfarm*	*Wage earner*	*Self-employed farm*	*Self- employed nonfarm*
Some primary	0.075 (0.42)	0.137 (1.01)	0.283 (1.14)	0.526** (2.22)	0.225** (2.35)	−0.017 (0.11)	−0.110 (0.47)	−0.044 (0.44)	0.309 (1.26)
Primary	0.128 (0.67)	0.253** (2.02)	0.382 (1.43)	0.308 (1.26)	0.071 (0.66)	0.118 (0.76)	−0.181 (0.82)	0.097 (0.96)	0.142 (0.69)
Lower secondary	0.529** (2.18)	0.654*** (3.42)	0.525 (1.55)	0.399 (1.48)	0.177 (1.20)	0.363* (1.80)	0.341 (1.06)	0.288** (2.25)	0.323 (1.18)
TVET	1.075 (1.28)	1.356** (2.17)	0.691 (1.05)	0.612 (1.00)	0.031 (0.07)	0.234 (0.53)	0.321 (0.55)	0.371 (0.73)	0.772 (0.92)
Higher secondary	0.834* (1.89)	1.870*** (3.73)	0.175 (0.21)	0.482 (1.08)	0.061 (0.17)	0.880* (1.74)	0.628 (1.21)	0.728** (2.11)	0.450 (0.91)
Postsecondary	1.262* (1.66)	2.214** (2.18)	0.199 (0.17)	0.352 (0.47)	0.326 (0.59)	1.102* (1.82)	1.770** (2.09)	1.959** (2.28)	1.226 (1.49)
Apprentice, low education	0.029 (0.17)	−0.038 (0.35)	0.255 (1.20)	0.210 (0.93)	0.083 (0.76)	−0.118 (0.87)	0.349 (1.28)	−0.053 (0.39)	0.230 (0.82)
Apprentice, medium education	−0.123 (0.65)	−0.075 (0.53)	0.177 (0.69)	−0.204 (1.02)	−0.007 (0.06)	−0.013 (0.07)	−0.401* (1.90)	−0.057 (0.32)	0.046 (0.14)
Apprentice, high education	−0.441 (0.86)	−2.009** (2.00)	0.780 (0.77)	0.058 (0.21)	−0.062 (0.15)	0.271 (0.51)	−0.295 (1.06)	−0.468 (0.61)	0.167 (0.35)
Experience	0.043* (1.72)	0.074*** (3.73)	0.044 (1.23)	0.034 (1.41)	−0.032 (1.61)*	0.080*** (2.76)	0.020 (1.05)	0.027 (1.26)	0.002 (0.06)
Experience squared	−0.001* (1.76)	−0.001*** (3.54)	0.000 (1.01)	0.000 (1.01)	0.000 (1.92)*	−0.001*** (3.21)	0.000 (0.57)	0.000 (1.18)	0.000 (0.45)
Married	0.112 (0.95)	−0.040 (0.52)	0.167 (1.25)	0.027 (0.19)	0.114 (1.64)*	0.175* (1.81)	0.134 (1.06)	0.184** (2.06)	−0.052 (0.36)
Men	0.297 (0.65)	1.076*** (3.40)	0.144 (0.26)	0.247 (0.76)	−0.193 (0.93)	0.272 (0.75)	0.697 (1.62)	0.573 (1.35)	−0.426 (0.47)
Formal job	−0.063 (0.33)	0.085 (0.31)	0.039 (0.27)	0.125 (0.87)	−0.195 (0.94)	−0.022 (0.21)	−0.141 (1.18)	0.398 (0.49)	−0.647 (1.40)
Union	0.169 (1.56)	..	..	0.294** (2.20)	..	1.893** (2.19)	0.179* (1.68)	..	−0.758* (1.91)

table continues next page

Table 5A.4 Earnings Regressions (OLS): Rural Areas *(continued)*

	Rural, age group 25–64								
	1991/92			1998/99			2005/06		
Variable	*Wage earner*	*Self-employed farm*	*Self-employed nonfarm*	*Wage earner*	*Self-employed farm*	*Self-employed nonfarm*	*Wage earner*	*Self-employed farm*	*Self-employed nonfarm*
Public	0.077 (0.66)	..	..	−0.167 (1.38)	..	..	0.158 (1.40)	..	..
Accra	..	..	..	..	..	..	..	..	..
Forest	0.171 (0.87)	0.488*** (3.87)	0.385* (1.75)	0.072 (0.32)	0.152 (1.19)	0.051 (0.25)	0.375** (1.97)	0.232 (0.97)	−0.165 (0.44)
Coastal	0.312 (1.51)	0.171 (1.14)	0.763*** (2.88)	−0.196 (0.59)	−0.428** (2.23)	0.091 (0.39)	0.476* (1.81)	0.047 (0.18)	−0.475 (1.04)
_m1	0.297 (1.11)	1.482 (1.57)	0.332 (0.68)	−0.050 (0.13)	−1.097 (1.17)	1.871 (1.44)	−0.331 (0.87)	0.509 (0.56)	−0.577 (0.51)
_m2	0.402 (0.40)	−0.253 (0.76)	0.568 (0.44)	1.677* (1.90)	−0.556 (1.53)	−0.598 (0.50)	−1.361 (1.58)	−0.634 (1.62)	−3.164* (1.65)
_m3	0.320 (0.18)	−1.350 (1.19)	0.710 (1.23)	1.096 (0.91)	0.138 (0.15)	0.102 (0.24)	−2.449* (1.79)	−1.303 (1.45)	−0.248 (0.44)
_m4	−0.102 (0.09)	−1.179 (1.03)	−0.987 (0.51)	−0.655 (0.63)	1.251 (1.46)	0.426 (0.38)	−2.189** (2.37)	−1.186 (1.12)	−0.148 (0.11)
Constant	3.043** (1.97)	1.199 (1.35)	1.912 (0.99)	6.128*** (4.13)	6.589*** (8.15)	4.519*** (4.15)	5.022*** (3.70)	5.847*** (3.85)	6.922*** (5.21)
Number of observations	350	1,838	633	394	2,353	968	488	2,976	1,060
R^2	0.200	0.088	0.042	0.217	0.107	0.077	0.215	0.056	0.053

Source: Adams and others 2009.

Note: Rural areas, workers 25–64 years of age. T-statistics in parentheses. .. = negligible; OLS = ordinary least squares; TVET = technical and vocational education and training.

Significance level: * = 10 percent; ** = 5 percent; *** = 1 percent.

Table 5A.5 Earnings Regressions (Accounting for Selectivity): Urban Areas

	Urban, age group 25–64								
	1991/92			*1998/99*			*2005/06*		
Variable	*Wage earner*	*Self-employed farm*	*Self-employed nonfarm*	*Wage earner*	*Self-employed farm*	*Self-employed nonfarm*	*Wage earner*	*Self-employed farm*	*Self-employed nonfarm*
Some primary	−0.250 (0.80)	0.088 (0.50)	−0.109 (0.74)	0.038 (0.12)	0.208 (0.83)	−0.236** (2.02)	−0.028 (0.17)	0.066 (0.35)	0.100 (0.87)
Primary	0.072 (0.34)	0.350 (1.39)	0.181 (1.17)	0.548 (1.46)	0.383 (1.37)	−0.003 (0.02)	0.148 (0.95)	0.074 (0.29)	0.047 (0.35)
Lower secondary	0.415*** (2.70)	−0.145 (0.41)	0.095 (0.61)	0.417** (2.00)	0.424 (1.46)	0.057 (0.48)	0.188 (1.59)	0.556** (2.23)	0.340*** (3.02)
TVET	0.539*** (3.27)	−0.164 (0.55)	−0.213 (0.85)	0.525** (2.26)		0.137 (0.78)	0.584*** (4.53)	1.037* (1.83)	0.515*** (3.60)
Higher secondary	0.725*** (4.39)	−0.120 (0.18)	0.499* (1.86)	0.838*** (3.86)	1.516** (2.53)	0.460** (2.38)	0.585*** (4.40)	0.006 (0.01)	0.581*** (3.71)
Postsecondary	1.183*** (7.12)		1.719*** (5.44)	0.911*** (4.42)	0.939 (1.51)	0.231 (1.03)	1.302*** (10.01)	0.421 (0.54)	1.001*** (5.28)
Apprentice, low education	−0.165 (0.83)	−0.756*** (3.26)	−0.186 (1.38)	−0.247 (0.79)	−0.474* (1.91)	−0.088 (0.77)	−0.046 (0.34)	0.206 (1.10)	0.127 (1.13)
Apprentice, medium education	−0.277*** (3.27)	−0.061 (0.22)	−0.053 (0.44)	−0.148 (1.43)	−0.318 (0.89)	−0.089 (0.88)	0.031 (0.46)	−0.396* (1.85)	−0.138* (1.74)
Apprentice, high education	−0.183 (1.34)		0.237 (0.79)	−0.241** (2.03)	−0.568 (0.69)	0.041 (0.26)	−0.284*** (3.13)	0.457 (0.72)	−0.221 (1.29)
Experience	0.047*** (3.15)	−0.003 (0.05)	0.010 (0.59)	0.029** (2.11)	0.003 (0.12)	0.035*** (2.76)	0.030*** (2.90)	−0.013 (0.33)	0.047*** (4.06)
Experience squared	−0.001* (1.91)	0.000 (0.47)	0.000 (0.42)	0.000 (1.58)	0.000 (0.14)	−0.001*** (2.91)	0.000** (2.17)	0.000 (0.18)	−0.001*** (3.74)
Married	0.076 (0.83)	0.235 (1.26)	0.016 (0.15)	−0.005 (0.06)	0.180 (1.02)	0.013 (0.17)	−0.011 (0.18)	0.206 (1.36)	0.007 (0.12)
Men	0.090 (1.18)	0.596** (2.38)	0.335*** (3.51)	0.143** (2.26)	0.368** (2.40)	0.389*** (4.91)	0.147*** (3.05)	0.201 (1.15)	0.406*** (7.22)

table continues next page

Table 5A.5 Earnings Regressions (Accounting for Selectivity): Urban Areas *(continued)*

	Urban, age group 25–64								
	1991/92			*1998/99*			*2005/06*		
Variable	*Wage earner*	*Self-employed farm*	*Self-employed nonfarm*	*Wage earner*	*Self-employed farm*	*Self-employed nonfarm*	*Wage earner*	*Self-employed farm*	*Self-employed nonfarm*
Formal job	0.427*** (3.44)	−0.188 (0.55)	−0.601**(2.19)	0.218* (1.83)	0.163 (0.30)	0.074 (0.44)	0.201*** (2.94)		−0.362 (1.19)
Union	−0.029 (0.38)		0.149 (0.45)	0.317*** (4.55)		0.046 (0.06)	0.159*** (3.09)		−0.254 (0.26)
Public	0.120 (0.95)			0.106 (1.28)			0.091 (1.52)		
Accra	0.228** (2.48)	−1.722*** (6.06)	0.126 (0.74)	0.434*** (3.90)	0.012 (0.03)	0.061 (0.48)	−0.056 (0.54)	−0.957* (1.77)	−0.240* (1.83)
Forest	0.072 (0.61)	−0.030 (0.08)	0.002 (0.01)	0.203* (1.69)	0.168 (0.43)	−0.170 (1.20)	0.125 (1.20)	−0.372 (1.21)	0.244* (1.94)
Coastal	−0.044 (0.41)	0.143 (0.39)	0.225 (1.30)	0.186 (1.60)	−0.313 (1.02)	−0.319* (1.92)	0.209* (1.75)	−0.303 (0.87)	0.174 (1.16)
Constant	6.364*** (28.27)	6.547*** (8.03)	7.473*** (22.63)	6.430*** (22.71)	6.335*** (11.58)	7.374*** (30.98)	7.099*** (39.44)	7.761*** (10.76)	6.958*** (31.90)
Number of observations	1,413	408	1,745						
R^2	0.319	0.064	0.077						

Source: Adams and others 2009.
Note: Rural areas, workers 25–64 years of age. T-statistics in parentheses; TVET = technical and vocational education and training.
Significance level: * = 10 percent; ** = 5 percent; *** = 1 percent.

Table 5A.6 Earnings Regressions (Accounting for Selectivity): Rural Areas

	Rural, age group 25–64								
	1991/92			*1998/99*			*2005/06*		
Variable	*Wage earner*	*Self-employed farm*	*Self-employed nonfarm*	*Wage earner*	*Self-employed farm*	*Self-employed nonfarm*	*Wage earner*	*Self-employed farm*	*Self-employed nonfarm*
Some primary	−0.017 (0.11)	0.059 (0.68)	0.056 (0.32)	0.480** (2.35)	0.134 (1.36)	0.003 (0.02)	−0.016 (0.08)	−0.015 (0.18)	0.364** (2.50)
Primary	0.104 (0.60)	0.182 (2.00)	0.203 (0.97)	0.267 (1.25)	0.126 (1.16)	0.144 (1.08)	−0.120 (0.78)	0.091 (1.01)	0.275* (1.94)
Lower secondary	0.367** (2.37)	0.336 (3.24)	0.185 (0.98)	0.432*** (2.78)	0.329** (2.50)	0.214 (1.47)	0.432** (2.31)	0.200** (2.05)	0.460*** (2.76)
TVET	0.937*** (3.03)	0.928 (1.78)	0.411 (0.82)	0.776 (1.71)	0.030 (0.08)	0.125 (0.33)	0.472** (2.26)	−0.035 (0.15)	0.452 (1.57)
Higher secondary	0.624*** (3.53)	1.060 (3.66)	−0.148 (0.26)	0.770*** (3.90)	0.275 (1.12)	0.324 (1.02)	0.637***(3.16)	0.326* (1.87)	0.391 (1.20)
Postsecondary	1.023*** (7.30)	0.846 (1.54)	0.244 (0.41)	1.086*** (5.92)	0.675*** (2.65)	0.148 (0.82)	1.230*** (6.26)	0.745* (1.76)	0.221 (0.70)
Apprentice, low education	0.020 (0.14)	0.001 (0.01)	0.176 (1.03)	0.145 (0.63)	0.106 (1.21)	−0.164 (1.55)	0.455*** (3.22)	−0.155* (1.88)	0.208 (1.50)
Apprentice, medium education	−0.131 (0.90)	−0.059 (0.58)	−0.020 (0.15)	−0.253* (1.67)	−0.088 (0.98)	−0.006 (0.05)	−0.256 (1.84)	−0.108 (0.97)	−0.152 (1.11)
Apprentice, high education	−0.302 (1.14)	−1.293 (4.46)	0.605 (0.81)	−0.137 (0.74)	−0.065 (0.23)	0.533 (1.50)	−0.200 (1.09)	−0.298 (0.43)	0.171 (0.54)
Experience	0.029* (1.95)	0.038 (2.86)	0.017 (0.73)	0.019 (1.36)	0.014 (1.17)	0.083*** (5.07)	0.018 (1.14)	0.025** (2.04)	0.036** (1.97)
Experience squared	0.000* (1.79)	0.000 (2.58)	0.000 (0.42)	0.000 (0.95)	0.000 (0.29)	−0.001*** (4.58)	0.000 (0.87)	0.000 (1.45)	−0.001* (1.94)
Married	0.136 (1.26)	−0.012 (0.16)	0.166 (1.31)	0.064 (0.52)	0.084 (1.23)	0.129 (1.37)	0.128 (1.21)	0.209*** (2.73)	0.029 (0.26)
Men	0.004 (0.04)	0.470 (6.50)	0.031 (0.26)	0.073 (0.67)	0.386*** (5.53)	0.329*** (3.35)	0.165 (1.48)	0.436*** (6.15)	0.220** (2.19)

table continues next page

Table 5A.6 Earnings Regressions (Accounting for Selectivity): Rural Areas *(continued)*

	Rural, age group 25–64								
	1991/92			*1998/99*			*2005/06*		
Variable	*Wage earner*	*Self-employed farm*	*Self-employed nonfarm*	*Wage earner*	*Self-employed farm*	*Self-employed nonfarm*	*Wage earner*	*Self-employed farm*	*Self-employed nonfarm*
Formal job	−0.047 (0.25)	0.108 (0.41)	0.046 (0.20)	0.145 (0.86)	−0.193 (0.89)	−0.010 (0.08)	−0.149 (1.27)	0.510 (0.62)	−0.559 (1.21)
Union	0.169 (1.59)			0.288** (1.96)		1.945*** (3.15)	0.207** (1.99)		−0.805*** (5.30)
Public	0.076 (0.65)			−0.184 (1.10)			0.142 (1.19)		
Accra									
Forest	0.020 (0.21)	0.195 (1.87)	0.287* (1.67)	−0.092 (0.62)	0.427*** (2.86)	0.025 (0.16)	0.069 (0.54)	0.167 (1.43)	0.250* (1.65)
Coastal	0.076 (0.63)	−0.123 (0.93)	0.348* (1.66)	−0.275* (1.76)	−0.302 (1.61)	−0.159 (1.01)	0.084 (0.58)	−0.102 (0.78)	−0.060 (0.36)
Constant	7.099*** (22.29)	6.031*** (24.14)	6.935*** (16.24)	7.129*** (25.83)	6.072*** (23.82)	6.163*** (18.93)	7.276*** (28.55)	6.467*** (28.83)	6.984*** (21.23)
Number of observations	488	2,976	1,060						
R^2	0.215	0.056	0.053						

Source: Adams and others 2009.
Note: Rural areas, workers 25–64 years of age. T-statistics in parentheses; TVET = technical and vocational education and training.
Significance level: * = 10 percent; ** = 5 percent; *** = 1 percent.

Notes

1. This chapter is largely based on World Bank (2009) and Adams and others (2009).
2. However, as noted by Coulombe and Wodon (2007), a possibility exists that the decrease in poverty observed in the Ghana Livings Standard Survey data may have been overestimated because of a weaker increase than expected in the official consumer price data for urban areas outside Accra, which tend to result in relatively low poverty lines for these areas.
3. Note that the terms "lower" and "higher" secondary education are synonymous with "junior" and "senior" secondary education. For the sake of comparisons across the five country cases, the former terms are used consistently in all chapters.
4. The logit function coefficients are relative odds ratios; thus a value of 1.321 for a primary education in the wage earner regressions for 2005/06 means that workers with a primary education have a 32.1 percent higher likelihood of being a wage earner than a worker with no education at all.
5. Both ordinary least squares (OLS) regressions and two-stage regressions taking into account the first stage of selection into sectors are presented in the annex tables.
6. Family circumstances can conceivably influence both access to education and access to specific sectors of employment. For example, families that are more affluent can afford to send children to school and may influence their children's opportunities in different sectors of employment. High levels of education and access to higher-earning jobs would then be correlated, but not because education directly influences opportunities. If this link is strong, omitting family influence from the estimations may overstate the direct effect of education. To test for this link, results from earnings regressions excluding and including father's education were compared; however, including the variable does not change the conclusions regarding the effect of education.
7. Labor force data for Ghana in 2000 show that male apprentices were mainly in auto mechanics, carpentry, tailoring, and driving, whereas females were primarily in dressmaking, hairdressing, and catering.

References

Adams, Arvil V., Harold Coulombe, Quentin Wodon, and Setareh Razmara. 2009. "Education, Employment, and Earnings in Ghana." In *Ghana: Job Creation and Skills Development*. Vol. II: Background Papers, annex 1. Report No. 40328-GH. Washington, DC: World Bank.

Atchoarena, David, and André Marcel Delluc. 2001. *Revisiting Technical and Vocational Education in Sub-Saharan Africa: An Update on Trends, Innovations, and Challenges.* IIEP/Prg.DA/1,320. Paris: International Institute for Educational Planning for the World Bank.

Coulombe, Harold, and Quentin Wodon. 2007. "Poverty, Livelihoods, and Access to Basic Services in Ghana." In *Ghana—Meeting the Challenge of Accelerated and Shared Growth: Country Economic Memorandum*. Vol. 3. Background Papers, 1–86. Report No. 40934-GH. Washington, DC: World Bank. https://openknowledge.worldbank.org/handle/10986/7662 License: CC BY 3.0 Unported.

Darvas, Peter, and Robert Palmer. 2011. "Demand and Supply Factors in Skills Development in Ghana: Performance and Recommendations for the Technical and

Vocational Education and Training System." Unpublished, Africa Department, World Bank, Washington, DC.

GSS (Ghana Statistical Service). 1991–92. *Ghana Living Standards Survey (GLSS) III 1991–1992*. World Bank SHIP Harmonized Dataset, GHA_1991_GLSS_v01_M_v01_A_SHIP. http://microdata.worldbank.org/index.php/catalog/1066.

———. 2005–06. *Ghana Living Standards Survey (GLSS) V 2005–2006*. World Bank SHIP Harmonized Dataset, GHA_2006_GLSS_v01_M_v01_A_SHIP. http://microdata.worldbank.org/index.php/catalog/1064.

Monk, Courtney, Justin Sandefur, and Francis Teal. 2009. "Apprenticeship in Ghana." In *Ghana: Job Creation and Skills Development*. Vol. II. Background Papers, annex 2. Report No. 40328-GH. Washington, DC: World Bank.

Rosholm, Michael, Helena Skyt Nielsen, and Andrew Dabalen 2007. "Evaluation of Training in African Enterprises." *Journal of Development Economics* 84 (1): 310–29.

World Bank. 2009. *Ghana: Job Creation and Skills Development Draft Report*. Vol. I: Main Report. Report No. 40328-GH. Washington, DC: World Bank. http://ddp-ext.worldbank.org/EdStats/GHAstu09a.pdf.

———. 2010. *World Development Indicators 2010*. Washington, DC: World Bank.

———. 2012. *World Development Indicators 2012*. Washington, DC: World Bank. http://data.worldbank.org/data-catalog/world-development-indicators.

CHAPTER 6

Skills Development in the Informal Sector: Kenya

In This Chapter

The informal sector in Kenya—the *Jua Kali* sector—accounts for 7 of 10 jobs available in the nonfarm sector and 1 in 3 of the total 10 million employed in 2006. The informal sector is large and growing. Comparing different definitions of the informal sector using household surveys does not alter this conclusion. Strengthening skills development in the informal sector is likely to help reduce poverty, but constraints to this development that face small household enterprises in the informal sector must be addressed. The chapter examines a number of skills development options and offers findings that would improve productivity and earnings in the informal sector.

Introduction

Since the mid-1990s, Kenya has experienced important swings in the rate of economic growth, with much of the volatility induced by political events.[1] In 2002, as a result of the political instability surrounding national elections, real gross domestic product (GDP) growth plunged to 0.6 percent, translating into losses in per capita output. The subsequent economic recovery was abruptly cut short by postelection violence and the 2008 global economic crisis (figure 6.1, panel a).

At the same time, a growing youth population looking for job opportunities has exerted demographic pressures on the economy. Kenya's population expanded by nearly 10 million people, from 29 million to 38 million, between 1998 and 2008, and the proportion of young adults increased. As in other African countries, high population growth is resulting in rapid growth of the young population. In 2008, nearly two in five Kenyans (38 percent) were between 15 and 34 years of age.

Because of increasing rates of job creation, unemployment rates fell from 14.6 percent in 1999 to 12.7 percent in 2006. However, youth unemployment rates remained significantly higher than overall unemployment rates and even

Figure 6.1 Economic Indicators, Kenya

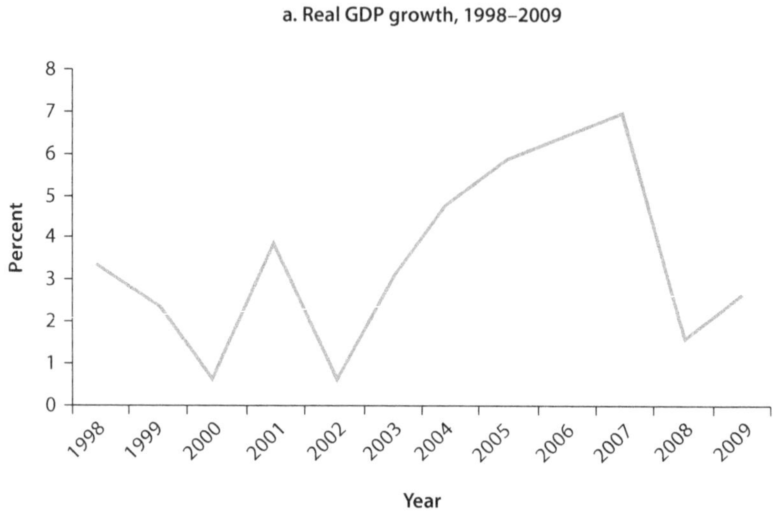

Source: KNBS (various years).
Note: GDP = gross domestic product.

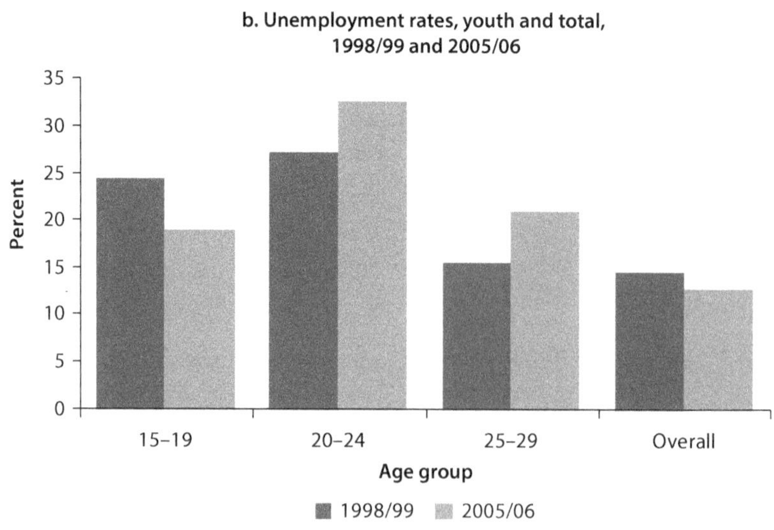

Sources: KCBS 2003; KNBS 2008.

increased quite substantially for the group 20–29 years of age (figure 6.1, panel b). The demographic pressures and worsening labor market outcomes for youth have been intrinsically linked to political instability.

Poverty has fallen, especially in urban areas. The period between 1998/99 and 2005/06 saw a reduction in poverty as the share of poor in the population fell from 52 to 46 percent. Urban poverty fell much more significantly than rural poverty; the share of poor fell from 49 to 34 percent in urban areas, compared with a reduction of four percentage points (53–49 percent) in rural areas (where a majority of the population lives).

Table 6.1 Key Indicators, Kenya

Indicator	*Measurement*
Growth, 1998–2009	
Average GDP	3.5
Average GDP per capita	0.8
Annual working-age population, 2000–09 (%)	3.1
Employment-to-population ratio (%)	73
Farm, share of employment (%)	47
Farm, share of GDP (%)	23
Rural poverty headcount index	49
Urban poverty headcount index	34
Income, share held by lowest 20 percent	4.7

Sources: World Bank 2011; elaboration of KNBS 2007.
Note: GDP = gross domestic product.

To continue to reduce poverty, Kenya will need to find ways of increasing growth and diversifying its sources. Most adults work, but almost half of them remain in farming, with overall low productivity and limited earnings (table 6.1). Much of Kenya's employment in the nonfarm sector is situated in the informal sector. Questions exist about the size of this sector and its employment characteristics. Who is working in these jobs? How do the earning opportunities differ from those of larger private firms, the public sector, or farming? What level of skills do workers and the self-employed in this sector possess? Where can they find opportunities to increase their skills? And what is the payoff of different skills levels in terms of earnings?

The informal sector in Kenya has long been seen as an integral part of economic development. It is referred to as the Jua Kali sector—literally "work under the hot sun"—alluding to the many employment opportunities that operate outdoors, without fixed location, in the street, and so on.

Skills, Employment, and Earnings

This chapter compares different definitions of the informal sector and then chooses one to compare the characteristics of workers in the formal and informal sectors, with a specific focus on skills and earnings. The evidence suggests that the informal sector is large and growing in Kenya and that significant numbers of women have entered the sector in recent years. Formal sector workers have higher levels of education than informal sector workers, earn more—and earn more at similar levels of education—and are by consequence significantly less poor.

Measuring the Informal Sector in Kenya

The measurement of the informal sector is based on the most recent household survey data available, the Kenya Integrated Household Budget Survey (KIHBS) 2005–06 (KNBS 2007). An earlier Labour Force Survey (LFS) 1998/99 (KNBS 1999) is first used to review different definitions of the informal sector in Kenya. The 1998/99 survey contains an informal sector module that, together with

Box 6.1 Definitions of Earnings, Education, and Training

Earnings: The measure of earnings includes wages and benefits, and profits from any business undertaking. For formal (public and private) sector or paid workers, earnings include the basic salary and any benefits in cash or in kind. For self-employed persons, business profits are used as the measure of earnings. Monthly earnings were truncated at 100 Kenya shillings (K Sh; approximately US$1.35) and K Sh 1,000,000 (US$13,513).

Education: Information on the highest level of education completed and highest educational qualification attained was used to generate six discrete categories of education completed and corresponding years completed, based on Kenya's 8-4-4 (primary, secondary, university) education system (see table B6.1.1).

Table B6.1.1 Education Levels in Kenya

Level	*Years*
No education or pre-primary	0
Some primary	7
Primary completed	8
Some secondary	11
Secondary	12
University	16

Training: The 2005/06 survey includes a question on whether individuals have training. However, the sample was adjusted for inconsistencies: for example, those with no complete primary education who reported commercial college training were excluded because secondary education certificates are required to enroll in commercial private or public colleges.

information on employment status and sector of employment, makes comparisons possible of different definitions of informal sector employment. In both survey periods, the sample used is taken from people 15–65 years of age. The definitions of key variables used in the analysis are detailed in box 6.1.

Different definitions of informal sector employment give similar results for informal sector shares and demographic characteristics. Table 6.2 summarizes four alternative measures of informal sector employment based on the 1998/99 LFS:

- *Reported:* The first definition focuses on direct responses from individuals to the question on whether their employment sector is formal or informal (in the Jua Kali sector). This reveals the respondent's perception regarding his or her sector of employment and thus reflects subjective rather than objective criteria.
- *Employment status:* The second definition includes people who reported themselves as self-employed or working employers, unpaid family workers, apprentices, or paid employees in the Jua Kali sector. Persons in these employment states constitute the second definition of informal sector.

Table 6.2 Comparing Definitions of Informality in Kenya, 1998/99

	Sector		
Definition of informality	*Formal*	*Informal*	*Total*
Reported			
Share of total nonfarm employment (%)	35.2	64.8	100.0
Mean age (years)	36.0	38.5	37.6
Mean years of schooling	10.4	7.3	8.4
Males (%)	74.0	56.0	63.0
Employment status			
Share of total nonfarm employment (%)	34.5	65.6	100.0
Mean age (years)	36.1	38.6	37.7
Mean years of schooling	10.4	7.3	8.4
Males (%)	75.0	56.0	63.0
Registration status			
Share of total nonfarm employment (%)	39.0	61.1	100.0
Mean age (years)	36.1	39.7	38.3
Mean years of schooling	10.4	7.1	8.4
Males (%)	75.0	52.0	61.0
Firm size			
Share of total nonfarm employment (%)	34.5	65.6	100.0
Mean age (years)	36.1	38.6	37.7
Mean years of schooling	10.4	7.3	8.4
Males (%)	75.0	56.0	63.0

Source: Elaborations based on KNBS 1999.

- *Registration status:* A third definition of informal sector employment is based on whether the business enterprise in which the individual was employed was registered with the Registrar of Companies.
- *Firm size:* Finally, a fourth definition is based on firm size: individuals employed in firms with fewer than 10 employees are considered informal sector workers.

The informal sector accounts for two-thirds of employment in the nonfarm sector. As seen in table 6.2, the share of informal employment shows little variation across the four definitions. Irrespective of the definition used, the share of informal employment in the nonfarm sector hovers between 61 and 66 percent. The same holds true for key variables: the mean age is around 39 years (and is higher for informal than formal); informal sector workers have around seven years of schooling, about three years fewer than formal workers; and males account for just over half the informal workforce but three-quarters of the formal workforce, across definitions.

The 2005/06 survey contains no informal sector module. Because all four of the preceding definitions produce similar results, this study uses employment status, which can be replicated in the 2005/06 survey, to define the informal sector. Informal workers are identified as nonwage workers (own-account

Figure 6.2 Employment by Nonfarm Formal, Nonfarm Informal, and Farm Sectors in Kenya

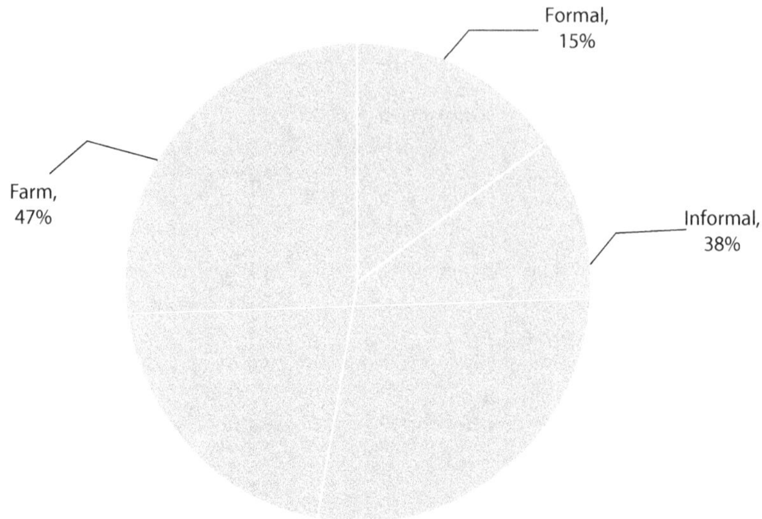

Source: Elaborations based on KNBS 2007.

workers, working employers, unpaid family workers), apprentices, and wage workers who are employed by individuals (self-employed). The data for this definition are available in the 2005/06 survey and are replicated in the 1998/99 survey.

Using this definition, the informal sector accounted for about 72 percent of nonfarm employment in Kenya in 2005/06. Nonfarm employment accounts for a little more than half of all employment in Kenya and is dominated by informal forms of employment (figure 6.2). In 2005/06, about 3.5 million workers of Kenya's total 10 million employed, about two-fifths, were in the informal sector.

Comparing the Formal and Informal Sectors

Because informal sector work accounts for a majority of nonfarm opportunities, understanding the characteristics, opportunities, and constraints of this sector is essential. The following subsections discuss the key socioeconomic characteristics of informal and formal sector workers. The analysis highlights the critical role of the informal sector for youth and female workers, and the links between sector of work, job opportunities, and welfare levels.

Demographics

The informal sector is by far the most important employer of youth in the nonfarm sector. Among labor market entrants and young workers (15–24 and 25–34 years of age), 42 and 41 percent, respectively, were employed in the informal nonfarm sector, compared with 52 and 42 percent in farming, and 6 and 17 percent in the formal nonfarm sector. The informal sector, thus, employs a vast

Figure 6.3 Share of Informal Workers in Nonfarm Sector in Kenya, by Age Group

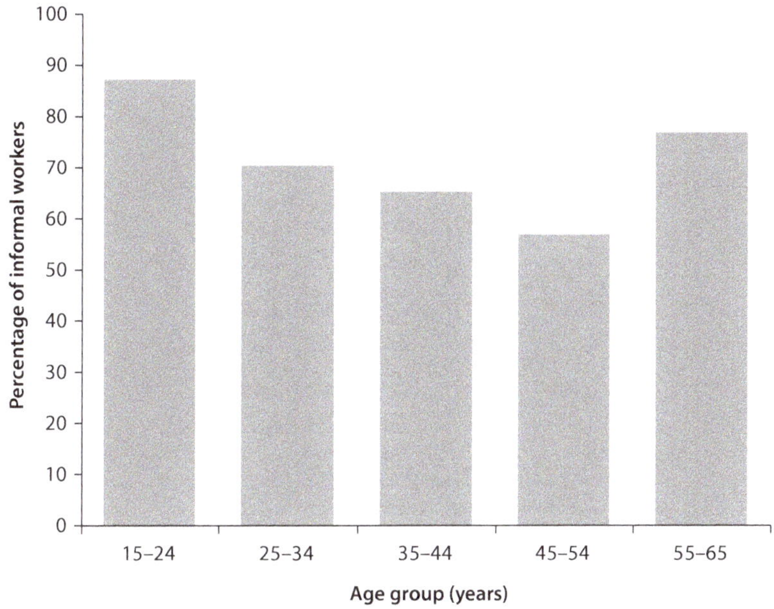

Source: Elaborations based on KNBS 2007.

Table 6.3 Gender, Location, and Age in Kenya, by Formality Status
Percent

Sector	*Male*	*Urban*	*Mean years*
Formal	71	49	37
Informal	60	37	33
Total	63	40	34

Source: Elaborations based on KNBS 2007.

majority of youth in the nonfarm sector (figure 6.3). The likelihood of a young worker being in the informal sector was higher than that of older workers, and the average age of workers in the informal sector is lower than for male workers.

Informal activities are predominantly rural, and women are more likely to work in the informal sector than the formal sector. Although male workers form a majority of both formal and informal sector work, the share of males is higher in the formal sector. Women, consequently, are overrepresented among informal workers. Informal sector activities are more prevalent in rural than in urban areas. Nevertheless, the proportion of urban informal jobs is quite high, at nearly 40 percent (table 6.3).

Women are more likely to be self-employed or unpaid workers than men (figure 6.4). Informal sector employment consists in equal measure of nonwage and wage work. In 2005, one of three nonfarm workers was self-employed. Differences exist between employment for women and men, however; for women, self-employment (mostly as own-account workers) is significant, with only one in

Figure 6.4 Occupational Share of Nonfarm Employment in Kenya, by Gender

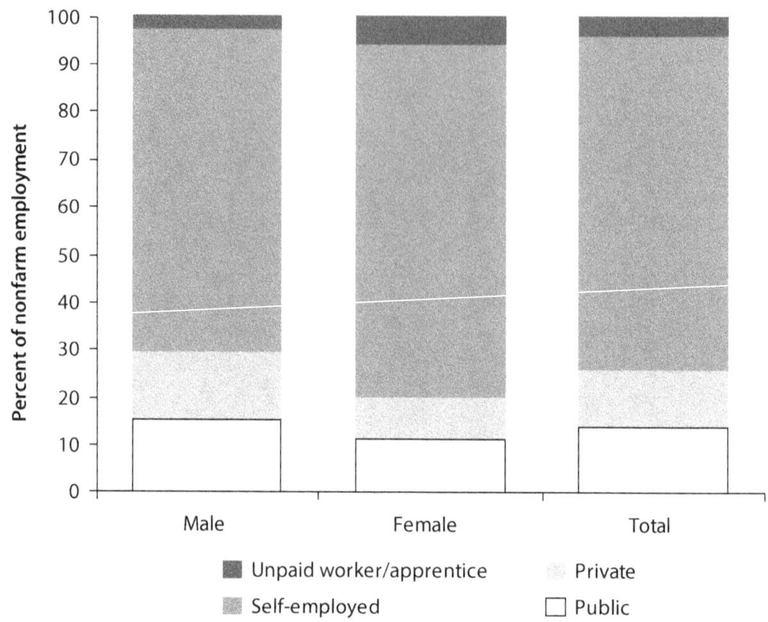

Sources: Elaborations based on KNBS 1999, 2007.

five in either the private formal or the public sector. Men are more likely to be in both public and private formal wage employment and to be employees rather than nonwage workers. Overall, this finding supports the notion of women in potentially more vulnerable employment conditions, with a higher share in the informal than the formal sector and a higher propensity for nonwage work.

Access to informal sector work, compared with farm work, is associated with higher welfare levels. In many cases, working in the informal sector is the first steppingstone out of poverty, as it raises household income. Figure 6.5 shows the median consumption levels of workers in the formal, informal, and farm sectors (consumption is a household measure, however, so the numbers refer to the averages for the household in which the worker lives). Not surprisingly, formal sector workers enjoy higher consumption levels than other workers. The median monthly consumption expenditures (of the households) of formal sector workers are significantly higher than for informal sector workers and several times that of farm workers. Thereafter, the consumption levels of informal sector workers are considerably higher than those of farm workers. This difference, together with the limited expansion of formal sector jobs—even assuming very high growth rates in the formal sector—suggests that informal sector jobs may provide an important part of a poverty reduction strategy in Kenya.

Skills and Access to Different Occupations

The skills profile of a worker can influence the accessibility to and earnings on the job in various sectors. For example, persons with some basic capacities like

Figure 6.5 Median Monthly Consumption in Kenya, by Sector of Work

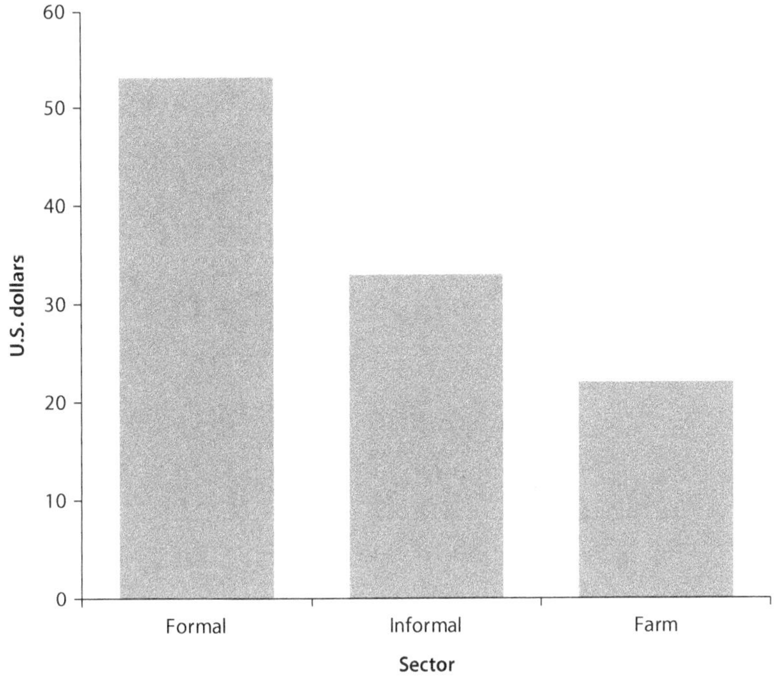

Source: Elaborations based on KNBS 2007.

reading and writing may be able to leave farming to take up a nonfarm activity, whereas public sector administration may employ only persons with university degrees. Thus, skills history can determine whether one accesses a particular sector with high or low earning opportunities. Once on the job in a higher- or lower-earning sector, earnings may or may not be further influenced by education. The following analysis shows that skills profiles differ and that more formal education is needed for access to formal sector work but that formal education does not favor the informal sector over farming. In contrast, lack of basic capabilities appears to keep people in farm occupations.

The level of basic literacy capacities is high in Kenya. The majority of workers in both formal and informal sectors can write in some language and can read a whole sentence. Although literacy and writing skills are higher in the formal sector for both men and women, most informal sector workers are literate. Women are comparatively worse off: 7 in 10 informal sector female workers can read a whole sentence, compared with 8 in 10 informally employed men and 9 in 10 formally employed women. The gaps between men and women appear somewhat higher in the informal sector than in the formal sector (figure 6.6).

Informal sector workers possess fewer years of schooling than formal sector workers. As shown in table 6.4, the mean years of schooling in the formal sector exceed those of the informal sector by nearly three years (10.8 and 8.2,

Figure 6.6 Literacy in Informal and Formal Sectors in Kenya

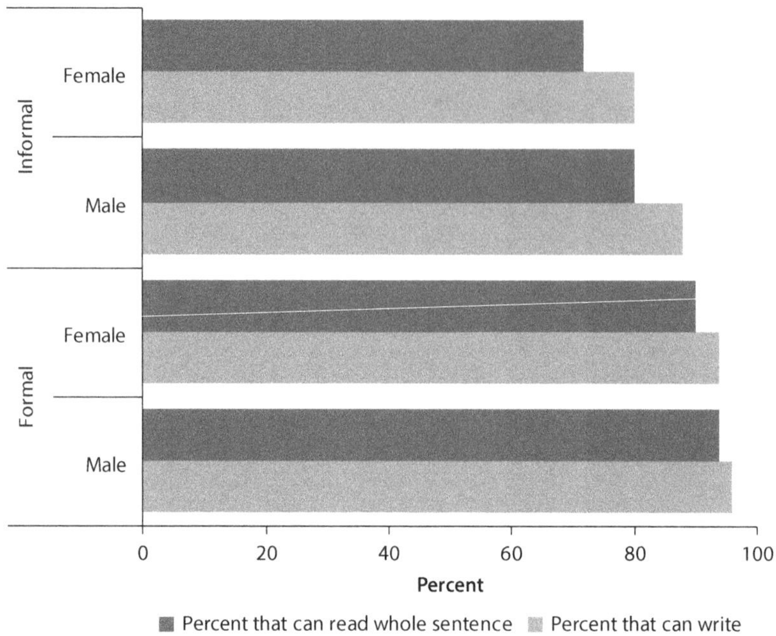

Source: Elaborations based on KNBS 2007.

Table 6.4 Average Years of Education in Kenya

Sector	*Male*	*Female*	*Total*
Formal	10.7	11.0	10.8
Informal	8.2	8.2	8.2
Total	9.1	8.9	9.1

Source: Elaborations based on KNBS 2007.

respectively). This implies that the average formal worker has some higher-secondary education, whereas the average informal worker has completed basic levels of education but no more. The informal sector workers are closer to the level of education in the farm sector (about seven years, not shown here) than to the formal sector.

Informal sector workers have had considerably less access to formal education and vocational training. Table 6.5 shows that about 4 in 10 informal sector workers have not finished primary levels of education, compared with 1 in 10 in the formal sector. Only one-fourth of informal sector workers have completed secondary, vocational, or university training, compared with two-thirds of formal sector workers. The gender gaps look very different across the sectors; although women have less education than men in the informal sector, they have more education in the formal sector.

Literacy and vocational training increase the probability of holding an informal sector job compared with formal sector work, controlling for other characteristics.

Table 6.5 Highest Education Level Completed in Kenya, by Sector and Gender
Percent

	Formal			Informal			Gender gap	
Education level	*Male*	*Female*	*Total*	*Male*	*Female*	*Total*	*Formal*	*Informal*
None or some completed	13	13	12	37	44	39	1.0	1.2
At least primary	23	17	22	36	33	35	0.7	0.9
Secondary completed	21	14	19	15	13	14	0.7	0.9
Vocational training	36	48	39	12	10	11	1.3	0.8
University	7	8	7	1	0.2	0.5	1.1	0.2
Total	100	100	100	100	100	100		
At least secondary, vocational, university	64	70	65	28	23	26	1.1	0.8

Source: Elaborations based on KNBS 2007.

Multinomial analysis (table 6A.1) suggests that vocational training has a positive influence on formal and informal sector employment compared to farming. Literacy is important for participating in the informal sector relative to farming but is insignificant for formal sector entry. Basic capabilities may thus provide a pathway into more lucrative nonfarm earnings but are irrelevant for the formal sector where higher levels of training are required. More years in formal education reduce the probability of entering informal sector work, controlling for other characteristics. It is nonetheless difficult to interpret this result without a better understanding of the opportunities in the farm sector. It may reflect omitted variables that influence participation and are correlated with education, entry barriers such as lack of credit, or attitudes to wage over nonwage work.

Age—a proxy for experience—increases the likelihood of finding employment in either the formal or informal sector, though the rate of increase declines as a worker becomes older. Because the comparison is with farming, the concave relationship between participation (in formal and informal employment) and worker's age suggests that as a worker grows older in the farming sector, the likelihood of exiting farming diminishes. Workers leave the farm sector primarily during youth. The likelihood of an older person searching for and finding work outside farming is low. In addition, men were more likely to find nonfarm employment (formal and informal employment) than women, relative to farming.

Skills and Earnings

On average, earnings in the informal sector fall below those of the formal sector, but some in the informal sector may earn more. The differences in consumption levels discussed previously are linked to differences in earnings. Informal sector workers on average earn significantly less than formal sector workers: median earnings in the informal sector were about one-quarter of those in the formal sector in 2005/06. Formal sector workers have an earnings advantage at all points on the earnings scale: the distribution of formal sector earnings is further to the right of the distribution of informal sector earnings (figure 6.7). Yet the overlap between the log earnings distributions means that some informal sector workers

Figure 6.7 Distribution of Log Monthly Earnings in Kenya by Formality Status, 2005/06

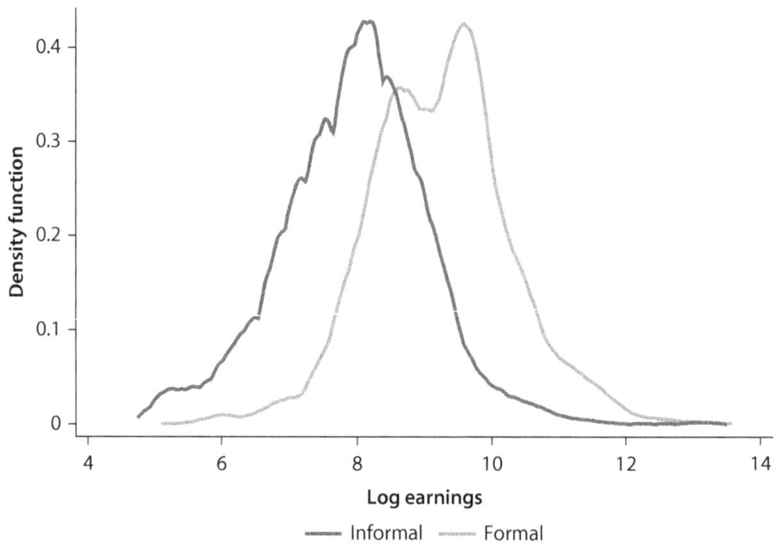

Source: Elaborations based on KNBS 2007.

Table 6.6 Monthly Median Earnings in Kenya by Sector, 2005/06

Gender	*Formal (U.S. dollars)*	*Informal (U.S. dollars)*	*Sector gap[a] (%)*
Female	85	14	0.16
Male	77	24	0.31
Total	80	19	0.24
Gender gap[b] (%)	1.1	0.6	n.a.

Source: Elaborations based on KNBS 2007.
Note: Earnings at 1998 prices. n.a. = not applicable.
a. Informal/formal ratio.
b. Female/male ratio.

earn as much or more than the formal sector workers and may, in fact, be in the informal sector by choice (Adams 2008; Maloney 1999).

The median earnings of women exceed those of men in the formal sector, while the opposite applies for men in the informal sector. This leads to a larger earnings gap for women between their earnings in the formal and informal sectors (table 6.6).[2]

Higher levels of education and training produce earnings gains. The age-earnings profile indicates that formal sector earnings peak earlier (35–44 years of age) than informal sector earnings (55–65 years of age), which may be evidence of a trade-off in terms of education and work experience, for which the latter counts more in the practically oriented informal sector (figure 6.8). The most significant payoff to education in the formal sector appears to kick in at the university level (note that informal sector workers with university education account for less than 1 percent of the total). Also noteworthy is that vocational training is associated with higher earnings in the formal sector than secondary

Figure 6.8 Mean Monthly Earnings by Age and Education in Kenya

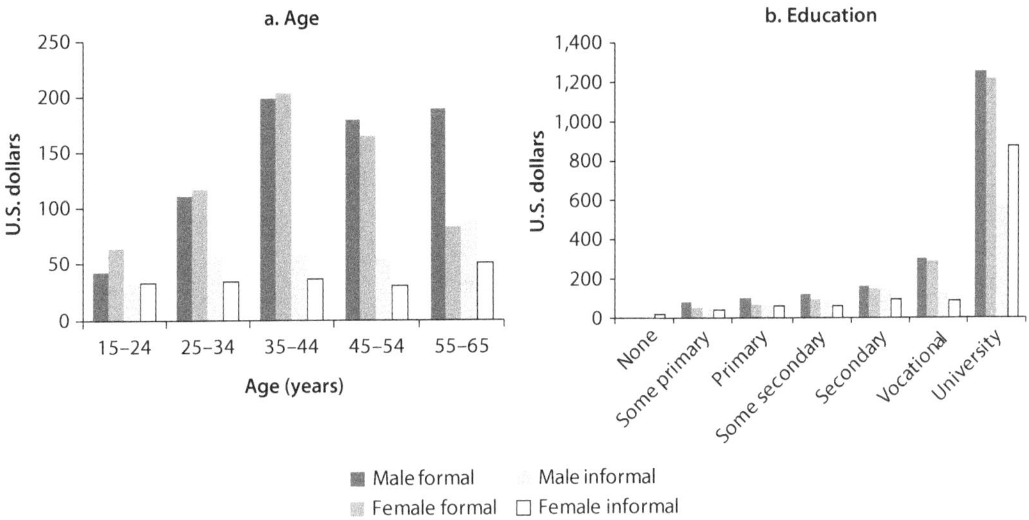

Source: Elaborations based on KNBS 2007.

general education, while the earnings of the two are about the same in the informal sector.

Formal education and vocational training have a positive effect on earnings, but returns are significantly higher in the formal sector than in the informal sector. Multivariate analysis (tables 6A.2–6A.5) also suggests positive returns to education and vocational training in both informal and formal sectors; however, the returns to education or vocational training are more than twice as high in the formal sector as in the informal sector. In the informal sector, vocational training, perhaps offering experience that is more practical and labor market relevant, pays off more than additional years of formal education; the reverse is true for formal sector earnings.[3]

Literacy does not influence earnings once other personal characteristics are controlled for. Thus, even for the informal sector, literacy does not influence earnings but, as shown earlier, may be an important precondition for working in the informal sector in the first place. Beyond formal education and vocational training, other socioeconomic characteristics influence earnings. Men earn more than women in both sectors, and the earnings gap appears to have widened over the period between the two surveys. Rural residence is associated with a significant earning disadvantage.

Even though apprenticeships are likely to be the most important source of skills for the informal sector, data are unavailable to measure their effect on earnings. Anecdotal evidence indicates that apprenticeships are an important form of skills training in the informal sector (see the following section), but it cannot be corroborated using the respective survey data, which do not offer information on apprenticeship training in Kenya. Thus, the roles apprenticeships play in accessing employment or influencing earnings cannot be analyzed. As in other countries, this form of training is generally the only one available for people who fail to meet the educational requirements to qualify for formal training and apprenticeship programs and, as such, is potentially catering to a large group of youth.

Overall, education plays a larger role for entry and earnings in the formal sector than in the informal sector. That said, some payoffs to different forms of education exist for the informal sector, with a stronger emphasis on more work-oriented skills (literacy, vocational training). In contrast, the formal sector requires certain levels of education (whether as a signaling device, for instance to enter a public administration job, or because of actual job requirements consistent with higher-productivity jobs), and the payoff to education is significantly higher in the formal sector.

Acquiring Skills for the Job Market in Kenya

Kenya offers many ways to acquire skills. Different types of public and private actors provide formal technical and vocational education and training (TVET). Providers of TVET include postsecondary technical institutions and colleges under the Ministry of Higher Education, Science, and Technology (MoHEST); postprimary youth polytechnics under the Ministry of Youth Affairs and Sport (MoYAS); the National Youth Service (NYS); specialized institutions under various government ministries; and a myriad of faith-based organizations (FBOs), nongovernmental organizations (NGOs), and community-based organizations as well as private commercial schools and institutions. In addition, public or donor-funded programs are intended to foster skills development, entrepreneurship, and employability among youth. Finally, the Jua Kali sector with its traditional apprenticeship system and a growing private training market provide access to skills development with particular emphasis on informal sector employment.

The importance of skills development beyond basic education has received significant attention in Kenya. A rapidly growing labor force and rising unemployment, accompanied with increasing social discontent and political unrest, have resulted in an increased focus on how to promote gainful employment for youth. The need for skills development also emerges as a transversal theme in different key strategy documents, including Kenya's Vision 2030, and various sectoral policy documents. Issues raised include the need to align skills development with labor market needs, increase quality by rehabilitating and improving facilities, improve equity by investing in underserved areas, and create centers of excellence for key occupational areas.

The National Technical and Vocational Education and Training Strategy was adopted in 2008 but has not been fully implemented. In reality, a lack of clarity surrounding TVET reform has impeded full implementation of reform measures. Institutional responsibilities remain unclearly defined, and the system continues to focus on inputs to training (defining strict training standards for institutions) instead of outcomes (defining benchmark competencies as requisite outcomes). This strategy effectively excludes formal recognition of nontraditional ways of learning. Trades testing, as explained below, offers a way around this problem.

The landscape for skills development includes a vibrant private sector and requires measures to bring these operators into the policy picture. Although responsibility for TVET is currently spread across several ministries, voucher initiatives have produced several important findings. First, significant unsatisfied demand exists among producers for training in the informal sector produced by constraints of time, limited space, cost, and flexibility of hours. Second, responding to this demand, the private sector skills providers have proven their capacity to increase the amount of training available (Adams 2001; Hicks and others 2011). Overall, the lack of rigorous monitoring and evaluation of training programs, including those of private providers, poses a problem for judging the effectiveness of these programs.

Education

Kenya has made significant advances and widened access to primary education. In 1999, the gross primary enrollment rate reached only 67 percent; 4 of every 10 students failed to finish primary school; and about 3 million children of school age were not in school (table 6.7). By 2008, the picture had changed. Primary gross enrollment rates and completion rates exceeded 100 percent, while the number of out-of-school children had been cut to less than one-tenth of the 1999 figure. The household data also showed that, on average, even farm workers had completed as much as seven years of education.

Progress at the higher levels has been slower, and a large number of youth still enter the labor market with less than a basic education. Although lower-secondary enrollment increased from 8 to 36 percent, higher-secondary enrollment hardly changed, and tertiary enrollment remained below 2 percent. As a result, the absolute number of youth that exit school before 15 years of age and end up in the labor market has been increasing markedly. Moreover, evidence exists of a disconnect between formal education and labor market relevance, because the focus remains on cognitive skills and theoretical

Table 6.7 Education Statistics, Kenya

Indicator	*1999*	*2008 or later*
Primary gross enrollment rate (%)	67	105
Primary completion ratio (%)	57	102
Out-of-school children, primary	3,185,000	268,000
Lower-secondary gross enrollment rate (%)	8	36
Higher-secondary gross enrollment rate (%)	3	4
Vocational and technical as percentage of secondary	9	—
Tertiary gross enrollment rate (%)	0.6	1.5

Source: World Bank 2011.
Note: — = not available.

education, at the disadvantage of noncognitive and more applied skills (Pina and others 2012).

Formal Sources of Skills Development

Critics complain that formal TVET is theoretical and lacks hands-on practical skills. The MoHEST is a large player responsible for postsecondary TVET, including 43 different institutions, with an annual intake of about 15,000 for full-time studies. The MoHEST also accredits private TVET institutions. Anecdotal evidence suggests that in the more technical trades, graduates frequently end up working as self-employed in the informal sector after graduation. The little entrepreneurial training offered is generally considered to be quite theoretical.

The MoYAS and its youth (village) polytechnics (YPs) play an important role in reaching school leavers after primary education. About 50,000 youth are currently enrolled in the YPs (30–35 percent women). They specifically target students with completed primary education although some secondary graduates are accepted. The YPs offer long-term training programs of two years, geared toward certification of qualifications through trades testing. The programs include traditional technical trades, information and communication technology (ICT), catering and hospitality, beautician, as well as some life skills and entrepreneurship modules. No evidence is available on labor market performance of graduates, and failure rates are quite high on exams, possibly as a result of the revamping of the YPs simultaneously with a large curriculum reform.

The MoYAS also offers an NYS program. The NYS provides two years of paramilitary training and service in public works, after which students are admitted to different skills development programs also amounting to qualifications at diploma level or trades testing. Graduates are assumed to be highly valued in the labor market, in particular because of life and work skills developed during the training. For those with lower levels of education who follow artisan training, self-employment is common; however, no support services (in terms of start-up kits, links with microfinance schemes, and the like) are included in the NYS. Other government agencies also provide TVET, a few with particular relevance for the informal sector. For example, the Institute of Business Training under the Ministry of Trade targets medium and small-scale operators, and Utalii College provides tourism and hospitability training at different levels.

The Directorate of Industrial Training (DIT) provides programs parallel to the formal TVET system that are perceived as more relevant to the needs of both informal and formal workers and operators. The DIT oversees the national trades testing system, administers the industrial training levy fund, and organizes a number of training schemes. The DIT administers a formal apprenticeship program of limited size (500–600 trainees per year) and provides a small wage subsidy for about 10,000 students annually, emanating from TVET and universities for on-the-job induction training for new recruits. It also oversees industrial skills upgrading and trades test preparation programs involving about 1,200–1,500 trainees per year.

The DIT's intake of trainees is limited compared to demand, and the high cost is a barrier to access. Although these programs officially are directed to both informal and formal agents, the cost is equivalent to four months of (median) earnings in the informal sector (more than US$80), which serves as a barrier to many who would enter the informal sector. The scale of DIT activities is low by comparison with the numbers of young people exiting the formal education system.

Trades testing is available to certify skills attained from diverse providers. The trades testing system is available for a fee (around US$25) to any person seeking recognition, regardless of mode of skills acquisition—apprenticeships, on-the-job training, or nonformal and formal training. More than 400 centers, mainly training institutions, are accredited trades testing centers, and the number of candidates is high (about 45,000 in 2010). The vast majority test for semi-skilled levels, indicating the attractiveness of the certification.

Nonformal Sources of Skills Development

As noted earlier, the private training market is vast and diverse, and it fills an important role in responding to demand. It has more than a thousand private TVET providers, including FBOs, NGOs, and community-run organizations as well as private commercial schools and institutions. About 500 institutes are currently registered with the MoHEST; many others are not registered and not subject to quality control. Some indicators point toward underused capacities, especially with the commercial providers. Fees can range from K Sh 1,000 to K Sh 100,000 per program, but in the case of donor-supported NGOs and FBOs, often only a commitment fee is charged. These last appear to focus largely on traditional techniques whereas commercial providers offer training in more modern occupations, including ICT.

Judging the quality and effectiveness of nonformal sources of skills development is difficult, like that of formal sources, because of the lack of monitoring and evaluation of training outcomes. As a result, knowledge is limited about effectiveness and efficiency of programs. Given the high diversity of the training supply in Kenya, finding out more about what works and what does not should be an important goal to support and replicate well-functioning systems. What can be discerned from a review of programs is summarized below. This review highlights the small scale of activities addressing the needs of the informal sector for skills, the key role played by private providers of these skills, and the features of programs that appear to offer benefits to people seeking employment in the informal sector.

Available information suggests the following:

- *Comprehensive packages with high-quality training and follow-up services are successful but may be costly*. Some privately provided (but noncommercial) programs appear to be comparatively successful in equipping graduates with a multifaceted set of skills for the workplace. For example, the Don Bosco skills training centers (FBO-run institutes) are known for high-quality training in a variety of traditional skills, ICT, and secretarial skills as well as for strong mentorship. Graduates are assisted in finding employment through a job placement center; application and interview training is also part of the curriculum. However, the program is costly at K Sh 120,000 (US$1,200) per year per trainee, making a national scale-up of the program problematic.

- *Close targeting of beneficiaries may facilitate the design of training to provide the right mix of technical, business, and soft skills, combined with other services to facilitate labor market entry and a reduction in occupational segregation.* The African Centre for Women, Information and Communications Technology (ACWICT) is piloting a program financed by Samsung. The Samsung Real Dreams program targets women in the informal settlements of Nairobi, aiming to provide them with relatively advanced ICT skills. A tracer study, however, suggested that 77 percent of graduates were working in regular (formal) employment. It also showed that graduates highly value the soft skills provided during training.

- *Where rigorous evaluation was applied to a pilot training program, the provision of private training proved able to provide stronger connections to the labor market and ensure more flexibility and better adaptation to changing needs, and the use of vouchers provided a means of stimulating this supply.* To gauge the potential for the private sector as a key provider, the Technical and Vocational Vouchers Program (TVVP) was launched in 2008 (see box 6.2). The pilot program is significant, because unlike the vast majority of interventions, it has been subject to a rigorous evaluation methodology. The evidence is positive.

- *The voucher program also indicated that subsidies can fill an important role in stimulating training for lower-income groups.* In particular, training has payoffs in both employability and earnings, and a larger private sector supply of training provides more flexibility. The program provides important findings for skills development policy: training costs appear to be too high, so subsidies may be necessary, and participants face many other constraints beyond financing, including training location.

For in-service training, Jua Kali operators are basically served by only the private sector. Many of the trainers are master craftspersons who have developed training as a complementary business activity—a legacy of an earlier government voucher program stimulating private sector supply of training. This segment of training providers is now organized in the National Association of Technology Transfer and Entrepreneurial Training. The quality of training and effectiveness in terms of raising productivity and earnings is not known, however.

Box 6.2 Increasing Access by Stimulating Private Provision: Kenya TVVP

The TVVP launched in 2008 in western Kenya (Busia) is a research project focusing on factors affecting demand for skills development and the economic and social effect of skills development. Among youth who applied for the project, 50 percent were randomly selected to receive a voucher, with the remaining 50 percent serving as a control group. Of those receiving vouchers, half were given restricted vouchers applicable only in public institutions.

Although final results are still unavailable, preliminary analysis points to interesting results from a policy perspective:

- High costs of accessing TVET are potentially a significant barrier to accessing skills development: 75 percent of the voucher holders had attended training, compared with 4 percent of the control group.
- Private training appears to increase the choice in the training market and improve the chances that young people will find a provider that matches their needs and individual circumstances. The share of unrestricted voucher holders making use of the voucher was 10 percentage points higher than the share for holders with the restricted voucher.
- Further evidence indicated the need for a large supply of institutions that can flexibly accommodate individual constraints, including family considerations. When asked the reasons for choosing a specific program, almost half the youth indicated "proximity to home," and almost a third said the "ability to find accommodation nearby the training center."
- Information on training supply and labor market contexts is low. Participants turned out not to be properly informed about labor market outcomes, including the likely returns.
- Vocational training can serve as an effective second-chance program for youth with low educational achievements. Participants with, at most, completed primary were more likely to finish their education than those with secondary levels of education.
- Systematic information on returns to training is not yet available, but there are some very preliminary indications that training helps in shortening job search and increasing remuneration (especially for women).

Source: Hicks and others 2011.

Public and NGO programs also specifically address the training needs of the informal sector. One example is the Informal Sector Business Institute (ISBI), which offers a "street MBA" to existing informal sector operators. The curriculum includes management, marketing, accounting, and business English. However, the scale is very small, with only 350 entrepreneurs having benefited from the program since 2004. ISBI also runs youth training programs, focusing on basic computer skills training. As for many of these programs, hard evidence on their costs and benefits is lacking. Table 6B.1 summarizes some key programs and highlights how (if at all) they address the constraints faced by new or established informal sector agents wishing to increase their skills. Although the programs may address some constraints, they rarely hit a majority of the key problems.

For example, many programs work on multiskilling, recognizing that self-employment requires more than technical skills, but few programs address the need for modular and flexible forms of training. Thus, the outreach and effect of programs may be limited.

Informal Sources of Skills Development

Traditional apprenticeships are, as in other parts of Sub-Saharan Africa, the most important skills development system available to youth for the informal sector. Estimates of apprentices date to 1999, but if the share of apprentices in the Jua Kali sector has remained constant over time or possibly grown, the sector now hosts at least 180,000 youth as apprentices. Informal sector associations are involved in setting standards for fees and fee arrangements and in informally supervising quality. Training fees are for tuition only and do not cover living expenses and transport, which the trainee must bear. Although traditionally these apprenticeships were accessible for youth with low education levels, some evidence indicates that educational requirements are increasing and that master craftspersons require potential trainees to have completed primary education.

The apprenticeships offer hands-on, production-oriented, and on-the-job training based on informal contracts. On the upside of apprenticeships is their strong labor market relevance and self-financing system. Although widely available, apprenticeships suffer from lack of access to newer technology, varied quality in teaching skill and methods, absence of second-chance education options for trainees with limited schooling, and poor business practices. Fees are perhaps surprisingly high—around US$15 per month—effectively limiting access by the poorest segments. Taking steps to address these weaknesses would strengthen this important source of skills development for the informal sector.

Efforts to train master craftspersons can provide wider benefits. An example of traditional apprenticeship support (Strengthening Informal Training and Enterprise, SITE) suggested that efforts to also target trainers (in this case master craftspersons) could be beneficial in improving skills outcomes, raising productivity, and increasing the supply of (higher quality) training through apprenticeships (box 6.3).

In summary, Kenya has made important progress in increasing access and equity in formal education at the basic education level, but more remains to be done for skills in the informal sector. Most children still exit school before entering secondary levels of education. How to equip young workers with adequate skills for the labor market outside the realm of formal education therefore remains a crucial policy issue. Compared with many other African countries, Kenya offers an unusually wide range of nonformal and informal training options for the formal and informal sectors. However, because of a lack of good evaluations and tracer studies, much uncertainty still exists about what works and what does not work in terms of creating sustainable employment among youth. Given the size and importance of the informal sector to the economy, more attention needs to focus on the constraints to acquiring skills for the informal sector.

Box 6.3 Training the Trainers in the Informal Sector: Traditional Apprenticeship Support by SITE

Between 1996 and 1998, with assistance from the United Kingdom, the NGO Strengthening Informal Training and Enterprise (SITE) ran a project to support and develop traditional apprenticeship training in Kenya. The project concentrated on metalwork, woodwork, and textiles. In total, 420 master craftspersons and 280 apprentices were trained directly, while an estimated 1,400 apprentices received improved training from the project's host trainers.

According to available information, the effect was positive by various accounts. Traditional apprenticeship training became more efficient (reduced time and costs) and effective (concentrated on productive activities), gaining from the training that the masters had received. Of the masters who participated, the number of apprentices increased by 15–20 percent. The masters themselves benefited through increased turnover and profits, assumed to be a direct result of new skills applied, new products, penetration of new markets, and better workshop layouts and production organization.

Some of the lessons learned from the project included the following:

- Skills training was not immediately interesting to master craftspersons, unless it was delivered in the context of a broader business improvement context.
- Training for the masters has to be delivered in a flexible manner, taking into account time constraints and opportunity costs.
- Masters get involved in training not necessarily to increase training fees but to increase income from production. Training turned out to be a good entry point for technology upgrading in the enterprises.
- Attempts to create links between the Jua Kali and the training institutions were disappointing: independent trainers (business development services providers) are more flexible and suitable.
- Collaboration with informal sector associations is important.

Overall, the intervention demonstrated that skills development, carefully and appropriately targeted, can be instrumental in improving the performance of informal sector enterprises. New skills appeared to lead to increased growth, innovation, and productivity.

Sources: Haan 2006; Johanson and Adams 2004.

Conclusions

Recent years have seen important economic, political, and demographic dynamics taking place in Kenya. Economic growth rates have fluctuated significantly, in response to domestic political instability (2002 and 2008) and the global financial crisis (2008). The Kenyan demographic and labor market structure has changed as more youth enter the labor market, lowering the average age of the working-age population and labor force. The employment structure has shifted, with nonfarm informal sector employment absorbing more new workers than both the farming and the formal sectors. Low-quality employment, underemployment, and open unemployment (especially urban youth) remain critical labor market and poverty reduction challenges. At the same time, Kenya has continued to invest in the education and training of the workforce.

Kenya needs to focus on the nonfarm informal sector because diversification into nonfarm activities offers earning opportunities that can lift families out of poverty. The Jua Kali sector is deeply imbedded in Kenyan society. However, the gap between earnings in the informal and formal sectors continues to be wide, and the question remains how to increase productivity and earnings opportunities for the rapidly growing informal sector workforce, most of whom work on their own account.

Access to schooling and other forms of training is important because training matters for earnings in several ways. Skills influence earnings in Kenya directly by raising productivity or earnings for the worker and indirectly by improving access into sectors with higher earnings. Importantly, literacy pays off to enter informal sector employment but does not facilitate access to formal sector work, where requirements on formal education are likely to be significantly higher. Formal education, including vocational training, pays off less in terms of earnings in the informal sector than in the formal sector.

As in many other African countries, progress on access at primary levels of education needs to be consolidated and reinforced by paying more attention to quality and opening up training opportunities at higher levels. Kenya has improved access to primary education and lower-secondary education. Building on these achievements will require focusing on the quality of education and on basic capacities like literacy. Increasing access at lower levels, however, will increase pressure on expanding access at higher levels of education and will require actions to support high-quality training through both formal and nonformal means. Given the abundance of public and private programs and initiatives, finding ways of improving the efficiency of the existing institutions and improving the relevance of skills training will be important.

Because most work opportunities will be as own-account workers and entrepreneurs, providing skills beyond technical skills will be integral to achieving results. This broader package of services includes life-skills training, business training, opportunities for apprenticeships, access to credit, counseling, and continued business services after training. The evidence is still limited on the cost-effectiveness of these types of programs on a larger scale, however.

The informal sector faces many constraints that formal wage workers or larger employers may not face, and programs that address these constraints are likely to reach out better to this important segment of the working population. For example, informal sector operators have lower earnings, have limited cash flow, depend on their income for survival and so cannot attend school during the day, and need to acquire a wide range of competencies because many are very small firms. Generally, they also have limited access to new technologies and pedagogical sources of training. Programs that target informal sector operators need to consider the following, among other things: (a) how to be flexible in provision of training; (b) what can make training affordable for low-earning groups; (c) how to provide access to relevant technology; and (d) how to provide the broad range of skills needed. Evidence from Kenya shows that vouchers can stimulate private sector supply of skills in this area, with positive results in terms of labor market outcomes.

Means of increasing the efficiency of apprenticeships as well as improving their value in labor (or credit) markets are needed. Although household survey information is lacking for the specific case of Kenya, apprenticeships in the African context are common and have several advantages, including self-financing and high labor market relevance. Some of their weaknesses, including lack of access to trainers with pedagogical skills and lack of training in modern technology and modern business practices, may be the target of specific programs to upgrade master craftspersons. The popularity of Kenya's trades testing system underscores the importance of formally recognizing informally acquired competencies and reflects the acuity of results-based approaches.

The informal sector is comparatively well organized in Kenya, and associations could be involved in strengthening training supply. With their strong connections to the informal sector needs, the National Association of Technology Transfer and Entrepreneurial Training and several Jua Kali associations could in various degrees be involved in (a) assessment of training and market demand, (b) advocacy on the benefits of training, and (c) supervision of training outcomes.

Much work remains to be done to build the evidence base on skills development in Kenya. Unfortunately, no information is available on apprenticeships or other forms of in-service training likely to contribute significantly to skills development in the informal sector, and there is a serious lack of evaluations of the long-term (or even short-term) effect of many of the public or private training programs on employability or earnings of its beneficiaries. Closer monitoring and evaluation would permit Kenya to improve its training system and focus resources on the most efficient programs.

Annex 6A: Tables

The annex contains multivariate regressions that form the basis for analyzing the links between education and sector of employment as well as earnings on the job. The first table consists of the multinomial regression that shows how years of education is related to sector of employment. Subsequent tables show the relationship between education and earnings on the job in the formal and informal sectors, both taking into account the effect of selection into sectors and without it.

Table 6A.1 Determinants of Labor Allocation across Employment Sectors in Kenya, Odds Ratios, 2005–06

Multinomial logistic regression

Number of observations = 13,588
LR chi²(20) = 7,226.32
Prob > chi² = 0.0000
Log likelihood = −10,374.003
Pseudo R^2 = 0.2583

Modern	*RRR*	*Standard error*	*z*	*p > z*	*95% confidence interval*
Formal					
Age	1.360	0.028	14.990	0.000	1.306 to 1.415
Age_2	0.996	0.000	−14.240	0.000	0.996 to 0.997
Gender	2.928	0.193	16.270	0.000	2.572 to 3.332
Drururb	0.071	0.005	−34.670	0.000	0.061 to 0.083
Vtraining	3.450	0.275	15.550	0.000	2.951 to 4.033
Edyrs	1.286	0.016	20.420	0.000	1.255 to 1.317
Literate	0.873	0.174	−0.680	0.495	0.591 to 1.290
Married	0.986	0.129	−0.110	0.913	0.762 to 1.275
Numagelt6	0.905	0.030	−3.020	0.003	0.848 to 0.966
Numage714	0.875	0.024	−4.900	0.000	0.830 to 0.923
Informal					
Age	1.089	0.013	7.020	0.000	1.063 to 1.115
Age_2	0.999	0.000	−8.950	0.000	0.998 to 0.999
Gender	2.154	0.099	16.740	0.000	1.969 to 2.357
Drururb	0.063	0.004	−44.620	0.000	0.056 to 0.071
Vtraining	1.503	0.117	5.240	0.000	1.290 to 1.750
Edyrs	0.953	0.008	−5.590	0.000	0.938 to 0.969
Literate	1.375	0.126	3.470	0.001	1.149 to 1.646
Married	0.597	0.051	−6.070	0.000	0.506 to 0.705
Numagelt6	0.990	0.021	−0.480	0.628	0.949 to 1.032
Numage714	0.903	0.017	−5.550	0.000	0.871 to 0.936

Source: Elaborations based on KNBS 2007 relative to working in farming.

Table 6A.2 OLS: Returns to Education in Formal Sector, 2005–06

Linear regression

Number of observations = 2,234
F(72,226)=185.45
Prob > F = 0.0000
$R^2 = 0.4441$
Root MSE = 0.79532

Lntot~Formal	*Coefficient*	*Robust standard error*	*t*	*p > t*	*95% confidence interval*
Age	0.092	0.015	6.330	0.000	0.063 to 0.120
Agesq	−0.001	0.000	−4.220	0.000	−0.001 to 0.000
Gender	0.070	0.036	1.910	0.056	−0.002 to 0.141
Drururb	−0.326	0.035	−9.430	0.000	−0.394 to −0.258
Training	0.013	0.035	0.380	0.703	−0.055 to 0.082
Edyrs	0.181	0.007	24.980	0.000	0.167 to 0.195
Literate	0.253	0.169	1.500	0.134	−0.078 to 0.584
_Cons	4.956	0.299	16.590	0.000	4.370 to 5.542

Source: Flaborations based on KNBS 2007.
Note: White's test for homoskedasticity indicates presence of heteroskedasticity (χ^2 (30) = 82.04; *p*-value = 0.0000). Hence, robust standard errors obtained. OLS = ordinary least squares.

Table 6A.3 OLS: Returns to Education in Informal Sector, 2005–06

Linear regression

Number of observations = 4,597
F(74,[illegible]) = 108.34
Prob > F = 0.0000
$R^2 = 0.1508$
Root MSE = 1.0315

Intot~informal	*Coefficent*	*Robust standard error*	*t*	*p>t*	*95% confidence interval*
Age	0.025	0.009	2.790	0.005	0.007 to 0.043
Agesq	0.000	0.000	−1.620	0.105	0.000 to 0.000
Gender	0.374	0.032	11.770	0.000	0.312 to 0.436
Drururb	−0.432	0.032	−13.510	0.000	−0.494 to −0.369
Training	0.111	0.050	2.210	0.027	0.013 to 0.209
Edyrs	0.083	0.007	12.100	0.000	0.070 to 0.097
Literate	0.090	0.069	1.300	0.195	−0.046 to 0.225
_Cons	6.610	0.159	41.700	0.000	6.300 to 6.921

Source: Elaborations based on KNBS 2007.
Note: White's test for homoskedasticity indicates presence of heteroskedasticity in the log earnings equation for the informal sector (χ^2 (29) = 184.17; *p*-value = 0.0000). Hence, robust standard errors reported. OLS = ordinary least squares

Table 6A.4 Log Earning Function: Correcting for Selection into Formal Sector, 2005–06

Heckman selection model

Number of observations = 13,514 (regression model with sample selection)
Censored observations = 11,288
Uncensored observations = 2,226
Wald $chi^2(7)$ = 389.08
Log pseudolikelihood = −7,036.723
Prob > chi = 0.0000

	Coefficient	*Robust standard error*	*z*	*p > z*	*95% confidence interval*
Lntotincome					
Age	0.129	0.020	6.550	0.000	0.090 to 0.167
Agesq	−0.001	0.000	−5.010	0.000	−0.002 to −0.001
Gender	0.180	0.056	3.210	0.001	0.070 to 0.290
Drururb	−0.491	0.069	−7.070	0.000	−0.626 to −0.355
Vtraining	0.200	0.075	2.650	0.008	0.052 to 0.347
Edyrs	0.226	0.018	12.720	0.000	0.191 to 0.261
Literate	0.219	0.179	1.220	0.221	−0.132 to 0.569
_Cons	3.171	0.690	4.590	0.000	1.818 to 4.525
Dformal					
Age	0.134	0.010	13.230	0.000	0.114 to 0.153
Agesq	−0.002	0.000	−11.820	0.000	−0.002 to −0.001
Gender	0.353	0.032	11.110	0.000	0.291 to 0.415
Drururb	−0.500	0.032	−15.680	0.000	−0.562 to −0.437
Vtraining	0.549	0.039	13.980	0.000	0.472 to 0.626
Edyrs	0.150	0.007	21.160	0.000	0.136 to 0.164
Literate	−0.207	0.095	−2.180	0.029	−0.394 to −0.021
Married	0.103	0.065	1.590	0.113	−0.024 to 0.230
Numagelt6	−0.044	0.017	−2.570	0.010	−0.077 to −0.010
Numage714	−0.038	0.013	−2.940	0.003	−0.064 to −0.013
_Cons	−4.925	0.218	−22.630	0.000	−5.352 to −4.499
/Athrho	0.534	0.190	2.800	0.005	0.161 to 0.907
/Lnsigma	−0.142	0.058	−2.480	0.013	−0.255 to −0.030
Rho	0.488	0.145			0.159 to 0.719
Sigma	0.867	0.050			0.775 to 0.971
Lambda	0.423	0.149			0.132 to 0.715

Source: Elaborations based on KNBS 2007.
Note: Wald test of independent equations (rho = 0): $chi^2(1)$ = 7.87 Prob > chi^2 = 0.0050. Hence, the measure of correlation (rho) between the error terms of the log earnings equation and formal sector entry equation is statistically different from zero at 1 percent.

Table 6A.5 Log Earning Function: Correcting for Selection into Informal Sector, 2005–06

Heckman selection model

Number of observations = 12,827 (regression model with sample selection)
Censored observations = 8,243
Uncensored observations = 4,584
Wald chi²(7) = 700.63
Log pseudolikelihood = −13,832.86
Prob > chi² = 0.0000

	Coefficient	*Standard error*	*z*	*p > z*	*95% confidence interval*
Lntotincome					
Age	0.0255	0.0091	2.8100	0.0050	0.0077 to 0.0433
Agesq	−0.0002	0.0001	−1.6500	0.1000	−0.0005 to 0.0000
Gender	0.3750	0.0335	11.2000	0.0000	0.3094 to 0.4407
Drururb	−0.4464	0.0585	−7.6400	0.0000	−0.5610 to −0.3318
Vtraining	0.1073	0.0515	2.0800	0.0370	0.0063 to 0.2083
Edyrs	0.0819	0.0078	10.5100	0.0000	0.0666 to 0.0972
Literate	0.0945	0.0707	1.3400	0.1810	−0.0441 to 0.2330
_Cons	6.6022	0.1604	41.1500	0.0000	6.2877 to 6.9167
Dinformal					
Age	0.0022	0.0069	0.3100	0.7530	−0.0113 to 0.0156
Agesq	−0.0003	0.0001	−3.3000	0.0010	−0.0005 to −0.0001
Gender	0.2639	0.0251	10.5100	0.0000	0.2147 to 0.3131
Drururb	−1.0671	0.0280	−38.0700	0.0000	−1.1220 to −1.0121
Training	−0.2519	0.0385	−6.5400	0.0000	−0.3273 to −0.1764
Edyrs	−0.0811	0.0046	−17.6500	0.0000	−0.0901 to −0.0721
Literate	0.3467	0.0529	6.5600	0.0000	0.2431 to 0.4503
Married	−0.3501	0.0467	−7.5000	0.0000	−0.4415 to −0.2586
Numagelt6	−0.0066	0.0128	−0.5100	0.6080	−0.0317 to 0.0185
Numage714	−0.0350	0.0106	−3.3100	0.0010	−0.0557 to −0.0143
_Cons	1.2409	0.1343	9.2400	0.0000	0.9777 to 1.5041
/Athrho	0.0195	0.0696	0.2800	0.7800	−0.1170 to 0.1559
/Lnsigma	0.0307	0.0137	2.2500	0.0250	0.0039 to 0.0574
Rho	0.0195	0.0696			−0.1165 to 0.1547
Sigma	1.0312	0.0141			1.0039 to 1.0591
Lambda	0.0201	0.0718			−0.1206 to 0.1607

Source: Elaborations based on KNBS 2007.
Note: Wald test of independent equations (rho = 0): chi²(1) = 0.08 Prob > chi² = 0.7798. Hence, the measure of correlation (rho) between the error terms of the log earnings equation and informal sector entry equation is not statistically different from zero at 1, 5, or 10 percent.

Annex 6B: Training Scheme Descriptions

The annex presents, first, a table that provides a detailed overview of the degree to which different programs and initiatives in Kenya cater to the skills development constraints faced by the informal sector, and second, a table that explains different factors that contribute to success in skills development programs.

Table 6B.1 Training Schemes and Approaches in Kenya for Informal Sector Relative to Informal Sector Skills Training

High opportunity cost	*Low cash flow of firms and workers*	*Multiskilling needs*	*Lack of skills for training*	*Information failures on benefits of training*	*Little supply catering to informal skills needs*	*Absence of economies of scale for training driving up cost*
• Kenya Youth Employment Program (KYEP): Preparation training of masters provided in evening hours.	• KYEP: Providing scholarships for trainees/interns and allowances for informal sector masters to provide training places.	• ACWICT: Preemployment, but including informal sector employment. Combined technical with entrepreneurial and life skills.	• KYEP: Attachments in informal sector are preceded by training master craftspersons in entrepreneurship, production, marketing, human resources development, and coaching/training methodologies.	TVVP (pilot research voucher program): Established and addressed information failures. However, this was targeting youth, not informal sector operators.	• All formal (recognized) TVET programs in Kenya include business management and self-employment modules. However, because of lack of appropriate instruction skills, this training is not perceived to be very relevant.	All programs providing subsidized access.
• SITE (1990s): Scheduling of training of master craftspersons during times and hours not interrupting the business work schedule.	• World Bank Informal Sector Voucher Program: Providing informal sector operators with vouchers to partially cover training costs.		• SITE (during the 1990s): Technical assistance support offering additional training to master craftspersons.		• World Bank Informal Sector Voucher Program: Stimulated demand, which was met by a newly emerging type of training providers (within the informal sector). Facilitated the emergence of a specialized informal sector training provider system (unintended effect).	

table continues next page

Table 6B.1 Training Schemes and Approaches in Kenya for Informal Sector Relative to Informal Sector Skills Training *(continued)*

High opportunity cost	*Low cash flow of firms and workers*	*Multiskilling needs*	*Lack of skills for training*	*Information failures on benefits of training*	*Little supply catering to informal skills needs*	*Absence of economies of scale for training driving up cost*
	• ISBI: Linking training to micro venture-capital scheme.				• ACWICT and ISBI: Inclusion of life skills alongside technical and entrepreneurial training trade testing: scheme to recognize informally acquired skills, including skills developed in informal sector work. This is complemented by upgrading and trade test preparation training offered by DIT. • Most microcredit schemes in Kenya (which are widespread) require some sort of short entrepreneurship or business management training for borrowers. • Training provided as part of value chain and subsector development programs.	

Source: Franz 2011.

Table 6B.2 What Makes TVET and Youth Employment Programs Successful?

Factor	*Sources/Evidence*
Job placement efforts by training providers	ACWICT, Samsung Real Dreams Follow-up Survey Results; Salesian Church/Don Bosco
Internships	ACWICT, Samsung Real Dreams Follow-up Survey Results; results of KYEP will add further evidence
Cooperation with industry in training	Formal apprenticeship system; results of KYEP to add further evidence
Appropriately comprehensive technical skills training in line with labor market requirements (avoid too short skills training programs)	ACWICT evaluation of Reaching the Unreached program; KYEP/Internships and Training Program (feedback from Jua Kali master craftspersons)
Life-skills training, counseling, and follow-up	ACWICT evaluation, evidence from NYS program; CfBT Education Trust 2009
Specific targeting; provision of tailor-made programs	CfBT Education Trust 2009; own observation; ISBI
Management commitment and capacities of training provider	Survey of government and nongovernmental training providers in Kenya, CfBT Education Trust 2009; own observations in visited training institutions
Appropriately competent instructors	Experience from other countries, own observations in training institutions; TVVP evaluations expected to provide more insight because relevant baseline data were collected
Appropriate resources	Experience from other countries, own observations in training institutions; TVVP evaluations expected to provide more insight because relevant baseline data were collected

Source: Franz 2011.

Notes

1. This chapter is largely based on Onsomu and Wambugu (2012) and Franz (2011).
2. Although median earnings are higher for women in the formal sector than for men, mean earnings are higher for men than for women in both formal and informal sectors.
3. Both ordinary least squares and Heckman corrected regressions, controlling for selection bias, give this result.

References

Adams, Arvil V. 2001. "Assessment of the Jua Kali Voucher Program." World Bank, Washington, DC. http://siteresources.worldbank.org/EDUCATION/Resources/278200-1099079877269/547664-1099079934475/547667-1135281552767/Jua_Kali_Pilot_Voucher_Program.pdf.

———. 2008. "Skills Development in the Informal Sector of Sub-Saharan Africa." World Bank, Washington, DC. http://siteresources.worldbank.org/INTLM/Resources/390041-1141141801867/2275364-1213970047519/Skills_for_Informal_Sector-6042008.pdf.

Franz, Jutta. 2011. "Realizing the Youth Dividend in Kenya through Skills for the Informal Sector: Institutional Assessment of Skills Development and Youth Employment Promotion Programs and Projects." Unpublished, Africa Department, World Bank, Washington, DC.

Haan, Hans Christiaan. 2006. *Training for Work in the Informal Micro-enterprise Sector: Fresh Evidence from Sub-Sahara Africa*. Dordrecht, Netherlands: Springer.

Hicks, Joan, Michael Kremer, Isaac Mbiti, and Edward Miguel. 2011. "Vocational Education Voucher Delivery and Labor Market Returns: A Randomized Evaluation among Kenyan Youth, Final Report for Spanish Impact Evaluation Fund (SIEF) Phase II." Policy Note Human Development Network, World Bank, Washington, DC.

Johanson, Richard K., and Arvil V. Adams. 2004. *Skills Development in Sub-Saharan Africa*. Regional and Sectoral Studies. Washington, DC: World Bank.

KCBS (Kenya Central Bureau of Statistics, Ministry of Planning and National Development). 2003. *Report of the 1998/99 Labour Force Survey*. Nairobi: KCBS.

KNBS (Kenya National Bureau of Statistics, Ministry of State for Planning National Development, and Vision 2030). Various years. *Economic Survey*. Nairobi: KNBS.

———. 1999. *Labour Force Survey-1999*. Version 1.2 of the public use dataset (November 2008), provided by the National Data Archive, Government of Kenya, Nairobi. http://www.nda_popstan.or.

KNBS (Kenya National Bureau of Statistics, Ministry of Planning and National Development). 2007. *Kenya Integrated Household Budget Survey 2005–2006*. Version 1.0 of the KNBS dataset, Government of Kenya, Nairobi. http://statistics.knbs.or.ke/nada/index.php/catalog/8.

———. 2008. *2005/06 Kenya Integrated Budget Survey: Labour Force Analytical Report*. Nairobi: KNBS.

Maloney, William F. 1999. "Does Informality Imply Segmentation in Urban Labor Markets? Evidence from Sectoral Transitions in Mexico." *The World Bank Economic Review* 13 (2): 275–302.

Onsomu, Eldah, and Anthony Wambugu. 2012. "Skills Development for Informal Sector Workers in Kenya." Unpublished, Africa Department, World Bank, Washington, DC.

Pina, Patricia, Tim Kotin, Vicky Hausman, and Edwin Macharia, Dalberg Global Development Advisors. 2012. "Skills for Employability: The Informal Economy." Paper prepared for the Innovative Secondary Education for Skills Enhancement (ISESE) project, Results for Development Institute, Washington, DC. http://www.resultsfordevelopment.org/sites/resultsfordevelopment.org/files/resources/Skills%20for%20Employability%20in%20the%20Informal%20Economy.pdf.

World Bank. 2011. *World Development Indicators 2011*. Washington, DC: World Bank.

CHAPTER 7

Skills Development in the Informal Sector: Nigeria

In This Chapter

In spite of strong and diversified economic growth, a majority of Nigeria's population remains in the farm and informal nonfarm sectors. Earnings and skills levels differ greatly between sectors. Compared with formal workers, informal workers are less literate and numerate and have much less formal schooling. They earn less, and education has a smaller payoff for earnings. Investment in skills is cumulative, and workers with higher levels of education continue to benefit through on-the-job training opportunities throughout their working life. Although more children than ever access basic education, one in four primary school students never graduates, and progression to secondary school remains low. Formal technical and vocational education and training (TVET) is very limited, but private institutions absorb some of the excess demand for training. Traditional apprenticeships remain the most important form of skills development for the informal sector but are not associated with higher earnings.

Introduction

Nigeria has experienced economic gains over the past decade.[1] Between 2003 and 2009, growth in gross domestic product (GDP) exceeded 7 percent per year on average. Although Nigeria possesses vast amounts of oil wealth, growth has been broad based, with growth in the nonoil sector, especially agriculture, manufacturing, and telecommunications, exceeding growth in the oil-mining sector (Treichel 2010).

The benefits of growth, however, have not been equally shared. In spite of Nigeria's solid economic performance and the strong growth in nonoil sectors, poverty rates have not fallen and almost two-thirds of the population lives on less than 1.25 international dollars per day (table 7.1). Subsistence farming continues to be the main source of meeting basic needs for the population and has even

Table 7.1 Key Indicators, Nigeria

Indicator	*Percentage*
Growth 2003–09	
Average GDP	6.7
Average GDP per capita	3.7
Annual working-age population	2.6
Employment-to-population ratio	52
Farm, share of employment	63
Farm, share of GDP	33
Rural poverty headcount index	64
Urban poverty headcount index	43
Income, share held by lowest 20 percent	5

Source: World Bank 2010.
Note: Data are for 2006 or latest available, unless otherwise indicated. GDP = gross domestic product.

increased its share of employment since the 1990s. In turn, wage employment has declined, because new industries have not replaced the jobs lost in the retrenchment of the civil service and state-owned enterprises. Fast-growing sectors include many informal workers (Treichel 2010). With an estimated 50 million youth unemployed, raising both the quality and quantity of employment remains a critical challenge.

Raising productivity in the informal sector would help reduce poverty. Most of the nonfarm workforce is employed in the informal sector, here defined as nonwage workers and wage workers without formal employment arrangements such as benefits. By 2004, the informal nonfarm sector accounted for some 21 percent of total employment, almost three times as much as the formal sector. In light of the significant and growing role of informal sector employment as an option, particularly for youth, and the pervasive poverty that is linked to insufficient earning opportunities, finding ways and means of increasing the productivity and earnings of those in the informal sector in Nigeria is important.

The chapter examines different measures of the informal sector in Nigeria and the profile of people working in the sector. It contrasts the profile with those working in the formal sector and compares the level of skills and their payoff in terms of earnings in the two sectors. It subsequently provides an overview of the institutional landscape for skills development in Nigeria, including formal and nonformal routes. The chapter includes a discussion of policy options to increase the productivity of informal sector workers.

Skills, Employment, and Earnings

How do different forms and levels of education and training correlate with entry into formal and informal sectors of employment, and what are the payoffs to skills in the two sectors in terms of earnings? Answering these questions starts with defining informal sector employment and understanding the characteristics of those working informally. This section looks at different definitions of

Box 7.1 Definitions Applied

Earnings: Respondents were asked if they received remuneration for their primary activity and then how much in various time units, which are standardized to monthly amounts. Unpaid workers or those with zero or negative income are excluded, as well as observations with blatantly inconsistent earnings or income answers between the two measures. To deal with outliers, measures are censored at the top and bottom 5 percent of values.

Occupational status: Respondents were asked whom they work for during their primary activity (private or public employer, self, and so on). Results from another question on self-reported employment status are not used because farm workers are not easily separated out. However, answers to these questions were compared and observations dropped where there were inconsistencies. Because only a small number of observations exist for secondary or subsequent activities, the analysis is limited to the primary activity.

Schooling: Respondents were asked the highest level of schooling completed as well as the highest certification attained. Information on other types of skills—apprenticeships, short-term courses, literacy courses, on-the-job training—is also available, as well as literacy and numeracy capacities. Education years are assigned in line with the 6-3-3-4 education system in place in Nigeria (see table 7A.1 of the annex to this chapter).

the informal sector in Nigeria and the impact the choice of definition has on the size of the sector.

The study is based on household survey data. The study looks at the population 15–65 years of age, using the National Living Standard Survey (NLSS) 2003 (NBSN 2004).[2] The variables of greatest interest are occupational status, earnings, and skills formation (here these comprise formal education, apprenticeships, on-the-job training, literacy and numeracy, and other courses). The definitions of these variables depend on the survey questionnaires and data quality and are explained in box 7.1.

Measuring the Informal Sector in Nigeria

Farming remains the main employer in Nigeria. Table 7.2 provides a breakdown of employment by occupational status (primary activity). As shown, almost two-thirds (63 percent) of the labor force engages in farming. More than half of those employed in the nonfarm sector work for themselves (that is, they are self-employed), and unpaid family workers make up a relatively small share. The sample proportion of self-employed (61 percent) is slightly higher for women than for men (52 percent), while the ratio of self-employed persons to paid employees is almost three times higher for women.

The measurement of informal sector employment depends on the questions asked in household surveys. Surveys in other chapters of this book provide the researcher with different options for measuring the informal sector. Some relate to the conditions of work (social security, formal contracts, and so on) and others to the level of incorporation of the hiring enterprise (registered with authorities,

Table 7.2 Employment in Nigeria, by Occupational Status
Percent

	All including farm[a]			*Nonfarm only*[b]		
Employment sector	*Male*	*Female*	*Total*	*Male*	*Female*	*Total*
Family farm	64	61	63	n.a.	n.a.	n.a.
Public	7	4	6	32	14	23
Private	3	2	2	11	5	8
Self-employed	13	16	14	52	61	56
Unpaid family	1	5	3	6	21	13
Other	11	12	11	n.a.	n.a.	n.a.
Self-employed ratio[c]	1.21	3.17	1.77	1.22	3.23	1.8

Source: Elaborations based on NBSN 2004.
Note: n.a. = not applicable.
a. "All including farm" refers to all respondents with a primary employment activity.
b. "Nonfarm only" excludes "Family farm" and the "Other" categories.
c. "Self-employed ratio" is ratio of "Self-employed" to "Public" and "Private" wage employees.

paying taxes, providing social security, and the like), size, or type of job. In the case of Nigeria's household survey, information is available on occupational status, job benefits, and size of firms. These are explored below.

Combining the preceding information with information on firm size and job benefits, four different definitions for the informal sector are considered, from narrowest to broadest:

- Self-employed or does unpaid family work (narrow definition, or nonwage workers).
- Self-employed or does unpaid family work, or works for a cooperative.
- Self-employed or does unpaid family work, or works for a cooperative, or is employed by a private firm with fewer than 10 employees and receives no benefits.[3]
- Informal if self-employed or does unpaid family work, or works for a cooperative, or is employed by a private firm with fewer than 10 employees (broad definition).

The differences between the narrowest and broadest definitions are small because of the dominance of nonwage workers. Both definitions are examined. The first definition simply considers all nonwage workers as informal and all wage workers as formal, whereas the broader definitions allow some wage employees in smaller firms to be informal. The share of wage employees in informal sector firms is relatively small. Table 7.3 shows that the differences between the narrowest and broadest definitions are only about 5 percent of the nonfarm workforce. In what follows, both definitions are reported.

Comparing the Formal and Informal Sectors

The formal and informal sector workers differ in many characteristics—in where they live, in their gender, and in the level and type of skills formation to which they have had access. The informal workers have fewer years of schooling and

Table 7.3 Distribution of Employment (Primary Activity) in Nigeria, by Sector with Different Definitions

Employment sector	*Narrowest definition*[a]	*Broadest definition*[b]
Farm (%)	71	71
Formal (%)	9	8
Informal (%)	20	21
Informal share of nonfarm work (%)	68	73
Total workers (thousands)	28,381	28,381

Source: Elaborations based on NBSN 2004.
a. Narrowest measure of informality refers to nonwage workers.
b. Broadest measure includes wage earners at cooperatives and small firms.

Table 7.4 Gender, Sector, and Age in Nigeria, by Formality

	Narrow		*Broad*	
Characteristic	*Wage*	*Nonwage*	*Formal*	*Informal*
Proportion of females (%)	30	54	30	53
Proportion of urban residents (%)	74	68	74	68
Mean age (years)	40.8	39.6	41.4	39.4

Source: Elaborations based on NBSN 2004.
Note: Population-weighted proportions.

have acquired fewer diplomas. Instead, they have had recourse to apprenticeships as a means of increasing their vocational skills. And importantly, they differ in their earnings.

Demographics

Females and rural residents are more likely than men and urban residents to be in the informal sector. Table 7.4 shows some key demographic data by sector: location, gender, and age. As shown, more than half of informal sector workers are females, compared with less than a third of formal sector workers, while the proportion of urban dwellers is slightly smaller in the informal sector than the formal sector. The age difference, nonetheless, is relatively small.

Skills and Access to Different Occupations

Skills levels differ significantly between formal and informal sectors. Different skills can affect earning opportunities through different channels. Skills acquired can influence the type of jobs and sectors workers may have access to and can directly influence the earnings capabilities within each sector.

Informal sector workers have some basic literacy and numeracy skills, though less so than formal workers. Nine of 10 formal workers read, write, or perform calculations. The majority of informal sector workers also have basic capacities; about 2 in 5 informal workers do not have these basic skills. Only a small minority (between 2 percent and 4 percent) of workers have actually attended a literacy course (table 7.5).

Table 7.5 Basic Skills across Sectors in Nigeria, by Gender
Percent

	Narrow		Broad	
Skill	*Wage*	*Nonwage*	*Wage*	*Nonwage*
Read	91	61	92	62
Write	89	57	91	58
Perform calculations	89	62	90	63
Attended literacy course	3	2	4	2

Source: Elaborations based on NBSN 2004.
Note: "Read" and "Write" refer to English.

Figure 7.1 Education across Formal and Informal Sectors in Nigeria

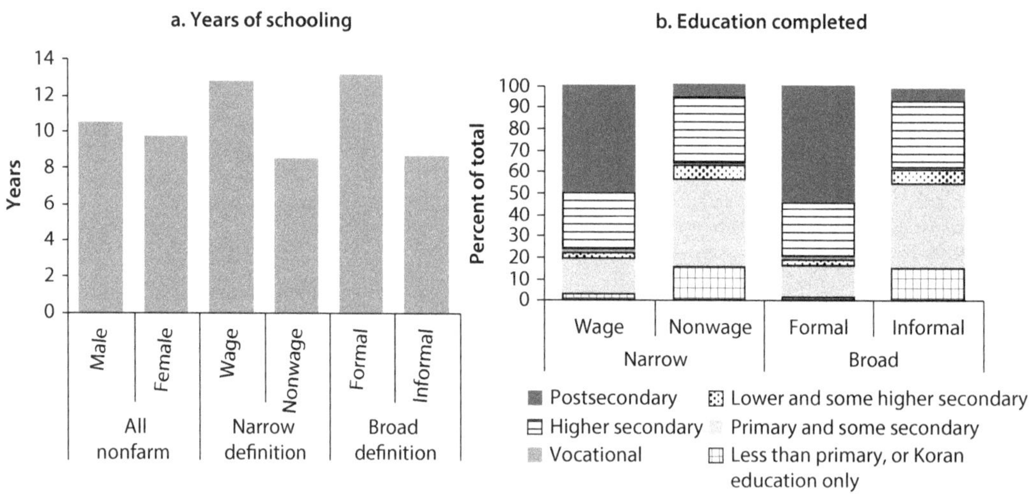

Source: Elaborations based on NBSN 2004.

Workers in the informal sector have less formal schooling than workers in the formal sector. Informal sector workers nonetheless have schooling levels above the total population mean of approximately eight years, because the mean includes farm workers who have less education. Formal sector workers (using the broad definition) have 13 years of education, compared with less than 9 years for the informal sector—a gap of 4.5 years. The gap between the formal and informal sectors is much more significant than, for example, that between males and females (figure 7.1, panel a). Three of five informal workers have not completed higher-secondary education, compared with one of five formal sector workers (figure 7.1, panel b). The main difference between formal and informal workers occurs at higher-secondary and postsecondary levels, because over 50 percent of formal sector workers completed postsecondary education, compared with only 6 percent of informal sector workers. Conversely, 15 percent of informal workers have not completed primary-level education, compared with 2 percent of formal workers. The proportion that completed vocational training is insignificant but the same across sectors (1 percent). In short, access to higher levels of secondary education and beyond is an important correlate of formal sector work.

The sources of skills vary between informal and formal sector workers. Enterprise-provided training (on-the-job training, or OJT) generally is rare in Nigeria, and the few opportunities that exist are mostly available in the formal sector, where some 7 percent of workers have had access to OJT, compared with less than 1 percent of informal sector workers. Informal workers instead are more likely to have received skills through apprenticeships. One in 5 informal sector workers did an apprenticeship, compared with 1 in 15 formal sector workers (table 7.6). Male workers were more likely than female workers to have undertaken apprenticeships. These apprenticeships lasted on average for more than half a year.

In the informal sector, people who can read, write, and calculate—or any of the three—are more likely to have been apprentices than those without these basic skills (table 7.7). Having some basic skills is thus important to an

Table 7.6 Apprenticeships by Gender and Informality in Nigeria

	All		*Narrow*		*Broad*	
Apprenticeship	*Male*	*Female*	*Wage*	*Nonwage*	*Formal*	*Informal*
Did apprenticeship (%)	21	12	8	21	6	21
Duration (weeks)	34.7	29.5	31.9	33.2	30.4	33.3

Source: Elaborations based on NBSN 2004.
Note: Weighted. Duration in weeks, conditional on undertaking an apprenticeship.

Table 7.7 Apprenticeship and OJT in Nigeria, by Informality and Other Possible Covariates
Percent

	Have been through apprenticeships		*Have had OJT*	
Variable	*Formal*	*Informal*	*Formal*	*Informal*
Male	6	27	8	1
Female	2	11	3	0
Urban	6	24	7	2
Rural	4	13	6	0
Education ≥ 10 years	4	24	7	5
Education < 10 years	11	27	2	0
Received OJT	6	5	n.a.	n.a.
No OJT	5	5	n.a.	n.a.
Can read	5	27	7	1
Cannot read	4	8	4	0
Can calculate	5	27	7	1
Cannot calculate	5	8	4	0
Can write	5	26	7	1
Cannot write	5	11	4	0

Source: Elaborations based on NBSN 2004.
Note: n.a. = not applicable; OJT = on-the-job training.

apprenticeship, but higher levels of skills may not be as important. In contrast, these higher-level skills, measured by education, do seem to be important to employment in the formal sector and to further opportunities for OJT offered by employers. Men and people living in urban areas are more likely to have been apprentices than women and people living in rural areas (table 7.7).

Formal education is an important market signal guiding employer investments in training on the job. Employers in table 7.7 prefer investing in workers through OJT if the workers have already demonstrated high levels of schooling or ability. This pattern is largely a formal sector phenomenon. The descriptive statistics are supported later in this chapter by probit analysis on the probability of being an apprentice or receiving OJT.[4]

Multivariate analysis also reveals that skills play an important role in accessing sectors with different earnings potentials. Probit equations (tables 7A.3–7A.6) indicate a positive relationship between years of education and the probability of entering the formal sector (wage work) and a negative relationship between years of education and entering the informal sector (nonwage work). As seen in figure 7.2, the predicted participation in farming falls with years of education levels while predicted participation in the formal sector rises at an increasing rate with education. For the informal sector, the predicted probability is relatively flat but falls beyond 12 years (postsecondary education).

Entry to the formal sector increases with education, and vocational training also appears to be a strong predictor. Table 7.8 presents marginal effects, each of which indicates the impact on the probability of selecting or being given access to the formal (or informal) sector after moving from no education to that

Figure 7.2 Probabilities of Being in a Sector in Nigeria, Given Years of Schooling

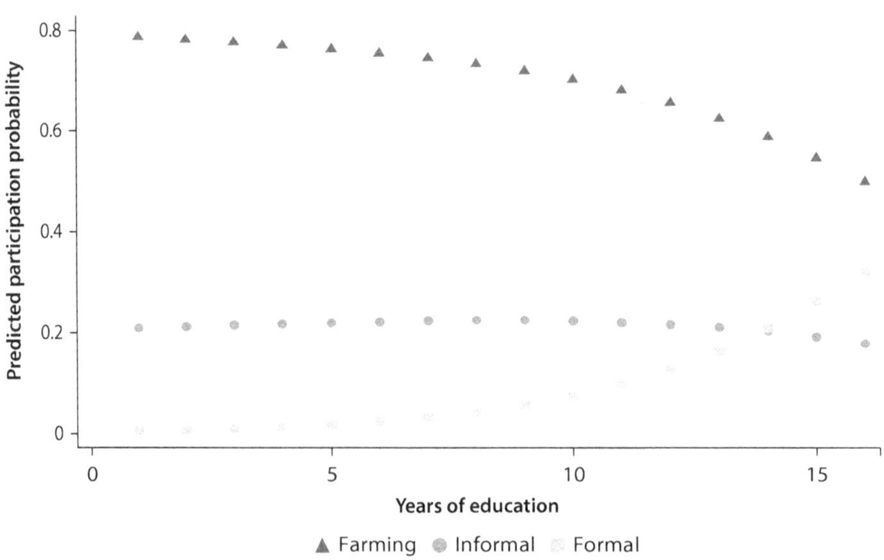

Source: Elaborations based on NBSN 2004. Predicted probabilities generated from multinomial logit.

Table 7.8 Selection into Sectors in Nigeria: Marginal Effects

	Nonwage		*Wage*	
Education level	*Effect*	*p-value*	*Effect*	*p-value*
Years of education	−0.014	0	0.036	0
Primary	−0.060	0.019	0.122	0
Lower secondary	−0.076	0.101	0.278	0
Vocational	−0.097	0.059	0.346	0.002
Higher secondary	−0.112	0.002	0.332	0
Postsecondary	−0.339	0	0.705	0
Apprentice	0.322	0	−0.075	0
Short course	−0.163	0.036	0.265	0.001
Literacy course	−0.088	0.059	−0.007	0.788

Source: Elaborations based on NBSN 2004, using narrow definition.
Note: Marginal effects from multinomial logit for selection into the formal or informal sectors. Evaluated for a discrete jump from no education and at means of all other variables.

particular level of attainment. Whether focusing on years of education or discrete measures, the evidence suggests that for the formal sector, the impact on participation becomes progressively larger. Note that the marginal effect of vocational training on formal sector entry is higher than that for higher-secondary attainment and is much higher than lower secondary despite being only one additional year. This finding tentatively suggests vocational training is a relatively fast way to enter the formal sector for a person with nine years of schooling, but the results are sensitive to the fact that there are relatively few observations of people having vocational training.[5]

Apprenticeships are an important source of skills for the informal sector, increasing the predicted probability of informal sector participation by more than 30 percentage points. This is consistent with apprenticeships being mostly a form of skills development taking place in the informal sector and serving primarily to access informal sector work. Conditional on being in the informal sector, an apprenticeship does not affect earnings significantly. Short courses, in contrast, are associated with formal sector participation. The effect of education on the probability of being in the formal or informal sectors corresponds to the slopes of the lines in figure 7.2 evaluated at just over eight years of education.

Skills and Earnings

Average earnings are higher in the formal sector than the informal sector, but informal sector earnings are higher than those of farming. Mean earnings in the formal sector exceed mean earnings in the informal sector by between 40 and 60 percent, depending on method of calculation and indicator used (table 7.9). Although the focus here is on comparing the nonfarm formal and informal sectors, it is important to note that informal sector workers typically make more income than those in farming.[6] Hence, off-farm income offers a potential for poverty reduction.

Table 7.9 Earnings by Sector in Nigeria
U.S. dollars

	Narrow		*Broad*	
Measure	*Wage*	*Nonwage*	*Formal*	*Informal*
Weighted mean	121	74	127	74
Unweighted mean	117	71	121	71
Median	100	48	108	50

Source: Elaborations based on NBSN 2004.
Note: Primary earnings censored at fifth percentiles of the distribution.

Figure 7.3 Distribution of Wages in Formal Sector Compared with Informal Sector in Nigeria

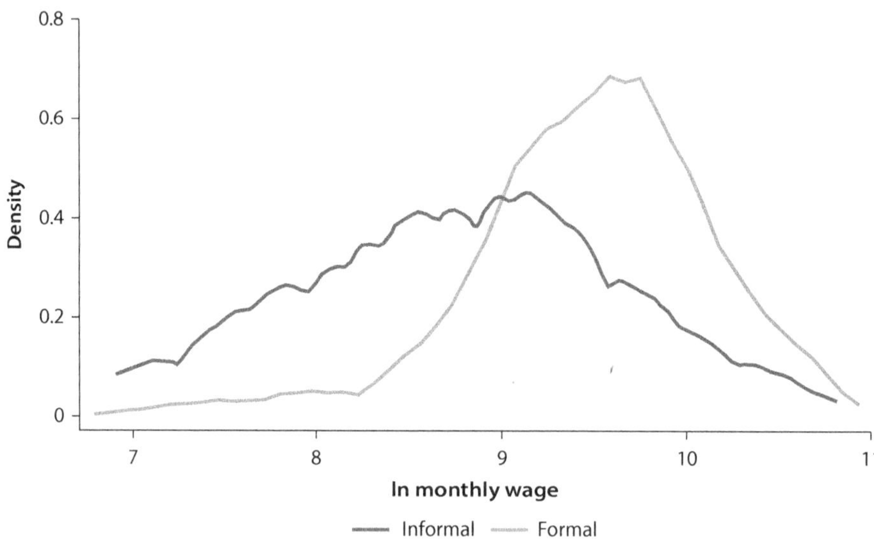

Source: Elaborations based on NBSN 2004.
Note: Distribution of log monthly wage (in naira) by sector. Primary earnings censored at 5 percent.

The dispersion of earnings in the informal and formal sectors, however, leads some in the informal sector to earn as much or more than those in the formal sector. Figure 7.3 compares the distribution of (log) wages in the formal and informal sectors. Although the distribution of informal earnings is to the left of that of formal earnings, a significant section overlaps, where informal workers are earning more than formal sector workers. As discussed in Adams and others (2009) and Falco and others (2009), this result supports the view that the informal sector is diverse and multitier and is not necessarily inferior to the formal sector.[7]

The formal sector earnings premium is largely owing to earning differences at higher levels of education. For example, using primary income measures, the earnings of men are in fact higher in the informal than in the formal sector, up to the lower-secondary level (figure 7.4). The overall male premium is caused in large part by a composition effect, because many people with a postsecondary education are in the formal sector and many people in the informal sector are at

Figure 7.4 Earnings and Returns to Education in Nigeria

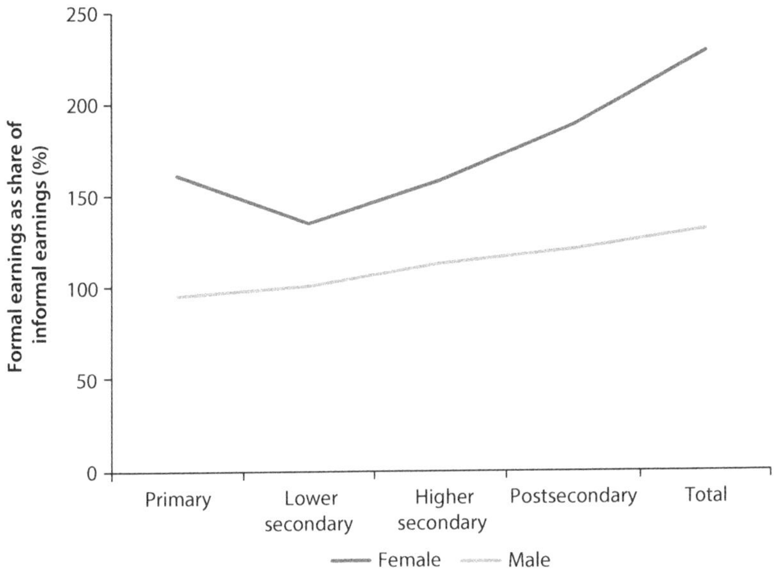

Source: Elaborations based on NBSN 2004.
Note: Primary earnings censored at 5 percent.

lower levels (e.g., completed primary). It follows that for the formal sector, earnings increase more for each level of education achieved than is the case for the informal sector. For women, formal sector earnings are higher than informal sector earnings at all education levels. (However, because low-educated women are virtually absent in the formal sector, the comparisons are not reliable at the lower levels of education.)

Men earn more than women, controlling for other characteristics, and gender gaps are more significant in the informal sector. The analysis suggests that men have higher earnings, controlling for other factors, and the male premium is higher for the informal sector than for the formal sector (tables 7A.3–7A.6). A possible explanation is that differences in hours worked are not accounted for here or in the types of activity engaged in. Although activities in urban locations render a premium over rural activities, no systematic evidence indicates larger differences in formal and informal sectors. These results hold across different specifications and measures of informality and education.

Formal sector wage workers enjoy an earnings premium over workers in the informal sector that is not related to their observable characteristics. This premium could be the result of some form of segmentation (for example, formal sector earnings may be driven by public sector wage policies, which may not be competitively determined). However, a number of alternative interpretations are available. For instance, the formal premium could in reality be the result of a firm-size premium, which is a robust empirical finding explained in part by the superior productivity big firms may have (Oi and Idson 1999).

Acquiring more education does not pay off in the informal sector as well as it does in the formal sector. Such low returns (ranging from negative to about 8 percent, depending on estimates) are not unique to Nigeria or this study. Recent Mincerian regressions for seven African countries (not distinguishing between formal and informal) result in an average of 7 percent (Behar 2009); the average marginal return for the informal sector from eight West African cities (Kuepie, Nordam, and Roubaud 2006) is calculated to be 5 percent. A pairwise estimate of returns to different levels of education in the informal and formal estimates shows that the payoff to education is always lower for the informal sector—and in many cases less than half.

The finding that returns to education are low in the informal sector is subject to a number of possible interpretations. First, it could mean the curricula of schools are not well suited to that form of activity. Second, it could reflect rationing into the formal sector. Individuals who acquire education but nonetheless fail to secure formal sector work end up in the informal sector, where their education is not needed and hence not remunerated. Whether this rationing is random or occurs because informal sector workers also go to bad schools, are less capable, or otherwise are disfavored for learning, is not clear. Third, it may reflect an inherently convex wage earnings profile in which informal sector workers tend to have low returns because they have low levels of education, and formal sector workers have high returns because they manage to get to the stage where returns are high. Fourth, it could reflect a less severe penalty to low education levels. Fifth, higher returns could reflect the use of education as signaling, which is likely to be more important in the formal sector, where wage employment is the main form of work and firing costs are high, so that observing the capacity of workers before hiring them (using the level of education as a proxy) is important. Vocational training may provide similar signals to employers.

The difference between the formal and informal sectors means earnings are driven by different returns at higher levels of education—above lower-secondary education—whereas differences are small or insignificant at lower levels.[8] Returns increase faster at higher levels and in particular kick in at postsecondary education levels. Much of the higher return to education in the formal sector is driven by the significantly higher effect of postsecondary education in the formal rather than informal sector. For primary wage earnings, the formal sector return is higher at most education levels but much higher for postsecondary education. Vocational training has no effect in either sector on primary earnings.

Apprenticeships appear to affect earnings weakly, with no robust statistical evidence. Nor do other alternative forms of skills development, such as literacy courses, short courses, and OJT, show evidence of measurably increasing earnings. The main effect of an apprenticeship thus appears to be its association with entry into an informal sector job, as discussed previously.

The results of the study are robust. Overall, the differences across the informal and formal sectors hold without respect to the definition of the informal sector used. Much of the higher formal return observed for the (linear) years of education is driven by postsecondary attainment because returns are more convex in the formal sector than in the informal sector. Apprenticeship is associated with working in informal activities relative to farming. Only workers in the formal sector have vocational training and short-term training.

Acquiring Skills for the Job Market in Nigeria

Private sector agents complain of lack of practical hands-on experience, information and communication technology knowledge, and communications skills. The question is how Nigeria can strengthen training opportunities (in the broad sense) to improve productivity and earnings in both the informal and formal sectors. The opportunities for skills development take several routes: (a) primary to postsecondary levels of education in the formal general education system; (b) accredited and formally recognized education and training in the formal technical and vocational stream; (c) nonformal, short-term vocational training; and (d) apprenticeships. As seen, employment in the formal and informal sectors reflects differences in the routes taken to skills development.

Education

Although access to basic education has increased, many children and youth enter the labor market with no or very little education. Nigeria's education system is based on a 6-3-3 system (primary, lower secondary, higher secondary), with four to six years of postgraduate studies. In the lower levels, school enrollment has improved significantly in recent years. Gross enrollment rates for primary and lower-secondary education increased by 10 and 12 percentage points, respectively, between 1999 and 2006. Nonetheless, more than 7 million children of primary school age remain out of school; one in four primary school students never graduates; and progression to secondary remains low, as evidenced by enrollment rates of 38 percent and 29 percent, respectively, for lower- and higher-secondary levels (table 7.10).

Table 7.10 Education Statistics, Nigeria

Indicator	*1999*	*2006 or latest available*
Primary gross enrollment rate (%)	91	101
Primary completion ratio (%)	—	86
Out-of-school children, primary (thousands)	7.6	7.3
Lower-secondary gross enrollment rate (%)	26	38
Higher-secondary gross enrollment rate (%)	22	29
Vocational and technical as a percentage of secondary enrollment	—	4
Tertiary gross enrollment rate (%)	6	10

Source: World Bank 2010.
Note: — = not available.

Table 7.11 Enrollment in Vocational Education Compared to General Postbasic Education in Nigeria
Thousands

Education type	*Enrollment*
General higher-secondary education	2,773
Technical colleges	73
Universities	725
Polytechnics	139
Monotechnics	21

Source: Billetoft 2010.
Note: Data are for 2004/05.

Formal Sources of Skills Development

Vocational formal training is very limited. In fact, the total enrollment in technical colleges is a mere fraction of that of general secondary-level education (table 7.11). Similarly, at the postsecondary level, a strong preference for academic rather than technical training is evident. The enrollment in polytechnics or monotechnics is less than one-quarter of university enrollment—even though very few make it to the university level in the first place. In total, very few young people enter the labor market with technical or vocational training acquired in the formal system.

TVET falls under the auspices of the National Board for Technical Education (NBTE). The role of the NBTE is to provide standardized minimum guide curricula and to supervise, regulate, and accredit institutions, including secondary and tertiary levels. It also has the responsibility of providing advice on the use of the Industrial Training Fund.

At both secondary and tertiary levels, TVET institutions are detached from labor market needs. Secondary-level technical colleges produce craftspersons and master craftspersons. The focus tends to be on traditional mechanical or technical vocations, such as electricians, vehicle mechanics, and masonry; women make up only 20 percent of students. These colleges are intended to equip students with job-specific skills (technical, agricultural, commercial, and economic) and, in parallel, assist them in building skills necessary for successful self-employment and independence—midlevel technical skills that are in short supply in Nigeria as in many other developing countries. However, the colleges remain largely supply driven, have a dated approach to content and teaching, and suffer from poor equipment and facilities. Tertiary-level polytechnics produce technicians, professionals, and engineers. The focus is primarily on nontechnical vocations. In particular, business-oriented vocational training dominates the overall picture with accounting, business studies, marketing, and banking and finance accounting for nearly half of all graduates (2004 data). The polytechnics appear to have lower status and fewer resources available for quality improvement than universities do, with ensuing problems of lower-quality staff and management. As in the technical colleges, the approach and content of the training offered are detached from labor market needs, and no partnering is done with the private sector to improve this situation.

Private institutions are meeting some of the excess demand for skills development. New types of institutions—vocational enterprise institutions and innovative enterprise institutions—have been established in Nigeria since 2007. They are private institutions allowed to offer TVET in the area of technical manpower. The focus is very much on technology and practical training, targeted to school leavers, persons who want to upgrade their skills, university graduates seeking employable skills, and second-chance education seekers. Demand has so far exceeded expectations, suggesting a significant need for and interest in skills development that remain unmet by the formal public system.

Overall, the education system and the demand from students show strong preferences for nontechnical vocations and for tertiary-level professions over secondary. This may well reflect the high earnings premium for postsecondary education (discussed previously).

However, a significant skills mismatch appears to exist in the labor market. Unemployment is high among university graduates, while simultaneously the Nigerian economy suffers from a lack of skilled craftspersons in various professions. Different technical and broad workplace skills are also in deficit. A recent study of the demand for vocational and technical skills that asked employers and stakeholders about their perceptions of graduates' skills showed deficiencies of technical skills in areas such as mechanics, electrical installation, and other areas where many programs in fact are offered and demonstrated a lack of more general competencies such as analytical, information and communication technology, or important workplace skills (table 7.12).

Nonformal and Traditional Sources of Skills Development

The mainstream education system is complemented by nonformal private training and traditional apprenticeships. Both of these streams are likely, by far, to exceed formal TVET in volume, with apprenticeships proving relevant to the informal sector.

Nonformal training systems are flexible but remain largely unregulated and of unknown quality. Although a flexible training system may be advantageous, the lack of standards in certification reduces the efficiency of training in terms of signaling of acquired competences, and the lack of direct connection to labor market needs further reduces the effectiveness of training in alleviating constraints in both job and product markets.

For a majority of nonfarm workers, training outside the formal system, especially traditional apprenticeships, is the main form of training available. A Nigerian study (NISER 2007) found that more than half the operators interviewed had acquired their skills through apprenticeships in one form or another. Of some importance, not only uneducated youth but also some of those who completed secondary education and beyond had attended some form of informal learning before setting up a business. The study also suggested that lack of basic skills (literacy) and lack of equipment tended to hamper skills development in the informal sector.

Nonformal training caters to a diverse range of students. The nonformal training modes usually result in some form of certificate of attendance but do not

Table 7.12 Priority Areas for Skills Development in Nigeria

Growth areas	*Broad occupations in demand*	*Specific occupations*	*Generic skills*
Farm	Livestock rearing	Poultry farming	Communications
	Crop rotation	Dairy farming	Supervisory
	Animal husbandry	Aquaculture	Numeracy
Manufacturing	Food processing	Food preparation	Work related
	Light manufacturing	Metal fabrication	Literacy
		Carpentry	Information and communication technology
		Furniture maker	
		Structural timber	
		Boat maker	Entrepreneurship
Services	Wholesale and retail	Garment/tailoring	
	Information and communication technology	Computer programming	
		Auto mechanics	
	Vehicle repair	Hairdressing	
		Motor vehicle mechanic	
Hotel and restaurant	Catering	Cooks	
	Hotel management	Supervisors	
	Tourism	Pottery making	
Construction	Masonry	Electrician	
	Carpenters	Electrical installation	
		Brickmaking	
		Scaffolding	
		Arc welder	
		Bricklayer	
		Carpenter	

Source: Billetoft 2010.

provide a recognized qualification. These types of training are generally short term (less than a year), provided by different entities, and directed at many different audiences and at different stages in life. They include unschooled youth and dropouts as well as older workers wishing to complement an existing qualification. Training is provided by ministries and regional authorities as well as by nongovernmental organizations and private for-profit institutions. The evidence suggests that demand outstrips supply of places in the public programs, explaining why a relatively vibrant parallel private market exists.

Overall, public initiatives (training programs, trade certification, formal apprenticeship systems) face problems of limited access and excess demand, uneven quality, lack of connection to labor markets, and lack of monitoring and evaluation of program impact and outcomes:

- *Public training programs specifically intended to combat mass unemployment face significant quality problems.* These programs are governed by the National Directorate of Employment and target unemployed new entrants to the labor market and other persons who lack productive and marketable skills. The main programs are the Open Apprenticeship Scheme, the School-on-Wheels program, and the Entrepreneurial Development Programs. These programs are limited by a large volume of applicants, a lack of resources to meet this demand, and serious quality problems related to lack of monitoring and evaluation of skills at completion as well as labor market outcomes for graduates over the long run. In addition to the National Directorate of Employment, the Ministry of Youth provides short-term skills training for unemployed youth, focusing on farming and agrifood sectors. Private initiatives at different levels complement these public initiatives, often in some form of public-private partnership or with support of international partners.

- *The trades testing system effectively excludes those with lower skills.* The government also provides trades testing, the official system for assessing and classifying artisans and craftspersons in different skills. Only past apprentices or those with vocational training qualify to take the test even at the lowest level. The capacity of the testing system is strained by lack of testing of practical skills, lack of skilled testers, and infrequent updating (every five years) of the curriculum used, making the system unlikely to pick up new and changing skills.

- *The Open Apprenticeship Scheme is hampered by lack of skilled trainers and lack of relevance.* The scheme provides vocational skills acquisition for out-of-school unemployed youth and dropouts in approximately 80 trades. The entrants work with master craftspersons for between 3 and 24 months, depending on the trade, and are provided with a certificate of attendance at the end. The annual intake is significant, about 37,000 per year. The National Directorate of Employment authorizes only a limited number of craftspersons, resulting in a very high apprentice-master ratio. Another constraint is that the scheme is not adjusted to labor market needs: the course content is not linked to economic, technological, or labor market developments; there is no quality monitoring or evaluation; and the trainers often lack up-to-date technical and pedagogical skills.

Traditional apprenticeships remain the most important form of skills development. These have both important strengths and weaknesses. Although no official numbers on traditional apprenticeships exist, the household survey analysis presented previously (see table 7.7) shows that apprenticeships provide the most significant form of training to informal sector workers and are likely to exceed other forms of vocational training by a large margin, including the Open Apprenticeship Scheme. Apprenticeships, as a self-financed system, generally display high flexibility, combine work with learning, are accessible for youth with very little or no prior training, and are connected to labor markets in ways that formal training forms rarely manage to be. Yet their efficiency is generally hampered by the limited knowledge of master craftspersons, who generally lack the ability to continuously upgrade knowledge. In addition, the lack of standardized certification is problematic. When the master craftsperson considers the apprentice qualified, he or she is released, usually with a certificate of qualification, but this does not comply with any official standards that could be recognized nationally.

In all, the institutional framework for skills development suffers from several problems. First, the population's overall education levels remain very low and provide a weak base to build upon. Second, TVET, whether through formal or nonformal means, is provided in a fragmented system with no coherent overall approach to monitoring, certification, or accreditation that is pervaded by quality problems. Third, because of this fragmentation, few links exist between labor market developments and manpower needs, on the one hand, and training on the other. The lack of strategy for lifelong learning and opportunities to increase skills development for educated youth, older workers, the unschooled, and dropouts, means that no coherent approach exists for addressing skills and job gaps in the labor market.

Basic competencies appear important to provide access to the informal sector compared to farming, and as such to higher earnings options. Although much has been achieved in terms of increasing access to primary education, further work is needed to help the population ensure a certain level of literacy and numeracy through higher-quality basic education. At the same time, the private sector provides a significant amount of the available training, with a wider reach and higher accessibility to a diverse clientele, although it varies extremely in quality. Improving the outcomes of private sector training, for example by providing a transparent, uniform system of certification and trades testing, would be a means of increasing and standardizing the value of traditional apprenticeships.

Conclusions

Most adults in Nigeria work in the farm sector with most of the remaining 30 percent working in the nonfarm informal sector. They work for themselves and their families or, to a smaller extent, are employed in small informal firms.

The informal sector offers better earning opportunities than the farm sector, but earnings lag behind those in the formal sector. Mean earnings are significantly higher in the formal sector than in the informal sector. The formal sector premium occurs throughout the earnings distribution though some overlap occurs, indicating that some workers in the informal sector can earn more than those in the formal sector.

Different forms of skills provide entry to different sectors. Apprenticeships are an important form of entry into informal sector activity, and basic skills like reading, writing, and counting improve access to apprenticeships. Higher levels of education and vocational training increase the likelihood of a person being employed in the formal sector. The most important effects appear to kick in beyond primary levels of education. However, an education "overlap" exists because a substantial number of workers in the informal sector have higher-secondary education levels or above.

The economic gains from education and skills development are higher in the formal than in the informal sector, though the magnitude and degree of statistical significance of the results depend on the specifications and variables used. Returns to education appear to be convex, in both the informal and formal sectors; much of the difference in returns between formal and informal sectors occurs at post-secondary attainment. There are no clear returns to apprenticeships, however. It is conceivable that the major role of apprenticeship is to create the basis for establishing oneself as an independent worker, rather than remain in the farm sector.

Although access to basic education has increased, many youths enter the labor market with little education, and TVET and labor market–oriented training are limited. Most children do not complete basic education, and enrollment in formal vocational training is low at all levels. The nonformal and traditional sectors provide much more training, and to a much more diverse clientele, but are ridden with their own quality problems.

Reforms are important for skills in both the formal and informal sectors. A significant mismatch appears to exist between job opportunities (demand for skills) and the type of qualifications provided (offer of skills) in the education system, compounded by a general lack of practical training and a disregard of vocational education in favor of tertiary levels of education. Traditional apprenticeships fill an important gap but have their own limits, in terms of lack of common standards, and appear not to raise productivity per se. The informal sector is not the focus of policy. Little systematic evidence is available on the effectiveness of different small- or large-scale program initiatives for the informal sector that could be explored to inform policy.

Access to quality formal education at the lower level and a shift toward competence-based learning and relevance of skills for the job market and private sector needs are key to skills development. Basic literacy and numeracy together with workplace skills are important for successful work as a self-employed entrepreneur and are strongly associated with access to apprenticeship. But post-basic levels of education are those that pay off in terms of higher earnings. Thus, continuing to expand these options while building a stronger foundation is important.

A stronger focus on policies for the informal sector is needed to help this important and growing sector develop higher productivity and increase mobility into formal sector activities. As documented elsewhere in this book, people working in the informal sector face several constraints in terms of skills development, including lack of resources or at least cash flow to pay for training, lack of time to attend daytime courses, and needs for multiple skills. Programs that reach out to small-scale businesses need to consider these constraints.

Involving the private sector can significantly strengthen the currently weak links between demand for skills (by employers or customers of goods and services), the availability of skills in the population, and the provision of skills through private and public actors. In Nigeria, associations of micro- and small enterprises exist in several trades. These can be involved in facilitating course upgrading, overseeing apprenticeship training, issuing certificates, or taking part in trades testing for the informal sector. They can also be involved in raising awareness of the importance of skills development and of available schemes. Smaller organizations with strong local coverage may be more suitable for this type of engagement than larger associations

The government could tap into the demand for training visible in the apparently important—but largely unregulated—private supply of training. For example, more innovative ways of financing skills development, such as using voucher systems as in Kenya, could be envisaged, while the public sector could be responsible for quality control. Finally, the content and signaling effect of traditional apprenticeships could also be strengthened by standardized certifications.

Annex 7A: Tables

The annex tables provide additional information related to the analysis. Table 7A.1 relates to method while table 7A.2 presents mean earnings for different categories. Tables 7A.3–7A.5 provide the multivariate analysis that explains links between level of education, sector of employment, and earnings on the job.

Table 7A.1 Assigning Years to Levels of Education

Education completed	*Years*
None	0
Some primary or Koranic education only	3
Primary complete or some lower secondary	6
Lower secondary complete or some higher secondary	9
Vocational	10
Higher secondary complete	12
Postsecondary	16

Source: Elaborations based on NBSN 2004.
Note: Aggregate education categories (based on education completed) and years assigned. Vocational training is given a value of 10 (between lower and higher secondary). Koranic education is assigned the same value as having some primary education.

Table 7A.2 Monthly Mean Primary Earnings by Level of Education, Sector, and Gender
Nigerian naira

	Males		*Females*	
Level of education	*Informal*	*Formal*	*Informal*	*Formal*
None	12,942	17,000	4,508	n.a.
Some primary or Koranic	11,778	9,715	6,003	13,400
Primary complete	12,105	11,496	6,577	10,556
Lower secondary	11,592	11,682	6,052	8,173
Vocational	7,543	11,139	5,200	8,550
Higher secondary	12,171	13,660	6,733	10,593
Postsecondary	16,823	20,188	9,498	17,820
Total	12,454	16,399	6,664	15,165

Source: Elaborations based on NBSN 2004.
Note: n.a. = not applicable (no women in the formal sector have no education).

Table 7A.3 Earnings Functions: Wage Workers/Nonwage Workers, with Years of Education

		OLS		*Heckman*		*Multinomial logit*	
Stage	*Variable*	*Nonwage*	*Wage*	*Nonwage*	*Wage*	*Nonwage*	*Wage*
Second	Main						
	Male	0.615***	0.158***	0.594***	0.226***	0.582***	0.131*
	Urban	0.120*	0.105*	0.107*	0.207*	0.001	0.274**
	Education	0.025***	0.054***	0.008	0.099***	−0.006	0.069***
	Age	0.055***	0.069***	0.043***	0.123***	0.032*	0.097***
	Age squared	−0.001**	−0.001***	−0.000**	−0.001***	0	−0.001***
	Apprentice	−0.065	−0.076	0.016	−0.272**	0.007	−0.093
	Short course	0.526***	−0.003	0.388	0.207	0.352	0.050
	Literacy course	0.127	0.057	−0.111	0.034	−0.099	0.023
	Literate/numerate	0.023	0.095	0.084	0.162**	0.075	0.138
	Informality		−0.302***				
	Lambda			0.107	0.367		
	Selection_ag					−0.009	−0.234
	Selection_formal					−0.680	0.148
	Selection_informal					−0.089	0.520*
First	Male			−0.416***	0.301***	−0.396***	0.353***
	Urban			0.247***	0.498***	2.087***	1.778***
	Education			−0.141***	0.153***	0.026**	0.287***
	Age			−0.0401*	0.136***	0.064***	0.226***
	Age squared			0	−0.001***	−0.009***	−0.002***
	Apprentice			0.824***	−0.328***	1.524***	0.176
	Short course			−0.544**	0.750***	−0.012	1.266***
	Literacy course			−0.247	−0.052	−0.343*	−0.152
	Literate/numerate			−0.096	0.147**	0.071	0.293**
	Hh_kids			0.002	−0.023**	−0.035**	−0.060***
	Married			0.146**	−0.068	−0.058	−0.170*
	Government grants					−0.000*	−0.000*
Number of observations		1,995	1,565	4,127	13,429	12,546	12,546

Source: Elaborations based on NBSN 2004.
Note: Dependent variable is monthly wages from primary activity in Log Naira. First stage is either probit equation for participation in formal (wage) or informal (nonwage) sectors (binary) or a multinomial logit simultaneously estimated for the formal and informal sectors relative to farming; lambda indicates correlation between errors (the inverse Mills ratio) in probit and second stage while m_ terms are control terms for participation in each of the three sectors. Standard errors clustered in linear estimate, adjusted for two-stage procedure in Heckman and bootstrapped in multinomial logit; population weights are used in OLS and Heckman. OLS = ordinary least squares.
Significance level: * = 10 percent; ** = 5 percent; *** = 1 percent.

Table 7A.4 Earnings Functions: Informal/Formal Workers (Broad Definition), with Years of Education

		OLS		*Heckman two-stage*		*Multinomial logit*	
Stage	*Variable*	*Informal*	*Formal*	*Informal*	*Formal*	*Informal*	*Formal*
Second	Main						
	Male	0.607***	0.115**	0.637***	0.130**	0.6187***	0.093
	Urban	0.110*	0.122*	−0.199	0.118*	−0.0869	0.2753*
	Education	0.0250***	0.0605***	0.0379***	0.0660***	0.0054	0.0672*
	Age	0.0563***	0.0636***	0.0442**	0.0650***	0.0393*	0.0723*
	Age squared	−0.0005***	−0.0006**	−0.0004*	−0.0006**	−0.0003	−0.0007
	Apprentice	−0.0606	−0.0741	−0.271*	−0.111	−0.0897	−0.0734
	Short course	0.281	0.0202	0.425	0.0432	0.2302	0.0278
	Literacy course	0.148	0.0279	0.199	0.0365	−0.0664	−0.004
	Literate/numerate	0.0337	0.0803	−0.0188	0.092	0.0806	0.1321
	Selection_ag					0.1902	−0.0597
	Selection_formal					−0.2389	0.0863
	Selection_informal					−0.0896	0.4987
First	Male			−0.0902*	0.339***	−0.3287***	0.2994***
	Urban			0.997***	−0.127	2.097***	1.730***
	Education			−0.0568***	0.161***	0.0297***	0.313***
	Age			0.0444***	0.125***	0.0585***	0.2858***
	Age squared			−0.0006***	−0.0013***	−0.0008***	−0.0030***
	Apprentice			0.859***	−0.701***	1.487***	−0.0574
	Short course			−0.438*	0.821***	0.053	1.313***
	Literacy course			−0.270*	0.193	−0.4111**	−0.0392
	Literate/numerate			0.199***	0.179*	0.0764	0.3447***
	Hh_kids			−0.0214**	−0.0001	−0.0384***	−0.0613***
	Married			0.0489	−0.160**	−0.0837	−0.1453*
	Government grants					−0.00001**	−0.0000*
Ancillary statistics	Number of observations	2,169	1,391	12,542	5,014	12,546	12,546
	Lambda			−0.393	0.0512		

Source: Elaborations based on NBSN 2004.
Note: Dependent variable is monthly wages from primary activity in Log Naira. First stage is either probit equation for participation in formal (wage) or informal (nonwage) sectors (binary) or a multinomial logit simultaneously estimated for the formal and informal sectors relative to farming; lambda indicates correlation between errors (the inverse Mills ratio) in probit and second stage while m_ terms are control terms for participation in each of the three sectors. Standard errors clustered in linear estimate, adjusted for two-stage procedure in Heckman and bootstrapped in multinomial logit; population weights used in OLS and Heckman. OLS = ordinary least squares.
Significance level: * = 10 percent; ** = 5 percent; *** = 1 percent.

Table 7A.5 Earnings Functions: Wage Workers/Nonwage Workers, with Highest Education Attained

		OLS		*Heckman*		*Multinomial logit*	
Stage	*Variable*	*Nonwage*	*Wage*	*Nonwage*	*Wage*	*Nonwage*	*Wage*
Second	Main						
	Male	0.593***	0.160***	0.599***	0.134*	0.584***	0.201***
	Urban	0.123*	0.119*	0.094	0.068	−0.060	0.313***
	Primary	0.023	0.17	0.005	0.128	−0.028	0.195
	Lower secondary	0.022	0.302*	−0.012	0.212	−0.091	0.354*
	Vocational	−0.001	−0.022	−0.149	0.163	−0.249	0.383
	Higher secondary	0.099	0.227	0.049	0.197	−0.058	0.420**
	Postsecondary	0.504***	0.665***	0.338	0.556	0.169	1.085***
	Age	0.055***	0.057***	0.044***	0.070***	0.033**	0.095***
	Age squared	−0.001**	−0.001**	−0.000**	−0.001**	−0.000*	−0.001***
	Apprentice	−0.037	−0.071	0.004	−0.149	−0.029	−0.111
	Short course	0.483**	0.023	0.383	0.025	0.340	0.189
	Literacy course	0.057	0.012	−0.16	−0.006	−0.146	−0.04
	Literate/numerate	0.058	0.158	0.108*	0.142*	0.089	0.195***
	Informality		−0.292***				
	Lambda			0.024	−0.088		
	Selection_Ag					0.031	−0.847*
	Selection_Formal					−0.636	0.062
	Selection_Informal					−0.175	−0.238
First	Male			−0.435***	0.303***	−0.319***	0.417***
	Urban			0.235***	0.492***	2.096***	1.783***
	Primary			−0.293*	0.404***	−0.074	0.677***
	Lower secondary			−0.576***	0.661***	0.189	1.387***
	Vocational			−0.969**	1.038***	0.195	1.881***
	Higher secondary			−0.716***	0.945***	0.291**	1.853***
	Postsecondary			−1.978***	2.092***	0.005	3.713***
	Age			−0.029	0.121***	0.064***	0.213***
	Age squared			0	−0.001***	−0.001***	0.002***
	Apprentice			0.764***	−0.268***	1.530***	0.302*
	Short course			−0.470**	0.667***	0.168	1.303***
	Literacy course			−0.185	−0.107	−0.322*	−0.246
	Literate/numerate			−0.182*	0.207***	0.085	0.421***
	Hh_kids			−0.001	−0.022**	−0.032**	−0.057***
	Married			0.204***	−0.081*	−0.055	−0.233
	Government grants					−0.000*	−0.000*
Number of observations		1,893	1,525	3,965	12,286	11,558	11,558

Source: Elaborations based on NBSN 2004.

Note: Dependent variable is monthly wages from primary activity in Log Naira. First stage is either probit equation for participation in formal (wage) or informal (nonwage) sectors (binary) or a multinomial logit simultaneously estimated for the formal and informal sectors relative to farming; lambda indicates correlation between errors (the inverse Mills ratio) in probit and second stage while m_ terms are control terms for participation in each of the three sectors. Standard errors clustered in linear estimate, adjusted for two-stage procedure in Heckman and bootstrapped in multinomial logit; population weights used in OLS and Heckman. OLS = ordinary least squares.

Significance level: * = 10 percent; ** = 5 percent; *** = 1 percent.

Table 7A.6 Earnings Functions: Informal Workers/Formal Workers, with Highest Education Attained

		OLS		*Binary*		*Multinomial logit*	
Stage	*Variable*	*Informal*	*Formal*	*Informal*	*Formal*	*Informal*	*Formal*
Second	Main						
	Male	0.588***	0.115**	0.636***	0.122*	0.6167***	0.1467*
	Urban	0.114*	0.137**	−0.253	0.147*	−0.0701	0.2778**
	Primary	0.0367	0.106	0.0184	0.17	0.0212	0.227
	Lower secondary	0.0461	0.247	−0.0171	0.307	−0.0154	0.4124
	Vocational	0.0572	−0.0624	−0.0507	0.237	−0.1118	0.3908
	Higher secondary	0.107	0.211	0.0327	0.309	0.0321	0.4579
	Postsecondary	0.506***	0.643***	0.656***	0.752	0.4021	1.04*
	Age	0.0561***	0.0570***	0.0278	0.0660*	0.0417	0.0813**
	Age squared	−0.0005***	−0.0005**	−0.0002	−0.0006*	−0.0004	−0.0007**
	Apprentice1	−0.0349	−0.055	−0.282*	−0.12	−0.0788	−0.1113
	Short course1	0.269	0.0424	0.283	0.0817	0.254	0.1618
	Literacy course1	0.0855	−0.0243	−0.0537	−0.0396	−0.1214	−0.0446
	Literate/numerate	0.0709	0.133	0.0853	0.144*	0.1068*	0.175*
	Selection_Ag					0.02	−0.4047
	Selection_Formal					−0.1875	0.064
	Selection_Informal					−0.1462	−0.0784
First	Male			−0.121***	0.269***	−0.2536***	0.3573***
	Urban			0.980***	0.419***	2.104***	1.729***
	Primary			0.0299	0.460***	−0.0859	0.9841***
	Lower secondary			0.0984	0.751***	0.1945	1.72***
	Vocational			−0.147	1.239***	0.1089	2.419***
	Higher secondary			0.133*	1.049***	0.2955**	2.26***
	Postsecondary			−0.797***	2.197***	0.1128	4.174***
	Age			0.0618***	0.142***	0.0589***	0.2670***
	Age squared			−0.0008***	−0.0015***	−0.0008***	−0.0029***
	Apprentice1			0.910***	−0.388***	1.499***	0.0773
	Short course1			−0.102	0.652***	0.225	1.340***
	Literacy course1			−0.276**	−0.0378	−0.3908*	−0.1429
	Literate/numerate			0.0811	0.214***	0.0883	0.4555***
	Hh_kids			−0.0273***	−0.0185*	−0.0348***	−0.0585***
	Married			0.00074	−0.052	−0.089	−0.1936*
	Government grants					−0.00001*	−0.0000*
Ancillary statistics	Number of observations	2,058	1,360	11,530	12,367	11,558	11,558
	Lambda			−0.477	0.037		
	Rho_Ag					0.034	−0.7876
	Rho_Formal					−0.3186	0.1246
	Rho3_Informal					−0.2485*	−0.1525

Source: Elaborations based on NBSN 2004.
Note: Dependent variable is monthly wages from primary activity in Log Naira. First stage is either probit equation for participation in formal (wage) or informal (nonwage) sectors (binary) or a multinomial logit simultaneously estimated for the formal and informal sectors relative to farming; lambda indicates correlation between errors (the inverse Mills ratio) in probit and second stage while m_ terms are control terms for participation in each of the three sectors. Standard errors clustered in linear estimate, adjusted for two-stage procedure in Heckman and bootstrapped in multinomial logit; population weights used in OLS and Heckman. OLS = ordinary least squares.
Significance level: * = 10 percent; ** = 5 percent; *** = 1 percent.

Notes

1. The chapter is largely based on Behar (2010) and Billetoft (2010).
2. The NLSS is also analyzed in Haywood (2007) and Haywood and Teal (2010).
3. Access to benefits implies at least one of the following is true: worker has a formal contract; has a pension; has entitlements to paid holidays, sick leave, medical care, or other benefits, or works for a firm that is unionized.
4. Results are available on request.
5. Possible reasons are discussed in Adams and others (2009).
6. Based on the (limited number of) responses for farm income, the median amount received is about US$30, less than half of the corresponding informal earnings measures.
7. However, the analysis of the cumulative distribution functions (available on request) confirms that distribution for the informal sector is everywhere above that for the formal sector. Thus, a greater proportion of informal sector workers than formal sector workers is always earning less than a certain amount, regardless of that amount.
8. Convexity in returns, where the return is higher at higher levels of education, has been found in a number of studies; see, for example, Colclough, Kingdon, and Patrinos (2009).

References

Adams, Arvil V., Harold Coulombe, Quentin Wodon, and Setareh Razmara. 2009. "Education, Employment, and Earnings in Ghana." In *Ghana: Job Creation and Skills Development*. Vol. II: Background Papers, annex 1. Report No. 40328-GH. Washington, DC: World Bank.

Behar, Alberto. 2009. "Directed Technical Change, the Elasticity of Substitution and Wage Inequality in Developing Countries." Economic Series Working Paper 467, Department of Economics, University of Oxford, U.K.

———. 2010. "Nigeria: Skills Development in the Informal Sector." Unpublished, Africa Department, World Bank, Washington, DC.

Billetoft, Jorgen. 2010. "Labor Market Trends and Skills Development." In *Putting Nigeria to Work: A Strategy for Employment and Growth*, edited by Volker Treichel, 167–202. Directions in Development. Washington, DC: World Bank.

Colclough, Christopher, Geeta Kingdon, and Harry Anthony Patrinos. 2009. "The Pattern of Returns to Education and Its Implications." Policy Brief No. 4, RECOUP (Research Consortium on Educational Outcomes and Poverty), Cambridge, U.K.

Falco, Paolo, Andrew Kerr, Neil Rankin, Justin Sandefur, and Francis Teal. 2009. "The Returns to Formality and Informality in Urban Africa." CSAE WPS/2010-03, Centre for the Study of African Economies, Oxford University Press, Oxford, U.K.

Haywood, Luke. 2007. "The Performance of the Labor Market in Nigeria: A Report on the 2003–2004 Nigeria Living Standards Survey." Unpublished, Centre for the Study of African Economies (CSAE), Oxford University, Oxford, U.K.

Haywood, Luke, and Francis Teal. 2010. "Employment, Unemployment, Joblessness, and Incomes in Nigeria, 1999–2006." In *Putting Nigeria to Work: A Strategy for Employment and Growth*, edited by Volker Treichel, 167–202. Directions in Development. Washington, DC: World Bank.

Kuepie, Mathias, Christophe Nordam, and François Roubaud. 2006. "Education and Labor Market Outcomes in Sub-Saharan West Africa." Working Paper DT/2006/16, DIAL (Développement, Institutions et Analyses de Long terme), l'Université Paris Dauphine and l'Institut de Recherche pour le Développement (IRD), Paris.

NBSN (National Bureau of Statistics, Nigeria). 2004. *National Living Standard Survey 2003*. Federal Government of Nigeria, Abuja. http://www.nigerianstat.gov.ng/nada/index.php/catalog/28.

NISER (Nigerian Institute of Social and Economic Research). 2007. "Report of Baseline Study on Employment Generation in the Informal Sector of the Nigerian Economy." African Capacity Building Foundation/International Labour Organization Project on Strengthening the Labor Market Information and Poverty Monitoring System in Africa, Nigerian Institute of Social and Economic Research, Ibadan, Nigeria.

Oi, Walter, and Todd Idson. 1999. "Firm Size and Wages." In *Handbook of Labor Economics*. 1st ed., Vol. 3, edited by Orley Ashenfelter and David Card, chapter 33, 2105–214. Amsterdam: Elsevier.

Treichel, Volker. 2010. "Employment and Growth in Nigeria." In *Putting Nigeria to Work: A Strategy for Employment and Growth*, edited by Volker Treichel, 9–60. Directions in Development. Washington, DC: World Bank.

World Bank. 2010. *World Development Indicators 2010*. Washington, DC: World Bank.

CHAPTER 8

Skills Development in the Informal Sector: Rwanda

In This Chapter

In Rwanda, the past decade brought economic growth, poverty reduction, and an increase in employment in the nonfarm sector, most of it in the informal sector. Skills remain in short supply, however. Having some, even limited, education increases the chances of working in the informal sector rather than in farming, but secondary education or more is needed in the formal sector. Education also affects earnings earlier in the informal sector than in the formal sector. Because of the limited reach of public provision, private providers dominate training services in Rwanda's technical and vocational education and training (TVET) system, relying on tuition and other fees. Their popularity bears witness to the willingness to pay for skills acquisition. Programs addressed to informal sector skills development are not thoroughly evaluated, but available information suggests that whereas fostering informal sector skills and productivity is difficult, comprehensive and targeted programs may be more successful.

Introduction

Rwanda is a poor, densely populated, and landlocked country.[1] In 2009, the vast majority of the population of around 10 million lived in rural areas (World Bank 2011). Four of five working adults are employed in farming, most of it subsistence farming. Because of the devastating civil war that raged in the country during the 1990s, Rwanda has faced paramount challenges over the past decade: rebuilding trust, securing peace, and reversing the collapse in per capita income, the extremely high poverty levels, and the devastating effects on health, education, and output.

After this lost decade, the Rwandan economy has been growing at a steady pace with real per capita growth in gross domestic product (GDP) reaching 4.4 percent between 2000 and 2009. The main driver of the economic recovery has been the services sector, followed by industry. As a result, the services sector now accounts for nearly half of GDP (48 percent in 2006), compared with 38 percent for the farm sector (figure 8.1). In parallel to the changing composition of output, the employment structure has undergone an important transformation. Most particularly, and as discussed in detail by the World Bank (Cichello and Sienart 2009), the share of farm employment fell significantly between 2000 and 2006, from 90 percent to 77 percent. Workers shifted into

Figure 8.1 Structural Shifts in the Economy and Labor Markets in Rwanda, 1990–2006

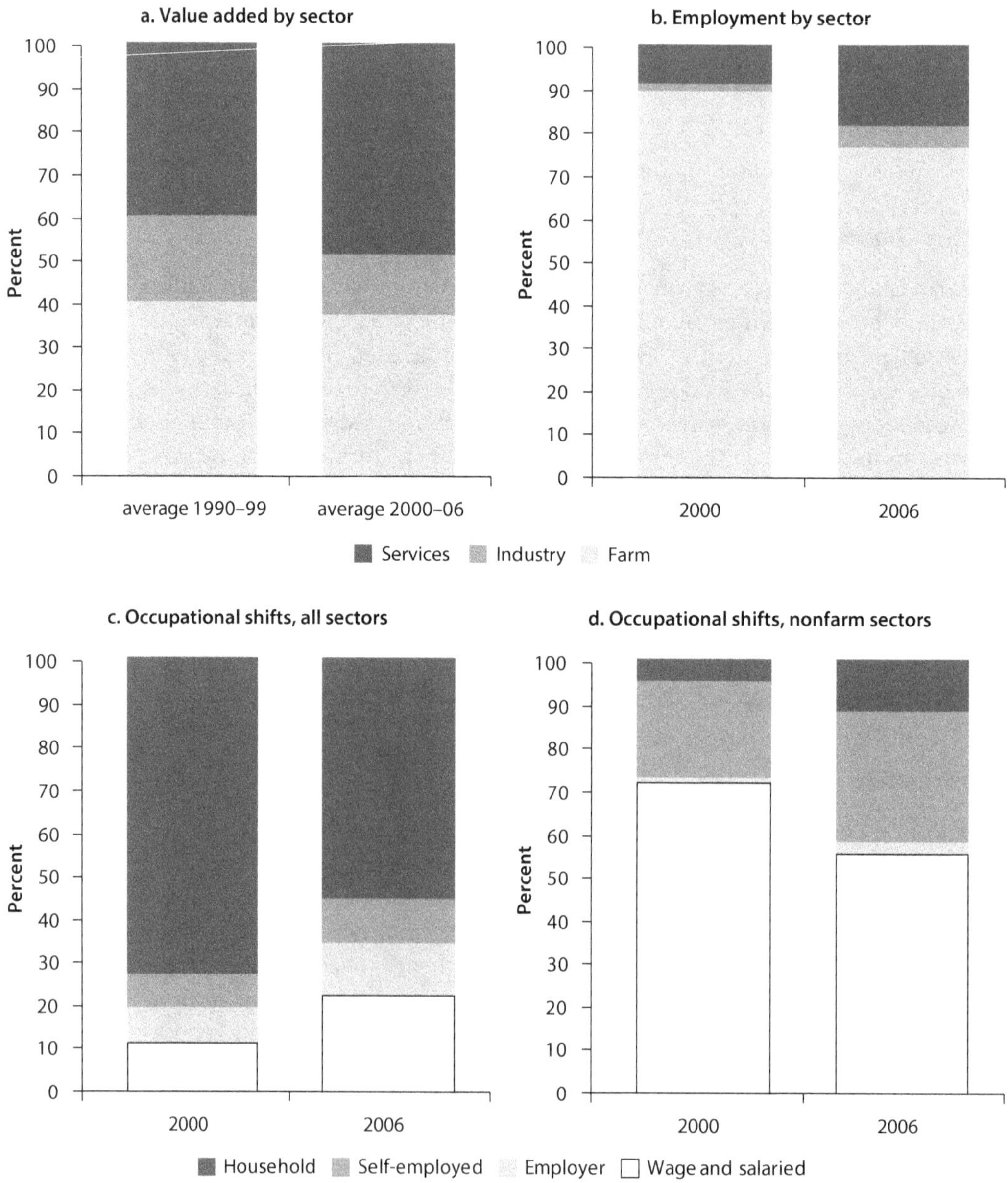

Sources: World Bank 2011; elaborations based on NISR 2007.

the services sector. Simultaneously, more paid than unpaid jobs were created in the nonfarm sector.

New jobs paid better than older ones. Median real earnings increased by an estimated 10 percent between 2000 and 2006 (about 1.7 percent per year). However, earnings fell for all occupational groups except those of household enterprise workers in the farm sector. This apparent puzzle—increases in overall earnings coupled with earnings reductions everywhere except in the poorest-paid category—is explained by the structural shift in employment. New workers flowed into better-paid sectors (nonfarm) and occupations (paid or self-employed), and although these new workers received lower earnings than was the case in 2000, they were still better off than in the lowest-paid occupations left behind.

Poverty rates declined. Higher earnings led to a fall in poverty rates; yet half of rural and one in five urban residents remained in poverty (table 8.1). According to the 2005/06 household survey data, poverty rates are highest among unpaid household workers and among wage workers in farming, although the latter is a very small group (Cichello and Sienart 2009). Because of high population growth following the genocide, Rwanda's population and workforce are very young, even by African standards. Raising earnings for the large cohorts of youth entering the labor market each year, as well as for older workers, is a critical challenge to the country. Farming remains a major employer, but the simultaneous effects of pressures on land and the limited potential to increase productivity and employment mean the nonfarm sector is critical to future gains in earnings.

Raising productivity among the self-employed will be important to future reductions in poverty. As seen in figure 8.1, panel d, some 45 percent of those employed in the expanding nonfarm sector were nonwage workers in small and household enterprises. Raising productivity and earnings in these enterprises will pose a challenge for the future. Studies of small, unregistered, unincorporated firms and household enterprises identify lack of skills and poor education as one

Table 8.1 Key Indicators, Rwanda

Indicator	*Percent*
Growth 2000–06	
Average GDP	7.1
Average GDP per capita	4.4
Annual working-age population	3.6
Employment-to-population ratio	79
Farm, share of employment	77
Farm, share of GDP	38
Rural Poverty Headcount Index	49
Urban Poverty Headcount Index	22
Income, share held by lowest 20 percent	2.3

Sources: World Bank 2012; World Bank staff calculations.
Note: Data are 2006 or latest available, unless otherwise indicated. GDP = gross domestic product.

of many constraints to expansion (Abbott and others 2010; NISER 2007). Other constraints in the Rwandan context include poor transport and power infrastructure, high cost of financing, and limited markets. Addressing the need for skills will require a significant lead time because such investments typically take a long time to bear fruit.

This chapter provides an overview of the level of skills in Rwanda's labor force and the supply of skills available through different forms of training. The focus is on the nonfarm informal sector where significant growth has occurred. The chapter uses household labor force surveys to describe the growth of the informal sector and its skills profile. The findings stress the importance of skills to the changing structure of the economy and future earnings gains. Programs that address the skill needs of the informal sector are examined and recent innovations are highlighted.

Skills, Employment, and Earnings

Household labor force surveys provide data that help quantify the growth of the informal sector and its socioeconomic characteristics. The data in this chapter come from the Rwanda Integrated Household Living Conditions Survey (Enquête Intégrale sur les Conditions de Vie de Ménage, or EICV1 and EICV2) conducted in 1999/2000 (NISR 2001) and 2005/06 (NISR 2007), respectively. The analysis is based primarily on the most recent survey.[2] The sample is restricted to individuals between 15 and 65 years of age and focuses on primary activities in the nonfarm sector. Box 8.1 explains how the key variables for education and earnings are constructed for analysis.

Measuring the Informal Sector in Rwanda

Several definitions of the informal sector are constructed to determine what effect different measures may have on the profile of those working in the sector. The definitions use employment status of the worker and characteristics of the firm in terms of its registration and payment of social protection benefits. The comparison of formal and informal sectors is based on the information available in household surveys for these features and takes into account comparability issues across years.

Six potential definitions are summarized in table 8.2. Starting with those employed in the nonfarm sector, workers were asked a number of questions about their employment status, and firm characteristics are used to determine whether they work in the formal or informal sector. No information is available on the size of firms (smaller firms are more likely to be informal). For employers, the self-employed, and household enterprise workers, questions are asked about registration with a government agency and whether the firm keeps accounts. This information is combined to produce the different definitions of the informal sector. Definition 0 starts with all nonwage workers and adjusts this measure for those working in unregistered firms or firms that do not pay social protection benefits. A subjective measure of informal sector employment is also considered.

Box 8.1 Earnings and Education in the Rwanda Integrated Household Living Conditions Survey

Earnings and education levels—two key variables for the analysis—are calculated as follows: *Earnings:* For wage workers, earnings include cash, in-kind payments, tips, bonuses, and other extras. For employers, the self-employed, and household enterprise workers, earnings are constructed by reported profits (net income) or by the differences between revenues and costs from the household business. These earnings are divided equally among all household workers. Income is measured in 2001 Rwanda francs (RF) and deflated using regional price deflators. For the sake of completeness, the socioeconomic profile is based on an uncensored sample, while the earnings profile and regressions are based on the sample censored at 5 percent. In the multivariate analysis, income is measured per hour; annual working hours are capped at 4,160 (16 hours a day, 5 days a week, 52 weeks a year); and individuals reporting to work less than two hours per day are dropped from the sample to avoid the effect of outliers. The number of hours worked declined across all jobs between the two surveys, possibly because of changes in the questionnaire. The discrepancy could artificially boost growth in earnings per hour between the surveys. When comparing earnings between surveys, annual earnings are therefore used.
Education: Respondents were asked to report the highest level of schooling completed and the highest certification attained. The questions do not allow us to separate out how many years a person actually spent in school, so that for a respondent reporting to have completed higher secondary, the number of years of schooling is reported as 12, irrespective of whether the person spent two years in every class. The second question provides information on achievement rather than attendance. A discrete measure has been constructed using both of these questions:

- Edu0 → No education
- Edu1 → Some education but less than completed primary education
- Edu2 → Completed primary and some lower-secondary education
- Edu3 → Completed lower-secondary and some higher-secondary or vocational education
- Edu4 → Completed higher-secondary or extended vocational education and above

Table 8.2 Definitions of Informal Sector in Rwanda

Definition 0	Self-employed, employer, and household enterprise worker
Definition 1	Self-employed, employer, and household enterprise worker in enterprise unregistered with government agency
Definition 2	Self-employed, employer, and household enterprise worker plus self-declared informal sector wage worker
Definition 3	Self-employed, employer, and household enterprise worker in enterprise unregistered with government agency plus self-declared informal sector wage worker
Definition 4	Self-employed, employer, and household enterprise worker in enterprise unregistered with government agency plus self-declared informal sector wage workers who get no benefits (medical care/retirement/paid leave)
Definition 5	Self-employed, employer, and household enterprise worker in enterprise unregistered with government agency plus wage workers who get no benefits (medical care/retirement/paid leave)

Note: In 2006, a number of individuals who declare to be nonwage workers in a family enterprise are not listed in the corresponding nonfarm business module of the survey or the household does not report running such a business. In a few cases, there is information about the family enterprise, but the answer about registration with a government agency is missing. In all these cases, the workers are classified as informal.

Table 8.3 Employment Shares of Informal Sector in Rwanda, 2000 and 2006
Percent

	Share of nonfarm employment			*Share of total employment*		
Definition	*2000*	*2006*	*Change*	*2000*	*2006*	*Change*
Definition 0	28.5	44.8	16.4	3.0	10.4	7.5
Definition 1	20.9	32.9	12.0	2.2	7.7	5.5
Definition 2	63.5	64.1	0.6	6.6	14.9	8.3
Definition 3	55.9	52.2	−3.8	5.8	12.1	6.3
Definition 4	55.6	52.1	−3.5	5.8	12.1	6.3
Definition 5	77.6	79.5	1.8	8.1	18.5	10.4

Sources: Elaborations based on NISR 2001, 2007.

Definitions make a difference in the case of Rwanda. Because of a relatively high share of wage workers without benefits, the choice of definition will, indeed, strongly affect the size and dynamics of the informal sector. Table 8.3 shows the informal sector's share of nonfarm employment varying between one-third (Definition 1) and four-fifths (Definition 5). Partly as a result of the movement of labor toward nonwage work (as described in figure 8.1, panel d), trends also differ depending on whether or not informal wage workers are included. If they are excluded, as in Definitions 0 and 1, informal sector employment would have increased between 2000 and 2006. If they are included, as in Definitions 2–5, the informal sector's share of nonfarm employment stagnated. Thus, nonwage work has increased at the expense of wage work, but among wage workers, informality has fallen.

Using the more comprehensive Definition 5, the informal sector accounts for one-fifth of total employment and four-fifths of all nonfarm employment. The numbers employed in the informal sector have increased with this definition. The increase from 2000 to 2006 represented around 450,000 jobs, while another 100,000 jobs were created in the formal sector (figure 8.2). At the same time, nearly 70,000 jobs were eliminated in the farm sector. In all, the informal sector accounted for 80 percent of all gross job creation between 2000 and 2006, as a measure of its importance to the economy.

Most of the increase in nonwage employment took place in the informal sector. Workers leaving the farm often moved into self-employment. Table 8.4 shows the declining share of employment in farming, dropping from 90 percent to 77 percent between 2000 and 2006. The nonfarm sector thus doubled from 10 to 23 percent. Virtually all the gains in nonfarm employment were concentrated in the informal sector. Gains in the share of wage employment in the informal sector nearly matched the gains in nonwage employment, 5 percent compared with 6 percent, but the growth of nonwage employment outpaced that of wage employment in the informal sector (table 8.4).

Comparing the Formal and Informal Sectors

Who are those employed in the informal sector, and how do they compare with other workers? The findings show that informal sector workers are mostly male,

Figure 8.2 Total Employment by Sector in Rwanda, 2000 and 2006

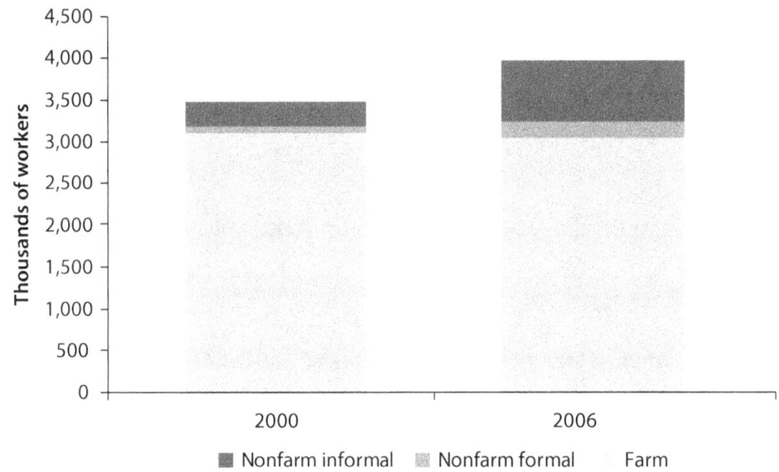

Source: Elaborations based on NISR 2007.

Table 8.4 Employment in Rwanda by Wage or Nonwage and Sector, 2000 and 2006
Percent

	2000			*2006*			*Change*		
Sector	*Wage*	*Nonwage*	*Total*	*Wage*	*Nonwage*	*Total*	*Wage*	*Nonwage*	*Total*
Farm	4	86	90	10	67	77	6	−19	−13
Nonfarm	7	3	10	13	11	23	5	8	13
Formal	2	1	2	2	3	5	1	2	3
Informal	6	2	8	11	8	19	5	6	10
Total	11	89	100	23	78	100	..	..	..

Source: Elaborations based on NISR 2007.
Note: .. = negligible.

although the gender gap is smaller in urban areas. Youth (15–24 years of age) are more likely than adults (25–65 years of age) to be in the informal sector. Overall, the informal sector is associated with lower poverty than farm employment, pointing to its potential for higher earnings and better livelihoods. Education levels are lower in the informal sector, and apprenticeships provide an alternative route to acquiring skills.

Demographics

In rural areas, women are less likely to be in informal sector work than men, but in urban areas, gender gaps are smaller. Female workers are slightly more likely than male to be in the informal sector (82 percent of female workers in the nonfarm sector are in the informal sector, compared with 78 percent of male workers), but because of higher participation rates among men, nearly two-thirds of the workers in the informal sector are male (table 8.5 and figure 8.3). The differences between men and women are largely driven by differences in rural areas,

Table 8.5 Informal vs. Formal Sector Employment in Rwanda, by Gender

	2000		*2006*		*Change (share)*	
Gender	*Formal*	*Informal*	*Formal*	*Informal*	*Formal*	*Informal*
Percentage by gender						
Female	21	79	18	82	−3	3
Male	23	77	22	78	−1	1
Percentage by sector						
Female	34	38	31	37	−4	−1
Male	66	63	70	63	4	1

Sources: Elaborations based on NISR 2001, 2007.

Figure 8.3 Informal Sector Employment in Rwanda, by Gender and Location

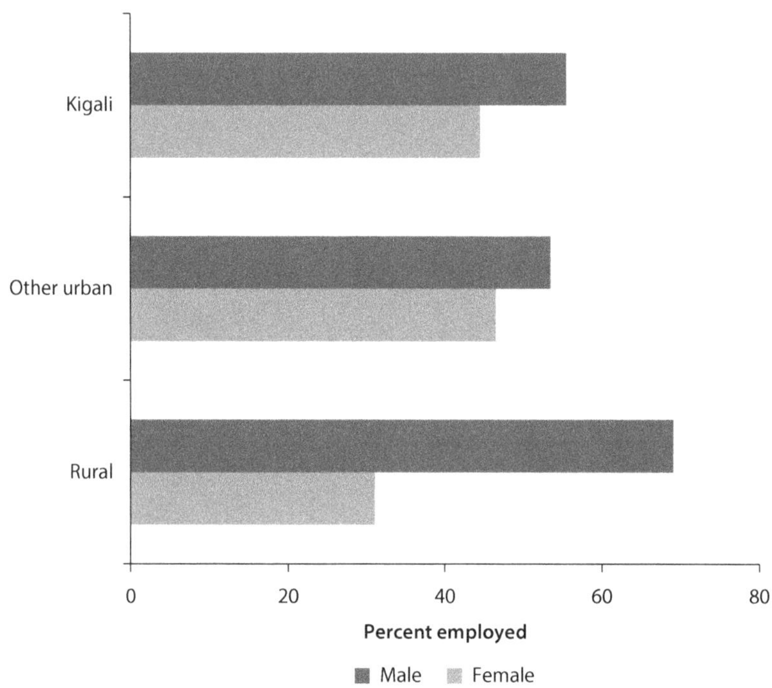

Sources: Elaborations based on NISR 2001, 2007.

because women are more likely to be in the farm sector. In fact, in Kigali as well as in secondary cities, the informal sector is made up of almost as many women as men.

Most youth find their way into the labor market through the informal sector. One-third of all workers (15–65 years of age) in the nonfarm sector were under 25 years of age in 2006. However, youth (15–24 years of age) accounted for less than one in five formal workers, compared to two in five informal workers. The share of youth among formal sector workers nonetheless increased between 2000 and 2006 by 4 percentage points (figure 8.4).

Evidence indicates labor mobility between the formal and informal sectors, but more so in urban areas. In urban areas, the share of employment in the informal

Figure 8.4 Workers in the Formal and Informal Sectors of Rwanda, by Age Group

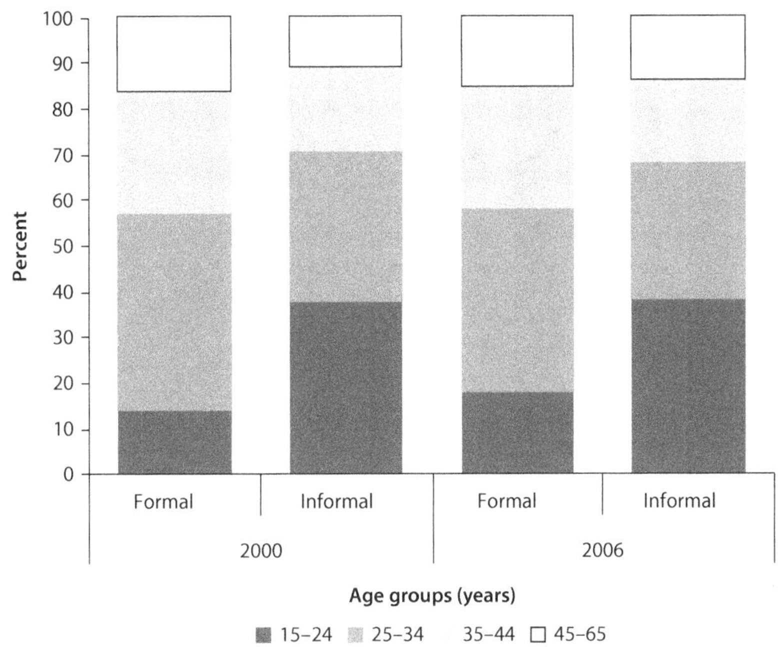

Sources: Elaborations based on NISR 2001, 2007.

sector declines with age up until about 45 years of age, when it begins to rise. The pattern exists but is less pronounced in rural areas. This possibly reflects a combination of separate and distinct patterns of adjustment that are age specific. Youth who start in the informal sector may gradually find their way into a formal sector job, thus leading to a decline in the share of employment in the informal sector. Conversely, those who start in the formal sector after acquiring knowledge and experience on the job may elect to start their own businesses. The urban market appears to be more dynamic in this respect than rural markets (figure 8.5).

Caution is needed in trying to infer patterns of change over time, however. Without panel data, sorting out patterns like the preceding from cross-sectional data is difficult. Whether today's youth will be less likely to enter the informal sector as they grow older, whether women will be more likely to remain there as they grow older, or whether older adults will leave the formal sector to enter self-employment cannot be assessed with confidence from cross-sectional data. The patterns observed in 2006 possibly reflect the realities of what happened to youth and older adults after the civil war. Older adults formerly working in government and other formal sector jobs may no longer have the option for these jobs and may be left with the informal sector as an option. Youth today may face more difficulties in finding a formal sector job and choose instead the informal sector.

The services sector was by far the most important employer in the formal and informal sectors, but with differences between the two (table 8.6). Informal

Figure 8.5 Share of Employed in the Formal and Informal Sectors of Rwanda, by Age Group, Gender, and Geographical Area, 2006

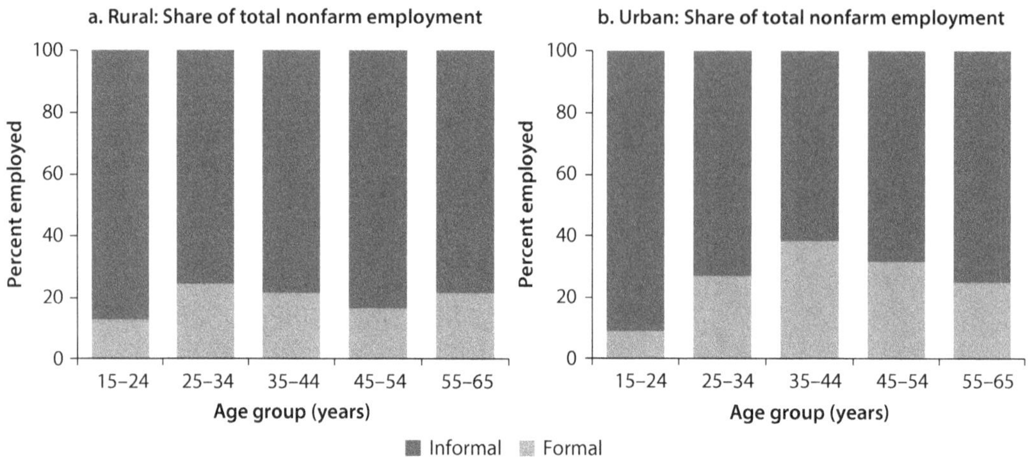

Source: Elaborations based on NISR 2007.

Table 8.6 Distribution of Workers in Rwanda by Sector and Gender, 2006

	Formal		*Informal*	
Sector	*Female*	*Male*	*Female*	*Male*
Mining	2	3	1	4
Manufacturing	5	8	6	10
Utilities	1	0	0	0
Construction	1	14	2	14
Commerce	45	32	62	38
Transport, storage, communication	7	6	1	10
Financial, insurance, real estate	3	1	0	0
Public administration	29	5	0	1
Other services	9	31	29	23

Source: Elaborations based on NISR 2007.

sector workers were more likely to be in construction and "other services" while formal sector workers were more likely to be in commerce and public administration. Within the informal sector, there were also significant differences between women and men. In particular, women were highly likely to be involved in commerce of some sort. Although commerce was also the most important subsector for men, they were considerably more likely than women to be working in the construction or transports/communications sectors.

Poverty

Working in the informal sector lifts more people out of poverty than farming, but not as many as working in the formal sector does. Poverty remains widespread in Rwanda. Nevertheless, sectoral differences are important (figure 8.6).

Figure 8.6 Consumption Levels and Informality in Rwanda

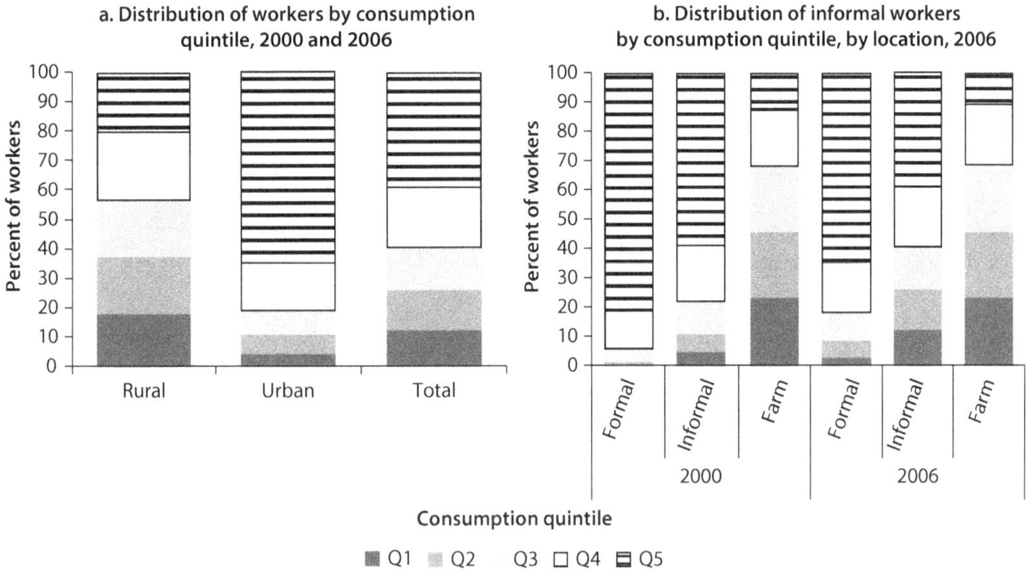

Source: Elaborations based on NISR 2001, 2007.

Some 69 percent of farm workers were living in households among the three poorest quintiles. For the informal sector, this percentage was 40 percent, and for formal sector workers it was 17 percent. The share of informal workers among the poorest quintiles increased between 2000 and 2006. This result is consistent with the drop in earnings for the nonfarm sector over time and with the inflow of workers from the farm to the nonfarm sector. Informal sector work in urban areas offers different opportunities than in rural areas. Only 18 percent of urban informal workers lived in households with consumption levels among the three poorest (national) quintiles, compared with 57 percent for rural areas.

Skills and Access to Different Occupations

Raising productivity in the Rwandan economy will require increasing human capital and will be a significant challenge. In 2006, over half the nonfarm workforce had not completed primary school, and some 12 percent did not have any education at all. (Note that because of the inflow of farm workers to nonfarm activities, the average skill level fell in the nonfarm sector between 2000 and 2006.)

Education levels were significantly higher in the formal sector than in the informal sector. Nearly 2 in 3 workers in the informal sector had less than a primary education or no education at all. Only 1 in 50 (2 percent) had completed higher secondary or higher levels of education. This stands in contrast with the formal sector where more than 1 in 5 has higher levels of education or above, and 3 in 5 had completed at least primary education (table 8.7).

Table 8.7 Education Levels by Formal/Informal, 2000 and 2006
Percent

	2000			*2006*			*Change (share)*		
Education level	*Formal*	*Informal*	*Total*	*Formal*	*Informal*	*Total*	*Formal*	*Informal*	*Total*
No education	4	13	11	8	15	12	5	2	1
Less than primary	14	37	32	32	49	42	18	12	10
Completed primary and some secondary	24	26	26	27	28	28	3	2	2
Completed lower secondary and some higher secondary or vocational	24	14	16	10	6	8	−14	–8	–8
Completed higher secondary or extended vocational, and above	35	10	16	23	2	10	−12	–8	–5
Total	100	100	100	100	100	100			

Source: Elaborations based on NISR 2001, 2007.
Note: Columns may not add to exactly 100 percent because of rounding.

Figure 8.7 Education Levels in the Informal Sector of Rwanda by Gender and Location, 2006

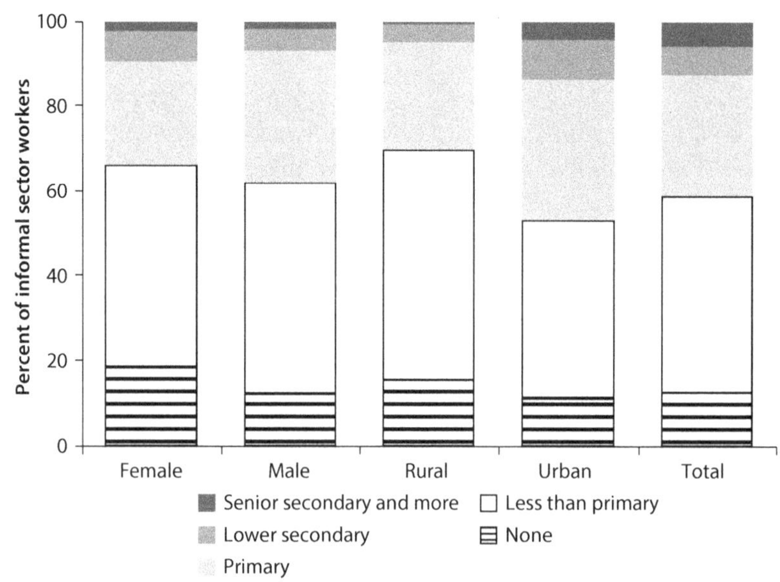

Source: Elaborations based on NISR 2007.

Within the informal sector, urban areas have a more educated pool of workers than rural areas. Some 70 percent of rural informal workers did not have any education or at least did not complete primary education, compared with 53 percent for urban areas (figure 8.7). The share of female workers without education was higher than for males, but the share of females with higher levels of education (lower or higher secondary and above) was higher than for males. These patterns point to the importance of policies for improving productivity in the informal sector that distinguish between rural and urban areas by gender.

Table 8.8 Apprenticeships in Rwanda, 2006
Percent

	Frequency of apprenticeships and training, by sector							
	Have been an apprentice in the past						*Have attended other training*	
		Informal						
	Formal	*Total*	*Women*	*Men*	*Rural*	*Urban*	*Formal*	*Informal*
Yes	20	21	15	24	19	23	30	14
No	80	79	85	76	81	77	70	68

Source: Elaborations based on NISR 2007.

Table 8.9 Training in Rwanda, 2006

Sector of apprenticeships			
Formal	*%*	*Informal*	*%*
Driver	23	Tailor	23
Mason	22	Mason	15
Other	11	Carpenter	12
Tailor	10	Driver	9

Source: Elaborations based on NISR 2007.

Apprenticeships are an alternative mode of skills acquisition in the formal and informal sectors, especially for male and urban workers. They offer a potential route to developing and adapting skills to labor market needs. In Rwanda, apprenticeships have been a relatively important form of training for both formal and informal sectors. In 2006, the share of informal sector workers who went through apprenticeship was only slightly higher than that of formal sector workers: about one-fifth of workers in each sector reported having had an apprenticeship in the past (tables 8.8 and 8.9). Urban residents and men were more likely to have been apprentices than rural residents or females. Some 37 percent of the informal sector workers reported having paid a fee for the training, suggesting demand and willingness to pay for in-service training.

Apprenticeships offer access to different sectors for men and women. Informal and formal sector workers alike had acquired their apprenticeships in the construction and services sector. Among the informal workers, tailoring was the most common form of apprenticeship (linked to female workers), whereas among formal workers, drivers and masons were the dominating categories of acquired skills. Past apprentices who worked in the informal sector were predominantly employed in construction, commerce, and manufacturing, and they were particularly more prone to work in manufacturing than informal sector workers without apprenticeships or than formal sector workers.

Short-term training is more frequent among formal sector workers and is linked with some level of formal education. A 2006 enterprise survey shows that in a group of 11 African countries, Rwanda is the country with the lowest share of firms in the manufacturing sector offering formal training to their employees.[3] On the basis of the household data, short-term training opportunities appear to be twice as likely in the formal sector as in the informal sector (tables 8.8 and 8.9). Training and formal education also appear to be complements in the informal sector, because workers with higher education were more likely to have gone through training. As an example, less than one in five of those with no education had had training, while one in three with higher-secondary education was likely to have been trained.

The role of formal education differs for apprenticeships and short-term training in the informal sector, as confirmed by multivariate analysis (tables 8A.1 and 8A.2 in the annex to this chapter). Men and workers living in urban areas were more likely to have participated in an apprenticeship, holding other factors constant. People with education at less than a primary level were 13 percent more likely than those with no education to have been apprentices in the past; this increases to 16 percent for those with completed primary. The probability falls, however, for higher levels of education. Some basic education, given its practical orientation, is needed for an apprenticeship, but higher levels of education may not be necessary. For short-term training, in contrast, the probability of receiving training increases monotonically with education (figure 8.8). Education is complementary to short-term training because it increases the chances of training at each education level.

Basic and secondary education (compared with none) open access to the informal sector from farming, while a university-level education increases the likelihood of being in the formal sector. Education and employment opportunities are closely linked. Multivariate analysis (table 8A.3) shows that the likelihood of being employed in the informal sector rises with education but reaches a plateau

Figure 8.8 Predicted Probability of Apprenticeships and Training for Different Levels of Education in Rwanda

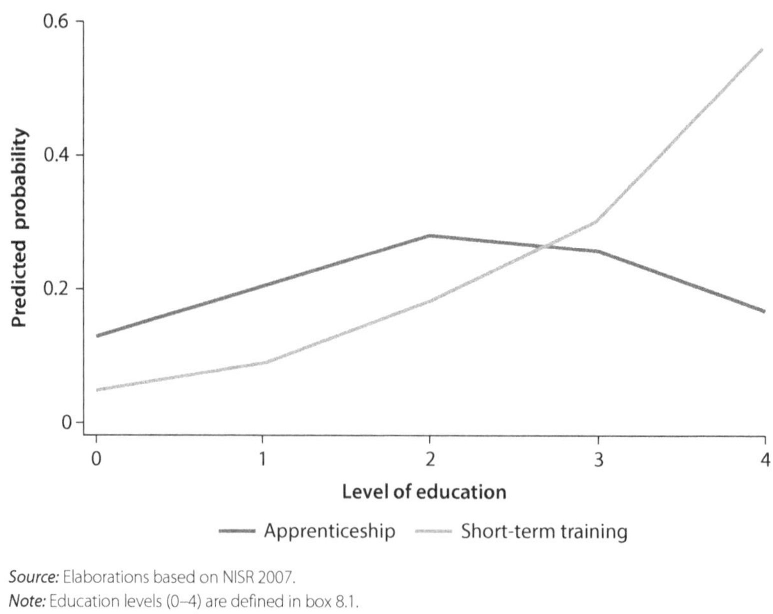

Source: Elaborations based on NISR 2007.
Note: Education levels (0–4) are defined in box 8.1.

Figure 8.9 Predicted Probabilities by Educational Attainment in Rwanda from Multinomial Logit, 2006

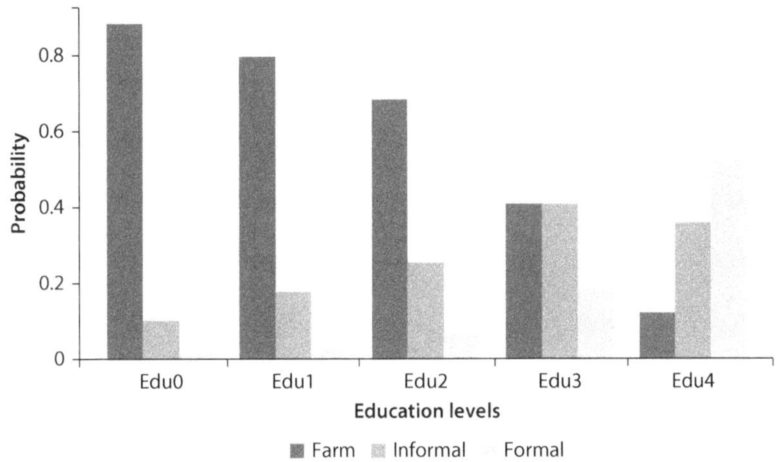

Source: Elaborations based on NISR 2007.
Note: Education levels (0–4) are defined in box 8.1.

at higher education (figure 8.9). Employment in the formal sector continues to rise with higher education. For farming, the predicted probability drops with education, from about 80 percent for individuals with no education to less than 20 percent for those with completed lower-secondary education.

Apprenticeships are a path for entry to informal sector jobs. People with an apprenticeship experience are more likely to be in the informal sector than farming but are less likely to be in the formal sector. Technical or vocational training or other forms of training do not significantly affect entry.

Women as primary caregivers may influence access to different sectors. For men, being married increases the probability of formal, informal, and farm work relative to inactivity. However, being married increases the probability of a woman being in farming, though the possibility of being in the informal sector is smaller—in fact, smaller than being in the formal sector. This result can be interpreted as an influence of the multiple roles of women in the Rwandan socio-economic structure. Women who have access to the formal sector can combine a well-paid job with family responsibilities: they may possibly afford child care, household services, and buying rather than growing food. Rurally based women can combine work on the family plot with household chores. The nonfarm informal sector, as an intermediate, may offer more difficult working conditions (less pay than the formal sector, long hours, perhaps more precarious work) that are not compatible with family responsibilities.

Skills and Earnings

The informal sector offers lower earning opportunities than the formal sector—though higher than the farm sector. The earnings hierarchy mirrors the consumption poverty levels discussed previously, and they are of course strongly related;

Table 8.10 Mean Annual Earnings by Sector in Rwanda, 2000 and 2006

	2000 (2001 RF, thousands)			*2006 (2001 RF, thousands)*			*Change (%)*		
Variable	*Formal*	*Informal*	*Farm*	*Formal*	*Informal*	*Farm*	*Formal*	*Informal*	*Farm*
Total	6	249	47	273	138	48	−47	−44	2
Gender									
Female	464	220	47	279	106	47	−40	−52	1
Male	544	266	47	270	154	49	−50	−42	4
Area									
Rural	434	199	47	209	106	48	−52	−47	1
Urban	575	281	47	346	177	52	−40	−37	10
Education									
None	520	146	45	159	88	45	−70	−40	0
Less than primary	458	182	47	178	102	46	−61	−44	0
Completed primary	397	263	52	236	124	55	−40	−53	5
Completed lower secondary	500	326	61	322	239	65	−36	−27	5
Completed higher secondary and above	643	481	51	403	344	67	−37	−28	31

Sources: Elaborations based on NISR 2001, 2007.
Note: RF = Rwanda francs.

poverty is highest among farm workers because they earn the least from their work. In 2006, mean formal earnings were about twice as high as mean informal earnings (table 8.10). But in turn, informal earnings were almost three times as high as mean farm earnings. In line with the Rwandan earnings and employment structural changes discussed earlier, the earnings in formal and informal sectors (with inflows of workers) fell, whereas those in the farm sector (with outflows) increased marginally. Formal and informal earnings were compressed by nearly half, with the most significant changes occurring for rural areas and for lower levels of education.

In 2006, the earnings of women remained significantly lower than those of men in the informal sector, and there was no earnings gap in the formal or farm sectors. The formal wage premium was consequently significantly higher for women than for men and increased over time, although earnings fell in both formal and informal sectors. In contrast, the urban-rural wage gap was, albeit significant, of the same magnitude for informal and formal sectors.

The payoff to education varies by sector of employment. Additional years of schooling acquired are associated with higher earnings in both formal and informal sectors. However, the returns at each level of education appear to be higher in the formal sector than in the informal sector. The differences between the returns for the formal and informal sectors diminishes at higher levels of education.

Formal sector earnings, at every point of the earnings distribution, are higher than informal earnings, even though some informal workers have comparatively high earnings. The dominance of the formal sector holds for both men and women, but many workers in the informal sector are in fact earning more than those in the formal sector (figure 8.10). The overlap is particularly large for men.

Figure 8.10 Distribution of Log-Hourly Earnings in Rwanda by Gender and Sector, 2006

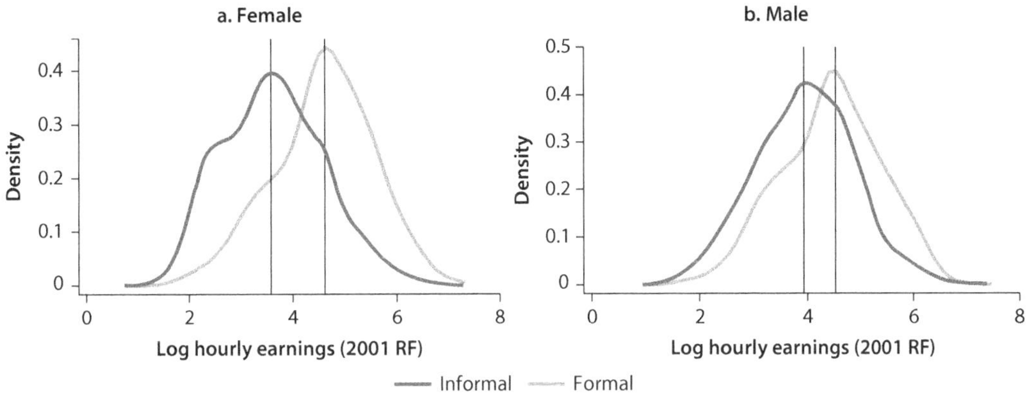

Source: Elaborations based on NISR 2007.
Note: Vertical lines indicate mean values. RF = Rwanda francs.

A breakout (table 8A.4) shows the following: (a) earnings are higher for men than for women at all levels of education except for women with no education in the formal sector; (b) the gender gap is highest at medium levels of education; and (c) formal sector workers in rural areas earn more than informal sector workers in urban areas at lower and medium levels of schooling but not after completed lower-secondary education.

Apprenticeships and short-term training have an earnings premium, especially in the informal sector. Formal sector workers with some form of short-term training or apprenticeship earn on average 30 percent more than workers with no access to training. In the informal sector, trained workers earn on average 65 percent more than others. Moreover, in the informal sector, the earnings premium for women is higher than for men; the reverse is true for the formal sector. Thus, in the informal sector, women are generally paid less than men and are less likely to have accessed training. When they do, however, it pays off in terms of earnings.

The effect of education on earnings in the informal sector begins at lower levels of education than in the formal sector. Multivariate analysis provides further evidence of the role of education in the informal and formal sectors (tables 8A.5 and 8A.6). In the formal sector, there are no significant returns to lower levels of formal education; the effect starts from lower-secondary schooling. In the informal sector, in contrast, all levels of education carry an important additional premium, although the premium increases with level of education. Apprenticeships and attending a technical or vocational school turn out to be a significant factor for earnings only in the informal sector, and the effects are in magnitude similar to those of getting some education (still less than primary) compared to no education at all. Compared with 2000, in 2006 the returns to education and apprenticeships had fallen slightly in the informal sector, especially at higher levels of education (table 8A.7). Using years of schooling instead of completed levels of education, the return to one additional year is slightly higher in the formal sector than the informal sector (8.3 percent compared with 7.6 percent).

Compared with other countries, smaller differences in returns exist between formal and informal sectors in Rwanda. Set against estimates for seven West African cities (discussed in Kuepie, Nordam, and Roubaud 2006), these results place Rwanda at the lower end for formal sector returns but at the higher end for informal sector returns. Other significant variables behave as expected. Earnings increase with age (but the effect becomes smaller over time); there is an urban premium; and the southern and western provinces of Rwanda offer lower earnings opportunities, all else equal. Moreover, there is an earnings premium for men in the informal sector, while this is not the case for the formal, regulated sector.

In summary, the informal sector has become a growing source of employment for Rwanda, and skills are making a difference to earnings and poverty reduction in the sector. The informal sector is an intermediate point on a continuum between low-productivity agriculture (where the majority of the population still works) and the higher-paying jobs in the formal sector. It includes the self-employed, family workers, and informal wage workers. Several different forms of skills acquisition pay off in the informal sector (i.e., apprenticeships, some formal education, even at lower levels, and vocational training). In the formal sector, higher levels of education are needed for access, and only higher levels of education are associated with higher earnings.

Acquiring Skills for the Job Market in Rwanda

National policy acknowledges, but does not clearly develop, the role of skills development for the informal sector. The importance of the small and household enterprise sector and the role of training for work in this sector are partially acknowledged in the Rwandan national policy framework (that is, Umurenge Vision 2020), the Economic Development and Poverty Reduction Strategy 2008–12, the National Employment Policy, the Action Plans for Youth Employment and for Women's Employment, and the Small and Medium Enterprise Development Policy (GoR 2000, 2007a, 2007b, 2009, 2010). However, it is missing from other key strategies, including the National Youth Employment Policy and the Education Sector Strategic Plan (GoR 2006, 2008a). The Rwanda national TVET policy (GoR 2008b) does not provide a specific objective to target training for the informal sector, although it specifies the importance of improving access to TVET for vulnerable groups and promoting entrepreneurship. Overall, however, few specifics are stated about objectives or policies for training the informal sector.

Education

The education system in Rwanda is based on a 6-3-3-4 system (primary, lower secondary, higher secondary, and university bachelor). Access to schooling has increased significantly at the primary and secondary levels. Almost all children (96 percent) of the relevant age group are enrolled in primary school. Completion rates have increased significantly as well. Yet nearly half the children still do not

Table 8.11 Key Education Statistics, Rwanda

Indicator	*1999*	*2008 or latest available*
Primary gross enrollment rate (%)	100	151
Primary net enrollment rate (%)	75	96
Primary completion ratio (%)	28	54
Out-of-school children, primary (thousands)	—	60
Lower-secondary gross enrollment rate (%)	11	28
Higher-secondary gross enrollment rate (%)	8	16
Vocational and technical as a percentage of secondary	25	16
Tertiary gross enrollment rate (%)	1	4

Source: World Bank 2011.
Note: — = not available.

complete primary school and are thus entering the labor market without fundamental capacities (table 8.11).

Enrollment at the postprimary levels has also increased, but only one in six youths is enrolled in higher-secondary education. Lower-secondary school enrollment has nearly tripled, and higher-secondary enrollment has doubled since 1999. Recently, lower-secondary school was made compulsory, but the surge in enrollment preceded this policy change. Women appear to have relatively equal access to school; about half the pupils are females (51 percent for primary levels and 48 percent for secondary levels). Increased school enrollment has, in fact, contributed to lowering employment rates in Rwanda for both youth and children, because more adolescents are studying before entering working life. However, the share of secondary-level students who choose TVET has also fallen.

Formal Sources of Skills Development

Three main sources can be identified in Rwanda for informal sector training: training institutions, informal sector enterprises, and service providers. Figure 8.11 shows a typology for informal sector training.

- Technical secondary schools (TSSs) are part of the formal TVET system, cater to upwardly mobile youth, and prepare students both for postsecondary education (though few continue at this level) and entry to the labor market.
- Vocational training centers (VTCs) are institutions mainly for preemployment training for basic education graduates or dropouts. They are terminal in the sense of not feeding graduates into higher levels of education or training.[4]

Two types of informal sector enterprises provide skills for employment in the informal sector.

- Training and production enterprises, including microenterprises, deliver short, intensive, organized curricula mainly to out-of-school youth, combined with practice in producing goods.

Figure 8.11 Typology of Informal Sector Training

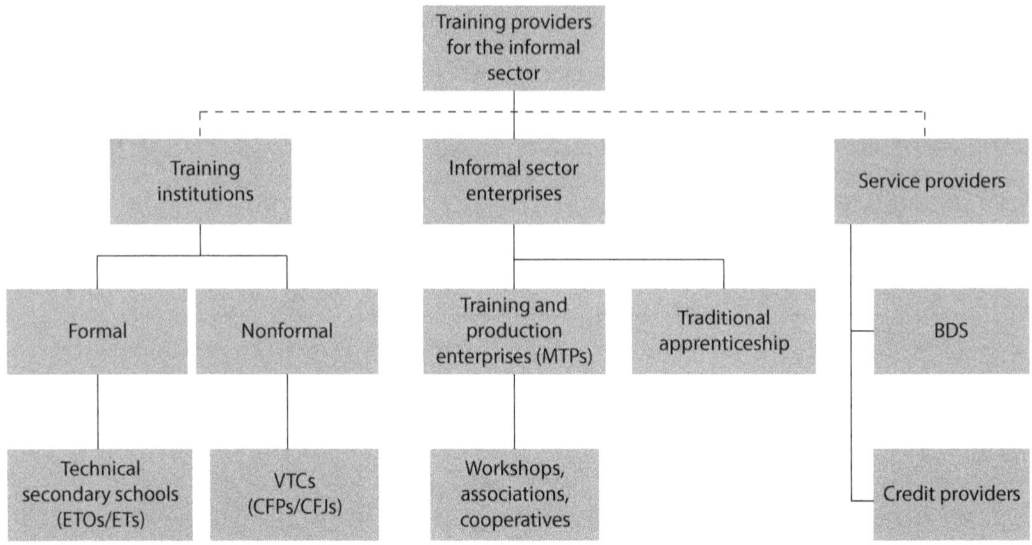

Source: Johanson and Kayiranga Gakuba 2011.
Note: BDS = business development services; CFJ = Centre de Formation des Jeunes; CFP = Centre de Formation Professionnelle; ET = École Technique; ETO = École Technique Officielle; MTP = microtraining provider; VTC = vocational training center.

- Traditional apprenticeships cater mainly to young males in the labor market. The training is based on ad hoc assignments given by master craftspersons, is not organized, and is characterized as learning by observing and learning by gradually doing more difficult tasks.
- Service providers of various types also provide business or entrepreneurial skills for self-employment and those wishing to start their own businesses. (This category is not covered here.)

Vocational-level training is provided through VTCs. Currently, the courses are mainly for primary school graduates but are expected to receive graduates of the nine-year cycle of basic compulsory education in the future. These courses typically last from six months to one year and operate at a low skill level in various crafts and trades, such as tailoring, hairdressing, woodworking, electrical installation, and masonry. The VTCs are terminal, in the sense that one cannot then proceed to further education or training.

The enrollment in VTCs and TSSs is low compared with general secondary education. VTCs enroll just over 10,000 trainees, about 4,700 of them in public centers. This number is modest, compared with the total number of students enrolled in the secondary level (exceeding some 400,000, according to the World Bank [2012]), and in relation to the more than 2 million children enrolled in primary school. TSSs (École Technique Officielle for the public sector and École Technique for the nongovernmental sector) operate at the higher-secondary level. They take in graduates of lower-secondary school and provide three years of training, leading to a craftsperson certificate. Enrollment in TSSs is significantly higher than in VTCs, with some 55,000 students.

A mismatch exists between the TVET supply system and the labor market, including lack of relevant and practical skills and lack of common standards and certification systems that help regulate the quality of private provision. First, the system is not sufficiently connected to labor market needs, with both important skills gaps and overproduction of other skills as a result. The lack of relevant skills produced results from lack of market information about skills demands and trainee absorption into the labor market; lack of links between providers and potential employers; insufficient training in entrepreneurship skills for self-employment and informal sector work; and limited enterprise-based training, owing mainly to weak interest in, and incentives for, training by the private sector. The government is aware of these issues and is now working on addressing them.

In addition, employers tend to see TVET graduates as weak on practical skills, owing to lack of up-to-date curricula, insufficient qualified training personnel, and high attrition caused by low pay, lack of equipment for practice, and no serious testing of practical skills. Dated and nonfunctional equipment is a common challenge for public providers, and no system ensures minimum standards through registration or accreditation of private providers.

Access also remains unequal, with women and low-income groups facing higher barriers. Total enrollment in VTCs represents only about 2 percent of the total population 16–18 years of age. Enrollment in TSSs amounts to about 9 percent of the same age group. The pressure to expand enrollment in VTCs and TSSs is expected to grow substantially with the move toward compulsory lower-secondary education; moreover, VTCs are expected to address in part the backlog of primary school dropouts. Females make up 37 percent of trainees in public VTCs (43 percent in private VTCs) but only 25 percent in public TSSs, and reportedly much less for the technical colleges at the postgraduate level. A strong gender dimension biases the different crafts (similar to apprenticeships in the informal sector) because women make up a strong majority of trainees in tailoring, cooking and food processing, and hairdressing, whereas men dominate in trades such as plumbing and welding, carpentry, and the like (Johanson and Kayiranga Gakuba 2011). Furthermore, school dropouts as well as completers have a low chance to acquire skills in the TVET system relevant to work over the life cycle, and low-income groups cannot access financial support for skills acquisition.

Finally, the TVET system appears underfunded. Although total public expenditure on education amounts to around 4 percent of GDP (World Bank 2011), TVET funding has historically amounted to only about 2–3 percent of the education budget. Private sources are also limited; there is no cost-sharing system with enterprises; and households are in turn limited in what they can afford to pay for tuition. Lack of funding reduces the providers' ability to pay competitive salaries, provide adequate equipment, and regularly update human and physical capital.

Because of the limited reach of public provision, private providers dominate training services in Rwanda's TVET system. They rely on tuition and other fees and operate almost entirely without government support, which demonstrates the willingness of students or their parents to pay for skills acquisition.

Nonformal and Informal Sources of Skills Development

Private providers are the main suppliers of nonformal training and appear to meet the demands of females more successfully. Statistics for the TVET system tend to focus on the main public and private training providers. However, a recent survey of training providers showed that when smaller and microtraining providers (MTPs) are included, the private sector dominates training provision in Rwanda, accounting for about 90 percent of all enrollment in training. These private providers differ from the public providers inasmuch as they accommodate a higher share of female trainees—possibly because one-third focus on tailoring—and have considerably fewer trainees per teacher or instructor. Courses average 12 months, with about 70 percent of the time dedicated to practical activities. The private training providers derive income from trainee fees and from the sale of goods and services.

The majority of training providers were very small scale. MTPs have 12 or fewer trainees enrolled, on average only 6 trainees per provider, and 3 trainees per teacher or instructor. They account for less than 10 percent of total private enrollment registered in the survey but nonetheless enrolled twice as many trainees than the public TVET institutions taken together. They are young institutions (half were established between 2006 and 2009), and half are under individual proprietorships, with the other half being associations or cooperatives. Four of five MTPs derive income through tuition and four of six from sales of goods and services. One can fairly assume that this segment is serving women to a higher extent than any other type of provider, especially because MTPs are concentrated in a few categories: two-thirds of enrollment is in tailoring (45 percent), carpentry (14 percent), and beautician services (8 percent).

These findings indicate that private training providers are responding to strong popular demand for skills acquisition and compensating for weaknesses in public provision. In particular, they appear to compensate for lack of a place for women in public training institutions. They constitute the overwhelming majority of training providers in the country, and their numbers indicate an ease of access for clients. A vast majority is fee based, which suggests people are willing to pay to acquire skills. Two-thirds also derive income from production of goods. They operate, apparently successfully, without government regulation or support.

Household-level data as well as a recent survey of African countries suggest that apprenticeships are less important in Rwanda than in similar African countries. Still, one in five employees in the informal and formal sectors has been an apprentice in the past. Results from a small reverse tracer study, while not nationally representative, suggested that a high share of enterprises do have at least one apprentice, that many of the employers with apprentices pay their apprentices, and that these apprentice earnings are comparatively high (box 8.2).

Box 8.2 Enterprise-Based Training Is Important in the Informal Sector: Findings from a Reverse Tracer Study of Micro- and Small Enterprises

To identify sources of training among informal sector workers, Johanson and Kayiranga Gakuba (2011) conducted a "reverse tracer study," using a stratified sample of 32 microenterprises. About 32 micro- and small enterprises, with an average of 5.9 employees, of the stratified sample were equally divided between urban and rural areas. Over 70 percent of the enterprises were in tailoring, automobile mechanics, construction, carpentry, metalworking, and catering. The survey covered almost 160 employees with an average age of 30 years, 80 percent of whom were male and two-thirds of whom had received more than primary education. The survey showed the following:

- Apprenticeships were important in the informal firms. First, a vast majority—81 percent—of the enterprises had apprentices, averaging 2.6 apprentices per enterprise with apprentices. Only 23 percent of apprentices were required to pay fees; other apprentices were instead compensated, at an average rate of RF 12,770 per month. Second, some 43 percent of employees had undergone training as apprentices in the past, two-thirds within informal sector enterprises.
- The incidence of apprenticeship, and length of training, varied considerably, pointing to the problem of standardization. Apprenticeship training was most frequent in four occupations: tailoring, welding, automobile repair, and carpentry. They varied widely in length between and within occupations, ranging from a few weeks to several years; in carpentry, the shortest apprenticeship identified was for three months, and the longest for four years. Metal works, information technology training, tailoring, and air conditioning and refrigeration take the lead in terms of having the highest percentage of apprentices.
- Informal firms continued to provide enterprise-based training after apprentices "graduated" into regular employment especially for male dominated trades. Some 41 percent of employees interviewed said they had received on-the-job training (OJT) after becoming regular employees. Of these, 30 percent received OJT in training institutions, 56 percent in the enterprises, and 14 percent in other locations. OJT was most prevalent in occupations dominated by males, such as construction, carpentry, and welding. OJT was largely funded by enterprises (38 percent) but also by donors (22 percent) and government programs (16 percent).

Employers remain interested in upgrading their own skills as well as those of their employees. Some 32 employers were also interviewed about training. One-fourth of these had gone through apprenticeships themselves, and another fourth had a TVET background. Almost all employers indicated a strong interest in receiving training themselves, and about 80 percent indicated a willingness to pay for it. Almost 70 percent of the employers stated their willingness to pay for training of their workers. Most employers would pay part but not all of the costs.

Source: Johanson and Kayiranga Gakuba 2011.

These findings suggest that the apprenticeship process has a value for employers. Nearly half of employees had been apprentices in the past. A relatively high proportion of employees also received additional training, nearly half outside the firm—probably by the MTPs discussed previously. This finding again suggests value to the enterprise of further skills development. However, the variation in length in apprenticeships within occupations suggests, among other things, a lack of standardized approach to what is considered a fully learned apprentice.

MTPs differ from traditional apprenticeship in several ways. MTPs market their training services and sometimes even have "training" in the title of the enterprise. They follow an organized curriculum designed by the enterprise itself. Training tends to be shorter and more intensive (average 30 hours per week in training) than traditional apprenticeships. Most (80 percent) charge fees for training services. They offer certificates from the enterprise on completion of training. In contrast, traditional apprenticeship has no established curriculum, involves observation and doing progressively more difficult tasks, usually compensates the apprentice for work performed, is of longer and variable length depending on individual progress, and usually offers no certificates on completion.

Although informal systems of training have strong merits, little information exists about its effect on skills, employment prospects, or earnings. These two systems of training within the informal sector operate successfully with little or no government support or regulation and compensate to some extent for weaknesses in public provision of training (table 8.12). They can be highly relevant to employment because they are linked with actual production. However, little is known about the quality and standards of training provided. Because they depend on individual enterprise owners without minimum standards, one can assume that quality varies considerably.

Table 8.12 TVET System vs. Private, Informal, Small-Scale Providers in Rwanda

Characteristic	*Weaknesses in TVET system*	*MTPs and traditional apprenticeship system*
Relevance	Lack of employer involvement	Training by enterprise producers
	Lack of responsive training provision	Relatively short training (MTPs)
		Training responds to immediate market requirements
Coverage	Low coverage overall	Wider coverage by MTPs than public VTCs
	Low coverage for females	Relatively high enrollment of females in MTPs but not in traditional apprenticeships
Skills taught	Lack of equipment	Equipment used because training is practical
	Lack of practical skills	Useful skills taught
		Extensive workplace exposure for trainees
		Venture into less traditional areas (information and communication technology and others)
Financing	Inadequate public financing	Self-financed, often combine fees with production

Source: Johanson and Kayiranga Gakuba 2011.
Note: MTP = microtraining provider; TVET = technical and vocational education and training; VTC = vocational training center.

Programs to Improve Skills Development in the Informal Sector

Raising productivity in the informal sector may call for policy interventions, but policies, projects, and programs face challenges in terms of relevance and outreach. In Rwanda, as in many other African countries, examples of training programs exist that are funded by donors, nongovernmental organizations, and governments and could or should be relevant for the informal sector. Some important programs evaluated for the purpose of this study are presented in box 8.3.

The projects show that training programs have had limited effectiveness and that more rigorous evaluations are needed. First, no data are available on cost-effectiveness,[5] and what data are available suggest that the effectiveness of most

---

Box 8.3 Case Studies: Programs Relevant for the Informal Sector

KURET-Rwanda by World Vision: Vocational training for vulnerable youth. The project covered four countries, including Rwanda. The objective was to enable vulnerable youth to be removed from, or avoid, unsafe work environments through acquisition of skills that would raise their incomes. The training reached about 830 youth in Rwanda, of whom about 70 percent are female. Training was provided either through VTCs or informally through local artisans.

CARE-NIPS: Assessment of the impact of vocational training and apprenticeship. The purpose was to increase the incomes of orphans and vulnerable children through acquisition of vocational skills. The project provided vocational training for almost 1,400 youth, of whom 63 percent were female. The training was provided through two different types of providers: apprenticeship training and VTCs.

"Education Offers Perspective" with Dutch assistance. Dutch assistance was provided from 2005 to 2008 to training centers operated by a German nongovernmental organization, SOS Children's Villages, in three countries: Ethiopia, Kenya, and Rwanda. The goal of the project was to combat poverty by creating sustainable employment through provision of relevant, quality vocational training. The project cost €1.9 million. It targeted preservice training for labor market entrants and upgrading informal sector operators. Informal sector training was delivered into two parts: (a) entrepreneurship, training about 140 vocational training staff in entrepreneurship; (b) training for informal sector enterprises, based on surveys and development and delivery of training modules.

Case study of two vocational training centers located in Nyanza. The youth training center, Centre de Formation des Jeunes (CFJ), caters to preemployment training for youth and ex-combatants. The Centre de Formation Professionnelle (CFP) provides preservice training as well as continuous in-service upgrading for adults in employment. Both provide training for the informal sector. The CFJ provides training to about 200 youth in one-year courses, mainly in traditional trades: masonry, carpentry, welding, plumbing, and tailoring. CFJ also provides occasional training for ex-combatants through separate (donor and government) financing. The CFP provides training to about 500–800 adults per year in three- to-six month courses. Over half the graduates have taken various levels of driver training, followed by automobile repair (24 percent of total).

Source: Johanson and Kayiranga Gakuba 2011.

---

programs is quite limited, with tracer studies showing poor employment rates for many participants. Pretraining preparation is required. When interviewed, employers commonly indicate a willingness to pay for themselves and their employees to acquire skills (as, for example, in the household surveys and the reverse tracer study in box 8.2). In practice, however, employers may be less appreciative of the potential benefits of training. Initial market surveys that canvass demand for training as well as tracer studies on absorption of graduates are therefore important to determine occupations in demand to avoid market saturation.

The training process itself benefits from sufficient length of time and mix with production and hands-on experience. The process needs to be of sufficient duration to guarantee a minimum of essential skills. The use of competency-based training—allowing different lengths of time to acquire specified skills—could solve this problem and improve information and signaling in the labor market. Where training is combined with production for sale (a common approach in the MTPs discussed above previously), apprentices and trainees have a direct link to goods and services markets that help ensure relevance and quality standards of the work performed. Apprenticeships have a clear advantage in relevance, and may raise earnings, but suffer from quality problems owing to lack of equipment and uneven teaching skills.[6]

The case studies suggest that comprehensive approaches work better and that innovative approaches are needed to ensure their cost-effectiveness. Overall, several programs suffer from low employment rates after training, lack of employment in the sector or occupation the trainees were trained for, and low earnings. The limited evidence suggests that training is incomplete if not part of a wider package—including not only training for self-employment but also assistance with credit and follow-up business services. Innovative models are needed to ensure cost-effective interventions (e.g., linking with financial institutions for arranging credit as part of a graduation package).

In-service training in programs receives little attention. Because many youth enter the labor market very early, they may have very few skills from the outset. As seen in box 8.3, the private sector may provide both apprenticeships and OJT. However, public or donor-funded programs tend to look less at reaching youth or adults after they are employed. In doing so, it will be important to try to alleviate some specific constraints that informal sector business operators face, including the opportunity cost of time (suggesting modular training and flexible timing are needed) and cash flow issues (pointing to need for either subsidies or more flexible payment methods, such as opportunity costs of time, cash flow issues) of the informal sector operators.

Conclusions

The nonfarm informal sector has been expanding in Rwanda, absorbing farm workers. The informal sector is the main employer in the nonfarm sectors, absorbing 80 percent of the nonfarm workforce. Although Rwanda remains a very rural economy, with almost 80 percent of the total workforce in farming, informal sector employment is taking on a more important dimension in total employment over time, with jobs growing at a rate of about 17 percent per year between 2000 and 2006. In this period, the informal sector absorbed a large share of farm workers who left farming for new opportunities in nonfarm activities. The vast majority of young workers who start in the nonfarm sector enter the labor market through a job in the informal sector—9 in 10 youth who are active in the nonfarm sector (and thus not in the farm sector, school, or otherwise "inactive") work in the informal sector.

The shift into nonfarm activities is positive for household earnings, because earnings in the informal sector are considerably higher than in the farm sector. Although earnings in all but the farm sector fell between 2000 and 2006, they still offered much better opportunities than subsistence farming. With a rapidly growing working-age population and an economy set to grow rapidly in the coming years, the informal sector is likely to be a fundamental source of income and livelihoods for an increasing share of youth, including in rural areas.

More years of schooling are associated with work in better-paid sectors, pointing to the benefits of increasing access to education. Although the formal sector appears to favor those with highest levels of education, there are significant returns to education at all increments for the informal sector. Reinforcing the education system bottom-up could therefore have a considerable payoff, which implies focusing on quality of education at all levels. Those who are most vulnerable in terms of low and variable income are also likely to have lower levels of education. From this perspective, ensuring that all children at least finish a primary education appears to be vital, while opening up opportunities for further education as well.

The study shows important payoffs to apprenticeships—founded on a minimum education—and vocational and technical training in the informal sector. Ways of increasing technical skills before, or during lifelong work, could clearly raise earnings in this sector. Although apprenticeships are as frequent in the formal sector as in the informal sector, in the informal sector, they visibly affect earnings. Importantly, the premium to any form of training is higher for females than for males in the informal sector.

So where could more labor market–relevant skills come from? A comprehensive and coordinated policy with respect to informal sector skills development is needed in Rwanda as elsewhere. The formal TVET system has institutions that cater to training for the informal sector, but they enroll relatively few, concentrate on youth, and teach little entrepreneurship. Access is a problem: women are in a minority, especially in formal institutions, and low-income groups are also largely excluded, because of the direct and indirect costs associated with training. Virtually no in-service training (programs for people already working in the informal sector and wishing to improve their skills) exists.

The private sector is providing a majority of nonformal training opportunities, especially for the informal sector workers, but more information is needed on effectiveness. The importance of private institutions indicates a willingness of parents and caregivers to finance skills acquisition for youth. However, most skills training for the informal sector comes not from formal training but from within the informal sector itself, in the form of MTPs, traditional apprenticeships, and OJT. These two systems operate without government support or regulation, are linked with actual production, and as such are likely to be relevant. However, little is known about the quality and standards of training provided.

When assisting the informal training systems, care must be taken not to damage or distort their effectiveness, including self-financing. Types of support that might be considered include assistance in identifying market opportunities, access to instructor training (adapted to those without formal training qualifications), development of competency-based training programs, and simple teaching aids. Vouchers may help boost trainee demand from lower-income groups, provided safeguards can be created to avoid collusion.[7]

Training programs need to be comprehensive and integrated with other services. Evidence suggests that unless training programs are comprehensive and cover more than technical skills, they will be ineffective. Similarly, they need to be a sufficient length of time. Moreover, benefits of coupling training to other business development services, like credit, should be explored. For example, programs could provide an integrated services package, with access to start-up capital through links with credit providers well in advance of training and follow-up advice (both technical and business). The value of entrepreneurship training for a large group of workers who will end up as self-employed also needs to be emphasized.

The public sector could assist in improving information flows in an environment of fragmented provision. For example, although training needs analyses or tracer studies are central to successful training for the job market, training providers are unlikely to have the capacity individually to undertake such studies. A central capacity could be established, with outreach of market analysis services to diverse providers. These should also assess more carefully the willingness of employers and workers to pay for training and assist in marketing courses better, including information dissemination among enterprises on the value of training.

Annex 8A: Tables

The tables in this annex contain the multivariate analyses underpinning the findings of the chapter. The analyses address the determinants in Rwanda of apprenticeship, short-term training, sector of employment, and earnings.

Table 8A.1 Determinants of Apprenticeship in the Informal Sector, 2006

Variable	*Marginal effect*	*p-value*	*Standard error*
Male	0.081	***	0.069
Age	0.028	***	0.017
Age squared/100	−0.028	***	0.023
Some education but less than completed primary	0.129	***	0.102
Completed primary and some lower secondary	0.159	***	0.106
Completed lower secondary and some higher secondary or vocational education	0.103	**	0.138
Completed higher secondary or extended vocational and above	0.019		0.145
Urban	0.055	**	0.094
Southern province	−0.039		0.106
Western province	−0.013		0.119
Northern province	−0.038		0.134
Eastern province	−0.004		0.136
Number of observations	2,991		

Source: Elaborations based on NISR 2007.
Note: Estimates account for the complex survey design. Taylor-linearized standard errors are reported next to marginal effects. Dependent variable equals 1 if an informal sector worker reports to have done an apprenticeship in the past and zero otherwise. Reference category: education, no schooling; province, city of Kigali.
Significance level: *$p < 0.1$, **$p < 0.05$, ***$p < 0.01$.

Table 8A.2 Determinants of Short-Term Training in Informal Sector, 2006

Variable	*Marginal effect*	*p-value*	*Standard error*
Male	0.033	**	0.067
Age	0.019	***	0.017
Age squared/100	−0.018	***	0.023
Some education but less than completed primary	0.109	***	0.135
Completed primary and some lower secondary	0.223	***	0.134
Completed lower secondary and some higher secondary or vocational education	0.387	***	0.149
Completed higher secondary or extended vocational and above	0.688	***	0.161
Urban	−0.029		0.111
Southern province	0.008	***	0.137
Western province	−0.018		0.135
Northern province	0.025		0.136
Eastern province	0.073	**	0.133
Number of observations	3,134		

Source: Elaborations based on NISR 2007.
Note: Estimates account for the complex survey design. Taylor-linearized standard errors are reported next to marginal effects. Dependent variable equals 1 if an informal sector worker reports to have done an apprenticeship in the past and zero otherwise. Reference category: education, no schooling; province, city of Kigali.
Significance level: *$p < 0.1$, **$p < 0.05$, ***$p < 0.01$.

Table 8A.3 First-Stage Multinomial Logit Sector Selection, 2006

	Informal			*Formal*		
Variable	*Relative risk ratio*	*p-value*	*Standard error*	*Relative risk ratio*	*p-value*	*Standard error*
Male	1.064	***	0.020	1.202	***	0.045
Age	0.904	***	0.022	0.779	***	0.039
Age squared/100	1.240	**	0.127	1.603	**	0.323
Some education but less than completed primary	1.496	***	0.167	2.772	***	0.591
Completed primary and some lower secondary	3.583	***	0.839	12.429	***	3.943
Completed lower secondary and some higher secondary or vocational education	8.054	***	2.583	122.360	***	45.485
Completed higher secondary or extended vocational and above	6.421	***	1.107	6.627	***	1.370
Urban	0.175	***	0.039	0.237	***	0.069
Southern province	0.225	***	0.050	0.302	***	0.079
Western province	0.193	***	0.045	0.201	***	0.055
Northern province	0.201	***	0.052	0.222	***	0.070
Eastern province	2.706	***	0.245	1.400	**	0.190
Apprentice	1.279	**	0.146	1.723	***	0.232
Training	1.281		0.256	0.743		0.168
Technical/vocational school	0.960		0.108	1.300		0.247
Married	0.389	***	0.040	0.223	***	0.049
Married*female	0.370	***	0.052	0.878		0.223
Widowed	1.171		0.365	0.692		0.427
Widowed*female	0.579	*	0.190	2.003		1.300
Imidugudu	1.058		0.164	1.116		0.267
Imidugudu*female	1.143		0.201	0.617		0.205

Source: Elaborations based on NISR 2007.

Note: Relative risk ratios are presented instead of coefficients. Base outcome: agriculture. Estimates account for the complex survey design. Reference category: marital status, never married; education, no schooling; province, city of Kigali. The specifications also contain a dummy for whether the individual is part of Imidugudu, a low-cost housing scheme to resettle thousands of people who returned at the end of the genocide of the mid-1990s. In many settlements, the beneficiaries did not know each other well and this resulted in a low level of social cohesion with potentially negative effects on economic activities. At the same time, the cultural institutions are less strong and women have more freedom to perform activities in the labor market that are traditionally reserved to men.

Significance level: $*p < 0.1$, $**p < 0.05$, $***p < 0.01$.

Table 8A.4 Average Annual Earnings by Sector, Gender/Area, and Education, 2006
2001 Rwanda francs

	Formal		*Informal*	
Weighted mean	*Female*	*Male*	*Female*	*Male*
No education	199,975	142,610	76,046	95,557
Some education but less than completed primary	166,014	182,062	73,124	115,525
Completed primary and some lower secondary	214,734	242,329	108,584	171,755
Completed lower secondary and some higher secondary or vocational education	311,833	328,064	145,994	295,733
Completed higher secondary or extended vocational and above	365,774	431,778	316,527	365,851
	Formal		*Informal*	
Weighted mean	*Rural*	*Urban*	*Rural*	*Urban*
No education	128,907	241,768	76,898	106,099
Some education but less than completed primary	155,382	229,013	85,556	125,332
Completed primary and some lower secondary	196,120	276,665	124,431	184,552
Completed lower secondary and some higher secondary or vocational education	268,295	360,963	191,248	278,227
Completed higher secondary or extended vocational and above	314,931	465,374	216,291	425,840

Source: Elaborations based on NISR 2007.

Table 8A.5 Earnings Equations (OLS), 2006

	Basic		*Full*	
Model	*Formal*	*Informal*	*Formal*	*Informal*
Male	0.09	0.305***	0.074	0.285***
Age	0.076***	0.109***	0.076***	0.100***
Age squared/100	−0.085***	−0.125***	−0.086***	−0.115***
Some education but less than completed primary	0.007	0.227***	−0.005	0.199***
Completed primary and some lower secondary	0.154	0.422***	0.152	0.370***
Completed lower secondary and some higher secondary or vocational education	0.397**	0.716***	0.470***	0.587***
Completed higher secondary or extended vocational and above	0.913***	1.347***	1.072***	1.168***
Urban	0.163*	0.143**	0.159*	0.125**
Southern province	−0.207*	−0.279***	−0.205*	−0.280***
Western province	−0.253**	−0.200***	−0.252**	−0.202***
Northern province	−0.088	−0.082	−0.08	−0.075
Eastern province	0.058	−0.067	0.067	−0.082
Imidugudu	−0.372***	−0.035	−0.370***	−0.033
Imidugudu*female	0.314	−0.058	0.315	−0.04
Apprentice			0.064	0.222***
Training			0.07	0.02
Technical/vocational school			−0.205	0.188**
Constant	2.627***	1.338***	2.631***	1.484***
R-squared	0.26	0.27	0.27	0.28
Number of observations	646	2,292	646	2,292

Source: Elaborations based on NISR 2007.
Note: Dependent variable is the logarithm of hourly earnings (2001 RF). Estimates account for the complex survey design. Reference category: education, no schooling; province, city of Kigali. OLS = ordinary least squares.
Significance level: $^{*}p < 0.1$, $^{**}p < 0.05$, $^{***}p < 0.01$.

Table 8A.6 Selection-Corrected Earnings Equations (Second Stage), 2006

	Formal sector			*Informal sector*		
Variable	*Coefficient*	*p-value*	*Standard error*	*Coefficient*	*p-value*	*Standard error*
Male	0.116		0.082	0.400	***	0.050
Age	0.088	***	0.031	0.100	***	0.010
Age squared/100	−0.101	**	0.040	−0.117	***	0.015
Some education but less than completed primary	0.022		0.156	0.229	***	0.073
Completed primary and some lower secondary	0.212		0.182	0.407	***	0.080
Completed lower secondary and some higher secondary or vocational education	0.597	**	0.271	0.649	***	0.113
Completed higher secondary or extended vocational and above	1.308	***	0.422	1.161	***	0.117
Urban	0.220	*	0.129	0.314	***	0.066
Southern province	−0.222	**	0.104	−0.428	***	0.072
Western province	−0.259	**	0.122	−0.327	***	0.079
Northern province	−0.108		0.119	−0.216	***	0.082
Eastern province	0.043		0.124	−0.219	***	0.082
Apprentice	0.047		0.099	0.321	***	0.051
Training	0.098		0.073	0.046		0.058
Technical/vocational school	−0.228	*	0.126	0.235	***	0.090
Imidugudu	−0.363	***	0.120	−0.023		0.074
Imidugudu*female	0.270		0.352	−0.062		0.145
Selection term	0.158		0.227	0.305	***	0.085
Constant	2.015	**	1.029	1.041	***	0.202
Number of observations	646			2,292		

Source: Elaborations based on NISR 2007.
Note: Dependent variable is the logarithm of hourly earnings (2001 RF). Estimates account for the complex survey design. Reference category: education, no schooling; province, city of Kigali.
Significance level: *$p < 0.1$, **$p < 0.05$, ***$p < 0.01$.

Table 8A.7 Comparisons of Returns to Education (OLS), 2000 and 2006

	2000		*2006*	
Variable	*Formal*	*Informal*	*Formal*	*Informal*
Some education but less than completed primary	−0.196	0.191**	−0.009	0.199***
Completed primary and some lower secondary	−0.004	0.393***	0.146	0.370***
Completed lower secondary and some higher secondary or vocational education	0.416	0.716***	0.485***	0.588***
Completed higher secondary or extended vocational and above	0.740*	1.304***	1.094***	1.167***
Apprentice	−0.022	0.283***	0.096	0.223***
Training	0.052	0.147*	0.047	0.021
Technical/vocational school	−0.204***	−0.004	−0.208	0.190**

Sources: Elaborations based on NISR 2001, 2007.
Note: Dependent variable is the logarithm of hourly earnings (2001 RF). Estimates account for the complex survey design. Reference category: education, no schooling; province, city of Kigali. OLS = ordinary least squares.
Significance level: *$p < 0.1$, **$p < 0.05$, ***$p < 0.01$.

Table 8A.8 Comparisons of Returns to Education (Selection Corrected), 2000 and 2006

	2000		2006	
Variable	*Formal*	*Informal*	*Formal*	*Informal*
Some education but less than completed primary	−0.151	0.198**	0.016	0.228***
Completed primary and some lower secondary	0.083	0.404***	0.203	0.406***
Completed lower secondary and some higher secondary or vocational education	0.572	0.739***	0.605**	0.648***
Completed higher secondary or extended vocational and above	0.949*	1.334***	1.316***	1.158***
Apprentice	−0.013	0.292***	0.080	0.318***
Training	0.072	0.158*	0.073	0.047
Technical/vocational school	−0.224**	−0.002	−0.230	0.235***

Sources: Elaborations based on NISR 2001, 2007.
Significance level: $^*p < 0.1$, $^{**}p < 0.05$, $^{***}p < 0.01$.

Notes

1. This chapter is largely based on Ranzani (2011) and Johanson and Kayiranga Gakuba (2011).
2. Data sets are available in the World Bank Labor Market microlevel database: http://web.worldbank.org/WBSITE/EXTERNAL/TOPICS/EXTPOVERTY/EXTEMPSHAGRO/0,,contentMDK:22135862~pagePK:148956~piPK:216618~theSitePK:2743783,00.html.
3. The Rwanda enterprise survey was conducted in 2006. For methodology and data, see http://www.enterprisesurveys.org/data/exploreeconomies/2006/rwanda/.
4. In the new TVET strategy, VTCs are foreseen to have the same curriculum as TSSs and, therefore, to provide formal training.
5. No rigorous evaluations of training programs are available to date. The following conclusions are based on interviews and other qualitative material and, where available, some tracer studies.
6. The finding is consistent with other reviews that point to uneven quality as one of the weaknesses of traditional apprenticeship training (Johanson and Adams 2004).
7. See the *Jua Kali* project in Kenya (Johanson and Adams 2004).

References

Abbott, Pamela, with Serge Musan, Ivan Murenzi, and Lillian Mutesi. 2010. *Rwanda Country Study: Raising Productivity and Reducing the Risk of Household Enterprises; Diagnostic Report*. Kigali: Institute of Policy Analysis and Research.

Cichello, Paul, and Alex Sienart. 2009. "Making Work Pay in Rwanda: Employment, Growth, and Poverty Reduction." Unpublished, Africa Region, World Bank, Washington, DC.

GoR (Government of Rwanda). 2000. *Rwanda Vision 2020*. Ministry of Finance and Economic Planning, Kigali.

———. 2006. *National Youth Employment Policy*. Ministry of Youth, Sports and Culture, Kigali.

———. 2007a. *Economic Development and Poverty Reduction Strategy 2008–2012*. Ministry of Finance and Economic Planning, Kigali.

———. 2007b. *Five Year Action Plan for Women's Employment Promotion in Rwanda*. Ministry of Public Service and Labor, Kigali.

———. 2008a. *Education Sector Strategic Plan 2008–2012*. Ministry of Education, Kigali.

———. 2008b. *Technical and Vocational Education and Training (TVET) Policy in Rwanda*. Ministry of Education, Kigali.

———. 2009. *National Employment Policy*. Ministry of Public Service and Labor, Kigali.

———. 2010. *Small and Medium Enterprises (SME) Development Policy*. Ministry of Trade and Industry, Kigali.

Johanson, Richard K., and Arvil V. Adams. 2004. *Skills Development in Sub-Saharan Africa*. Regional and Sectoral Studies. Washington, DC: World Bank.

Johanson, Richard, and Théogène Kayiranga Gakuba. 2011. "Rwanda: Training for the Informal Sector." Unpublished, Africa Department, World Bank, Washington DC.

Kuepie, Mathias, Christophe Nordam, and François Roubaud. 2006. "Education and Labor Market Outcomes in Sub-Saharan West Africa." Working Paper DT/2006/16, DIAL (Développement, Institutions et Analyses de Long terme), l'Université Paris Dauphine and l'Institut de Recherche pour le Développement (IRD), Paris.

NISER (Nigerian Institute of Social and Economic Research). 2007. "Report of Baseline Study on Employment Generation in the Informal Sector of the Nigerian Economy." African Capacity Building Foundation/International Labour Organization Project on Strengthening the Labor Market Information and Poverty Monitoring System in Africa, Nigerian Institute of Social and Economic Research, Ibadan, Nigeria.

NISR (National Institute of Statistics of Rwanda). 2001. *Enquête Intégrale sur les Conditions de Vie de Menage 2000-2001 (EICV 2001)*, Version 1.0. NISR, Kigali. http://www.statistics.gov.rw/survey-period/integrated-household-living-conditions-survey-1-eicv-1.

———. 2007. *Enquête Intégrale sur les Conditions de Vie des Ménages 2005–2006 - Overview- 10 -2005-2006 (EICV 2005)*, Version 1.1. NISR, Kigali. http://www.statistics.gov.rw/survey-period/integrated-household-living-conditions-survey-2-eicv-2.

Ranzani, Marco. 2011. "Skills Development and the Informal Sector in Rwanda." Unpublished, Africa Department, World Bank, Washington, DC.

World Bank. 2011. *World Development Indicators 2011*. Washington, DC: World Bank.

———. 2012. *World Development Indicators 2012*. Washington, DC: World Bank. http://data.worldbank.org/data-catalog/world-development-indicators.

CHAPTER 9

Skills Development in the Informal Sector: Tanzania

In This Chapter

In Tanzania, employment off the farm in small household enterprises of the informal sector is growing much faster than in the formal wage sector and is helping absorb the wave of youth now entering the workforce. Women are overrepresented in these enterprises, as are urban areas. Better earnings can be found in the formal sector, but the earnings of the informal sector offer gains when compared with those in agriculture. Education and skills are shown to be effective instruments for attaining employment off the farm and improved earnings. The Tanzania case, like others in this volume, illustrates the challenges to improving skills for the informal sector. It provides examples of programs that address these challenges but highlights the need for more rigorous evaluations.

Introduction

Tanzania's economy has experienced a significant and positive turnaround in recent years.[1] In the 1990s, real gross domestic product (GDP) increased by less than 3 percent per year (figure 9.1, panel a). Although the economy performed better than that of many Sub-Saharan Africa countries, low growth rates coupled with high population and labor force growth still meant that GDP per capita and labor productivity fell by 0.3 and 0.5 percent per year, respectively. The past decade has seen a reversal of this pattern. GDP growth rates exceeded 6 percent per year between 2000 and 2009, translating into GDP per capita growth, with sustained labor productivity growth of close to 4 percent per year—almost twice the Sub-Saharan average. The services sector increased by over 6 percent per year, second only to farming (figure 9.1, panel b).

Still, in spite of the economy's dynamics, Tanzania's economic structure, social indicators, and labor markets remain representative of a typical low-income country (table 9.1). Farming continues to dominate the economy. Employment rates are high (around 80 percent for men and women), reflecting high poverty

Figure 9.1 Economic Indicators, Tanzania and Sub-Saharan Average, 1990–99 and 2000–06

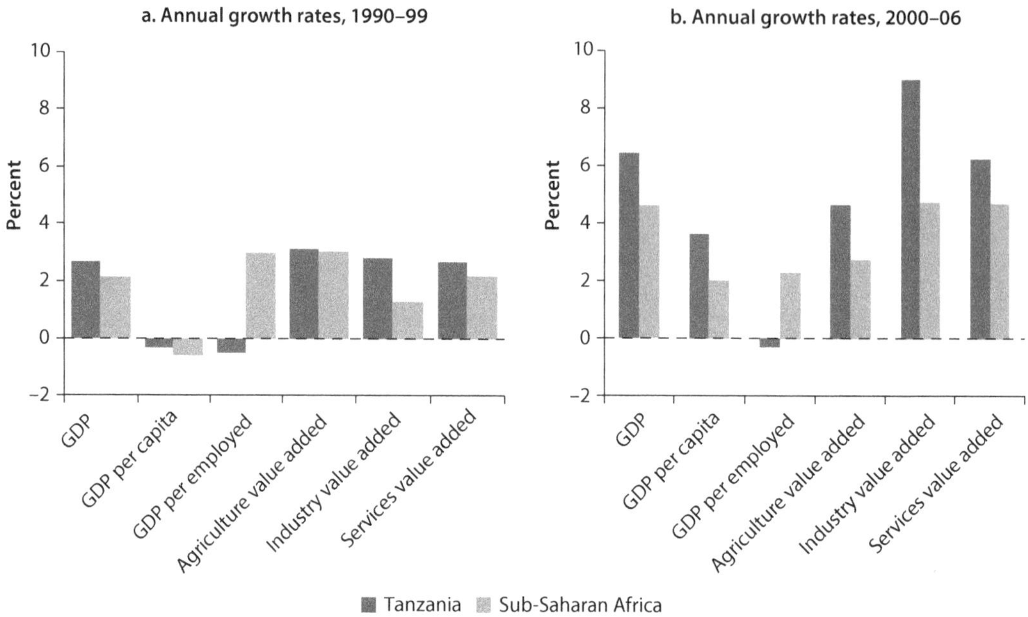

Source: World Bank 2011.
Note: Data are for 2006 or latest available. GDP = gross domestic product.

Table 9.1 Key Indicators, Tanzania

Indicator	*Percentage*
Growth 2000–09	
Average GDP	6.7
Average GDP per capita	3.8
Annual working-age population	2.1
Employment-to-population ratio	78
Farm, share of employment	82
Farm, share of GDP	45
Rural Poverty Headcount Index	37
Urban Poverty Headcount Index	22
Income, share held by lowest 20 percent	7.3

Source: World Bank 2011.
Note: Data are for 2009 or latest available. GDP = gross domestic product.

that obliges most people to be employed in some way or another. An overwhelming share of this employment is in subsistence farming.

Diversification of employment from low-productivity farming into the nonfarm sector offers a pathway out of poverty. The link between the high prevalence of low-productivity jobs in farming and poverty is incontestable. Recent analysis shows that rural households in Tanzania that operate nonfarm household enterprises and have access to markets and infrastructure improve their livelihoods (Kweka and Fox 2011). Opening employment opportunities in the nonfarm sector promises better earnings and the reduction of poverty.

Small-scale enterprises in the nonfarm sector are a likely source of employment for the growing influx of youth. With a population growth of about 3 percent, Tanzania is still in the early stages of its demographic transition,[2] and its population is very young, with the share under 15 years of age accounting for 44 percent of the population in 2002. Current population projections up to 2025 show a steady increase, with an average of more than 850,000 people a year coming of working age. The majority of these will find employment in farming and, increasingly, as self-employed in small enterprises of the nonfarm sector. Improving the productivity of the latter will be a key ingredient to increasing the earnings of Tanzania's low-income households.

This chapter sets out to provide a better understanding of employment off the farm in small household enterprises of the informal sector of Tanzania. Different definitions of the informal sector are examined. The chapter looks at the statistical importance of this employment and its demographic structure in relation to the formal economy. It examines the skill level of workers in the formal and informal sectors of the economy and how different sources of skills influence employment opportunities and earnings potential. It highlights different sources of skills development open to workers, particularly those in the informal sector, and factors influencing accessibility and outcomes.

Skills, Employment, and Earnings

Household survey data from the Integrated Labour Force Surveys (ILFSs) of 2006 and 2001 (NBS 2002, 2007b) provide an overview of employment in the informal sector. In Tanzania, informal activities are mostly undertaken as own-account work. The sector is more open to male workers and more prevalent in urban areas; women remain relatively more likely to be informal than formal workers than do men. Informal workers are younger than formal workers, especially in urban areas. They have some formal education although less than formal sector workers, and informal sector workers are almost as likely as private formal sector workers to have been exposed to some form of training, mostly in the form of apprenticeships.

Measuring the Informal Sector in Tanzania

Informality in the labor market can be examined through several prisms. In Tanzania, the national definition of the informal sector adopted for statistical purposes follows the definition adopted by the 1993 15th International Conference of Labour Statisticians. The informal sector is considered as a subset of household enterprises or unincorporated enterprises owned by households. They are enterprises that are not separate legal entities independent of the households or household members who own them. They do not have a complete set of accounts that permit a clear distinction of production activities of the enterprises from the other activities of their owners and the identification of flows of income and capital between enterprises and owners. The enterprises may or may not employ paid labor, and the activities may be carried out inside or outside the owner's home. All or at least some of the goods or services of the business have to be produced for sale (NBS 2007a).

The informal sector includes the self-employed, unpaid workers, and those informally employed. The definition of the informal sector begins with the self-employed. This includes employers who work on their own account and with unpaid family members and other employers who engage workers for wages. Those working on their own account or as employees in these enterprises are considered to be working in the informal sector. The self-employed who work on their own account comprise a larger share of the self-employed in most developing countries. The definition of the informal sector used in this chapter follows the national definition in which a nonfarm enterprise is considered to be in the informal sector if it meets the following criteria:

- It falls into the following categories: household economic activities (other than fetching water or firewood); unregistered cooperatives; private own-account enterprise; unregistered partnership; and other private enterprises.
- If employs fewer than 10 employees.
- It does not keep written records or accounts to monitor the activities of the enterprise.

Almost half of all Tanzanian employment off the farm is engaged in the informal sector, mostly as own-account operators (table 9.2). The focus here is on the primary job. People working in the informal sector as a secondary activity are excluded. In 2006, the number of workers 15 years of age and older (15+) in the informal sector was estimated at around 2.2 million. With total employment of about 19 million people, and three-quarters in farming, the informal sector

Table 9.2 Informal Sector for Main Economic Activity in Tanzania, 2006

Sector	*Share of total nonfarm employment (%)*	*Absolute number of workers (thousands)*	*Share of informal sector (%)*	*Median monthly earnings (T Sh)*	*Females (%)*
Informal employers[a]	4.7	226	10.1	72,000	33
Informal wage workers (regular)[b]	0.1	4	0.2	92,500[e]	52
Own-account operators[c]	40.6	1,947	86.9	40,000	46
Informal wage workers (casual)[d]	0.6	27	1.2	30,000[e]	38
Unpaid family workers	0.7	34	1.5	n.a.	56
Total informal sector	46.7	2,238	100	40,000	45
Total nonfarm employment	n.a.	4,789	n.a.	n.a.	43

Source: Elaborations based on NBS 2007b.
Note: Column totals may not sum exactly because of rounding. n.a. = not applicable.
a. "Informal employers" correspond to "self-employed with employees."
b. "Informal wage workers (regular)" are those with permanent contracts.
c. "Own-account operators" correspond to the "self-employed without employees" operating in the informal sector.
d. "Informal wage workers (casual)" includes both written and oral casual contracts, those "on contract," and those with no contract.
e. Median paid employment income.

accounted for about 12 percent of total employment. As elsewhere in Africa (cf. Becker 2004 and Haan 2006), a vast majority of the informal sector is composed of own-account operators: in 2005, they constituted 87 percent of the informal sector in the primary economic activity and contributed 41 percent of total nonfarm employment. Similarly, those reporting to be self-employed without employees are also more likely to be located in the informal sector: 93 percent of the self-employed without employees were in the informal sector in 2006, compared with 77 percent of the self-employed with employees.

Using this definition, informal sector activities have expanded much faster than total employment, helping absorb the large waves of new labor force entrants. From 2001 to 2006, the number of workers whose primary activity was in the informal sector increased by 700,000 on a net base, equivalent to a rate of roughly 9 percent per year. This is considerably faster than the 4 percent annual growth rate of overall employment (for the 15+ age group). This phenomenon is common among African economies, where rapidly expanding populations result in labor markets being continuously flooded by new job seekers and the formal sector is unable to absorb the new entrants (Fox and Gaal 2008).

Comparing the Formal and Informal Sectors

Distinct employment patterns separate the formal and informal sectors with age, gender, residence, education, and earnings playing important roles.

Demographics

Younger workers in Tanzania are more likely to be in the informal sector than older workers, particularly urban workers (figure 9.2).[3] This is in line with Perry

Figure 9.2 Share of Employed across Sectors within Each Age Group (15+) in Tanzania

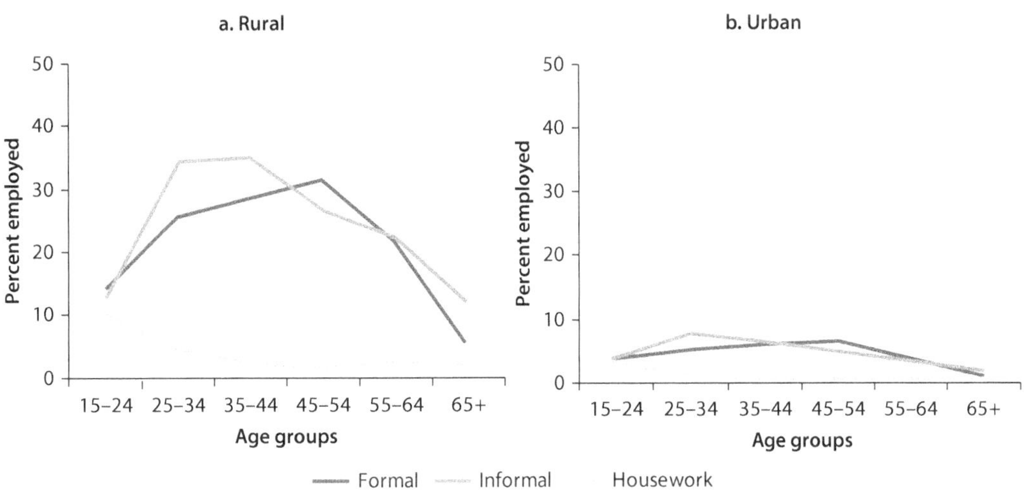

Source: Elaborations based on NBS 2007b.
Note: "Housework" in the International Labour Force Survey data corresponds to the "household employed" sector, which includes those employed as household servants.

and others (2007), who suggest that in Latin America, the informal sector serves as a point of entry into the labor market among the young, as they queue to find a job in the formal sector or accumulate more experience (unfortunately the ILFS data do not allow us to test the job-queuing hypothesis explicitly). As seen in figure 9.2, urban youth (where there is an inverted *U*-shape pattern) enter the informal sector. Possibly with age and experience, some find a job in the formal sector, but only panel data could give evidence of such mobility. It is also possible that youth today will not have the opportunities in formal sector employment when they grow older that older workers have today, and that the share of informal activities in the nonfarm economy is increasing. In that case, today's youth will remain in the informal sector into older ages.

Women remain overrepresented in the informal sector, even though the male share of informal activities is dominant and increasing. In 2000/01 and 2006, men accounted for more than half of those employed in the informal sector. In the main economic activity, the share of men increased from 51 percent in 2000/01 to 55 percent in 2006, a statistically significant change (table 9.3). However, the dominance of male workers is because of their higher participation rate. Although the share of women in the informal sector may appear low if compared with such other African countries as Benin, Kenya, Mali, or South Africa, where women account for 60 percent (or more) of total informal sector employment (Chen 2004), women are nevertheless overrepresented in the informal sector, as compared with other sectors of the economy. For instance, in the government sector men accounted for 68 percent of employees in the 15+ age group in 2006, and in the private formal sector they accounted for more than 70 percent of the total (table 9.3). The figures above also show that women in

Table 9.3 Distribution of Informal Sector Employment in Tanzania, by Type of Activity and Gender
Percent

	2000/01			*2006*		
	Male	*Female*	*Total*	*Male*	*Female*	*Total*
By type of activity						
Paid employee	47	53	100	60	40	100
Self-employed (with employees)	69	31	100	67	33	100
Self-employed (without employees)	50	50	100	54	47	100
Unpaid family worker	40	60	100	44	56	100
Total	51	49	100	55	45	100
By gender						
Paid employee	11	13	12	2	1	1
Self-employed (with employees)	12	6	9	12	7	10
Self-employed (without employees)	77	80	78	85	90	87
Unpaid family worker	1	2	1	1	2	2
Total	100	100	100	100	100	100

Sources: Elaborations based on NBS 2002, 2007b.
Note: Totals may not sum exactly because of rounding.

the nonfarm sector are more likely to be in the informal sector than the formal sector. This is not the case with men.

Women are relegated to more vulnerable and lower-paid occupations within the informal sector. Male workers in the informal sector are more likely to be higher up in the occupational pyramid or hierarchy. Although for both men and women self-employment without employees is by far the most prevalent category of employment in the informal sector, the share is higher for women. Men are more likely than women to be self-employed with employees: more than two-thirds of those in this category for the main economic activity were men. Given the generally lower earnings among own-account workers (see table 9.2), this highlights the higher level of vulnerability among women employed in the informal sector, who tend to be unpaid employees in smaller-scale household enterprises (table 9.3).

Informal sector activities are concentrated in trade. Three-quarters of informal employment is in the services sector, more than half of it in trade alone, and women are less diversified in their sectors of work. In fact, more than two-thirds of informal sector jobs were in the trade, and hotel and restaurant sectors in 2006 (table 9.4). Wholesale and retail trade was the main sector of activity in the informal sectors among both males and females, accounting for more than half the total in both categories. Hotels and restaurants occupied a further 20 percent of the total among females, with a much lower share (5 percent of the total) among males, who instead were in areas such as mining, construction, and transport. Manufacturing is one of the biggest categories for both men and women, although the occupations represented in this sector are quite different by gender.

Among males, almost half the workers in the informal sector who are in manufacturing are "extraction and building trades workers," with a further

Table 9.4 Sector Distribution of Informal Sector Jobs in Main Economic Activity in Tanzania, 2006

Main sector	*Male*	*Female*	*Total*
Farm	2	1	1
Industry	27	19	23
Mining and quarrying	5	1	3
Manufacturing	16	18	17
Electricity, gas, and water supply	0	0	0
Construction	7	0	4
Services	71	80	75
Wholesale and retail trade, repair of motor vehicles	56	56	56
Hotels and restaurants	5	21	12
Transport, storage, and communications	5	0	3
Other	6	4	5
Total	100	100	100

Source: Elaborations based on NBS 2007b.
Note: Totals may not sum exactly because of rounding.

30 percent in the "other crafts and related trades workers" category; whereas among females, the latter constitutes 80 percent of the total. Overall, women are less diversified than men, thereby adding to their vulnerability. Manufacturing, trade, and hotels account for 94 percent of all female employment. The sectors accounting for the three largest groups of employment for males (trade, manufacturing, and construction) account for 77 percent of total male employment.

Informal sector activities are largely urban. Urban areas accounted for two-thirds of total informal sector employment, and Dar es Salaam alone contributed 28 percent of informal sector employment in 2006. The service sector accounted for the largest share of informal sector employment in both urban and rural areas. Service and shop sales workers accounted for more than 50 percent of informal sector workers in urban areas and for 48 percent of the total in rural areas (figure 9.3).

Push factors (lack of other options) seem to dominate over pull factors (attractive opportunities) in motivating informal sector activities. A full 70 percent of workers in the informal sector in 2006 cited inability to find other work, additional income needs of the family, or release from other employment as the reasons for being in the informal sector. Less than 20 percent of those operating in the informal sector invoked good business opportunities or low capital requirements, while only 4 percent chose the informal sector for reasons of independence and flexibility.

Figure 9.3 Main Occupations in Informal Sector of Tanzania, 2006

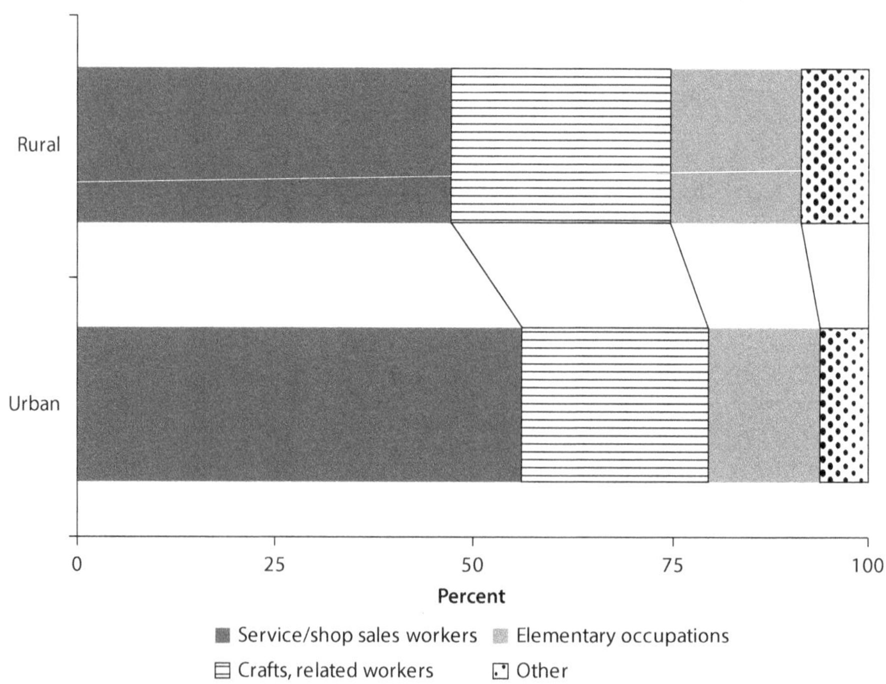

Source: Elaborations based on NBS 2007b.

Pull factors play a more important role for men than for women and for rural than urban areas. Women work in the informal sector mainly because of their need for additional income, whereas men are there because they see more attractive business opportunities. Pull factors play a larger role in rural areas where the option is lower-paying farming. Employment in the formal sector in rural areas is limited, and farming is the residual low-earnings option. Employment off the farm in the informal sector becomes the "preferred" option for many in rural areas. This pattern follows rural workers who move to urban areas because migrants in urban areas are more likely than nonmigrants to be in the informal sector (see tables 9A.1–9A.3).

Skills and Access to Different Occupations

Informal sector workers have less education than those working in the formal sector but more than those engaged in farming (table 9.5). The education system in Tanzania is based on a 7-4-2-3 system, including seven years of primary education, four years of lower-secondary education, two years of higher-secondary education, and three years (or more) of university education. The hierarchy of education levels is consistent with evidence from other countries (see, for example, Liimatainen 2002) and from the other country studies presented in this book. Overall, 12 percent of workers in the informal sector had no education, compared with 31 percent of those in small-scale farming. In urban areas, the share of workers with no education in the informal sector falls between the numbers for the government and private formal sectors and those of farming. Similarly, in urban areas, only 10 percent of workers in the informal sector have completed lower-secondary levels of education or more, compared with 21 percent in the formal private sector and 61 percent in the government sector. This level is nonetheless higher than the cumulative share of completed

Table 9.5 Education Profile by Main Sector in Tanzania, 2006

	Overall				*Urban only*			
Education level	*Government*	*Private formal*	*Informal*	*Farm*	*Government*	*Private formal*	*Informal*	*Farm*
No education	1	8	12	31	1	5	9	20
Incomplete primary	4	10	11	18	3	7	10	18
Completed primary	35	63	66	49	32	65	69	55
Incomplete lower secondary	2	3	3	1	2	3	3	3
Completed lower secondary	40	13	7	1	39	16	9	4
Higher secondary or university[a]	18	4	1	0	23	5	1	1
Total	100	101	100	100	100	101	101	101

Source: Elaborations based on NBS 2007b.
Note: Columns may not add to exactly 100 because of rounding.
a. "Higher secondary or university" category includes "some or completed higher secondary" and "some or completed university."

Figure 9.4 Education Profile of the Informal Sector in Tanzania

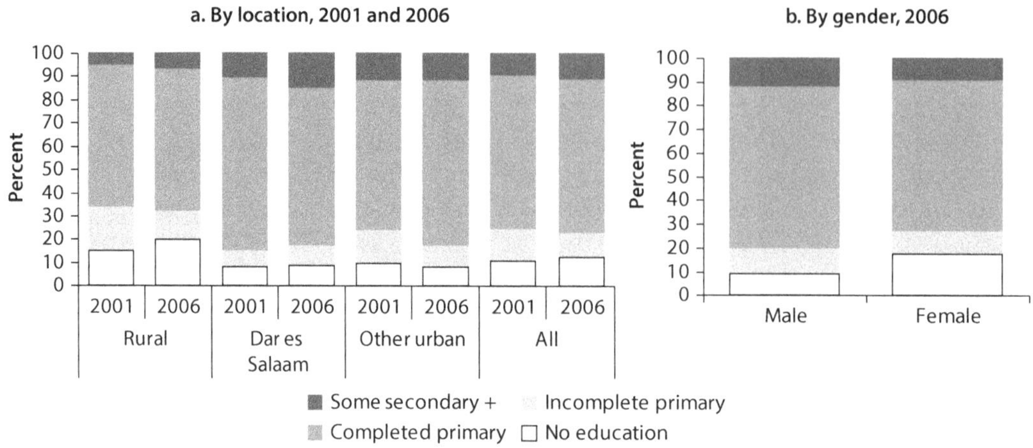

Sources: Elaborations based on NBS 2002, 2007b.

lower-secondary education and above for farming (4 percent of total). A majority of informal sector workers has completed primary education.

Education of informal sector workers favors those in urban over rural areas, and the education gap has increased over time. In Dar es Salaam, the share of workers in the informal sector in 2006 with some secondary education was twice that in rural areas, while those with no education were half the level registered in rural areas (figure 9.4). Overall, education levels did not improve with the expansion of the informal sector between 2001 and 2006. As the education levels increased in Dar es Salaam (at higher levels) and other urban areas (with higher levels of completed primary), rural areas saw a decline in education. The rural-based informal sector accounted for this with an increase of workers with no education. People leaving farming without education were finding their way into rural informal sector activities. Women are likely to have less education than men because 17 percent of women had no education, compared with 8 percent of men.

Skills development also takes place outside the formal education system with a bias toward those in the formal sector. Close to one in four workers in the informal sector received some form of training in 2006. About 1.7 million workers had benefited from some type of training—enterprise training, apprenticeships, vocational training—in 2000/01. The number increased in 2006 to over 2 million. Those working in the formal sector were more likely to receive training than those in the informal sector. A vast majority of government sector workers had training opportunities. One-third of workers in the formal private sector participated in these training opportunities. This percentage fell to 23 percent of workers in the informal sector, much higher than the training incidence among those engaged in small-scale farming or employed by a household (table 9.6).

Table 9.6 Training Incidence across Sectors in Tanzania, 2006

Main sector	*Percent who received training*
Government	82
Parastatals	60
Private formal	34
Informal	23
Traditional farm	5
Household employed	7
Total	12

Source: Elaborations based on NBS 2007b.

Table 9.7 Types of Training within Informal Sector of Tanzania, 2006

Type of training	*Urban*	*Rural*	*Total*
Informal apprenticeship	46.8	39.4	45.0
OJT	22.6	35.6	25.7
Vocational certificate	15.4	13.4	14.9
College/certificate	12.3	8.8	11.4
Diploma	1.4	0	1.1
Advanced diploma/university degree	0.5	0	0.4
Other	1.0	2.8	1.5
Total	100.0	100.0	100.0

Source: Elaborations based on NBS 2007b.

Apprenticeships are the primary mode of training for the informal sector, followed by on-the-job training (OJT) and vocational certificates. Together, these three categories account for 86 percent of total training in the informal sector (table 9.7). The difference between urban and rural areas among these modalities is generally insignificant (in the statistical sense) with the exception of OJT, which accounts for a higher share of those trained in rural areas. Most of the training is concentrated in (a) craft or trade and industrial programs and (b) construction at 41 and 31 percent, respectively (table 9A.4). The training incidence (percentage of employees with training) is highest in construction, manufacturing, and real estate but low in the sectors where most people are employed. Thus, in the wholesale and retail trade sector, and in the hotel and restaurant sector (which together account for two-thirds of informal sector workers), training incidence is relatively low (16 and 11 percent, respectively).

The type of training in the informal sector varies by industry. Across sectors of the informal economy, the training differences are notable (figure 9.5). Although informal apprenticeships dominate as a source of training, OJT is more prominent in sectors such as manufacturing, construction, real estate, and farming than in trade or hotels and restaurants. The cumulative share of vocational certificates and college certificates or diplomas is relatively low in the construction and manufacturing sectors, compared with the transport, storage, and communications sectors or the wholesale and retail sectors. In construction

Figure 9.5 Distribution of Training Modalities in Informal Economy of Tanzania by Sector, 2006

Source: Elaborations based on NBS 2007b.

Table 9.8 Training and Formal General Education in Informal Sector of Tanzania, 2006

	Training incidence across education levels			*Training incidence by education level*		
Level of schooling	*None*	*Some*	*Total*	*None*	*Some*	*Total*
No education	15.3	3.1	12.4	94.3	5.7	100.0
Incomplete primary	11.6	7.9	10.7	82.9	17.1	100.0
Completed primary	65.7	67.5	66.2	76.2	23.8	100.0
Incomplete lower secondary	2.0	4.0	2.5	62.7	37.3	100.0
Completed lower secondary	4.9	15.0	7.3	51.9	48.1	100.0
Higher secondary or university	0.4	2.5	0.9	36.3	63.7	100.0
Total	100.0	100.0	100.0	76.7	23.3	100.0

Source: Elaborations based on NBS 2007b.
Note: Numbers may not sum exactly because of rounding.

and manufacturing, informal training appears to substitute for, rather than complement, formal technical training.

Education influences access to training. Those who report any form of training at all also report higher levels of education, and only 3 percent of those with some training had no education, compared to 15 percent of those with no training (table 9.8). The training incidence in the informal sector increases with education level: 6 percent of those with no education report training, compared with 64 percent of those with advanced secondary or university education.

This pattern is confirmed in the multinomial analysis of table 9A.5. Even in the informal apprenticeship system, formal education is an important determinant of receiving training. The education level of those seeking to become an apprentice is reported to be one of the main criteria applied by master craftspersons to select apprentices (Haan 2006; Nübler, Hofmann, and Greiner 2009).

Access to training varies by residence and gender. Urban and male workers are more likely to have access to some form of training than rural or female workers. A regression of the incidence of training against individual characteristics supports much of the simple correlations discussed above (see also table 9A.5). People completing a primary education have a 40 percent higher likelihood of having training than those with an incomplete primary education, and those completing a secondary education are three times as likely to have had training. The chances of receiving training also increase with age, are considerably smaller for female and rural workers as well as own-account operators (compared to employers), and are higher in the manufacturing and construction sectors than elsewhere. The nature of training modalities may be one important reason why women have a lower training incidence: most training in the informal sector occurs either through informal apprenticeships or, in the case of formal vocational training, through faith-based training centers, both of which favor men (Johanson and Wanga 2008).

Training favors those in urban areas and in larger enterprises of the informal sector. The likelihood of training is 50 percent higher for urban than for rural workers, controlling for the sector of employment. Supply factors likely play a role in this pattern with more training centers available in cities than in the countryside. The likelihood of training is 70 percent higher for those working in informal sector enterprises that hire wage workers than those who do not. The self-employed who have reached a stage of profitability where they can afford to expand and hire wage workers are more likely to be able to invest in training for their workforce. They may also use more modern methods of production and require workers with skills to use the capital available.

Education also plays a role in attracting individuals to the informal sector to pursue good business opportunities. The motivation for being in the informal sector varies significantly for different levels of education. Of people with no formal education, only 8 percent were attracted into the informal sector by good business opportunities, whereas 41 percent claimed to be in the informal sector because of their inability to find other employment. Among people with more than a secondary education (higher secondary and university), 21 percent identified good business opportunities in the informal sector as the reason for undertaking their main economic activity there, and only 18 percent invoked inability to find other employment.

Like training, education is connected with the sector where one works. Multinomial logit regressions over the sample of those employed across different sectors show education to be associated with a higher probability of being employed in sectors with higher levels of formality relative to farming (tables 9A.6 and 9A.7). People who have a secondary education or more are also more likely to be employed in the public and private formal sectors, controlling for other factors. This highly educated group is more likely to be in wage work, or to work as employers, than as own-account workers or unpaid household workers. Higher levels of education are associated in particular with a higher probability of working in the government and parastatal sectors.

People leaving the farm receive more training. Having some training beyond general education—on the job, apprenticeship, vocational, or college certification—is associated with a greater probability of working off the farm in the formal or informal sector. Apprenticeships appear to be associated with a higher probability of being both self-employed and wage employed relative to being in small-scale farming. The probability is in fact higher for employers than for the self-employed without employees, suggesting that these apprenticeships serve to raise skills and lead to occupations that offer higher earnings. The likelihood estimates associated with informal apprenticeships are on par with those for OJT or vocational certificates for self-employment with or without employees. The estimates also confirm the fact that being female, young, and rurally based is an obstacle to accessing higher-paying sectors.

Skills and Earnings

Education and skills go beyond the type of job held to influence the earnings attained in the job. Multivariate analysis was used to investigate the returns to education and training, focusing on wage employment compared with self-employment.[4] It showed the following:

- Higher levels of education are associated with higher wage incomes among those in paid employment and with higher earnings among the self-employed, and the returns increase more rapidly at higher levels of education (table 9A.8). These findings are consistent with those of a recent study by Quinn and Teal (2008), using urban panel data for Tanzania. Here the earnings function was found to be convex in education, suggesting that investments in primary education may have limited effect on poverty (except for those who proceed to higher levels of education).

- Returns to education are higher in the wage sector. For all levels of education, except for incomplete secondary, the effect of having a given education level relative to the no-education baseline is higher in the wage sector than for the self-employed. And although the coefficient on completed secondary education is 1.6 times higher than the coefficient on incomplete secondary education in the wage equation, it is actually lower in the earnings equation, suggesting that among the self-employed, completing secondary education does not seem to convey an obvious premium beyond its effect on type of employment. The completed primary dummy is significant in both the income and earnings equations.

- Vocational training is also associated with higher hourly wages, particularly for training modalities other than informal apprenticeships. At the same time, only vocational and college certificates offer statistically significant earnings gains among the self-employed over the baseline of no training. OJT does not appear to have a statistically significant effect on the earnings of the nonfarm self-employed, while the effect of apprenticeships is significant only at the 10 percent level. Thus, apprenticeships seem to influence earnings only through access to higher-paying sectors.

Beyond education and training, experience and gender also influence earnings. Both incomes and earnings increase concavely with age, which can be viewed as a proxy for experience in the labor market and thus would be expected to positively affect earnings. Women earn less, accounting for age, education, and training profiles, as well as for the area of residence, the negative effect being twice as high for the self-employed as for those in paid employment.[5]

The informal sector is a diverse entity shaped by the education and skills of those who work in it. Education levels in the informal sector are higher than those in the farm sector—a majority of operators have finished primary school—but lag behind those of formal sector workers. Access to training is also limited. Such skills development outside formal education mostly comes in the form of apprenticeships. Apprenticeships and some formal education appear important to access the informal sector, but higher levels of education (secondary) are needed to access the formal sector and raise earnings. In contrast, apprenticeships offer no premium in terms of actual earnings in the informal sector, unlike vocational training.

Acquiring Skills for the Job Market in Tanzania

Constraints exist to attaining skills in the informal sector. The question is how informal sector workers can access skills from different providers—public and private, formal and informal. Access to skills development will depend not only on what the level of supply is, but also on how well different institutions or specific programs can cater to the constraints that informal sector workers face: among other things, their initial low level of education; their lack of time and money to spend on training; and their need for entrepreneurial, business management, and technical skills as mostly self-employed.

Skills for the informal sector are often neglected as a policy issue. The assumption seems to be that what works for the formal sector will also work for the informal sector. However, the preceding data show otherwise. Constraints to acquiring skills faced by those in the informal sector appear to be more binding than those of the formal sector. Although the role of technical and vocational education and training (TVET) is formally recognized in policy, little evidence exists of its adaptation to the special circumstances of the informal sector. The limited outreach of the formal TVET system implies that whatever training is taking place in the informal sector is in enterprises, the vast majority through apprenticeships.

Education

Education levels and literacy rates are rising in Tanzania, yet progress at postprimary levels is limited. In the 20 years after independence (1961–81), primary enrollment rates increased from 33 percent to 93 percent for the 7–14 age cohort, decreasing during the 1980s and then recovering to 84 percent by 2000. In contrast, secondary enrollment rates increased considerably from the early 1980s onward (Kahyarara and Teal 2006). By 2008, primary gross enrollment rates reached 105 percent, the number of out-of-school children (under 15) had been cut by 90 percent compared with 10 years earlier, and lower-secondary enrollment rates had more than quadrupled (table 9.9).[6] However, access to postprimary education remains limited; less than 6 percent proceed beyond lower secondary, and two-thirds do not go beyond primary levels.

Formal Sources of Skills Development

The national education strategy mentions the importance of strengthening TVET and training for the informal sector, yet few concrete steps have been taken to implement changes to the system. At the policy level, both the National Employment Policy and the National Strategy for Growth and the Reduction of Poverty recognize the importance of training for the informal sector. Action plans, grounded in careful analysis of labor market and training needs, are lacking to implement the policy pronouncements. Moreover, which agency is charged with executing the policies is unclear. The system remains fragmented and underfunded and does not cover key sections of the population, such as those in the informal sector.

The formal TVET system does not cover informal sector firms or workers. The system is divided between two regulatory and accreditation agencies also in charge of the direct provision of training: the National Council for Technical Education (NCTE), which regulates and provides relatively higher levels of skills (diploma and above), and the Vocational Education and Training Authority (VETA), which focuses on lower levels of skills training (technical skills mainly

Table 9.9 Education Statistics, Tanzania

Indicator	*1999*	*2008 or latest available*
Primary gross enrollment rate (%)	67	105
Primary completion ratio (%)	57	102
Out-of-school children, primary (thousands)	3,185	268
Lower-secondary gross enrollment rate (%)	8	36
Higher-secondary gross enrollment rate (%)	3	4
Vocational and technical as a percentage of secondary	9	—
Tertiary gross enrollment rate (%)	0.6	1.5

Source: World Bank 2011.
Note: — = not available.

at the certificate level or below a diploma). Established in 1994, VETA coordinates policy, sets standards, provides training, and tests skills. Yet the emphasis of vocational training for the informal sector appears to be in the early stages, and the tendency within VETA veers toward the continuation of traditional training methods and focus areas (Haan 2006). Indeed, training for the informal sector did not appear among the eight strategic issues in VETA's Corporate Plan III (2007–11), which focused on building VETA systems, enhancing training capacity in VETA training institutions, and implementing competency-based training and training of instructional staff.

The system is financed by a 2 percent vocational education and training levy collected by the Tanzania Revenue Authority on behalf of VETA. Only a third of that contribution is spent on VETA; the rest is considered government revenue and reallocated to other vocational training activities, such as the NCTE. Both VETA and NCTE activities are reputed to be undersourced by employers, and there have been calls for the two entities to merge. Moreover, donor funding for TVET has waned in recent years.

The enrollment in formal TVET is limited. As seen from table 9.9, only 1 in 10 students at a postprimary level is enrolled in TVET training. In 2007, only about 80,000 students were enrolled in different vocational institutions—less than one-third of the total number of out-of-school children. Females made up almost half (45 percent) of students enrolled and graduates. Nongovernmental institutions (private institutions, foreign-based owners, and nongovernmental organizations [NGOs]) accounted for about three-quarters of providers, and public providers (central government, local government, and VETA) the remainder. Throughout the country, VETA operates 21 training institutions, which in 2007 graduated 11,200 students. Only 18 informal sector training programs were conducted in 2006/07, with total enrollment of about 450.

Outreach to the informal sector is missing. A number of factors constrain the expansion of VETA training for the informal sector, including (a) the levy financing of VETA paid by the formal sector, which makes it more difficult to implement training for the informal sector; (b) high training fees, which are particularly constraining for informal sector workers (especially youth); and (c) pervasively negative opinions among informal sector operators about the quality of training offered by vocational training centers (VTCs). In addition to the VTCs, the government operates Folk Development Colleges, which are designed to develop farm, home economics, and technical skills as part of the efforts to stem rural–urban migration. Yet many of the Folk Development Colleges lack equipment and qualified personnel, and the effectiveness of training is unclear. Last, there is little demand orientation and partnership with informal sector operators in designing and running the programs.

Nonformal Sources of Skills Development

Most vocational training is provided by small-scale nongovernmental institutions. The training offered seems to focus predominantly on production skills, which contrasts with the need to provide training in basic bookkeeping and skills in marketing and product development that ongoing formalization efforts would generate. Generally, these small-scale institutions provide preemployment services and are financed through fees as well as production of goods during training. The quality of training and its relevance for the labor market, whether through donor-funded NGOs, churches, or private commercial operators, is undetermined.

Programs that successfully reach out to smaller informal operators with a package of services appear to have seen some success (table 9.10). An alternative model was designed with the help of GIZ (the German Agency for International Cooperation, formerly GTZ), targeting existing and potential informal sector operators. The Integrated Training and Entrepreneurship Promotion Program (INTEP) provided integrated training programs designed to cover both technical and business skills, plus literacy if necessary. The INTEP model included pretraining assessments of markets, target groups, and training capacity as well as provision of follow-up services.

Table 9.10 Programs That Partly Address Informal Sector Operators

Program or organization	*How does it address specific constraints for informal sector operators?*
SIDO provides a wide range of development business services, including technology, training, marketing, and financing to (a) people who have not yet started a business, (b) existing small enterprises, and (c) business service providers.	*Filling multiskilling needs:* Provides a range of training programs in business and technical areas to assist the small-scale self-employed.
Training programs are grouped in three areas: (a) entrepreneurship skills; (b) business management skills; and (c) acquisition and upgrading of technology, for example, in food processing and preservation, bamboo craft, leather products development, recycling, timber seasoning, and cashew nut processing.	*Lowering barriers to entry with respect to education and cost and payment method:* (a) no prior training or education is needed; (b) accepts in-kind contributions, easing the burden of payment and difficulties of cash flow. *Raising training capacity in the informal sector:* Generates potential master craftspersons who take on traditional apprentices.
Implemented from 1998 to 2002 by the government of Tanzania and GIZ (formerly GTZ), *INTEP*'s concept involved initial assessments of markets, target groups, and existing training capacity (potential suppliers of training) and subsequent provision of integrated training programs.	*Provided in-service training.* *Lowered barriers to entry,* through subsidized training schemes. *Filled multiskilling needs:* Provided technical and business skills plus literacy if needed.
An early assessment reportedly showed that the modules and courses were cost-effective, provided adequate training, and were successful in integrating trainers into the informal sector. Training resulted in improved quality of goods and services produced by the informal sector firms, which in turn led to greater sales and profits. The evaluation pointed to the importance of providing a mix of skills, providing follow-up services, and subsidizing training. It also suggested that the training for those already in business was more successful than for the unemployed, pointing to the payoff of in-service skills upgrading.	

Source: Based on Johanson and Wanga 2008.

The Small Industries Development Organization (SIDO) is another such example. It provides both in-service and preemployment programs with the purpose of developing small firms in both the formal and informal sectors, and business extension services, including loans. The training offered is intended to generate entrepreneurship, improve business management skills, and assist with technological upgrading. SIDO reduces barriers to entry by putting no preconditions on training and accepting fees in kind.

Recently, SIDO and VETA have started to cooperate so that VETA graduates are introduced to SIDO programs and services to generate successful businesses through self-employment. With a combination of entrepreneurship training, on-the-job placements with firms, incubators, stronger labor and product market information on demand and needs, and credit, the program set-up strengthens the link between graduates and the work of self-employment.

A failure to evaluate costs and effectiveness to ensure that programs can be scaled up in a sustainable way is problematic. The INTEP program, while judged to be successful, was ended because it was considered very costly because of the staff intensity required for initial surveys of markets and target groups, training, and follow-up services. More generally, no formal evaluations are available of SIDO's past or current activities, cost-effectiveness, or end results in terms of employment numbers and earnings. Although this finding is relevant to programs for the informal sector, it is equally relevant to those of the formal sector.

Traditional Sources of Skills Development

Apprenticeships can benefit from reforms. A small informal sector survey of 350 enterprises in Dar es Salaam concluded that more than half the operators had apprentices, with on average about two apprentices per firm (Nell and Shapiro 1999). Apprenticeship systems have appreciable advantages: they are entirely self financed and are cost-effective in transferring rudimentary skills. However, the Tanzanian apprentice system tends to exclude women, provides low-quality training, lacks appropriate instructional skills, and perpetuates old technologies. The apprentice system also appears less well organized than in other African countries. In Kenya, Zimbabwe, and West African countries, formal contracts and even payments to the master craftsperson are typical; in Tanzania, because of the connection with family or friends, no contracts exist to define the duration and type of skills to be offered.

Instructional reforms are needed. Learning on the job while producing goods and services for profit produces a strong link to the demand side and relevant technical skills but limits uptake of broader knowledge, such as business skills. The method of training is entirely skills based and focused on production; no theory is taught, and no training material is used. The apprentice observes and helps the master craftsperson and is expected to contribute as quickly as possible, often after only a few months, possibly creating a trade-off between wider learning and production in the firm. Indeed, trainees often learn only a part of the skills that are required for the enterprise—as an example, the apprentices in motor vehicle shops often learn only mechanics, auto electrical, or panel beating. Moreover, the skills are almost exclusively technical, rarely exposing apprentices to the commercial and business side of the firm. This weakness is significant (and prevalent in many more formal forms of training) because the most probable future for the apprentices is self-employment. The study by Nell and Shapiro (1999) showed that the vast majority of past apprentices had a job related to the trade in which they were trained: however, only 30 percent of the former apprentices were employees (10 percent remaining in the enterprise where they had been apprentices, 20 percent in another informal enterprise) while 50 percent had set up their own business.

Combining apprenticeships with education and formal training provides extra benefits. More recent evidence (Nübler, Hofmann, and Greiner 2009) suggests that workers often benefit from combining elements of formal education and training with informal training. Master craftspersons prefer apprentices with some formal education, though VETA graduates suffered in reputation. Incomes were found to be higher among those who combined apprenticeship training with formal training. This should be increasingly possible as a new "modular" approach to formal training is developed (box 9.1). Offering apprentices who lack basic education a second chance to acquire educational qualifications can further improve outcomes.

Addressing gender imbalances in the labor market is important. The distribution across trades, again drawing on the small Dar es Salaam survey, suggests significant division along traditional gender stereotypes. The male-dominated trades (motor vehicle mechanics, welding, carpentry, masonry) were more likely to offer apprenticeships, but only about one in four apprentices were females. Women held apprenticeships predominantly in tailoring, hairdressing, catering, and child care. In trades considered "male," the participation of women was strongly discouraged. The survey also suggested that actions and prejudices of enterprise operators served as a barrier for women entering the system; fear of pregnancy and loss of time while training a female apprentice underpinned these actions (Nell and Shapiro 1999).

The lack of formal recognition of skills achievements reduces the value of apprenticeship training in the labor market. Formal testing and certification of skills can provide employers with information about the potential productivity of a worker regardless of where he or she was trained. The recognition of skills is mostly informal. Although VETA offers certification through skills testing in some trades, few apprentices try to receive formal accreditation this way. No recognition is available in the marketplace for the skills obtained or use of certification to assess the quality of the training offered. The reasons underlying the lack of interest in pursuing skills certification include cost of preparatory courses, language barriers, and the low reputation of VETA among craftspeople.

Strengthening the organization of informal sector operators can help overcome constraints to training in the informal sector and advocate for further

Box 9.1 Informal Apprenticeship in Tanzania

A recent survey conducted in Mtwara and Lindi in southern Tanzania analyzed the practices, institutions, and labor market outcomes of informal apprenticeship in car mechanics, electricity services, tailoring, carpentry, plumbing, local arts, and food processing. The study found the apprenticeship system to be widespread and well established in the various craft sectors.

Training is based mostly on unwritten contracts between master craftspersons and apprentices. Training commonly lasts one to two years, with an average duration of 21 months. Unlike the situation in many West African countries, the average age of apprentices was quite high at 23.5 years, especially considering that most apprentices have only completed primary education (seven years). Master craftspersons had more education, on average, although most learned the skills of their trade in informal apprenticeships as well. The level of formal education is one of the three main criteria (together with age and talent for the work) for the selection of apprentices, reported by almost one-third of master craftspersons, who are concerned with the trainability and productivity of apprentices.

Most apprentices reported having decided to apprentice for pull reasons, such as (a) desire to learn the skills of the trade, (b) liking the trade, and (c) viewing apprenticeship as a cost-effective or good way of skills acquisition. At the same time, third parties (NGO workers, researchers, government employees) gave informal apprenticeships low rankings in terms of how well respected a skilled worker who learned through an apprenticeship is, or in terms of the contribution of apprenticeships to national development.

Skills recognition is mostly informal, through social networks and based on the good reputation of the master craftsperson in the community. Very few apprentices took the skills tests offered by VETA. Among reasons for not seeking formal recognition were the high cost of preparatory courses, language barriers (higher-level tests require knowledge of English), and the low reputation of VETA among craftspeople.

Skills acquired through apprenticeships are mostly technical; acquisition of theoretical or business skills is less frequent. Apprenticeships lead to employability of graduates, with most apprentices starting their own enterprises. Apprenticeships also appear to yield good returns in terms of income: a separate survey in Mtwar and Lindi suggests that incomes of unskilled daily laborers in urban areas are less than half the average wage of a skilled worker trained through an apprenticeship. At the same time, incomes are higher among those who combined apprenticeship training with formal training.

Source: Nübler, Hofmann, and Greiner 2009.

reforms. The informal sector in Tanzania is less organized than in other African countries (e.g., Kenya) and as such, the development of informal sector associations has been fairly recent. Some informal sector associations do exist,[7] and an umbrella organization, the Association of Small Informal Businesses, has been created. To date, it has done relatively little in terms of training services but sees training as an important priority for the future (box 9.2).

Box 9.2 Training Provision by Informal Sector Associations in Tanzania

The Association of Small Informal Businesses (VIBINDO) is an umbrella nonprofit NGO established in 1995 with 312 groups as members, representing 40,000 individuals. Since 2007, it has established offices in all 22 regions of Tanzania. The members are divided into three categories: producers, vendors, and service providers. Among other functions, VIBINDO's strategic plan calls for it to provide training services to members on the assumption that workers in the informal sector need to acquire skills through training to improve productivity as a necessary condition for formalization. So far, VIBINDO has organized two training programs for its members.

In collaboration with the United Nations Industries Development Organization, VIBINDO provided training to 500 members in 2003/04 in carpentry work, food processing, and business leadership and management skills. In 2006, with support from the International Labour Organization/United Nations Development Programme, VIBINDO helped train 30 trainers on acquisition and management of urban land for informal sector training activities. VIBINDO carried out a training needs analysis in 2007 that revealed a lack of knowledge and skills among informal sector operators in product quality, packaging, marketing, pricing, and bookkeeping.

One of the main constraints to expansion of its training services is financial, a consequence of the inability of most informal sector operators to afford the costs of training. Its new strategic plan (2009–11) is expected to feature training in business development.

Source: Johanson and Wanga 2008.

Conclusions

Growth in the informal sector has provided jobs for new labor force entrants in urban and rural areas. This growth is expected to continue. Its economic import has shifted and so must its position in economic policy and programs. Understanding what prevents informal sector operators from becoming more productive and from expanding employment through hiring workers on the market will be essential to improving the labor market outcomes of those employed in the informal sector (and particularly of youth) and capturing the characteristics of the jobs that the economy is creating.

Removing barriers to expansion will encourage small firms with the potential to grow. Addressing infrastructure constraints, such as energy and roads to improve connectivity, or improving the provision of credit to medium-size firms, could encourage expansion and presence of larger firms that are both more productive and more likely to train their employees. World Bank Investment Climate Assessment data suggest a particularly large productivity gap in Tanzania between small firms and medium or large firms as compared to Kenya and Uganda. Ensuring that the investment climate is friendly to new business start-ups is necessary, as is striking an appropriate balance in labor market regulations.

At the same time, a more general need exists to improve productivity in the informal sector through skills development, where training levels remain low.

Very few workers in the informal sector have any education beyond the primary level; yet earnings improve with higher levels of education or vocational training. In addition, the lack of business skills among own-account workers is hampering the growth of their enterprises. Although access to primary education has been improved, few children pursue secondary levels of education (general or TVET). For those who do not complete primary school, few options exist for further formal training. Gradual expansion of the secondary level will allow for improving quality and access. The likelihood of further training increases with education, even when other personal characteristics are controlled for.

Training for the informal sector is not sufficiently promoted in Tanzania by either the government or donors. Unlike the situation in many other countries, initiatives have been launched to address informal sector skills development. However, the government's institutional system is fragmented, with no clear assignment of responsibilities for informal sector strengthening. Furthermore, existing programs lack rigorous evaluations of cost-effectiveness and outcomes. In all, informal sector training initiatives, where they exist, tend to be one-off rather than continuous and only weakly linked with credit and business advisory services. Donors are not filling the training gap in the informal sector.

Recognition of the constraints to training faced by the informal sector operators is essential. The financing of training by the informal sector is constrained by low cash flow, limited ability to pay, and high opportunity cost of time away from work for training. These constraints can be addressed by providing subsidized training and modular forms of delivery to lower time constraints for those working. More consideration needs to be given to the share of the training levy allocated to informal sector training. The potential is there for the informal sector to become a valuable part of the value chain of formal sector firms by producing intermediate goods and services. The reform of the levy system could also include separating it from other levies for transparency and financing in-service rather than preemployment training for youth, as the former has proven more efficient.

A strategy to address gender imbalances is needed. Programs and policies should look at the specific constraints in terms of access and earnings. Women have less access to the informal sector than men (compared with the farming sector) and are more likely to be in the informal sector because of "distress work" (the family needs more income) than good business opportunities. They earn less and are relegated to specific sectors. They are generally excluded from some of the male-dominated trades, which offer higher earnings and have less access to private or NGO-run training schemes. These gender gaps may be the result of different household responsibilities as well as related cultural and societal norms, but they need to be considered in policy interventions. For example, efforts to increase information about payoff to less traditional female occupations may help women make choices that increase their lifetime earnings.

Upgrading master craftspersons can improve training. Apprenticeships will continue to be an important source of skills for the informal sector. The apprenticeship system can be strengthened by "training the trainers" (i.e., master craftspersons). Providing master craftspersons with upgraded technical skills and knowledge of how to deliver effective training programs can improve apprenticeship outcomes. Targeting master craftspersons and giving them business and pedagogical skills can improve the quality of informal apprenticeship training in Tanzania and the employment outcomes of those relying on apprenticeships for skills acquisition.

Strengthening informal sector associations is important. The informal sector is becoming more organized in Tanzania. Associations with close ties to the informal sector could be strengthened and encouraged to fill a more important role in terms of advising members of the benefits of training, overseeing quality of different initiatives, providing feedback on the type of training needed, or organizing training directly. Associations can aggregate the training needs of smaller members and deliver training on a more economical scale that can be afforded by members. Associations can also play an important role in policy development by encouraging attention to the needs of the informal sector.

The certification of skills required by the informal sector can improve labor market efficiency. Skills recognition for those who complete apprenticeships remains largely informal and thus primarily local in the geographical sense. This not only limits the portability of skills into formal markets but also makes it harder to promote quality in training and use apprenticeships for additional formal training. Certification through VETA, while available, is not common because of a combination of the associated fees for preparatory courses and certification tests, and the skepticism vis-à-vis VETA within the informal sector. Addressing these problems could lead to a more efficient labor market. Informal associations can work with VETA to ensure that apprenticeship skills are part of the testing and certification system.

More attention needs to be given to rigorous evaluation of programs providing skills for the informal sector. The improvement of skills in the informal sector is one of the steps needed to improve productivity and income in this sector. The evidence offered in this chapter from household surveys points to the importance of skills in reaching better-paying jobs in both informal and formal sectors. As in many other countries of the region, finding training programs in Tanzania whose effect on earnings and welfare has been rigorously evaluated is difficult to do. Careful monitoring and rigorous evaluation is a first step to identifying effective strategies for skills development and avoiding pitfalls. More attention to evaluation by government and donors will improve policy development for the informal sector and allow people to identify the best programs for their needs.

Annex 9A: Tables

This annex includes two sets of tables. The first describes the reasons for working in the informal sector and the types of training taken, as mentioned in the main text. The second contains the multinomial regressions results used in the text to explain the determinants of training in the informal sector and the impact of different levels and forms of education and training on the sector and type of employment and earnings.

Table 9A.1 Reasons for Informality in Main Economic Activity (15+), by Gender

	2000/01			*2006*		
Reason	*Male*	*Female*	*Total*	*Male*	*Female*	*Total*
Cannot find other work	43.8	48.1	45.8	37.9	35.2	36.7
Released from other employment	5.0	2.4	3.8	2.3	1.2	1.8
Retirement from other employment	1.6	0.9	1.3	1.2	0.6	0.9
Family needs additional income	19.9	28.6	24.0	25.1	38.6	31.2
Business has good income opportunities	8.6	4.1	6.5	15.8	7.9	12.2
Business does not require much capital	6.3	8.2	7.2	6.7	7.7	7.2
Can keep production costs low	0.4	0.6	0.5	0.6	0.4	0.5
Desire to be independent	2.7	1.4	2.1	2.2	1.9	2.0
Can choose hours and place of work	3.5	0.9	2.3	2.3	0.9	1.6
Can combine business and household responsibilities	2.2	2.2	2.2	2.4	4.2	3.2
Traditional line of business of respondent tribe	3.8	1.0	2.5	2.3	0.8	1.6
Other reasons	2.2	1.5	1.9	1.2	0.7	1.0
Total	100.0	100.0	100.0	100.0	100.0	100.0

Sources: Elaborations based on NBS 2002, 2007b.

Table 9A.2 Reasons for Informality in Main Economic Activity (15+), by Urban/Rural

	2000/01				*2006*			
Reason	*Urban (non–Dar es Salaam)*	*Rural*	*Dar es Salaam*	*Total*	*Urban (non–Dar es Salaam)*	*Rural*	*Dar es Salaam*	*Total*
Cannot find other work	56.7	31.9	44.9	45.8	38.8	27.4	45.0	36.7
Released from other employment	2.4	1.3	10.0	3.8	1.5	0.7	3.5	1.8
Retirement from other employment	1.4	0.9	1.6	1.3	1.0	0.4	1.5	0.9
Family needs additional income	22.5	30.6	17.8	24.0	33.7	32.1	26.8	31.2
Business has good income opportunities	4.7	10.5	4.1	6.5	10.4	16.4	9.6	12.2
Business does not require much capital	4.2	10.9	7.5	7.2	6.5	10.3	4.4	7.2
Can keep production costs low	0.3	0.6	0.8	0.5	0.5	0.5	0.5	0.5
Desire to be independent	0.9	2.8	3.5	2.1	1.5	1.6	3.3	2.0
Can choose hours and place of work	1.5	3.3	2.4	2.3	1.1	2.4	1.4	1.6
Can combine business and household responsibilities	1.3	2.5	3.5	2.2	2.4	5.1	2.2	3.2
Traditional line of business of respondent tribe	2.3	2.3	3.1	2.5	1.6	2.4	0.8	1.6
Other reasons	1.9	2.6	0.9	1.9	1.1	0.8	1.1	1.0
Total	100.0	100.0	100.0	100.0	100.0	100.0	100.0	100.0

Sources: Elaborations based on NBS 2002, 2007b.

Table 9A.3 Share of Migrants and Nonmigrants in Informal Sector Because of Inability to Find Other Work
Percent

	Male		*Female*	
Status	*Urban*	*Rural*	*Urban*	*Rural*
Nonmigrant	37.9	27.6	37.0	26.0
Migrant	52.9	37.1	43.3	25.5

Source: Elaborations based on NBS 2007b.

Table 9A.4 Main Subjects of Training in Informal Sector (15+), 2006
Percent

Training subject	*Urban*	*Rural*	*Overall informal*
Other craft, trade, and industrial programs	43.9	33.6	41.4
Construction trade programs	28.3	38.7	30.8
Transport and communication programs	5.9	4.9	5.7
Service trade programs	4.3	10.2	5.7
Commercial, clerical, business and public administration programs	6.0	1.5	4.9
Medicine and health-related programs	3.3	2.8	3.2
Education training	1.7	2.4	1.9
Fine and applied arts programs	2.0	1.4	1.9
Agriculture, forestry, and fishery programs	1.0	1.7	1.1
Other	3.7	2.9	3.6
Total	100.0	100.0	100.0

Source: Elaborations based on NBS 2007b.

Table 9A.5 Determinants of Training in Informal Sector (15+), 2006

Variable	*Overall informal*	*Manufacturing*	*Wholesale and retail*	*Hotels and restaurants*
Age	1.064*** (0.017)	0.993 (0.029)	1.067** (0.031)	1.042 (0.060)
Age squared/100	0.946*** (0.018)	0.999 (0.033)	0.961 (0.033)	0.978 (0.064)
Females	0.490*** (0.045)	0.406*** (0.074)	0.411*** (0.052)	0.968 (0.324)
No education	0.204*** (0.044)	0.152*** (0.064)	0.251*** (0.074)	0.273* (0.192)
Incomplete primary	0.626*** (0.102)	0.422*** (0.120)	0.704* (0.149)	0.439 (0.223)
Incomplete secondary	2.478*** (0.600)	1.498 (0.943)	2.701*** (0.815)	1.990 (1.326)
Completed secondary	3.148*** (0.457)	3.179*** (1.188)	3.113*** (0.592)	4.106*** (1.803)
Advanced secondary/university	4.884*** (1.866)	2.214 (2.245)	5.951*** (2.994)	1.358 (1.683)
Paid employee	1.029 (0.300)	0.289 (0.287)	0.546 (0.366)	2.875 (2.919)
Self-employed with employees	1.707*** (0.238)	1.259 (0.376)	2.474*** (0.556)	1.079 (0.339)
Unpaid family helper	0.732 (0.306)	0.202* (0.181)	0.961 (0.527)	
Urban	1.489** (0.234)	2.119*** (0.489)	1.173 (0.229)	1.379 (0.592)
Recent migrant (<5 years)	1.195 (0.178)	1.474 (0.366)	0.960 (0.238)	1.045 (0.564)
Migrant (5+ years)	1.520*** (0.174)	1.922*** (0.447)	1.306* (0.206)	2.337** (0.803)
Agriculture/hunting/forestry	0.676 (0.354)			

table continues next page

Table 9A.5 Determinants of Training in Informal Sector (15+), 2006 *(continued)*

Variable	*Overall informal*	*Manufacturing*	*Wholesale and retail*	*Hotels and restaurants*
Mining/quarrying	0.982 (0.398)			
Manufacturing	4.544*** (1.238)			
Construction	4.200*** (1.254)			
Wholesale/retail trade	0.620* (0.157)			
Hotels and restaurants	0.490** (0.145)			
Real estate/renting	1.464 (0.627)			
Public administration	3.910 (5.845)			
Education	0.662 (0.523)			
Health/social work	0.766 (0.422)			
Other community/social work	1.057 (0.310)			
Private household employed	1.122 (0.570)			
Constant	0.084*** (0.036)	1.402 (1.120)	0.036*** (0.023)	0.056** (0.075)
Regional and quarter dummies	Yes	Yes	Yes	Yes
Observations	4,966	817	2,794	542

Source: Elaborations based on NBS 2007b.
Note: Weighted estimates. Taylor-linearized standard errors clustered at primary sampling unit level in parentheses. Odds ratios reported in place of estimated coefficients. Dependent variable equals one if any training reported and zero otherwise. Education baseline: completed primary; migration baseline: since birth; sector baseline: real estate/renting; work-type baseline: self-employed without employees.
Significance level: *$p < .1$, **$p < .05$, ***$p < .01$.

Table 9A.6 Sector Location Logit (15+), 2006

Variable	*Government*	*Private formal*	*Informal*	*Household employed*
Age	1.355*** (0.037)	1.005 (0.012)	1.084*** (0.016)	0.819*** (0.013)
Age squared	0.713*** (0.023)	0.961*** (0.014)	0.900*** (0.017)	1.195*** (0.022)
Females	0.549*** (0.054)	0.361*** (0.022)	0.716*** (0.039)	3.986*** (0.369)
Education (baseline: no education)				
Incomplete primary	3.141*** (0.953)	1.153 (0.140)	1.112 (0.106)	0.544*** (0.100)
Completed primary	5.466*** (1.534)	1.743*** (0.177)	1.723*** (0.150)	1.052 (0.142)
Incomplete secondary	7.271*** (2.976)	1.536** (0.302)	1.550** (0.281)	2.135*** (0.483)
Completed secondary	49.063*** (14.630)	4.695*** (0.774)	3.338*** (0.537)	3.072*** (0.720)
Advanced secondary/university	73.021*** (29.474)	6.271***(2.104)	3.588***(1.213)	6.140***(2.881)
Training (baseline: no training)				
On-the-job training	16.698*** (2.894)	4.465*** (0.619)	2.699*** (0.365)	0.632 (0.200)
Informal apprenticeship	3.345*** (0.705)	2.941*** (0.386)	2.986*** (0.367)	1.323 (0.378)
Vocational certificate	13.524*** (2.839)	5.482*** (0.964)	3.560*** (0.660)	1.325 (0.453)
College certificate	45.179*** (7.347)	5.832*** (0.831)	2.101*** (0.312)	1.007 (0.326)
Diploma	24.187*** (8.724)	4.170*** (1.646)	1.114 (0.510)	0.226 (0.257)
Advanced diploma/university degree	18.050*** (9.698)	3.314** (1.870)	0.255** (0.175)	0.000*** (0.000)
Other training	6.502*** (2.151)	2.167*** (0.532)	0.567* (0.166)	0.000*** (0.000)
Urban	6.876*** (1.078)	9.988*** (1.547)	12.058*** (1.692)	6.669*** (1.222)
Constant	0.000*** (0.000)	0.032*** (0.011)	0.011*** (0.005)	0.159*** (0.093)
Observations	34,671	34,671	34,671	34,671

Source: Elaborations based on NBS 2007b.
Note: Weighted regression. Relative risk ratios presented instead of coefficients: baseline category: agriculture. Taylor-linearized standard errors clustered at primary sampling unit level in parentheses. Quarter-year and regional dummies included but not reported.
Significance level: *10 percent, **5 percent, ***1 percent.

Table 9A.7 Multinomial Logits for Work Type (Main Employment, 15+), 2006

Variable	*Wage employee*	*Self-employed with employees*	*Self-employed without employees*	*Unpaid family help (nonfarm)*
Age	1.032*** (0.011)	1.167*** (0.028)	1.084*** (0.016)	0.830*** (0.013)
Age squared	0.938*** (0.013)	0.829*** (0.026)	0.899*** (0.018)	1.181*** (0.021)
Females	0.384*** (0.022)	0.415*** (0.041)	0.734*** (0.042)	2.987*** (0.264)
Education (baseline: no education)				
Incomplete primary	1.212 (0.146)	1.616* (0.417)	1.118 (0.106)	0.633*** (0.106)
Completed primary	1.849*** (0.193)	3.246*** (0.640)	1.719*** (0.160)	1.117 (0.140)
Incomplete secondary	1.697*** (0.337)	4.263*** (1.403)	1.433* (0.265)	2.409*** (0.497)
Completed secondary	8.196*** (1.257)	11.271*** (2.677)	3.499*** (0.553)	4.624*** (0.958)
Advanced secondary/university	11.782*** (3.242)	11.361*** (4.965)	2.669*** (0.819)	4.955*** (2.160)
Training (baseline: no training)				
On-the-job training	6.584*** (0.891)	5.479*** (1.105)	2.666*** (0.346)	1.285 (0.458)
Informal apprenticeship	3.141*** (0.409)	4.214*** (0.730)	2.834*** (0.358)	1.244 (0.283)
Vocational certificate	7.016*** (1.161)	5.916*** (1.533)	3.391*** (0.662)	1.184 (0.394)
College certificate/diploma/university/other	10.585*** (1.497)	3.445*** (0.680)	1.294* (0.188)	0.660 (0.195)
Urban	9.367*** (1.325)	10.833*** (2.060)	11.769*** (1.644)	7.168*** (1.196)
Constant	0.021*** (0.008)	0.000*** (0.000)	0.009*** (0.004)	0.210*** (0.107)
Observations	34,671	34,671	34,671	34,671

Source: Elaborations based on NBS 2007b.
Note: Weighted regression. Relative risk ratios presented instead of coefficients: baseline category: agriculture. Taylor-linearized standard errors clustered at primary sampling unit level in parentheses. Quarter-year and regional dummies included but not reported.
Significance level: *10 percent, **5 percent, ***1 percent.

Table 9A.8 Selectivity Corrected Wage Regressions (15+), 2006

Variable	*Ln (hourly wage)*	*Ln (hourly earnings)*
Age	0.057*** (0.010)	0.041*** (0.010)
Age squared	−0.048*** (0.012)	−0.051*** (0.012)
Females	−0.179*** (0.041)	−0.390*** (0.038)
Education (baseline: no education)		
Incomplete primary	0.152 (0.119)	−0.011 (0.078)
Completed primary	0.317*** (0.080)	0.164*** (0.060)
Incomplete secondary	0.588*** (0.128)	0.512*** (0.133)
Completed secondary	0.966*** (0.109)	0.460*** (0.112)
Advanced secondary/university	1.537*** (0.136)	1.165*** (0.190)
Training (baseline: no training)		
On-the-job training	0.476*** (0.072)	0.096 (0.088)
Informal apprenticeship	0.251*** (0.064)	0.097* (0.057)
Vocational certificate	0.499*** (0.093)	0.308*** (0.092)
College certificate/diploma/university/other	0.970*** (0.112)	0.510*** (0.149)
Urban	0.023 (0.084)	0.102 (0.115)
m1	−0.017 (0.101)	0.748** (0.363)
m2	−1.368*** (0.264)	−0.056 (0.102)
m3	1.276*** (0.392)	0.341 (0.468)
m4	−0.661*** (0.232)	0.221 (0.291)

table continues next page

Table 9A.8 Selectivity Corrected Wage Regressions (15+), 2006 *(continued)*

Variable	*Ln (hourly wage)*	*Ln (hourly earnings)*
m5	−0.717*** (0.218)	0.411* (0.240)
Constant	2.362*** (0.308)	4.231*** (0.430)
Observations	3,629	4,540
R-squared	0.493	0.137

Source: Elaborations based on NBS 2007b.
Note: Weighted estimates. Bootstrapped standard errors (100 replications), clustered at primary sampling unit level in parentheses. Regional and quarter-year dummies included but not reported. m1–m5 are consistent estimators of conditional expected values of the residuals derives from the multinomial logit model, such that the coefficients estimate the covariance between the residual in the second-stage regression and the residuals from the multinomial logit.
Significance level: *$p < .1$, **$p < .05$, ***$p < .01$.

Notes

1. This chapter is based on Cojocaru (2010) and Johanson and Wanga (2008).
2. Fertility rates declined from 6.3 in 1991/92 to 5.7 in 2004/05; infant and child mortality declined from 115 to 95 and from 192 to 154 between 1988 and 1991/92 and between 1991/92 and 2002, respectively.
3. The omitted category in the age profile graphs is the sum of inactive, unemployed, and farm workers. Because farming is the prevalent employment category in rural areas, the remaining categories depicted in the graph account for only a small share of the total.
4. The underlying specification is based on the model outlined by Mincer (1958), modified as follows: (a) because employment experience cannot be inferred directly from the data, we use age and age squared instead; (b) education enters as a set of dummy variables for each additional education level, since we would like to investigate how wages or earnings vary across education levels and across different types of training. Given the underlying specification, the use of the term "returns to education" here is imprecise, as pointed out by Heckman, Lochner, and Todd (2005). Technically, we investigate the growth rate of earnings with additional schooling or training.
5. Some caution is nonetheless needed with regard to the earnings regressions, because the explanatory value of the regression is low: only 14 percent of the variation in earnings is explained by the variables included. Significant education variables may be picking up other effects that are omitted from the regression, including unobservables such as the innate ability of a worker.
6. The education system is based on a 7-4-2-3 system, including seven years of primary education, four years of lower-secondary education, two years of higher-secondary education, and three years (or more) of university education.
7. These include the Handcraft Organization of Tanzania, the Tanzania Crafts Association, and the Tanzania Food Processors Association.

References

Becker, Kristina Flodman. 2004. *The Informal Economy*. Stockholm: Swedish International Development Agency.

Chen, Martha. 2004. "Women in the Informal Sector: A Global Picture, the Global Movement." *SAIS Review* 21 (1): 71–82.

Cojocaru, Alejandru. 2010. "Tanzania: Skills in the Informal Sector." Unpublished, Africa Department, World Bank, Washington, DC.

Fox, Louise M., and Melissa Sekkel Gaal. 2008. *Working Out of Poverty: Job Creation and the Quality of Growth in Africa*. Washington, DC: World Bank.

Haan, Hans Christiaan. 2006. *Training for Work in the Informal Micro-enterprise Sector: Fresh Evidence from Sub-Sahara Africa*. Dordrecht, Netherlands: Springer.

Heckman, James, Lance Lochner, and Petra Todd. 2005. "Earnings Functions, Rates of Return, and Treatment Effects: The Mincer Equation and Beyond." Working Paper 11544, National Bureau of Economic Research, Cambridge, MA.

Johanson, Richard, and Goodwill Wanga. 2008. "Skills Training for the Informal Sector in Tanzania." Unpublished, Africa Department, World Bank, Washington, DC.

Kahyarara, Godius, and Francis Teal. 2006. "To Train or to Educate?: Evidence from Tanzania." Global Poverty Research Group Working Paper Series 051, Oxford, U.K.

Kweka, Josaphat, and Louise Fox. 2011. "The Household Sector in Tanzania: Why It Matters and Who Cares." Policy Research Working Paper 5882, World Bank, Washington, DC.

Liimatainen, Marjo-Riita. 2002. "Training and Skills Acquisition in the Informal Sector: A Literature Review." Working Paper 9, ILO InFocus Programme on Skills, Knowledge, and Employability, Informal Economy Series, International Labour Organization, Geneva.

Mincer, Jacob. 1958. "Investment in Human Capital and Personal Income Distribution." *Journal of Political Economy* 66 (4): 281–302.

NBS (National Bureau of Statistics, Ministry of Finance and Economics Affairs). 2002. *Integrated Labour Force Survey 2000–2001 (ILFS 2000–2001)*. Version 1.0 of the public use dataset (January 2002) provided by National Bureau of Statistics, Government of Tanzania, Dar es Salaam. http://www.nbs.go.tz.

———. 2007a. *Analytical Report for Integrated Labour Force Survey (ILFS), 2006*. Dar es Salaam, Tanzania: NBS, Ministry of Planning, Economy and Empowerment, Tanzania Gender Networking Programme, Ministry of Labour, Employment and Youth Development.

———. 2007b. *Integrated Labour Force Survey 2006 (ILFS 2006)*. Version 1.0 of the public use datasets (August 2007), provided by the National Bureau of Statistics, Government of Tanzania, Dar es Salaam. http://www.nbs.go.tz.

Nell, Marian, and Janet Shapiro. 1999. *Traditional Apprenticeship Practice in Dar es Salaam: A Study*. Consultancy report prepared for GIZ (formerly GTZ)/VETA, Dar es Salaam, Tanzania.

Nübler, Irmgard, Christine Hofmann, and Clemens Greiner. 2009. "Understanding Informal Apprenticeship—Findings from Empirical Research in Tanzania." Employment Working Paper 32, International Labour Organization, Geneva.

Perry, Guillermo E., William F. Maloney, Omar S. Arias, Pablo Fajnzylber, Andrew D. Mason, and Jaime Saavedra-Chanduvi. 2007. *Informality: Exit and Exclusion*. World Bank Latin American and Caribbean Studies. Washington, DC: World Bank.

Quinn, Simon, and Francis Teal. 2008. "Private Sector Development and Income Dynamics: A Panel Study of the Tanzanian Labour Market." Working Paper Series/2008-09, Centre for the Study of African Economies, University of Oxford, Oxford, U.K.

World Bank. 2011. *World Development Indicators 2011*. Washington, DC: World Bank.

Environmental Benefits Statement

The World Bank is committed to reducing its environmental footprint. In support of this commitment, the Office of the Publisher leverages electronic publishing options and print-on-demand technology, which is located in regional hubs worldwide. Together, these initiatives enable print runs to be lowered and shipping distances decreased, resulting in reduced paper consumption, chemical use, greenhouse gas emissions, and waste.

The Office of the Publisher follows the recommended standards for paper use set by the Green Press Initiative. Whenever possible, books are printed on 50% to 100% postconsumer recycled paper, and at least 50% of the fiber in our book paper is either unbleached or bleached using Totally Chlorine Free (TCF), Processed Chlorine Free (PCF), or Enhanced Elemental Chlorine Free (EECF) processes.

More information about the Bank's environmental philosophy can be found at http://crinfo.worldbank.org/crinfo/environmental_responsibility/index.html.

green press INITIATIVE

www.ingramcontent.com/pod-product-compliance
Lightning Source LLC
LaVergne TN
LVHW080034210926
848481LV00011B/3182